Dharma

The Categorial Imperative

Dharma

The Categorial Imperative

Edited by

Ashok Vohra
Arvind Sharma
Mrinal Miri

D.K.Printworld (P) Ltd.
New Delhi

Cataloging in Publication Data — DK
[Courtesy: D.K. Agencies (P) Ltd. <docinfo@dkagencies.com>]

Dharma : the categorial imperative /
edited by Ashok Vohra, Arvind Sharma,
Mrinal Miri.
vi, 466 p. 23 cm.
Contributed articles.
Includes bibliographical references (p.)
Includes index.
ISBN 8124602700

I. Dharma. 2. Hinduism. 3. Philosophy, Hindu. I. Vohra, Ashok, 1949- II. Sharma, Arvind, 1940- III. Miri, Mrinal, 1940-

DDC 294.548 21

ISBN 81-246-0270-0
First Published in India in 2005

Published and printed by:
D.K. Printworld (P) Ltd.
Regd. office : *'Sri Kunj'*, F-52, Bali Nagar
New Delhi - 110 015
Phones : (011) 2545-3975; 2546-6019; *Fax* : (011) 2546-5926
E-mail: dkprintworld@vsnl.net
Web: www.dkprintworld.com

Contents

Introduction

I

THE Indian Institute of Advanced Study, jointly with the Indian Council of Philosophical Research, the University Grants Commission and the Faculty of Religious Studies of McGill University held an international conference on "Dharma: The Categorial Imperative" during July 16-22, 1997 in Shimla on the campus of the Indian Institute of Advanced Study. The conference was attended by more than fifty scholars from various parts of the world. This volume comprises selected papers presented at the conference, which have been revised in the light of the discussions held during the conference.

II

The word *dharma* enjoys a unique semantic status in Indian civilization which is only enhanced when it is placed in a Western context. In such a context its semantic uniqueness is best teased out by juxtaposing it with the two English words: religion and ideology. The word religion of course deserves a treatise by itself, or even several treatises, but the dimension of its meaning most relevant at the moment is the fact that it often carries with it the connotation of singular religious adherence. In other words, it is not possible to be a follower of the religions of Judaism, Christianity or Islam, for instance, *at the same time*. This sense of exclusive belonging or singular adherence to a faith is a very important definitional marker of the Western concept of religion.

Likewise, the word *ideology* also involves a similar commitment to a single vision. Thus, it is difficult to be a capitalist and a communist together at the same time. Although both religion and ideology tend to imply exclusive adherence on the part of each, they however differ from one another inasmuch as religion involves a transcendental dimension while ideology does not have any. Ideology, like religion, consists of a systematic body of concepts especially about human life or culture but it typically excludes reference to a transcendental dimension such as might be represented by God, for instance. Marxism is a good example of an ideology, for it shares many formal aspects of religion but avoids being one because it is thoroughly immanent in character (although some have argued that history itself assumes an almost transcendental dimension within it).

If we now put *dharma* in this verbal soup and stir, then an interesting point emerges. *Dharma* shares many a semantic space with religion but differs from it in not being exclusive. And just as it differs from religion in not being exclusive, it also differs from ideology in possessing a transcendental dimension as well.

Indian civilization, as we know it now, stands exposed to all the three terms and concepts. The term *dharma* was chosen as the theme of this conference because it is often neglected as an organizing category in intellectual discourse in India, although widely represented in many other forms of discourse. The point may be further elaborated as follows.

Every civilization, from one point of view, could be looked upon as comprising two components: a material base and an ideational superstructure. Each major civilization of the world would thus consist of a distinct material base and a distinct ideational structure.

The all-embracing transformative impact of the West on India under the aegis of British rule since 1800 AD can also be analysed in these terms. The West profoundly affected Indian civilization at both these levels. One purpose of the conference was to analyse the impact of the idea of the Western notion of 'religion' on the Indian reality, and the tensions created thereby for the concept of *dharma*.

Each stable culture has an inherent mechanism to arrive at its own equilibrium between its material culture and its ideational structure. This equilibrium was disturbed in the case of India by the introduction of the Western concept of religion. This raises the question: To what extent does the continued use of the concept of religion in the Indian context reflect reality, and to what extent does it distort or misrepresent its dhārmic reality? It would be rash to assume that the word 'religion' nowadays totally misrepresents Indian reality inasmuch as the changes in the material realm brought about by the Western impact may have produced corresponding ideational transformations. These ideational changes could arguably be best understood in terms of the Western concepts of religion and ideology. However, since the transformation wrought due to the contact with the West was not total, the 'religious' life of India was, at least visibly, the sphere minimally affected by it. But the possibility — that the continued use of the word religion for *dharma* in the context of representing and comprehending Indian reality would seriously distort or misrepresent — cannot be overlooked.

It is clear, therefore, that neither the word religion nor *dharma* can be discarded while looking at the Indian reality. Neither of the two terms can be used as uncritically as might have been possible if India and the West had not come in close contact. The conference was devoted to the intellectual exploration of this existential situation.

III

It was with this in mind that the category of *dharma* was chosen as the lens for viewing the Indian reality. In fact it was felt that it was imperative that we do so. The imperative however was for us categorial rather than categorical in nature.

These two terms added a measure of creative confusion to the conference. However, these need to be clearly distinguished. The word categorical, made famous by Kant from 1827 onwards in his expression "the categorical imperative," refers to "moral obligation or command that is unconditionally and universally binding." The word categorial was chosen to emphasize its distinction from the word categorical in the above sense. It is true that the word categorical could also mean "of relating to, or constituting a category" but its heavy philosophical and ideational association with the expression 'categorical imperative' led us to prefer the word categorial to emphasize the point that we wished *dharma* to be used as a category for viewing Indian reality as an intellectual exercise.

This distinction gets further clarified if it is recalled that our enterprise was epistemological and not moral in character (even if *dharma* at times serves as a moral category), for, the purpose of the conference was to move towards an Indian epistemology for understanding Indian culture and civilization. For, the current Indian self-understanding is unique in one respect: This self-understanding of the Indians about themselves has been mediated through a Western intellectual intervention. This naturally raises the question: What form would such Indian self-understanding have assumed if it had not been mediated by such an intervention? Several significant consequences flow from this fact.

A central feature of this Western mediation was the writing of a history of ancient Indian civilization from an alien perspective, employing its method, vocabulary and terminology. Under the influence of the widespread, though contestable, view that ancient Indians lacked a sense of history, the modern Indian intellectual has almost axiomatically accepted the Western reconstruction of ancient India. This has led to the view that the Western modern studies in general are paradigmatic for studying, understanding and articulating ancient Indian values, culture and civilization. With the growing awareness even in the West itself of the culture-bound nature of any epistemology, even rationality, including its own, perhaps the time has come for intellectually sensitive Indians to examine the adequacy of applying Western categories of thought and understanding to the Indian context.

Crucial, then, to the recovery of an Indian self-understanding is the question: "Whether on the basis of the data now available, an alterative understanding of Indian civilization is possible, independent of Western presuppositions?" The theme of the conference crystallized this point. The papers presented here critically but constructively argue this issue. They do so by analysing the implications of the use of the words religion and *dharma* in the Indian Context.

Editors

1

'Religion' or 'Dharma': Meaning and Motivation

Primarily in Indian Context

R.S. Bhatnagar

ASSUMING that the understanding of a term is facilitated by locating the context within which it has its application, I first attempt to locate two such contexts — political and cultural — in order to understand the terms, 'religion' or '*dharma*'. Having noticed how these contexts compel attention in respect of the meanings of the terms, 'religion' and '*dharma*,' I would now like to lay down as to how these terms can be viewed on a scale having description and prescription as two nodes. Such a procedure finally suggests two kinds of motivations tending to the acceptance of two different ways of the application of the terms 'religion' and '*dharma*'.

At least two different contexts can be identified within which the word, 'religion' or '*dharma*,' assumes a problematic status and demands a semantic enquiry. These contexts can be called political and cultural respectively for the sake of convenience.

From the point of view of the history of our own country, we are apt to think that the existence of plurality of religions and consequently the problem of peaceful co-existence of different communities showing their allegiance to different religions are peculiarly germane to our society. However, as we now know, the problem is more widespread. Central Asia, Turkey, Middle East, Ireland and Indonesia are some of the countries where the plurality of religions following constitutes serious problem. Though the problem is general in character, yet obviously, specific features of the problem which affects religion would differ from country to country.

Political Context

Let us take communal tensions engendered by politically interested to begin with. It goes without saying that if the people of the various religious communities had not come in violent conflict with each other, some time or the other, and were living in mutual amity, religion would not have been an issue politically. It is interesting to note that the communities having different religious identities living together in the various parts of our country, as a matter of course, do not exhibit hostile relationship amongst them. Generally, people live more or less without thinking to overpower each other, without the fear of each other, even if no explicit social intercourse displaying intimate harmony is visible. If this is not a distorted or imaginary description, it becomes puzzling to find one fine morning that there has been a communal riot at such and such place. Unless the communal tensions have been long simmering and people were preparing themselves for such a broiling fray, how come that the peace loving people start plundering or killing each other? How does the normal way of life get suddenly shattered? At least, sometimes, it has been found and it has also been reported that some non-residents move in, locate some careless and irresponsible and unsocial elements as their allies, spread inflammable rumours, help their friends with arms and weapons, and finally succeed in generating a flare-up. This at least is the one sequence of events and there may be traced some others also.

Limiting ourselves to the one that is described here, it occurs to mind that such a planned and successful strategy cannot be staged for no reason. The question of motivation requires unravelling of the thread. Investigations suggest that links are often found to be rooted in some power or nucleus which has its operations performed in a surreptitious way, preying on the religious potential for that lends itself easily to an explosive situation. Communal tensions and communal flare-ups are political manoeuvres for very selfish narrow ends.

But, how come, the people could allow themselves to be so duped and manipulated by the unscrupulous, mischievous and diabolic agencies? One possibility is that the radically different and specific features of a religion having no common or meeting ground with some sort of radical and specific features of the other, are accentuated and high-lighted. Diametrically hostile attitudes are generated and nourished. Narrow sectarian and rigid attitudes sustain themselves on differentiating characteristics. Few are bothered or have leisure to think and find out if such differences really matter. Normally most of us think that we live a religious life without ever bothering to ask as to what such a life means. So most of us are caught as if in a sleep.

Communal flare-ups as traumatic events compel us to reflect, in cool moments, on the meaning of "religion" or *dharma*. Does religion or *dharma* really suggest that only those who accept our creed have a right to live or live with us and others not ? Is our *dharma* the only one that can lead to salvation, make people civilized and create paradise on earth?

Another well-known mode of the political context in which religion has been a target of polemics is Marxian. Marx said that religion is opium for people.[1] There is an aspect of religious beliefs

1. "Religious distress is at the same time the expression of real distress and also the protest against real distress. Religion is the sign of the oppressed creature, the heart of a heartless world, just as it is the spirit of spiritless conditions. It is the opium of the people.

   To abolish religion as the illusory happiness of the people is to demand their real happiness. The demand to give up illusions about the existing state of affairs is the demand to give up a state of affairs which needs illusions . . . the criticism of heaven turns into the criticism of the earth, the criticism of religion into the criticism of law and the criticism of theology into the criticism of politics." K. Marx, *On Religion*, p. 39, Moscow.

which tends to inculcate an inward attitude of withdrawal from the world in contrast to a positive involvement in the worldly life. People tend to accept their lot in the hope that their life in the other world or in future would compensate the miseries of this life by eternal happiness. This attitude prevents one from locating the roots of social ills in the structural dynamics and leads to an indifference and passivity so far as the resistance or struggle against the given system is concerned. That is how the metaphor of opium gains in meaning.

Slightly differently, the passive mode as linked with inward withdrawal is found to be associated with the *bhakti* trends specially those associated with the period of Muslim rule in India. Some historians believe that this was a defensive mechanism which allowed the Hindu psyche to put up with the coercion and oppression of alien rulers. Such a view may not appeal to those who look at the period of Muslim rule, not as causing any radical violence to the Hindu society but as leading to more and more integration of two cultures. This is not an occasion to enter into this controversy for it is not relevant for our present purpose. We only wish to point out the partial truth of the assertion that the so-called religious approach in our society too, has been partially responsible for detracting our attention from the ills as having their source in the social structure or the polity itself.

One may also hazard the guess that the notion of the two worlds — transcendent and mundane (*pārmārthika* and *vyāvahārika*) — has not merely led to the acceptance of the social structure as it is given, but it has also generated an approach to life for many which amounts to some sort of opportunism. When the two orders have nothing in common, the mundane has little to do with the transcendent. So one may act in the mundane realm as the occasion demands in view of one's own interest. Those who implicitly manage their lives with the two-world theory helping their composure may not like to be told that the hypocrisy now so rampant in life has its source in such a dual-world view. This dislike, however, does not diminish the force of the guess.

These assertions should not blind us to the strict self-discipline of those who would constantly guard themselves against worldly temptations and would follow a way of life which is strictly ascetic on the one hand, and the tremendous revolutionary force which those leaders of mankind have exercised whose teachings led to the establishment of a new religion or who were supposed to have taken birth in order to create a new order in society or sustain and strengthen an order which was being destroyed, on the other.

These individuals who had countered the given situation of their times, suffered on that account but finally succeeded in bringing about a changed awareness. It was a different matter that in course of time their teachings became ossified and were used as a source of oppression and exploitation by opportunists and pernicious people.

One is reminded of *dharmasya glāni*[2] and an *avatāra* descending to set things right, to punish the evil-doers and to protect the good ones. Obviously, the word *dharma* here refers to a certain social order. This is an order by which men ought to live but they do not.

Another mode of religion getting linked with politics needs to be mentioned. It is a well-known historical fact that wars were waged by one nation against the other on the pretext of religious command and with a view to reform. The avowed intention did not completely match the religious spirit for the simple reason that much destruction and havoc had been brought about by such wars on the land of countries invaded. The scars left on the psyche of the plundered countries sometimes get revived and invite

2. *Gītā*, IV. 7-8, *srajāmyaham* in *śloka* 7 may have a deeper meaning in the sense that it may be indicating a self-transformation of the individual and if that could be a possibility then it should be possible to dispense with the transcendental.

retaliatory reaction. One might raise the question of retrogressive justice in situations of this kind. A deeper reflection suggests that violence and counter-violence set in a vicious circle and damage the core religious spirit rather than getting motivated by it.

One encounters a strange paradoxical state in this connection. Every religion claims some sort of universality which is closely linked with the idea of universal brotherhood. The creator of the universe being one, the entire mankind is supposed to form a family. Yet, on the contrary, as the history testifies, these insights were not only pushed in the background rather they have been continuously violated by the so-called religious fanaticism.

It is important to ask whether the demand of retrogressive justice could ever be supported by genuine religious faith. In fact, often the religious recommendation is that the right of judging and consequently the right of punishment or reward does not lie within the purview of humans for it is the divine order itself that would take care of it.

We, thus, notice that within the political context, religion becomes an issue either because of the fact that a society has communities having different religious identities, or because religion as such has been considered as a source of resistance to social change and inimical to social justice for it supports *status quo*, or because it has served the purpose of some diabolic agency in a direct or an indirect way.

It is in this context, primarily, that we are now engaged in for quite some time to disentangle semantic issues relating to "religion," *dharma*, "Hindu *dharma*," "Hindutva," etc. Before these issues are taken up I would like to draw the attention of the reader to the following two questions:

1. What problem/s do I face in the society or the state of which I am a member because of the fact that I am a Hindu/Muslim/Christian?

2. Do I really have serious problems with my fellow beings belonging to different creed in the society just because I follow one religion, and they another?

The first question has a political context. The other one has a cultural context. We would take up the first to begin with. Our Constitution visualizes a society and a polity in which no discrimination would be made, so far as the rights of the people are concerned, on account of caste, creed, colour or sex. In actuality, it is no news to state, that we are far from having realized this non-discriminatory ideal fully. On the contrary, one or more than one of these components has been utilized for gaining undeserved benefits and for manoeuvering political power. The ills that have accrued as a consequence of this tendency are too evident to need mention.

Within this perspective the first question may elicit answers which may broadly differ according to the community to which the individual belongs. A Muslim might answer that the laws specific to his community are in jeopardy, that he is not getting his adequate share in jobs or governance and so on; while a Hindu might answer that he is being asked to keep his profile low unnecessarily; that a policy of appeasement is being followed by the government and this has adverse effect on his well-being. Members of both the communities may complain about the issue relating to the places of worship. Thus, the members of either community seem to feel that those in power are being partial to their interest and welfare just because they happen to belong to a particular religious community.

Problems of this type are different from the problems of a different nature. These other problems relate to civic amenities, proper public distribution system, ceiling on land and income, unemployment or inadequate employment, housing, etc. Obviously, they are not community specific, though political manoeuvering may some time tie them with the discriminatory components to gain political advantage. While these latter problems seem to form content of constant complaints, the former ones are heard when elections are at hand or consolidation of vote bank is in process. The point that I wish to bring home is that the problems having their source in the religious identity of a certain community are neither genuine nor pressing but they have a potential for formulating political strategies. Moreover, they often distract attention from the real problems of survival and good life.

The usual unrest that ensues as a consequence of dirty politics involving sham claims of various communities generally leads to asking what 'religion' or *dharma* really means, what role it has in our lives, to what extent it effects the governance of our society and so on. The fundamental question that may be raised in this context, to my mind, is whether the essence of religious spirit is *divisive* or *unificatory*, generating hate or love. Before proceeding further let us also have a look on the cultural context which too generates similar questions.

Cultural Context

The second question raised above relating to mutual relationship amongst the members of different communities has to do with cultural encounter of two different communities. It is basically germane to initial encounters and loses its inquisitive force with the gradual integration of two cultures. As a matter of fact, such encounters can be listed as ranging from very early ties to the present day as well as relating to various parts of the globe. Some general features can be noted.

Feelings of strangeness, repulsion, attraction, hesitation, inquisitiveness, withdrawal, aggression, etc., characterize the reaction of the members of one community towards the members of the other community. The objects of such reactions, are, obviously, the way people live — their habits and patterns relating to various activities of day-to-day living, their linguistic behaviour — expressions and pronunciation, their clothes, and above all their beliefs and values. Amongst these, the religious beliefs and practices have a special place.

Apart from a general curiosity, there arise occasions when we raise questions about our own religious beliefs and practices. This happens when closer ties are sought amongst the members of two communities and such attempts meet not only with great resistance but also with positive refusals, violent encounters leading to excommunication or even extermination. Such reactions are also encountered when we become aware that we have been following certain practices which though prescribed or recommended by convention or tradition but which turn out to be not only irrational but also inhuman and then we try to stop believing them. Gandhi had to respond to many questions relating to seemingly inhuman practices such as stoning, flogging, forbidding entrance of members of certain sections into temples, untouchability and so on. His general view was that no practice which discriminates between man and man, which is inhuman, which flouts a moral value, and which is irrational, can ever be a religious recommendation.[3]

Besides social practices in the form of cults and rituals, the creative freedom has also often been the target of attack on religious count. Nirmal Verma writing about the censor of Rushdie's *Satanic Verses*, compared such censor with the Stalinistic fanaticism. He wrote that the self-styled advocates of religion should "examine the fragility of their beliefs rather than try to seek imaginary blasphemies in what is supposed to be a work of imagination."[4] The burning of some paintings of Hussain is only a recent event.

---

3. Flogging "may be permissible in Prophet's time, but can't be defended as mentioned in Koran. . . . Every formula of every religion must submit to the acid test of reason and universal justice . . .

   Both reason and heart refuse to reconcile themselves to torture for any crime, no matter how vile the crime may be." M.K. Gandhi, *Young India*, 26.2.25.

4. These quotes are from a letter to editor. Unfortunately, the date and the name of particular newspaper is not available with me.

It can be said that the issues, relating to the meaning of 'religion' or *dharma*, that arise in political and cultural contexts are not unrelated to purely academic, i.e., sociological, psychological and philosophical, contexts. Yet, the former contexts bring the related issues into focus in a more pressing way and also reveal certain features relating to these issues for the academic disciplines. No theoretical exercise can ignore particularities of actual happenings. Why do we ask a question has to do with the kind of answer resulting from our inquiry in some important way.

Meaning of Religion or Dharma

Religion or *dharma,* do I take them as interchangeable? Permit me to answer this a little later. Let me first draw the attention of the reader to two ways of looking at 'religion' or *dharma* occurring in the considerations already presented. Either we look at *dharma* or religion in a very broad sense or in a very narrow sense. But I shall take up this issue after an explanation of the term *'dharma'*.

The first thing to note is that the various usages of the word *'dharma'* belong to Hindu tradition, which in itself is very complex. The word Hindu itself raises host of problems. There are communities which though normally are included in Hindus yet they themselves would like to keep their identities separate and would not prefer to call themselves Hindus. The distinctions between Jainas, Bauddhas, Sikhs and Hindus are accentuated in some contexts and are blurred in some others. Śāktas, Vaiṣṇavites, Śaivaites and many others would divide the remaining Hindus further. However, the word *'dharma'* is to be found in the vocabularies of most of these communities, though, not with the same meaning.

Buddhists have two important expressions: *dharma-cakrapravartana, dhammamśaraṇamgacchāmi.* In both these expressions, *'dharma'* refers to the four noble truths which constitute the earliest teachings that Buddha imparted to his first five disciples. These four noble truths may with some risk of generalization, be said to point to "things as they are" with the rider "for human beings." Jainas talk of *anantadharmī vastu* which again has an ontological connotation but within a human context, for the famous seven-fold assertions about the reality are formulated in terms of human cognition and expressibility.

Both these connotations are nearer to a very old concept of *dharma* as being "the support or basis of all that there is" as traceable to the Epics and Purāṇas. Once again *dharma* in this sense has both ontological and ethical import. *Ṛta* as a Vedic term had these connotations besides pointing to a cosmic order. *Dharma* as used in the phrases *dharmaśāstra, svadharma* or *sāmānya dharma* and even in *āpad-dharma* has mainly to do with what one *ought to do*. Thus, in a broad characterization *dharma* refers on the one hand to reality or its character, or its basis or support in some sense, and to action or desirable action on the other.

In the phrases, which have gained currency now but which are being constantly debated, *dharmanirapekṣa* and *sarva-dharmasamabhāva*, *dharma* is interchangeable with the term "religion" itself. Perhaps this was also the import involved in the solace which Kṛṣṇa offered Arjuna when he told him, "Give up all *dharma*s and come to me."[5] In this particular usage *dharma* is construed narrowly as to exclude the notion of duty. Kṛṣṇa here is not saying that Arjuna should give up all duties and then come to him.

We thus notice that both these terms — religion and *dharma* have a narrower as well as a liberal usages. The liberal or wider usage again gives us two different directions. In one case, we may include the different usages as forming a whole complex of beliefs and practices. It is in this wide application of the term, religion or *dharma*, that the beginnings of religious zeal and fervour can be marked. In an initial stage such beginnings are almost co-extensive with life itself, as they cover most of the aspects of living. From the

5. *Sarvadharmānparitajya māmekam śaraṇam vraja, Gītā*, XVIII. 66.

sociological point of view, the beginning of a religion reveals that religion functions as a source of information about all that there is, as determining value and significance of things as prescribing patterns of behaviour and aims of life. As differentiation begins, these functions are gradually taken over by the relatively independent fields which later on assume the form of specific disciplines and institutions. Functionally, 'religion' in its application to the various areas of life gets increasingly narrower and confined to other-worldly celestial realm and its concerns.

Strangely, while the field of application of the term gets narrower, the all-prevading meaning of the term continues to have a hold on the psyche of the protagonist. Not merely this, the cults and rituals which may have had their genesis in the local and temporal needs and conditions and which lose their meaning as we move on with the times, continue to occupy some place in the life patterns of the people. That they have lost their initial significance and function is to some extent supported by the fact that in most cases we do not know why we perform certain rituals yet we do perform them.[6]

Another important and very significant fact which is either

---

6. Such rituals and practices and the related beliefs have often been looked upon as preventing one at reaching the essence of religious spirit. Says Tagore, "The difference between the spirit and the form of religion, like that between fire and ash, should be borne in mind. When the form becomes more important than the spirit, the sand in the river-bed becomes more pronounced than the water, the current ceases to flow, and a desert is the ultimate result. . . . The spirit tells us to atone for evil thoughts and deeds by repentance and by performance of good deeds, but the form prescribes bathing in particular rivers at the hour of solar or lunar eclipse. The spirit advises us to cross seas and mountains and develop our minds by seeing the world, but the form puts an expiatory ban on sea voyage. The spirit tells us to reverse all good men irrespective of their caste, but the form enjoins respect for the Brahmin, however unworthy. In sum the spirit of religion leads to freedom, its form to slavery." Rabindra Nath Tagore, *Towards Universal Man*, pp. 188-89, Asia, 1961.

not noticed or deliberately ignored by the protagonists is the fact that hardly any religion retains its original form today and almost every religion has undergone processes which have introduced either subsects amongst its followers or have led to completely independent ramifications. The significance of this dynamic phenomenon in the growth of religious consciousness is that finality or rigidity are the only features which the followers unreasonably take for granted in respect of their creed.

In the other case, the direction of religious consciousness tends to move towards universality and generality in an all-inclusive way so far as the access to it for any individual is concerned. As Iqbal Singh points out in his biography of Raja Rammohun Roy, that Raja Rammohun Roy in his *Tuhaft-ul-Muwahhidin* sets out:

> . . . to turn Men's minds away from the formal diversities of religious practice to its supposed essence, and prove the underlying unity of all systems of faith since, according to him, they ultimately converge towards belief in the personality of One Being who is the source of all that exists and its governor. . .[7]

Rammohun Roy hoped that at some point of time people would realize that:

> . . . true system of religion which leads its observers to a knowledge and love of God, and to a friendly inclination towards their fellow-creatures, impressing their hearts at the same time with humility and charity, accompanied by independence of mind and pure sincerity.[8]

Every time someone within a certain religion takes courage and devotes himself to reform religious consciousness, the general emphasis is laid on the belief that all creatures have a relation of love and concern for each other, that there is one Supreme Being, that we should overcome negative, destructive and inhuman

7. *Rammohun Roy*, Iqbal Singh, vol. I, p. 69, Asia, 2nd edn., 1983.
8. *Ibid.*, p. 190.

tendencies and purify our hearts and minds. This insistence on a universal, underlying human, and inclusive religion being the true religion can be taken as indicative of the other wide connotation of the term, 'religion' — we may interchange it with *mazhab* or *dharma*.

In contrast to these two wider connotations, we may count the third narrower connotation which is basically characterized by a consciousness of exclusion.[9] Such a view of religion or *dharma* tends to be worried about its identity, about the number of its adherents, and about its exclusive claims to superiority, perhaps their funding sources as well as power over people.

Typological Characterization of the Concepts of 'Religion' or 'Dharma'

The three ways in which the term — religion or *dharma*, is used are not exhaustive. However, whatever the number of usages that we may be able to identify, the terms, unless taken in the sense of what is called 'family resemblance,' exhibits an open texture. To a large extent, a user exercises some independence of judgement while describing the usage or being himself engaged in using the term.

The debate about the usage assumes that there is some correct or preferred usage, or there is a possibility of a proper usage even though it is not fixed or given. The former sometimes may be based on the descriptive aspect of the usage. The term does purport to describe some features of a social reality, some set of beliefs that people have, some sort of practices that they follow, some texts that are supposed to be sacred, some places that are held pious, some dates or days of the year considered to be occasions for some kind of celebration.

---

9. Rammohun Roy remarked, as Iqbal Singh points out, "Followers of each religion" he complains, "believe that their own particular faith is the only way to salvation." This religious chauvinism sows, "seeds of prejudice, and disunion in their hearts" and they spend their time condemning "each other to deprivation of eternal bliss." *Ibid.*, p. 73.

On the other hand, the term has a normative-cum-prescriptive force and points to an attitude, to ideas, to considerations which, it is urged, people ought to pay heed to. Such a view is also linked with the kind of state of affairs that is considered desirable and which, it is so supposed, people ought to bring about.

Considering these two aspects as being co-mingled in the use of the term 'religion' or *dharma*, it would not be unreasonable to see it as placed within a range having for its nodes, description and prescription. The idea of such a range implies that no statement can be purely descriptive or prescriptive (or normative). The two extremes suggest only two logical possibilities.

Two motivations

These considerations, if sound, indicate that we tend to accept a certain usage of the term 'religion' or *dharma* which satisfies our motivation. Motivated in the direction of unity, friendship, mutual concern, universal brotherhood, we are inclined to accept one particular usage — religion as all-inclusive binding force and thus excluding the possibility of violence, torture, exploitation and inhumanity motivated by very narrow selfish ends (political, economic, commercial, and perhaps institutional). We tend to accept the other usage which requires division, exclusion, concern for identity, number of adherents and power.

Getting clear of these motivations, that is getting clear of our own inclinations and intentions, is, to my mind, getting clear about the meaning of 'religion' or '*dharma*'.

2

Philosophy, Religion, and Secularism
The Indian Context

Srinivasa Rao

SINCE I am discussing the notions of philosophy, religion and secularism together in their complex interrelationships, I will have to necessarily discuss at some length the nature of these concepts in the West as well as in India. The chief reason for discussing the Western as well as the Indian conceptions is that they are formulated and articulated in significantly different ways in the two traditions. A very important reason that necessitates dwelling at some length on these differences is the excessive enthusiasm that has existed in India, especially before as well as after it became an independent and sovereign Republic, for increasingly adopting the characteristic Western modes of thought and life as a replacement for the classical modes that existed for centuries. It was earnestly believed by most of our social reformers and leaders that this would cure our major social ills. Therefore, it is time that we ask ourselves seriously whether we have been entirely wise in seeking major, and in some cases forcible, replacement of our classical modes by certain Western modes in our attempts at modernizing our country and society and ridding it of its evils.

In human history, it is not uncommon for a civilization to adopt some new concept from another civilization. But normally, when such adaptation takes place, the concept gets indigenized in the sense that it gets fully adapted to the local environment and milieu.

Thus, the concept gets modified in the process and this modified concept, in turn, modifies the general environment and the milieu. But human history also provides us with examples of large-scale attempts at modifying the environment for the sake of adopting a concept. Probably, the adoption of communism in a good part of our globe in the early part of the twentieth century is a fair example of very serious attempts at changing a society in order to make it conform to a concept. To what extent the concept of communism was realized in the societies, that were forcibly or otherwise modified for its actualization, is something that is widely known and is also not very debatable today. No one can possibly question the genuineness of the Russian Revolution and the sincerity and dedication of its initial leaders; but that in no way mitigates the seriousness of the human tragedy that has trailed this Revolution from the days of its inception down to this day. The old Soviet Union has disappeared together with its Constitution, leaving its citizens in a state far from the promised paradise.

During some moments of hard thinking, I often feel that a fate similar to that of the Soviets might be waiting for the Indians round the corner. That is because, we are guided by the ideology of democratic socialism and secularism, which, in so far as I can make any sense of them, are essentially Western in conception; and we have been trying hard to make our country and society to conform to these ideologies exactly as they are found in the West. We want to modify our social and political reality in ways that will ultimately make us best conform to these ideologies and put us on par with the West.

The Western concept of secularism has its deep roots in the Western intellectual tradition and that concept is distinctly, and organically, related to the Western concepts of science, philosophy and religion. The Indians have had, for centuries, their own concepts of philosophy and religion, and also of science, although not exactly in the modern Western sense, and these are not at all adaptations from the West. In fact, the Indian conceptions of philosophy and religion differ quite significantly from their Western counterparts and therefore it becomes very important to investigate whether the Western concept of secularism is harmonizable with these Indian conceptions of religion and philosophy that continue to persist in democratic India. The Western concepts of man and society are very different from those that have held their ground for centuries in India and it is not wise to believe that the age-old Indian conceptions should be replaced, to our common benefit, by Western ones in the course of the large-scale Westernization that we have obviously been undertaking in India.

In fact, this phenomenon of Westernization is extremely complex and subtle. There are many stages in its development and we must clearly distinguish between its colonial and post-Independence phases. Sometimes, it appears to me that a fair critique of our secularism is in essence a critique of our post-Independence Westernizing process. But I would not pursue such a general, abstract, subtle and complex issue here. I confine myself to the task of exploring the basic notions of philosophy, religion and secularism in their Western as well as Indian contexts. This exploration is seriously meant as a basically conceptual exercise. My aim is not to criticize or evaluate the complex policies of our nation and its leaders especially in respect of secularism. My aim is to lay bare the conceptual structure and implications behind the State policy of secularism in India, and also to explore the deep and radical consequences of it on our political, social and intellectual environment and life today.

I begin by taking a brief look at the concepts of philosophy, religion and secularism as they have evolved in the Western environment. In ancient Greece, the cradle of all Western thought and philosophy began as an outcome of human curiosity and wonder about nature and man. Philosophy was an enterprise based on reason than on faith, and its aim was to offer a coherent, rational explanation of the universe and of man. 'Rational explanation' as one that can withstand scrutiny by reason, was the goal of the philosopher. Many of the ancient Greek philosophers were, and still are, examples of the most rational beings that we could ever find in the West. But, in general, human beings in all societies and at all times, have been usually intolerant of a very rational being as is evidenced by the death of Socrates and the later ban by the Church on reading the works of Plato and Aristotle, two great thinkers the West has produced — a ban that had been too readily accepted until Augustine and Aquinas changed the whole scene.

Though there has also been, in the West, "revolt against reason," such revolt has been directed more in the direction of emphasizing that reason should be supplemented by other elements than emphasizing a demand for supplanting and removing reason itself. That revolt is just symptomatic of a very valid point, — that the role and importance of reason should not be over-emphasized. Therefore, it may not altogether be wrong to hold the view that in the West, philosophy is and has always been a primarily rational enterprise whose goal is to 'explain' the universe of our experience and help us 'understand' it in clear theoretical terms. It may appear that there was a revolution in the nature of philosophizing in the West in the twentieth century because philosophy was no more regarded as a kind of 'theory' but as a kind of 'activity.' But, this is only the reformulation of the 'goal' of philosophy, without any substantial change in the nature of its 'role' in the world. System-building is no more the goal of philosophy in the modern West; analysis and clarification of human thought as expressed in language is the chief task of philosophy. This analysis and clarification aims at nothing more than removing confusions and misconceptions in human thinking, or just avoiding the 'misuse' of language. Philosophy did not have any *soteriological role* in the West before the advent of the modern 'activity view' of philosophy and it continues to be so even now. If salvation is the goal of any individual, then it is the religion which he should seek and not philosophy. There is no room for 'faith' in philosophy.

Philosophy has no followers as in a religion; it has only advocates and all its advocates do not necessarily see in the same way, very much like those of the advocates in the legal world.

The areas of philosophy, religion and science have eventually come to be clearly distinguished in the West though it might be the case that there are some fields where there is an occasional overlap. Clearly, in the modern West, there is no philosophy that is associated with a religious doctrine and there is also no religion that is associated with a specific school of philosophy. Religion and philosophy parted ways some centuries ago and science, which had all along been identified as "natural philosophy," has also developed a distinct identity of its own in the past centuries. There is also no formal relationship between science and religion. It was Galileo who forcibly initiated the move for the separation of science from religion by showing an interest in reinterpreting the *Bible* in the light of the scientific discoveries of his times — an interest that was deeply resented by the clergy that included very competent men of science of the day. But, it took centuries for this separation to take deep roots. That is why we see Newton, who is undoubtedly one of the greatest of scientists of all times, showing keen interest in the theological controversies of his day. He carried on a very bitter theological debate with Leibniz and it is quite interesting that nearly 75 per cent of Newton's writings are on theological subjects and not on physics! But this situation does not obtain today and except for a few rare physicists who are also cosmologists, we hardly hear any scientist speaking in a tone that seems accommodative of religion. The separation between the spheres of religion and science is complete.

While the separation of religion from purely speculative philosophy was natural and gradual in the West, the separation of religion from science was forced and bitter. This is very much due to the nature of Western religion itself. I think it is reasonable to identify "Western religion" with Judaism and Christianity. Both these are revealed religions that have their Holy Books which contain pronouncements about man and the universe he lives in. There is a "view of the world" in the *Bible* that came into sharp conflict with the view that science was led to formulate on the basis of observation and experiment. This conflict became intense as time went on and one very famous instance is the conflict between Darwin's thesis of evolution and the account of creation given in the Book of Genesis in the *Bible*. Philosophy did not come into similar conflict with science because philosophy was also a rational-theoretical enterprise like science, but not essentially relying on observation and experiment for arriving at its principles as science did. Though philosophers also sometimes appealed to sense experience in formulating their theories and principles, and also sometimes used the discoveries of the scientists to justify their general world-views, they never fundamentally relied on observation or experiment to finally validate their theories and principles. As time advanced, science and philosophy became further removed from each other.

But the case of religion was quite different. Christianity in particular, as embodied in the institution of the Catholic Church, tried to establish its authority not only over matters concerning the "natural world" through asserting the superiority of revelation over sense experience and reason, i.e., superiority of theology over science, but also over the "social world" of man through claiming temporal authority. God was the creator of man and since the Church represented God on earth, the Church claimed the right to exercise its authority over men on behalf of God. Thus, figuratively speaking, the Church claimed authority not only over the 'spirit' of man but also over his 'body.' The religious sphere was conceived as encompassing the intellectual as well as the social dimensions of human life. In course of time, this attempt of the Church to control and regulate the social and political aspects of life met with resistance and consequently we see the Pope declaring war against certain kings and some kings against the Pope in the history of the West. Finally, the Church and the State settled this long drawn-out dispute through agreeing to a separation of powers. Matters of State were removed from ecclesiastical jurisdiction and likewise, matters of religion were removed from the jurisdiction of the State. In Roman Catholic Law, anything becomes 'secular' when it is removed from ecclesiastical jurisdiction. Slowly, even a "secular morality," in which God and the Church are regarded as irrelevant in a well-rounded moral life, came to be developed and widely adopted in the West.

From the above account it is evident that the term 'secular' originally meant "outside the sphere of religion" or more strictly, "outside the jurisdiction of Church Law." That is because, originally, all spheres of human activity were within the sphere of control of the Church and subsequently certain areas of activity were released from that control. These released areas were subjected to a law of their own, the Common Law or the Civil Law that fell within the sphere of control of the State. Thus, religious matters were naturally excluded from the sphere of control of Common Law since such matters continued to remain within the sphere of control of Church Law. Therefore, there can be no doubt that the arising of the concept of secularism in the West is a direct consequence of the separation of the institution of religion or the Church from the institution of the State. In other words, secularism was born when there was a separation of the social-political aspects of life from the religious aspects. The religious aspect could be easily separated from other aspects of life only because the goal of religion was soteriological while the goals of other aspects of life like the social, cultural or the political were non-soteriological. Even the goal of the philosophical enterprise was non-soteriological.

Moreover, there was no linking of the soteriological and the non-soteriological aspects of human life in the Western tradition. Religious activities were conceived as affecting none but the individual who performed them and were therefore treated as falling within the sphere of private activities. Since the State was concerned with only that aspect of human behaviour which affected others, the religious activity necessarily fell outside the purview of the State. The State therefore ceased to make any legislation affecting any religion and it left the question of any religious legislation or reform to the religious institutions themselves. Secularism in the West evolved naturally, although the process was by no means totally painless, but it evolved in an environment of its own and was not transplanted from anywhere. As something naturally grown and not artificially foisted, a secular outlook has become a natural part of civilized life in the West. For all practical purposes, it can be said with a reasonable amount of fairness that secularism is an integral part of Western culture.

II

I shall now present a broad view of the nature of philosophy, science and religion in India. India did generate a very considerable amount of scientific knowledge in the past though, by contemporary standards, India is not now in the forefront. There is a very good reason for the non-development of science in India along Western lines. One major reason, at least as it seems to me, is that science in ancient India was not an offshoot of philosophy as in the West. In India, science developed independent of philosophy. Both science and philosophy in the West have their origin in man's curiosity and wonder about himself and his surroundings. But in ancient India, it was not curiosity and wonder that prompted men to philosophize or to attempt to 'understand' the natural world and man. The strongly felt presence of pain and evil in human life led to an inquiry about the nature of man and his world and the aim of this philosophical inquiry was, in general, to overcome pain and misery on a permanent basis. The fact that most schools of Indian philosophy unequivocally declare *mokṣa* to be the ultimate goal of man should be noted in this context. The main purpose of a philosophical system of this kind is to demonstrate to man how he is caught up in the web of sorrow and also to show him the way out of this web. Thus, the attainment of liberation is the chief goal of most

Indian schools of philosophy and in so far as this is the goal of religion as well, philosophy and religion have always been inseparable in India. Thus, most schools of Indian philosophy have a clear and unambiguous soteriological role unlike any typical school of Western philosophy. The chief role of philosophy consists in helping man attain salvation — a role that is not of philosophy but only of religion in the West.

Since the philosopher in the West was prompted by curiosity and wonder, his aim was to achieve an exact knowledge concerning the way the things really are and liberation was never his aim. In India also, the philosophers sought the knowledge of things as they are, but they never sought such knowledge for its own sake like their Western counterpart. They sought it for achieving liberation. Thus, philosophy in India was always soteriologically oriented while in the West philosophy was so only for a short period, during the age of scholasticism. Because of this soteriological orientation, many of the Indian philosophical schools also became religious. Thus, Buddhism and Jainism are both religions and philosophies at once, and so are Advaita, Viśiṣṭādvaita, Dvaita, Śaiva Siddhānta, Vīraśaivism, Sikhism, Vaiṣṇavism and so on. If we sort the Indian schools of thought with their discussions concerning the nature of man and the universe as the principal focus, we arrive at their philosophical aspects; if we sort them instead with the goal of their investigations as the primary focus, we get at the religious aspects. Thus, there is a blend of philosophy and religion in Indian thought which has no parallels at all in the West. This is one reason why some of the Western thinkers mistake many schools of Indian philosophy for theological systems. In the modern West, the understanding is that if a system of thought has a distinct soteriological dimension, it *cannot* be philosophy. But there is no such conception in India.

Perhaps it might be useful to dwell a little on the nature of science in the Indian context. An investigation into the nature of a thing *for its own sake* is a characteristic feature of Western science, but no investigation of any kind in India was undertaken for its own sake. This is true of all branches of knowledge. There must be a distinct *purpose* behind any kind of investigation or quest. Even when a book is written, the author has to first state the purpose of his writing it. Every *śāstra,* without exception, has to have a purpose (*uddeśya*) and an intended result (*phala*) and these must be declared in clear terms at the beginning of the work embodying that *śāstra.* Because of this factor, the nature of scientific knowledge has been very different in India. A lot of knowledge concerning plants is available in the works on *Āyurveda,* but all these plants are, without exception, *useful plants.* There has been no work that describes plants *in general.* The ancient Indians tamed elephants to use them in wars; hence they must have had a very intimate knowledge of that species. But they never undertook any study of animal species in general with the exclusive aim of knowing them as they are, i.e., the science of zoology. The whole of *Śilpaśāstra* incidentally contains very valuable information about the nature of different kinds of rocks, metals and minerals — a kind of knowledge that can be found only in treatises on modern Western geology and metallurgy. This knowledge was painstakingly acquired only because the temples and statues had to be created out of rocks and metals for purposes of worship. In the process of acquiring such knowledge, certainly every available type of rock and metal must have been tested and investigated; but detailed information only about the useful ones among them was preserved as a science.

It might be argued that the ancient Indians were very much like ancient Egyptians who, for example, knew a good number of geometric truths, but did not evolve any *science* of geometry out of them. The Greeks, who borrowed geometric knowledge from ancient Egyptians, axiomatized and developed it into the science of geometry. Presumably, the ancient Egyptians were good observers and experimenters, but lacked a capacity for axiomatization and theorization. While this might be true of ancient Egyptians, the same cannot be said of ancient Indians.

We have the very model of an axiomatized system in the Sanskrit grammar of Pāṇini which is believed to have been compiled around the fourth century before Christ. This proves that the ancient Indians possessed the capacity for axiomatization and theory-building that is characteristic of the Western sciences, but did not exercise that capacity to build scientific systems simply because their goal in the pursuit of knowledge about things was practical and not theoretical. They never sought knowledge for its own sake.

If any further proof is required, we only need to look at the very exact knowledge the ancient Indians possessed about the movement of the planets — the kind of knowledge which Tycho Brahe possessed in Europe, from which Kepler later deduced the laws of planetary motion — but the ancient Indians did not deduce any such laws. Kepler looked for a 'pattern' in the data that Tycho Brahe had accumulated and found it; he expressed it in the form of his laws of planetary motion. That was because his sole aim was to find out "what was out there" for its own sake. But, the ancient Indians were not interested in planetary movement for its own sake; their interest in it was solely to enable them just to construct a very accurate almanac which could help them predict the future as accurately as possible. Had they been interested in just 'understanding' planetary movement for its own sake and nothing more, they would certainly have long ago found the 'pattern' which Kepler found a couple of centuries later. Even today there are thousands of astrologers in India who can accurately predict the movement of the planets, but are not aware of either Kepler's laws or modern astronomy. I have chosen to dwell on this point at some length solely in order to drive home a very important fact about the thoroughly practical orientation of Indian scientific thought which it shares in common with much of Indian philosophical as well as religious thought.

Returning to the consideration of life in ancient India, it must be noted that religion was not a major factor of social organization.

Ancient Hindu society was not divided into religious groups; it was divided into caste groups. These castes also many times had very close links with religion and this linking of castes with specific religions is still a living phenomenon that can be observed in contemporary India. Those who follow the Viśiṣṭādvaita philosophy and religion are a distinct group called Iyengars in the southern regions of India. Those who follow Advaita are called Iyers. The followers of Vīraśaivism are called Liṅgāyatas. There are many people of sub-sects among brāhmaṇas who follow Advaita but are not Iyers, but this point is unimportant for our purpose. The important and main point to be noted here is that there are many castes and sub-castes in India which subscribe to a particular religion exclusively or in common with other castes or sub-castes. Many castes were, in their origin, pre-eminently occupational groups and this nature of caste is borne out by a very large number of caste names that are also the names of a particular profession like goldsmith, cobbler, barber and so on; such names survive till today although the members of these castes may not all be following the relevant profession.

Each caste had its own *dharma* or code of conduct. The castes were also arranged in a hierarchy and there were superior and inferior castes. But still, all castes were involved in the life of the community and had their own place and importance. Many public, religious rituals in Hindu society are still of such a nature that they involve and require the participation of several caste groups and sometimes even of people of other religions like the Muslims. The most important point for my purpose here is the fact that although Indians belonged to distinct religious groups, yet they did not live in those groups but lived in specific caste groups. Caste was the undisputed and primary determining factor of stratified social life and not religion, though religion often played a very crucial and important role in the life of many of the caste groups.

Though caste rules tended to divide men in society into distinct groups, yet religion helped these diverse groups to remain together to form a harmonious whole. One outstanding feature of religion as practised by the majority of Indians has been an underlying realization that whatever gods one may worship in an astounding variety of forms, they are all forms of one single divine being. If there have been no large-scale religious conflicts in ancient India — conflicts of the kind that were once rampant in the West — it must largely be attributed to this underlying assumption of the oneness of all divinity.

In pre-Independent India, even when there was conflict among different castes, religion was not a factor that initiated or contributed to it. If we talk to an illiterate Indian of any caste even today, he will come out with his belief in the oneness of divinity in no time. The deep religious faith that the same divinity was present in all beings seems to have prevented religion-based conflicts among the various castes. The caste never was, like any other institution in any other society anywhere in the world, a perfect social institution. It did possess its shortcomings, and the emergence of the Bhakti cults on a large scale in India from the eleventh century onwards, which also eventually led to the emergence of new castes, seems to have its roots in the failure of the caste system in certain respects. The condemnation of the notion of caste superiority in the light of the oneness of the Divine Being who pervades the whole of creation, is a recurring theme in all popular compositions and songs belonging to the Bhakti tradition. In fact, we can find a criticism of the caste system almost throughout the later history of India at different periods. One of the peculiarities of the innumerable Bhakti cults was that though their avowed goal was to unite men regardless of their caste barriers, many of them ultimately ended up as new caste groups. Repeated emergence of the contradictory phenomenon of the "casteless castes" is something peculiar only to India. The institution of caste has simply refused to die, despite the best efforts of some of the best men of our country, not only in the past but even during our own times.

The Bhakti movement also reinforced a recurring theme of most Indian religious thinking, viz., that there is only one divinity manifesting itself in a multitude of forms. It is also responsible, in no small measure, for the development of a syncretic religious tradition which flourished in thousands of places all over India and is living even today. While the Christians and the Muslims of the West have in the past fought pitched religious battles spread over centuries, the Indians, by and large, have lived in such harmony despite their believing in countless number of different gods, that it can be safely said that social conflict rooted in religion is the exception rather than the rule, at least until very recent times. That was because there could be a God for the whole caste, another God for the whole clan or a family within that caste, a God for the whole village and innumerable, different "gods of one's choice" (*iṣṭadevatā*) for different individuals within the same family. Thus, several gods were worshipped simultaneously as well as at different times by different castes and individuals belonging to different clans in order to obtain different kinds of favours. Yet there was absolutely no conflict among the worshippers belonging to these different castes.

One very characteristic feature of social life in India has been that there was no strict division between its religious and secular aspects. The soteriological and the non-soteriological goals were never kept separate in India. There was an interesting blend of the two. This becomes evident through the concepts of *varṇāśrama-dharma* and *puruṣārtha* as advocated in India. The first *āśrama*, the *brahmacaryāśrama* (stage of studentship) prepares an individual for both worldly life and the pursuit of liberation. The worldly ideals are pursued during the second *gṛhasthāśrama* (stage of the householder) and the last two, *vānaprastha* and *saṁnyāsa āśrama*s are exclusively meant for the pursuit of liberation. The "goals of human life" (*puruṣārtha*) are also four. They are the well-known *dharma, artha, kāma* and *mokṣa.* The stage of studentship prepares one for the remaining stages of life by imparting the knowledge necessary for them. In the stage of the householder, one is expected to pursue worldly wealth (*artha*) and desires (*kāma*) in a manner not opposed to the more basic value and ideal of *dharma*. In the terminal stages of the *vānaprastha* and *saṁnyāsa āśrama*s, one is expected to pursue the ideal of liberation or *mokṣa* exclusively.

The idea underlying all this is that liberation should be aimed at in and through one's worldly existence. In fact, it is a commonly accepted idea among many Indians brought up in the classical mould that one is born a human being just in order to enable oneself to achieve liberation. The secular, social life is the gateway to liberation. Thus, the whole of one's social existence comes to acquire a distinct and unmistakable soteriological orientation. Because of the existence of such soteriological orientation and also because in many cases the caste itself constitutes the religious group as well, a neat separation of the religious aspects of life from its secular aspects cannot be easily made. All religious and social duties of an individual are performed only within the all-pervasive framework of caste. There is no social life of any kind outside caste. It may be noted here that in many cases, the giving up of one's caste is also the giving up of one's religion.

It is also important to note that the kind of institutionalization of religion that took place in the West did not take place in India. It is not quite correct to equate the Indian religious institution, the *maṭha*, with the Church of the West. In the West, no one is born Christian; one is made Christian through baptism and one is baptized only by an accredited and ordained priest of the Church. In India, on the other hand, one belongs to a religious group simply by virtue of being born in that group which is usually a caste group and such caste groups are hereditary ones. Also, in India, priests are involved in religious ceremonies connected with naming, marriage, death and so on but these priests are not either ordained or licensed by any *maṭha*. The priestly class exists, but it is not institutionalized. Quite often people of different castes owe their allegiance to the same *maṭha* because their religious beliefs and practices are similar. It is a well-known fact that even the same gods, like Lord Viśvanātha of Kāśī and Lord Veṅkaṭeśvara of Tirupati are worshipped by widely different castes who do not either inter-dine or inter-marry among themselves. In fact, religious faith not only often cuts across the caste barrier, it also many times cuts across the inter-religious barrier as well. There are too many Christian and Muslim shrines that regularly attract a large number of Hindu worshippers; there are also Hindu shrines at which Muslims, and sometimes Christians too, offer worship. There are also some temples where people of lower castes have been priests for centuries and people of higher castes have no hesitation in worshipping at these temples. Catholicity of faith and acceptance of the belief that different religions are just different doorways to the same Divine has been the dominant characteristic of the religious frame of mind of a typical, ordinary Indian. Though the institution of caste stratified Indian society in extremely complex and unfortunate ways, still the society was mostly prevented from breaking up into warring segments because of the overpowering belief in the oneness of all existence and divinity. The co-operative economic structure of the caste system also definitely helped.

The belief in *varṇāśrama-dharma, puruṣārtha, karma* and rebirth also jointly contributed to harmony among the castes besides the very vital fact that the castes were economically too closely interdependent on one another to permit any serious conflict among them. Non-cooperation among the various castes in a community would immediately paralyse social life itself. Though the institution of caste is much reviled in contemporary India, perhaps justifiably so because of its alleged irrelevance today, it must still be conceded that despite all its alleged iniquities the institution of caste played a very significant social role for centuries. Caste as an economic institution was very greatly responsible for the generation of enormous wealth in ancient India and eventually India became so famous for its prosperity in the ancient world that for centuries in succession it remained a great attraction for marauders and colonizers from many parts of the globe.

Thus, what endured for centuries in India was a complex social life in which philosophy, religion and caste were inextricably combined and was so combined that it almost always contributed to peace, prosperity and harmony in public life over the centuries; although this "peace, prosperity and harmony" might now be dismissed by some as peace and harmony at the cost of equality and social justice.

One last poin I would like to dwell on is about the 'State.' The institution of the State as found in the modern West does not seem to have existed in India. Nothing higher than a feudal system can be found in ancient India. Even the structure of very large kingdoms and empires was feudal in nature. Politics never made a difference to the life of the common man who was not at all a significant political entity. The unit of social life was the caste group or the village, the caste council, and the village *pañcāyat* had complete control over the social life of an individual. There was an administrative bureaucracy attached to every king or emperor but it took care of some general aspects of social life like currency, revenue collection, defence, means of communication and so on. The entire set-up was something like a huge joint family; it was nowhere near the modern Western State in its structure, power or function. The king or emperor hardly was the law-maker; he was rather just in charge of upholding the law or *dharma* expounded by Law-givers or writers of the Dharmaśāstras. These Law-givers were not legislators as found within the modern structure of a 'State.' Even the term 'law' is a typically Western term, and it is not at all a proper substitute for what is represented by the Indian concept of *dharma*. Whether one was a king or a commoner, it was equally one's duty to act according to *dharma* and uphold the *dharma*. Even the recluse who largely lived outside society had his own *dharma*. No one was above *dharma*. Therefore, the idea of a sovereign authority, the State, that lords above everyone in society, is totally foreign to the classical Indian modes of life. The ruler as a legislator, i.e., as the sole authority who *makes* laws, is also unknown to the classical Indian way of life. Therefore, anyone who wanted to change Indian society — whether it was our colonizers or our own elected representatives — had this kind of a society to deal with. It was this society that was expected to assimilate the new ideas and conceptions like democracy, socialism and secularism that were transplanted into its environment after Independence, through the Indian Constitution.

III

So far, I have given a brief sketch of the nature of philosophy and religion in India and the West and while discussing the Western ideas I have also given a brief account of how secularism arose in the Western context. I have not entered into any detailed discussion of the implications of this concept or how it is operative in the West. I have also not spoken anything about secularism in India. Now I wish to dwell on these matters.

I have pointed out how the development of scientific thought and the development of the institution of the State eventually contributed to the emergence of the concept of secularism in the West. Before the emergence of the State as a distinct entity, the Church was the sole seat of all power and authority in society including political authority and power. When the State emerged as a distinct institution, the political power and authority was transferred to the State. But the Roman Catholic Church did not cease to be a State altogether, since the Pope was accepted as a sovereign by other States, but as a sovereign whose jurisdiction was confined to what we now know as the Vatican City in Rome where the Pope resides. Even today, the Pope has his ambassadors stationed in several countries, although in international politics the role of the Pope as a Head of State is probably at its barest minimum or even non-existent.

After transferring political power and authority to the State, the Church ceased to legislate in secular matters, but it continued to have sovereign powers to legislate over ecclesiastical matters.

Since the sovereignty of the Church in all religious or ecclesiastical matters was indeed recognized by the State itself, the State could not, naturally, exercise legislative powers in those matters. In the process of their struggles against the Church or the Pope for securing political autonomy, some of the kings had even declared themselves the Supreme Head of the Church within the geographical regions that were under their control. It is common knowledge that power once achieved is not easily given up and hence, even now we have cases of political sovereigns who are also heads of the churches. For example, the present Queen of England is also the Head of the Church of England following a long-standing tradition in which the Monarch of the British Realm is also the Head of the Church of England and even has the title "The Defender of Faith," a title given by the Pope himself long ago to King Henry VIII for defending the Catholic Church against attack from Protestants. The rulers of England later became Protestant, but still they merrily retained the title given by the Pope. That is because, I think, even the titles once acquired are not easily given up. Probably as a symbol of the political sovereignty the Church once enjoyed, the Archbishop of Canterbury who is the Primate of All England, continues to have a permanent place in the House of Lords. For obvious reasons, in the early stages the Church and the State were still closely interwoven, but gradually there was a realization of complete separation of powers.

Even though the Monarch of England who is the highest political authority in all England is also the Head of the Church of England, England is very much a democracy and it is also a secular democracy. Religious freedom is a notable aspect of British democracy. Even though the Protestants are in majority, as citizens they have no special privileges which are denied to persons professing other religions. But then again, probably it is not quite so since no Roman Catholic can ascend the British throne. This is because of a very natural reason that the Church of England is non-Catholic and as such the British Monarch who heads that

Church has also to be non-Catholic. Although the Head of a Church is the Head of the State in the United Kingdom, the most important point is that the State is a fully secular institution and it also remains thoroughly secular in practice.

There can even be a State that declares itself as theocratic, but it can still profess a secularity in outlook. For example, from the Article 9 of the Sri Lankan Constitution it is clear that it is a Buddhist state, but its Constitution grants the freedom of thought, religion and conscience to all its citizens and these freedoms are absolute. Article 14 of the Sri Lankan Constitution gives the right to every citizen to practice the religion of his choice and this right is absolute and it cannot be interfered with by anyone. Only the State may interfere with this freedom but only when an exercise of this freedom by an individual results in harm to public order, morality or the security of the nation.

The Swiss do not subscribe to the theory of the constitutional separation of the State from the Church. This can be inferred from Article 50(4) of their Constitution which stipulates that the establishment of bishoprics in Switzerland requires authorization by the Confederation. Nearly 97 per cent of the Swiss population is Christian, but there is absolute freedom of religion in Switzerland.

The reason why the United Kingdom is a *de facto* secular state is that it is a democracy. In fact, the very concept of democracy involves the concept of secularism. In a democracy, any individual has an absolute right to freedom of thought, opinion and belief as long as the public expression, profession and practice of them does not endanger public order, morality or security. That is, the State *cannot* interfere with the public expression of any kind of thought or opinion about anything whatever, by any of its citizens, as long as such expression does not endanger public order, morality and security. Therefore, any citizen of a democratic state has an absolute and fundamental right to believe in any religion whatever and follow its precepts. A democratic State cannot look upon the practitioners of any particular religion more favourably than it does on the practitioners of any other religion. A democratic State cannot discriminate among its citizens on grounds of religion. Showing any kind of special favour to any religious group would, *ipso facto*, render a State discriminatory and a State that thus discriminates among its citizens is not true to the democratic spirit. It of course naturally ceases to be perfectly secular in character.

Therefore, in the West where the institution of the State, as we know, took its birth, due to various complex factors that cannot be discussed here, the State gradually evolved into a democratic institution. As the State went on shaping itself in a democratic mould, it also naturally developed a thoroughly secular character. Thus, though a State need not necessarily be democratic, *if it is democratic, it also has to be invariably secular*. In such a State, not only do all its citizens have the right to practice any or no religion, but they also have the right not to be discriminated against any other citizen on grounds of religion. If we look at it from another angle, the individual or the Church can be a perfectly legitimate religious entity, but such entities cannot also be valid *political units* of public life in the eyes of that State. Such a State is a genuinely democratic State. This is not a picture of an *ideal* democratic State that might be unattainable in reality because indeed there are States around the world, as shown above, that are secular in the sense described and these States have no religious conflict as a recurring feature of their public life. But, unfortunately, there are also "democratic" States that have fallen short in many respects, particularly in respect of being secular. Their secular policies obviously seem not to have fared very well since serious religious conflict is a recurring feature of social life in these States.

Then, why has the secular policy failed in some of these States while it has not failed in the others? Why does a policy fail? A policy fails either due to failure in its conception or due to failure in execution of the conception. If a policy is correct in conception but its execution alone faulty, probably there is an easier solution to it; that solution is just to adopt correct measures. But, if there is an error at the level of conception itself, no amount of sincere efforts will lead to the realization of the desired end. From this angle, if secularism has not been faring very well in India, we need to ask whether the defect lies in the policy itself or in the execution of that policy. Hence I would devote the rest of this paper to an examination of at least some of the issues concerning secularism in India. I am certainly not equal to this enormously complex task because I am not a specialist in either politics or religion. But specialists in these areas have been in charge of things for quite a few years, and with consequences which are obviously there for all to see. Therefore, I do not think that my joining in the fray would make the situation any worse. But I would caution you about the very tentative nature of my thoughts and perceptions since they are not very thorough and it is so only due to my own imperfect knowledge of matters, religious as well as political.

What am I going to say is perhaps also controversial but then, I still say it because what is a philosopher's worth if he is afraid of controversies? I think that controversy and argumentation is what keeps philosophical thought alive but that is so only when what is challenged and argued about is something vital and not trivial. Secularism is very vital to our survival as a nation and a State, although what I say regarding secularism may not prove to be equally vital.

IV

India attained Independence in 1947 after a long struggle with the British, its colonial masters, but unfortunately, only after a bloody fight within the country between the Hindus and the Muslims. Therefore, when the Constituent Assembly composed a Constitution for the Republic of India, it included Articles 25 to 30 to preserve the right to religion and also the religious rights of the minorities. The term 'minority' is nowhere defined in the Constitution while the rights of the minorities are clearly specified. The right to freedom of religion conferred by Article 25(1) is not just confined to all citizens of India but extends to all 'persons' thus including even aliens. This right is conferred, like in Western democracies and in Sri Lanka, subject to public order, morality and health and "other provisions." The right extends to profession, practice and propagation of the religion of one's choice. The "other provisions" are found in clause 2(*a*) and (*b*) of Article 25. These empower the State to make any law

(*a*) regulating or restricting any economic, financial, political or other secular activity which may be associated with religious practice, and

(*b*) providing for social welfare and reform or the throwing open of Hindu religious institutions of a public character to all classes and sections of Hindus.

Explanation II in the Article 25 runs as follows:

> In sub-clause (*b*) of clause (2), the reference to Hindus shall be construed as including a reference to persons professing the Sikh, Jaina or Buddhist religion, and the reference to Hindu religious institutions shall be construed accordingly.

This Article treats all citizens of India, excluding Muslims, Christians and other smaller communities of religions of non-Indian origin, as just one religious bloc called 'Hindus.' The clear implication of this, at least in so far as the Hindus are concerned, is that the Constitution treats them all as belonging to one religious group irrespective of the specific religious or caste groups to which they might belong. Not only this, Hindus are treated on par with Jainas, Buddhists and Sikhs. The close association of religion with castes, a peculiar feature of Indian social life to which I have drawn attention earlier, is not recognized by the Constitution. The Constitution does not thus distinguish between one Indian and another as a Jaina, a Buddhist, a Sikh or a Hindu on the basis of the religions they profess. While the Constitution does not recognize a

Sikh as a Sikh *vis-a-vis* a Hindu, a Jaina or a Buddhist, it does recognize him as a Hindu *vis-a-vis* a Muslim, a Christian or a Jew. In other words, the Constitution does take note of a citizen's religion in distinguishing between its citizens as belonging to minority religions (i.e., specifically religions of non-Indian origin) and as not so belonging.

Since religion has a close association with caste which is essentially a social group, naturally religion also exercises control over several secular aspects of social life in addition to exercising control over its purely religious aspects. If, as in a genuinely secular State, complete freedom of religion is granted, in the caste-ridden Indian society that would amount to virtual surrendering of certain spheres of social life to religion when, in fact, they legitimately fall within the jurisdiction of the State. Since it was widely believed that the caste system was responsible for severe inequalities and backwardness in India, it was thought to be necessary as well as wise to interfere with the secular aspects over which the caste group — which was also a religious group — had control, in order to promote social welfare and reform. This seems to be the justification for including clauses 2(*a*) and 2(*b*) referred to above.

But this has certain consequences. State intervention in secular matters concerning castes requires a clear separation of the secular aspects of a caste from its religious aspects and also, an equally clear separation of the purely religious aspects of a religion from its non-religious or secular aspects. How does the Constitution go about in identifying the purely religious aspects of a religion? Since the Constitution does not do this identification, our only guide in this very vital matter is the vast body of judgements delivered by the High Courts and the Supreme Court in India. But, unfortunately, no writer on Indian secularism I know of has made any extensive, systematic study of these judgements. Therefore, I will make a very cursory attempt here. In the cases of *Stainislaus* vs. *State of Madhya Pradesh* (1975), the court ruling has been that what constitutes the essential part of a religion is primarily to be ascertained with reference to what the practitioners of that religion itself regard as its essential part; but, in the cases of *Quareshi* vs. *State of Bihar* (1959), *Digyadarsan* vs. *State of Andhra Pradesh* (1970) and *Ramanuja* vs. *State of Tamil Nadu* (1972), the Supreme Court has ruled that the determination of what constitutes the essential parts of a religion is subject to judicial scrutiny.

Before the Supreme Court gave this ruling, there were several different rulings. In the case of *Sarup Singh* vs. *State of Punjab* (1959) and *Ram* vs. *State of Orissa* (1959), the ruling was that each religious denomination or organization enjoys complete autonomy in the matter of deciding as to what rites and ceremonies are *essential* according to the tenets of the religion they follow. But in the case of *Moti Das* vs. *Sahi* (1959) and *Durgah Committee* vs. *Hussain* (1961), the Supreme Court ruled that the Court has the right to determine whether a particular rite or observance is to be regarded as essential by the tenets of a particular religion. Accordingly, the Supreme Court has ruled in the case of *Quareshi* vs. *State of Bihar* (1959) that the sacrifice of a cow is not an obligatory act according to Islam. The same Court had ruled earlier in the case of *Ramprasad* vs. *State of Uttar Pradesh* (1957) that marrying a second wife during the lifetime of the first wife cannot be said to be an integral part of Hinduism. It also ruled that a similar act of taking a second wife even by a Muslim cannot be said to be a part of Muslim religion in the case of *Badruddin* vs. *Aisha* (1957).

A highly disconcerting feature of Indian life after it became a Republic is that hundreds of cases involving some practice claimed to have been enjoined by one's religion, have gone up to the Supreme Court and I can readily remember one here concerning whether a temple elephant should be adorned with a Y *nāmam* or a U *nāmam* on its forehead, these two *nāmams* (marks) being religious symbols used by two different sects of Śrīvaiṣṇavas in south India. It is very clear from the above that the disputes that the followers of a religion would have previously solved among themselves by arriving at a consensus or a working solution are now being dragged to the courts, thus permanently dividing them into petitioners and respondents, thereby bringing down seriously the quality of religious life. It must also be noted that the Supreme Court has held in the case of *Venkataraman* vs. *State of Mysore* (1958) that the excommunication of a member ordered by a religious sect on religious grounds is a purely religious act protected under Article 26(*b*) ("Right of every religious denomination to manage its own affairs in matters of religion") and therefore cannot be interfered with by the courts even when such excommunication would severely affect the civil rights of that member. Some years ago there was an instance of a Chief Minister of a State who did something in the course of his normal duties as the chief executive of his State but whose acts were perceived by the Supreme Religious Council of his community as violative of their religion, for which it punished him by ordering him to clean the shoes of the devotees.

An important point to be considered here is that when the State reserves for itself the power to interfere in matters of religion which do not stand clearly separated from secular matters, there will be serious restraints on the effective use of such power. Even when this power is very fairly exercised by the State in public interest, it will eventually encourage the religious communities to think that whatever the State does not interfere with is, for that very reason, right and will never think of reforming their patterns of behaviour. This danger is particularly great when the religious community in question is a minority community enjoying special protection under the right to non-interference by the State guaranteed by the Constitution. If this minority community is not also socially advanced (unlike the Parsis), and a large number of its members are socially and economically backward, the harm done by such protection can be really deadly. With most educated individuals moving away from formal religion, religion increasingly becomes the exclusive preserve of fanatics and bigots who use the religious sentiments of the community to further their personal agendas. There is thus very little scope for any kind of reform to come from within the fold of the religious communities themselves. Under such circumstances, I do not think that the freedom given to the religious denominations under Article 26(*a*), (*b*), (*c*) and (*d*) are indeed useful and would also be used by the communities in a manner contributory to their general welfare.

Articles 29 and 30, and in particular Article 30, give protection to minorities to preserve their culture and religion and also to further their interests through establishing and administering educational institutions of their choice. The sections of the Constitution that were incorporated to specifi-cally protect the interests of the minorities are the unfortunate legacy of the bloodbath that preceded our Independence. As a further tragic consequence, every allegation of the infringement of the rights of the minorities has tended to make the minorities feel insecure and has made them resist any kind of reformation in their codes that would bring them closer in their practices to other communities. They seem to feel safe in remaining different from the rest of their brethren. Their attempts to remain distinct and different is also well-protected by the Constitution. This has made it increasingly difficult for them to integrate themselves with the other communities. Meanwhile, the majority communities seem to be getting impatient about the special privileges enjoyed by the minorities as well as the efforts of the minorities to continue to remain as exclusive groups. Fringe groups among the majority communities have developed which have adopted unmistakably anti-minority agendas. The situation is hotting up as days are rolling by and religious fundamentalism has already become an inalienable feature of certain segments of the Indian population thus vitiating national life as a whole.

There is a reason why this unfortunate crisis is developing. It is, in my opinion, clearly due to the politicization of religion and caste in post-Independent India. This politicization probably would have become quite hard to accomplish had the Indian State earnestly fulfilled the constitutionally envisioned promise of complete literacy. Education has the power to broaden vision and basically alter world-views and lifestyles. Had education reached the minorities on a large scale, they would have become less susceptible to fundamentalist influences. The secular ideal of the Constitution which itself was not very well conceived — because it was conceived under pressure, in haste and also disregarding ground realities of Indian society — has contributed to this mess. When the religious and secular aspects of the Indian society were themselves neither easily distinguishable nor separable, the Constitution intervened to let the State assume control over those aspects of community life that were social and secular in character. While reformist legislation was forced down the throats of the Hindus, no similar legislation was enacted for the religious minorities as the Constitution itself came in the way of any such attempt.

But most caste groups or communities were reluctant to give up their centuries-old social and secular privileges, but they also knew that fighting the Constitution was an uphill task. Therefore, many of them quickly realized that the way to preserving their privileges was by getting closer to the corridors of power and in the process of getting there they got themselves transformed into little reservoirs of power — political power. The institution of caste had no political power of any kind in the past and with the Constitution declaring its resolve to completely ignore the caste of a person in matters of public life, the institution of caste should have quickly declined. It would certainly have quickly declined or lost most of its power had the country embarked upon a massive literacy programme in earnest right immediately after Independence. Gutenberg, who invented the printing press, had an important role in the success of the social revolution in Europe and the ultimate triumph of democracy and secularism. The printed word gave a new power to the vast majority of people — a power that was so far confined only to the clergy who were in charge of all knowledge and learning. But, the State in India failed miserably in bringing literacy to the masses and its achievement even after more than 50 years is most disappointing. Therefore, the inevitable has happened.

The few who were educated or were the leaders in each community were able to get closer to the centres of power and since the communities had great faith in these educated men and leaders, it became relatively easy for the political parties to get the votes of these communities in the elections through winning over the leaders of such communities by fair or foul means. Caste, which had been sentenced to death by the Constitution, received a new lease of life as the handmaiden of the newly emerging political class. Misuse of State legislation concerning backward classes for amelioration of the poorer sections of the population further contributed to this politicization process. Progressive social legislation unfortunately developed a pernicious political dimension. Once the caste groups tasted political power or certain special privileges, it was impossible for them to stay away. Exploiting the minorities, who were mostly backward and ignorant, became the standard political game in which the different political parties in the country vied — and still vigorously vie — with one another.

Coupled with the decline of true religious fervour and a simultaneous acquisition of political power, the caste has still managed to remain the most important functional unit of social life. To live as a caste or religious group and to display this identity with shameless pride has become a normal feature of public life. The enormous increase in the caste associations in the post-independence era is a clear demonstration of the rise as well as legitimization of caste and community feelings at the level of national life.

Therefore, the war that the Constitution declared against the institution of caste and religious animosities has been nearly silenced in later years. The war against caste has dramatically transformed itself into war among castes and this war has only contributed to the hardening of caste differences and thus strengthening the institution of caste. The catholicity of religious outlook that once cut across caste barriers and even barriers of religion has been impaled by the communal riots that have become all too frequent. While the democratizing process in the West slowly moved in the direction of humanism, India has become more dehumanized after Independence. Civic values and finer sentiments have taken a back seat in public life. Ego and selfishness, the two factors against which the Indian religious and cultural tradition had always carried on an attack, have returned into our public life with renewed vigour.

Many believe that we have made progress after independence although certain undesirable factors are still found in our public life. But is this true? Are we really better than our ancestors whom we characterize as reeking in religious superstition and caste discrimination? This indeed is an important question that requires an objective investigation and answer. It is true, for example, that the Harijans were severely discriminated against by caste Hindus in the past centuries. But that was at a time when liberty, equality and fraternity in the modern sense were not heard of by Indians. Even though they had not formally adopted these noble social ideals, still, I do not think that they ever tied a Harijan to a pole and beat him to death or burnt him down in the presence of his helpless relatives and fellowmen. Such incidents did not take place in ancient India that was hopelessly caste-ridden, but they are taking place today in a democratic India. I firmly believe that the level of progress of any society is to be measured by the level of brutality it allows and tolerates in public life. By this standard, our ancestors were much more civilized, democratic and secular than we have been in independent India. I honestly feel that there is not really much for our ancestors to be ashamed of; if they have something to be most ashamed of it is certainly us — their successors and heirs to a great tradition that had some unrivalled excellences of its own. No doubt, it had some defects just like any other tradition anywhere else always had. It was up to us to preserve the excellence and remedy the defects in a free India in the light of our own modern education and classical wisdom. But what did we do in this important matter? We have largely thought that we should necessarily discard our past tradition in order to modernize our social life.

The fathers of our Constitution were all very well educated, of course in the Western tradition of education which we are continuing even today. They were thoroughly conversant with Western democratic traditions and wanted to transplant the best elements of it into our soil. In their enthusiasm, they did not stop to ponder over how the ideals of liberty and equality could be made to take roots in a soil that had known only subordination and hierarchy. They tried, and certainly very honestly, to provide a blue print to change our society into a democratic, socialistic and secular republic by transplanting certain Western ideas and ideals. Our Constitution is the framework of concepts to which, like the Soviets, we have tried to make our society conform. Our story as a free nation is just the story of an attempt to fit our society into a beautiful framework of ideas brought from the West. We have been trying hard, but it has not been fitting in quite well. Do you think we should still keep on trying in the same way as we have been since Independence?

3

Dharma — Its Normative Base and Orthopraxeic Frame

Concept of Dharma and its Implications in Dharmaśāstras

Godabarisha Mishra

yajñena yajñamayajanta devāḥ tāni dharmāṇi prathamānyāsan ।
te ha nākaṁ mahimānaḥ sacanta yatra pūrve sādhyāḥ santi devāḥ ।।

Gods [Nature's Bounties] worshipped the Supreme Lord with the sacrifice. These have been the earliest ordinances (*dharmas*). They, the great ones, thus attained heaven, where the earlier realized ones dwell in their resplendence.

— *Ṛgveda*, 10.90.16

The association of ritual with morality is clearly a consequence of the well-known blending of religion and philosophy in India. But that is not its only explanation. There is also a striking resemblance between them, which must have led to their being thus mixed up with each other. Morality as conceived in India by all excepting only the Cārvākas, has a reference to a future life, just as much as ritual has. Eschatological considerations are not separated from worldly ones in *ṛta*, *ṛṇa* and *dharma*. In all alike, the idea is based on a perspective, which extends beyond this life.

— M. Hiriyanna, *Indian Conception of Values*, 1975, p. 158

The term 'Hinduism' can be retained but with a shift of meaning. It is not *one* religion, but a group of distinct Indian religions.

> Once this connotation is accepted, one can go a step further and realise the enormous challenge which Hinduism, as a matter of fact, offers to the other religions today. For in Hinduism it was possible to create a culture of accepted multiformity, able to develop generous liberality and tolerance between religions and ideologies to a degree which civilisations based on Judaism, Christianity and Islam were never able to achieve.
>
> — Heinrich, Von Stietencron,
> "Hinduism on the Proper Use of a Deceptive Term,"
> In *Hinduism Reconsidered*, 1991, p. 21.

Introduction

Dharma is a loaded concept in Indian tradition. Since its connotations vary from time to time and author to author, it becomes well-nigh impossible to offer its equivalent expression in English. The Dharmaśāstras, the treatises dealing with *dharma*, do not provide a particular view on the topic. Rather they provide a framework for orthopraxis which partly explains the things as they are and lays down what they ought to be. Thus, the concept stands for various privileges, duties, obligations and normative behaviour. Given this complex background, the term has come to mean a religion, namely 'Hinduism' as understood in the West. It has been identified with a particular way of life based on a belief system and more conventionally on a set of "do's and don'ts." The construction of modern Hinduism is not bereft of such assumptions even though its oneness is hardly evident. As a product of the amalgamation of multiple traditions, Hinduism has to face the problem of ambiguity and the essence of this so-called "Hindu religion" is difficult to pinpoint. As a consequence, the concept of *dharma* has been subjected to varied exegetical analysis in order to remove the vagueness pertaining to the word 'Hindu.' Now the question may be raised as to how do we envision Hinduism as a *dharma* based on a tradition which has roots in the past and consequences for the future. Keeping in view the changing formulations of the religion in the present which is neither totally divorced from the past nor adheres to the tradition completely, there is a need to review Hinduism as a concept of spiritual liberalism. In this enterprise of selection and modification, we need to examine our early texts of Dharmaśāstra to understand how the changing views of *dharma* were accommodated from time to time in ancient India.

The present paper tries to address the above questions and deal with the concept of *dharma* by alluding to the views available in the post-Vedic, viz., Sūtra and Smṛti period.

Dharma — A Multi-dimensional Problematic

The concept of *dharma* has been basically understood in two distinct ways in Indian tradition. First, it has been understood as an "order," a social 'order,' that goes with the concept of *varṇa* or social stratification which meant a simple social structure (*varṇa-dharma*) in the early days of its conception. Secondly, it has been understood as a moral order, which owes its allegiance to the former since social order is not possible to be attained without the moral order. This is called *sādhāraṇa-dharma*. In the six systems of Indian Philosophy, the topic has been taken up for extensive discussion and *dharma* has been explained variedly as an action, as unseen (merit), quality and so on. After the advent of Christianity and Islam in India, the word *dharma* developed new connotations of faith of a race and got a new appellation called "Hindu *dharma*."[1]

Thus, *dharma* which was used in the sense of social and moral order and which was meant for strict observation steadily lost its hold with concessions creeping into the system. So the normative nature of this so-called religion was never very rigid as it has to be

---

1. The word "Hindu" was of a peculiar origin. The Pārsīs identified the inhabitants who lived on the banks of river Sindhu by this name as distinguished from Christians, Muslims and others. In course of time the term "Hindu *dharma*" was used to identify the faith of those inhabitants in the sense of religion like that of Christianity, Islam, etc. In this paper the word Hindu is used in the same sense.

based more on orthopraxy (correct behaviour) than orthodoxy (approved opinion). The idea is that, rationalism is valued more than the textual orthodoxy which ascribes injunctions primarily relevant to a period in the past. This being the case, Hinduism may not be taken as a religion in the strict sense of the term as it may go against the very definition of the term 'religion,' which has to be founded on certain stipulations since the time of its origin. So despite all self-contradicting features, the term "Hinduism" emerged as a fairly acceptable appellation referring to a religion-like concept if not strictly a religion.

Here I would endeavour to highlight how the term *dharma* has been dealt with differently in various Indian texts. Later, I would also try to explain that it is social workability that has been the criterion in its formulation and hence there is nothing wrong in identifying it with a cultural system which is no more geographically bound. I would also discuss the flexible nature of the texts, which can adapt to the needs of the changing times rather than being imposing eternal fixed laws.

Dharma — Types and Scope

The real significance of *dharma* lies in the profound Vedic perception of man's existence as a rational being who harmonizes the different purposes of life to be realized here and hereafter. Hence, it was deemed necessary that people be committed to respect *dharma* and act accordingly to conduct their personal and social affairs. In keeping with these dual requirements the concept was basically divided into two types, viz., *sādhāraṇa-dharma* (man's universal duties) and *varṇāśrama-dharma* (specific or class duties). In the former, the word *dharma* denotes a social or moral order which holds the society together. In the beginning, this was a simple social structure, which in due course of time became differentiated into four classes or castes namely, brāhmaṇas, kṣatriyas, vaiśyas and śūdras. Initially, it was a social necessity that gave rise to this stratification. For example, a society must secure itself from external threat and maintain internal order which necessitated the class of kṣatriyas. Similar needs led to the formation of other classes. In order to avoid chaos in regulating these classes the concept of *dharma* evolved. It must be noted here that the Vedic Indians who were nature worshippers over a period of time changed their way of worship and the rituals became predominant means of worship. It was during this period when the brāhmaṇa priests got superior positions in the sacrificial activities; the caste system lost its original character and the idea of *jāti* was substituted for the *varṇa* system and later on it came to be identified with the very birth of a person.

The concept of *svadharma* which later on was understood with relation to the job assigned to a particular caste was not intended in the initial days of its adoption. Thus, the *varṇāśrama-dharma*s were not determined by the birth of a person or like the present-day caste system. Rather, a person was qualified to be of a particular *varṇa* because of his innate ability to do a particular job. A person born to any parents can choose to adopt any profession he is eligible for; he can become a brāhmaṇa, kṣatriya, vaiśya or śūdra. A brāhmaṇa's son can become śūdra if he lacks such dispositions as possessed by a brāhmaṇa and vice-versa.[2] In the *Bhagavad-Gītā*, Kṛṣṇa clearly states that the four *varṇa*s were made by him in accordance with the characteristics possessed and actions performed.[3]

As regards the precise character of *dharma*, there are three views. For Mīmāṁsakas, *dharma* is an action (*yāgādireva dharmaḥ*). Through the intermediacy of *apūrva* (unseen potency) it yields its fruit. According to Naiyāyikas, *dharma* is a quality that is present in the self. For theistic schools, *dharma* is neither a quality nor an action. It is through meritorious deeds that one accumulates *dharma* and it is instrumental in getting the desired result which is either

2. *śūdro brāhmaṇatāmeti brāhmaṇaścaiti śūdratām*
kṣatriyāj jātamevaṁ tu vidyād vaiśyāt tathaiva ca — *Manu-Smṛti*, 10.65.

3. *cāturvarṇyam mayā sṛṣṭam guṇakarma-vibhāgaśaḥ*
— *Bhagavad-Gītā*, 4.13.

attainment of something good or avoidance of some evil. In the Vedas, it is used in the sense of religious ordinances.[4] In the Upaniṣads, the word *dharma* is equated with the word *satya*.[5] In the *Chāndogyopaniṣad*, it is described in terms of three features, viz., sacrifice, study, and charity. Here *dharma* denotes the peculiar duties assigned to different *āśrama*s.[6] P.V. Kane describes *dharma* as five-fold: *varṇa-dharma*, *āśrama-dharma*, *varṇāśrama-dharma*, *naimittika-dharma*, and *guṇa-dharma* (like the duty of the king is to protect).[7]

In the scheme of *puruṣārtha*s (human values), *dharma* is viewed as having intrinsic value and as being related to *ṛta* and *ṛṇa*. There are four *puruṣārtha*s, viz., *dharma* (righteous-ness), *artha* (security or wealth), *kāma* (pleasure) and *mokṣa* (liberation). While *artha* and *kāma* are taken as empirical values, the other two are taken as spiritual values. Philosophy is directly concerned with the two higher values of *dharma* and *mokṣa* and the right means to realize them. Hiriyanna views that philosophy, in this sense of grading the values, is a criticism of values.[8] In the *Bhagavad-Gītā*, we find that *dharma* is a regulating principle of *kāma*.[9] Thus, we may say that in the scheme of Indian conception of values, i.e., *puruṣārtha*, *dharma* is taken as a regulatory principle and thus we have *dharma-artha* and *dharma-kāma*, the empirical values as they ought to be rather than as they usually are. The ethical theories extended by

---

4. *Ṛgveda*, I.181.1. Also refer P.V. Kane, *History of Dharmaśāstra*, BORI, Poona, 1968, vol. I, p. 1.
5. *Bṛhadāraṇyakopaniṣad*, I.14.14.
6. *trayo dharmaskandhā yājñodhyayanaṁ dānamiti* — *Chāndogyopaniṣad*, 2.23.
7. P.V. Kane, *op cit.*, pp. 1-10.
8. M. Hiriyanna, *Indian Conception of Values*, Kavyalaya Publishers, Mysore, 1975, p. 16.
9. *dharmāviruddho bhūteṣu kāmo'smi bharatarṣabha* (I am the source of pleasure, if not conflicting with righteousness.) — *Bhagavad-Gītā*, 7.11.

different philosophical schools had liberation as their end and in that direction they formulated their ethical practices. Radhakrishnan says :

> Any ethical theory must be grounded on metaphysics, in a philosophic concept of the relation between the conduct and the ultimate reality. As we think the ultimate reality to be so we behave; vision and action go together.[10]

The *Arthaśāstra* enumerates *dharma* as six-fold: *ahiṁsā, satya, śauca, anasūyā, anr̥śaṁsya* and *kṣamā*. Jaiminī defines *dharma* as the object of injunction.[11] In the Vaiśeṣika School, *dharma* is defined as that from which results happiness, i.e., prosperity (*abhyudaya*) and liberation (*niḥśreyas*).[12] In the *Manu-Smr̥ti*, that which is practised by the learned who lead a moral life freed from hatred and partiality is called as *dharma*.[13] In the *Āpastamba* and such other Dharmasūtras, it is said that *dharma* is that activity which is praised by the wise. In the *Gautama-Dharmasūtra*, it is said: "The Vedas are the sources of *dharma*."[14] Buddhist conception of *dharma*, the earliest document of which is found in the fourth rock-edict of emperor Aśoka, lays emphasis on non-injury. However, in Buddhist philosophical literature, it is used in the sense of an entity similar to that of early Advaita. In Sanskrit, the term *dharma* is derived from the root *dhr̥*, meaning to hold, bear, support, or to nourish. As has been already seen above, it is translated contextually. The word has been interpreted severally in English to mean 'virtue,' 'righteousness' and religion conveying certain nuances of its import. The whole concept of *dharma* thus seems to be related to the Vedic ideal of *r̥ta* (universal order) and *r̥ṇa* (the debts one is

---

10. S. Radhakrishnan, *Eastern Religion and Western Thought*, 1958, p. 80.
11. *codanālakṣaṇārtho dharmaḥ* — *Pūrvamīmāṁsā-Sūtra*, I.1.2.
12. *athāto dharmaṁ vyākhyāsyāmaḥ, yatobhyudayaniḥśreyasasiddhiḥ sa dharmaḥ* — *Vaiśeṣika-Sūtra*, 1.1.2.
13. *Manu-Smr̥ti*, 2.1.
14. *vedo dharmamūlam* — *Gautama-Dharmasūtra*, I.1.2.

supposed to repay) and seems to be the particularization at the human level of the ethical order prevailing in the universe.

Dharma in the Dharmaśāstras

The Dharmaśāstric literature exercised substantial influence on the Indian perception of an ideal man in society from the Vedic period onwards. The Dharmasūtras form a part of Kalpasūtras, which are referred to as Smṛtis. The Kalpasūtras deal with the practical side of the Vedas which deal with ritual as well as common morality. In the process of their systematization and social adoption, newer materials have been incorporated into it to suit the demands of different places and different periods. One aspect of these Sūtras deals with the elaborate details of the Vedic rituals and has very little relevance for the common man.[15] Another category of Sūtras deals with the domestic rites, such as rites relating to birth, marriage and death.[16] The third category relates to the conduct of the individual and their religious duties emphasizing social and personal ethics. These are termed as Dharmasūtras which have enormous significance to society as they serve as guiding principles to decide right or wrong and merit or demerit (*pāpa* and *puṇya*).[17] Different Dharmasūtras were composed separately for different Vedas. These Sūtras were codified later after consolidation and necessary adaptation. The texts have been interpreted in different ways in successive periods giving rise to enormous literature in this field. These works have been broadly authoritative because of availability of wide range of options. The subject-matter of these treatises deals with three aspects : (1) code of conduct (*ācāra*), (2) expiation (*prāyaścitta*), and (3) jurisprudence (*vyavahāra*).

---

15. Those are called Śrauta-Sūtras which mainly discuss the norms of various *yāgas* and modes of their performance.
16. These are Gṛhya-Sūtras which contain the rituals to be performed by a householder.
17. The Dharmasūtras and the Smṛti are otherwise known as Dharmaśāstras.

In later periods, we find the texts of Manu, Yājñavalkya, Parāśara, Nārada and others, who codified the necessary social features based on their observations. Dharmaśāstras represent a sanctified tradition, and are accorded high respect next to only Śruti.[18] For example, Dharmaśāstras classifies actions in terms of obligatory (*nitya*), optional (*kāmya*), prohibited (*pratiṣiddha*) and occasional (*naimittika*) deeds. The last type, i.e., occasional deeds, are similar to obligatory deeds since one ought to perform them on the specified occasion. The first and the last type of deeds may be referred to as categorical imperatives.[19] The optional one deals with desired ends, which are performed for personal well-being aiming at a goal in this world or hereafter. The seeker should purify himself in accordance with the stated rituals which make him eligible to perform such actions (*kāmya-karma*s). Hence, these are hypothetical imperatives, which involve moral disciplines in a right direction. Thus, the Dharmaśāstras contains the disciplines of life which modify the external behaviour as well as the inner disposition of man. *Dharma*, as enunciated in the Dharmaśāstras, is the comprehensive umbrella term denoting all moral laws, ethics, codes of conduct and religious acts. *Ṛta* is the logical concept underlying *dharma*. *Ṛṇa* represents the obligation of man to make his life conform to *dharma* and *ṛta*.[20]

Dharma — Echo of the Universal

Many of the disciplines stated in the Dharmaśāstras are universal in nature. These texts have considered man as an individual as well as a social being. The two types of *dharma*s discussed above

18. Even during the period of Kālidāsa, the Śruti commanded a superior position than that of Smṛti. It is known from the verse *śruterivārthaṁ smṛtiranvagacchat* — *Raghuvaṁśa*, 2.2.

19. M. Hiriyanna, *op cit.*, p. 190.

20. S.S. Barlingey, *A Modern Introduction to Indian Ethics*, Penman Publishers, New Delhi, 1998, p. 81.

were put forth as the (1) universal duties, *sādhāraṇa dharmas*, in which we come across ethical facets which even deal with the protection of animals and honouring the feelings of immovable entities; and (2) the duties of an individual person in accordance with his state of life, which are called as *varṇāśrama dharmas*. For the former, i.e., *sādhāraṇa dharmas*, Manu asserts that the observation of the tenets of his Dharmaśāstra alone is sufficient to lead a fulfilling and rewarding life. His definition of *dharma* goes thus:

> Contentment, forbearance, gentleness, respect for other's property, purity, self-control, knowledge, philosophic wisdom, veracity and patience are the ten facets of *dharma*.[21]

In his commentary on the *Yogasūtra*, Vyāsa defines *dharma* as the universal goodwill.[22] Thus, we see that the normative aspect of *dharma* has a universal implication in the sense that it regards other's interests in the society without harming one's own interests. As Hiriyanna puts it:

> Thus, when a person practices the virtue of contentment, his conduct is sure to result in some positive advantages to others. . . . If the duties are negative and self-regarding, they generally point to rights of others as their correlatives.[23]

The ideals put forth here have undertones of universal ethics which promote self-discipline for an individual and his social well-being. Yājñavalkya says that *kāma* or desire as such is not bad and need not be suppressed, but it needs to be properly regulated.[24] Its social implications are so strong that one may tend to feel that *dharma*

21. *dhṛtiḥ-kṣamā-damo' steyaṁ saucamindriyanigrahaḥ*
dhīrvidyā-satyamakrodhaḥ daśakam-dharma-lakṣaṇam
— *Manu-Smṛti* 6.92.

22. *sarvathā-sarvadā sarvabhūtānām anabhidruhaḥ*
— *Vyāsabhāṣya* on *Yogasūtra*, 2.30.

23. M. Hiriyanna, *op cit.*, pp. 193-94, *ātmanaḥ pratikūlāni pareṣām na samācaret.*

24. *samyak saṁkalpaḥ yaḥ kāmaḥ* — *Yājñavalkya-Smṛti*, 1.7.

focuses more on bettering the society as a whole than the individual. In the *Mahābhārata*, we come across the same concept of *dharma* as being in the mind and one should do good to all.[25] Thus, *dharma* represents the moral order of the universe which is meant for providing a sustainable society. It implies an order which has an existence above the ordinary human requirements. As Taylor puts it:

> To fulfil the true impulse of nature in us is not just to meet the biological needs but also to satisfy higher aspiration. It is at the same time, a moral fulfilment. From Rousseau on[wards], the true voice of nature is at one and the same time both the impulse of biological needs and an aspiration to what is experienced as moral self-realization.[26]

It is for this reason that in the Indian context, that duty is more important than rights. This may be the idea why in the Dharmaśāstras there is so much emphasis on the community and the ideal of *dharma* conceives of society as an organic unity where individual interests are subordinated to the interests of the society.[27]

Dharma — Its Normative Base

Though there are many kinds of *dharma*, they all, in different ways, involve the notion of regulation, and are therefore, basically, rules of action. Thus, the normative ordering of anything is said to be *dharma*.[28] The Śruti or the Vedas are the basic sources of *dharma*. The vast literature of Śruti is considered as sacred and *apauruṣeya*, of superhuman origin and it has an overriding authority over the

25. *cittamūlo bhavet dharmaḥ* — *Mahābhārata*, 13.211.220.
26. Charles Taylor, *Hegel and Modern Society*, Cambridge University Press, Cambridge, 1979, p. 75.
27. S.S. Rama Rao Pappu, "Hindu Dharma, Western Liberalism and Contemporary Indian Society," in *Search of Hinduism*, ed., Cromwell Crawford, Unification Theological Seminary, New York, 1986, p. 138.
28. John M. Koller, "Dharma: An Expression of Universal Order," in *Philosophy East and West*, vol. 22, 1972, p. 131.

other texts, like Smṛtis and Sūtras which are *pauruṣeya* (human-origin).

The Śruti contains two types of statements (1) *vidhi* — injunctive statements, and (2) *arthavāda* — statements containing praise, etc., Āpastamba, an early Smṛti writer, is of the opinion that the source of the Smṛti should be *vidhi vākyas* or injunctive statements.[29] Jaiminī on the other hand, says that the whole Veda consisting of *vidhi* as well as *arthavāda* can be taken to be authoritative. In the Smṛti and their commentaries, a lot of efforts have been made to show that the rules of Smṛti literature were based on the Śruti. Kumārila Bhaṭṭa is of the view that the Vedic authority to a Smṛti can be given either by quoting the actual words or if the text is lost by giving its contention which would be equally valid like those of Śruti.[30]

Manu, one of the early authorities on the subject, quotes Śruti only once.[31] Though there is an underlying effort to align with the Śruti, it is never satisfactorily done by the Smṛti writers as the Vedas themselves have very little to convey so far as the subject-matter of Smṛti is concerned. The content (*viṣaya*), and the eligible person (*adhikārī*) are different and hence the results one could obtain thereby are also different.[32] The modes of reference are different

29. *Āpastamba-Dharmasūtra*, II.14.13.

30. *vedo hīdṛśa evāyaṁ puruṣairyaḥ prakāśyate*
sa paṭhadbhiḥ prakāśyeta smaradbhirveti tulyabhāk
tataśca śrutimūlatvāt bādhyodāharaṇena tat
vikalpa eve hi nyeyyastulyakakṣa pramāṇataḥ
— *Mīmāṁsādarśana* with *Śābarabhāṣya* and *Tantravārttika*, vol. 1, ed., Subba Sastri, Anandasrama Sanskrit Series No. 97, Pune, 1929, pp. 187-88.

31. *yanme mātā pralulubhe vicarantyapativratā* — *Manu-Smṛti* 9.20; Refer A.S. Altekar, *Sources of Hindu Dharma in its Socio-Religious Aspects*, Institute of Public Administration, Sholapur, Sain Das Foundation Lectures, 1952, p. 59.

32. *athāpi nityānuvādamavidhi māhurācāryāḥ* — *Āpastamba-Dharma-sūtra*, 2.14.13, ed. A. Mahadeva Sastri, Government Oriental Library Series No. 15, Mysore, p. 296.

in different texts. In other words, the normative status of the Śruti is never violated but at the same time social thought and institutions were recognized in the Dharmaśāstra literature.

Now for the texts which dealt with *dharma* in the later periods, the earlier Dharmaśāstras become authoritative. Like the Vedas, this later literature was recognized till the beginning of the last century. Since it was mainly meant for giving sanction to a certain prevalent custom in the society, its content went on changing and many things which were in vogue during the earlier days were prohibited in the later period.[33]

Orthodoxy versus Orthopraxy

Gautama, Manu and other earlier *smṛtikāra*s are of the opinion that the Vedas, *smṛti* (memory) and *śīla* (conduct) of those who know Vedas, are the sources of *dharma*. So an amalgamation of conventions and traditions as remembered by the Vedic scholars (which was learnt by rote) constitutes the Smṛti and hence they became authoritative. In the Vedic period, the society definitely did not need a Dharmaśāstra in the manner it was found later. After the Vedic period, during the period of rituals (around 600 BC), a few of the Dharmaśāstras were conceived and composed. Āpastamba views that Smṛti is based on *samaya* (tradition) and *ācāra* (convention).[34] Śaṅkara and following him Madhusūdana Sarasvatī regard the *Bhagavad-Gītā* as Smṛti.[35] Hence, though the

33. In the Vedic literature, we find references to inter-caste marriage, women's right to Vedic initiation, unmarried daughter's right to father's property and the like which were prohibited in the later ages.

34. *athāto samayācārakān dharmān vyākhyāsyāmaḥ* — *Āpastamba-Dharmasūtra*, 1.1.1. Commenting on this, Haradatta says: *samayaḥ samayamūla ācāraḥ, teṣu bhavaḥ samayācārika evambhūtān dharmān, samayācārikān pauruṣeyi-vyavasthā*, Refer A.S. Altekar p. 60.

35. *smarati ca bhagavān vedavyāsaḥ gītāyāṁ bhagavadvacanam*, Madhusūdana Sarasvatī in *Gūḍhārthadīpikā*, Verse 1.

Śruti is recognized to be eternally a valid source of knowledge, in due course of time, by the accommodation of social changes and practices, Smṛti too gained significant validity. In the seventeeth century, Lakṣmaṇa Bhaṭṭa, the author of the *Ācārasāra*, says that a direct conflict with the Śruti does not invalidate the injunctions of the Smṛtis.[36]

There are many instances where the normative base has been violated and overruled in favour of a social practice. As the changes occur frequently, the necessity for codifying them too becomes necessary. For example, the Smṛti texts, authored by Devala and Gobhila, were written to cater to the then fresh needs of the society as old Smṛtis became obsolete. After the Muslim conquest of India, many people were converted forcibly into Islam. Later on, there came a need for re-conversion. Śruti and the earlier Smṛtis never faced such a situation. This gave rise to the *Devala-Smṛti* which codified the ways for re-conversion to one's own religion.[37] *Samaya* and *ācāra* also differed from place to place and from time to time. For example, fish eating was sanctioned for the brāhmaṇas of eastern Indian States, the land named as Matsyadeśa. Meat eating was permitted for Kāśmīrī's and certain other people living in the northern part of the country.

Hence the writers of the Smṛti texts kept themselves open to the needs of their time. Medhātithi, an earlier commentator on Manu, says that during his time new Smṛtis were composed for the future generation.[38] Choices were open as there were many

---

36. *pratyakṣaśrutivirodhe'pi smṛtīnāmaprāmāṇyaṁ nāstītyuktamacāryaiḥ — Ācārasāra of Lakṣmaṇabhaṭṭa*, Quoted in A.S. Altekar, *op. cit.*, p. 15.

37. *sindhutīre sukhāsīnaṁ devalaṁ munisattamam*
sametya munayaḥ sarve idam vacanamabrūvan
bhagavan mlecchanītā hi kathaṁ śuddhima-vapnuyuḥ
— *Devala-Smṛti*, 1.3. Also refer A.S. Altekar, *op.cit.*, p. 19.

38. *adyatve ca evamvidhairguṇai yuktaḥ īdṛśenaiva ca hetunā granthamupanibandhiyāt, sa uttaresām manvādivat prāmāṇyam bhavet* — Medhātithi on *Manu-Smṛti*, 2.6.

Smṛtis available. The Purāṇas and the Nibandhas interpreted the Smṛti dictums and were considered to be authoritative in the areas of *dharma*. For example, in the *Nārada-Smṛti*, we find that widows have no right of inheritance. But Mitra Miśra, while commenting upon the text, observes that since the word *strī* is used and words like *patnī* or *bhāryā* are not used, Nārada is not opposed to the inheritance of a legally wedded wife but to a concubine.[39] Certain customs which were practised in earlier Smṛtis were prohibited later like inter-caste marriage, levirate and other practices. In legislating the means and end of liberation for all in the society, Smṛtis have pointed out that by the study of Purāṇas, those who do not have access to the Vedas may get liberating knowledge. Mitra Miśra stated that since *ātmajñāna* is the means for salvation, the śūdras can have it by the study of Purāṇas.[40]

The next source of orthopraxy as per *dharma* is one's contentment or *ātmatuṣṭi*. Its scope is comparatively limited as one has to follow a standardized path if a particular practice is not found in the Śāstras. Nyāya, reason, has been recognized as a source and such a source has been testified by authorities like Manu, Gautama, Nārada and Yājñavalkya. After the codification of Dharmaśāstra, there was no scope for *sadācāra*, "the path followed by the wise" to be treated as a different mode of deciding good or bad. But before the codification and after, at the time of a sheer necessity where the text is silent, it has been invoked in the Smṛti texts. For example, the *Baudhāyana-Dharmasūtra* says that certain practices are to be invoked from the Smṛtis and thereafter the social customs are to be followed.[41] *Sadācāra* (the conduct prescribed by

---

39. *yadyapi nāradaḥ tatstrīṇām jīvanam dadyāt iti tadavaruddhā strīparaṁ patniśabda grahaṇāt — Vīramitrodaya-Prakāśa, Vyavahārakāṇḍa, Satpratibandha-adhyāya*. Also refer A.S. Altekar, *op.cit.*, p. 64.

40. *veda anadhikarīṇām śūdrāṇām kathamātmasākṣātkāra iti cet purāṇaśravaṇāditi brūmaḥ — Vīramitrodaya-Paribhāṣa*, p. 36; refer *ibid.*, p. 62.

41. *śeṣakriyāyām tu loko anuroddhavyaḥ*

— *Baudhāyana-Gṛhyasūtra* — 1.5.131.

the wise) is relative in nature since what is good for a particular place may not be good for another. Hence, in the *Mahābhārata*, we find that the respectable people alone determine the nature of *dharma*.[42] In the same epic, in the context of Pāṇḍava's marrying Draupadī we come across a dialogue between Drupada, her father, and Yudhiṣṭhira, the eldest brother of the Pāṇḍavas. Drupada turns down the proposal of Yudhiṣṭhira to marry Draupadī to all five brothers since it was not *dharma*. For this, Yudhiṣṭhira pleads that *dharma* is too subtle and cannot be scrutinized by ordinary persons.[43] Marrying uncle's daughter and other such practices, though opposed in the earlier Smṛtis, were not prohibited in the later Smṛtis as those are *deśa-dharma*s (practices pertaining to particular places).[44] Śaṅkara, defending the slaughter of animals in sacrifices, argues that what is *dharma* of a particular place and on a particular occasion and with a purpose is *adharma* in other such contexts.[45] In *Yājñavalkya-Smṛti*, we come across the fact that the council of elders is an authoritative body to decide the *dharma* related topics.[46]

To sum up, my attempt here is to remove the pervading doubt that the Hindu law is static and does not show any sign of change

42. *tarko'pratiṣṭhaḥ śrutayo vibhinnāḥ*
naiko muniryasya matam pramāṇam
dharmasya tattvam nihitam guhāyam
mahājano yena gataḥ sa panthāḥ
— *Mahābhārata*,12. 373.117.

43. *sūkṣmo dharmo mahārāja nāsya vidmo vayaṁ gatiḥ*
— *Mahābhārata*, 3.195.21.

44. *udūhyate dākṣiṇātyaiḥ mātulasya sutā dvijaiḥ*
madhyadeśe karmakarāḥ (steyaratāḥ) śilpinaśca gavāśinaḥ
matsyadāśca narāḥ sarve vyabhicāraratāstriyaḥ
— Refer A.S. Altekar, *op.cit.*, p. 68. Also refer A. Mahadeva Sastri, *Social Reform on Sastric Lines*, Mysore, 1909, p. 69.

45. *yasmin deśakālanimitte ca yo dharmo'nuṣṭhīyate sa eva deśakālanimittāntareṣu adharmo bhavati* — Śaṅkara's *Brahma-Sūtra-Bhāṣya*, 3.1.25.

46. Dominic Goodall, *Hindu Scriptures* (ed. with new tr.), University of California Press, Berkeley, 1996, p. 296.

or participation in the social transformation. Such a contention is wrong. In fact, in Hinduism, orthopraxy is more venerated than the orthodoxy. It has been a flexible tradition and that is the reason why in spite of various onslaughts, it has survived the test of time. As Vasudha Dalmia remarks:

> Such a construction is based on "tradition" — an entity which is neither a permanent and unchanging heritage of the past, nor entirely fictitious, but constantly being selected and modified in response to social change and to visions of the future. The process however need not always be an entirely natural one. It is usually propelled and steered by individuals and by spokesman of interested groups. These may be tempted to take advantage of the fact that the constant adjustment and rearrangement of the constituents of tradition renders them particularly amenable to manipulation.[47]

In the foregoing pages, I have given an account of the concept of *dharma* as found in the original texts, i.e., in the Dharmaśāstric literature from post-Vedic period up to the modern age. To suit multi-formed society like India, and in the absence of any religious text (in the strict sense of the term as understood in Christianity and Islam) the necessity of the Dharmaśāstras cannot be gainsaid. In and through the ages, the Hindu society has been trying to surcharge itself with modernity and has kept itself flexible to adopt the modes of living which have been felt to be beneficial and good. The *śreyas* (absolute good) has not been completely rejected nor the *preyas* (temporal enjoyment) blindly accepted. Thus, the flexibility of the dicta has given adequate authority to its base, the ground on which the Dharmaśāstras have operated and negotiated their boundaries with the orthopraxy (correct behaviour) rather than orthodoxy (correct opinion).[48] The older the Smṛti is, the orthopraxy relating to social behaviour is much less and because

47. Vasudha Dalmia and Heinrich Von Stietencron, *Representing Hinduism*, Sage Publications, New Delhi, 1995, p. 21.

48. Dominic Goodall, *op. cit.*, Introduction, p. XVII.

of interpolations many times we find ambiguous and contradictory features in these texts.

Hinduism versus Hindu Dharma

Now I would like to deal with one more misunderstanding which has characterized the modern scholarship. This is about the use of the word *dharma* with the word Hindu signifying Hinduism, the religion of Hindus. The very term 'Hindu' has been derived from the word 'Sindhu,' which stood for the river and the valley adjacent to it. During the period of Muslim invasion, the word 'Hindu' was used in the sense of religion to distinguish itself from other religions. The problem here was that since the native way of living *in the sense of a religion*, which may be called as *saṁpradāya* or *mārga*, did not have a name for itself nor was there a need for it, the affiliation with the *dharma* as 'religion' was an outcome and it was associated with the place and the people who lived near the river Sindhu. As the oldest living religion of the world, Hinduism has passed through several phases, different practices and schools of Philosophy.

Starting from the period of the Vedic religion up to the twentieth century this has undergone different changes giving rise to many 'isms' in its fold. The Mīmāṁsaka's period of Brāhmaṇism, the formations of different orthodox and heterodox schools and modern Hinduism which imbibes the thinking processes of modern thinkers — all have brought about many variants in Hinduism. The term Hinduism has created a lot of difficulty for the Western Indologists who try to perceive it through the mirror of religions. In order to include Hinduism in the fold of religion, the traditional understanding of the term is not sufficient. It has to widen its scope so as to include a complex phenomenon of being and becoming a 'religion.' Heinrich Von Stietencron argues against the Hinduism being designated as a religion and his arguments are based on the fact that the core of this religion cannot be identified and the Hindus do not have uniformity in their thinking or in their practices. He says:

> There is hardly a single important teaching in "Hinduism" which can be shown to be valid for all Hindus, much less a comprehensive list of teachings. What some groups of Hindus believe to be true is contradicted by statements held to be true by other groups of Hindus. Animism and polytheism, pantheism, panentheism and henotheism, dualism, mono-theism and pure monism exist side by side.[49]

To him, it is the peaceful coexistence of the Hindus and the unifying term 'Hinduism' which favoured a tendency to neglect the differences and to emphasize the common elements and this is the reason, he argues, why the Western scholars saw Hinduism as a unity. To me, it is the strength of the religion that it permits multiple possibilities and becomes a universal phenomenon. Hence, the word *dharma* (universal order) came to be associated with 'Hindu' and the multifarious connotations of *dharma* were qualified to the term 'Hinduism' which has become an all-inclusive phenomenon.

In the absence of an essential factor, there was enough scope for other faiths to gain the status of religion. Modern (so-called) orthodox movements like Ārya Samāj, Brahmo Samāj, and heterodox ones like Neo-Buddhism and Draviḍian movements gained momentum within the broader canvas of Hinduism. And of late, the BJP's claim of Hindutva and Hindustan came into existence which may be because of the flexibility found in 'Hinduism' as a religion. The Gandhian conception of religion extending to *sarva-dharma-samabhāva* added a different dimension as Gandhi wanted to bring about a unity in his perception of religions. In the process of cleansing the system, he could not give much emphasis to the inherent problems of castes and their subaltern nature. Hence, he, at times, is criticized for not giving attention to these subaltern issues of caste hierarchy. The reformers, like Dayananda of Ārya Samāj, Raja Rammohun Roy, even in pre-

49. Heinrich, Von Stietencron, "Hinduism On the Proper Use of a Deceptive Term," *Hinduism Reconsidered*, ed. G.D. Sontheimer & Hermann Kulke, Manohar, Delhi, 1991, p. 14.

Gandhian days laid emphasis to this new dimension of Hinduism and worked for the subaltern people.

Here I present some thoughts which might offer some clues as to how the multiformity of Hinduism and its inherent liberality have the strength to integrate future "isms" into its vast fold.

1. We have seen that in the Indian context, there is no basic dogma or belief which constitutes the *dharma* or for that matter "Hindu *dharma*." The central idea is to sustain a society. This ideal is throughout nourished in this phenomenon called Hinduism. Hence, the accommodation of new thinking and new practices can be sanctioned by looking into the Dharmaśāstras which offer manifold choices for thinking and action.

2. One more pertinent point which may be noticed among the writers of the Dharmaśāstras is the glaring inconsistencies in their works. For example, in the same *Manu-Smṛti*, we find contradictory statements on the treatment of women and people of lower birth. Interpolation, wrong interpretation, and such other factors leave us with little scope for coherent thinking. But an important outcome of such opposite statements is that these give us the clue that in the Dharmaśāstras, which have a long history of social relevance, there is a possibility of accepting opposite ways as per their circumstantial necessities and the like.

3. The Indian schools of philosophy have an inherent tendency to complement each other. For example, *vyavahāre bhāṭṭanayaḥ*, i.e., as far as empirical *pramāṇa*s are concerned, the Advaitins agree with the Bhaṭṭas. Śaṅkara in his *Brahma-Sūtra-Bhāṣya* talks of Kapila, the first Sāṅkhya proponent with due veneration (*pradhānamalla*). In all the schools we find some types of dualism or monism in one form or the other. For example, Advaita believes in

empirical duality while Dvaita believes in Absolute independence of Viṣṇu. Hence, there is a filial atmosphere in Hinduism which is shared by all the schools. This can be expressed forming a basis for a concept of *dharma*.

4. What has been prevalent in Hinduism could be the case in any religion if there is scope for free thinking, independence of mind, which is set free from small considerations. In its long history, Hinduism has maintained its pristine nature because of these possibilities of adaptability to the practical needs of life. This may not happen in certain other religions as the original stipulations will stifle their approach towards newer and radical adoptions. In due course of time the necessity to accommodate the new things and allow acceptable concessions will not be there if the rigidity of the tenets are not transformed to suit the modern temperament. The case of science versus Christianity can be given as an example in this case. There was no such dichotomy in Hindu religion. If scientific world would have to be named after a religion, then it has to evolve as the biggest antidote to any religion of the West. But compromises are possible, as happened in the case of science and religion which go side by side everywhere.

5. Hinduism as a religion is not just a particular approach to life. It may be a theory (for schools) or practice or both. It has a place for innovation and that is how its relevance is maintained. That being the case, the Indian Constitution has almost replaced or has been created as a modern Dharmaśāstra for the people to follow. Even the incorporation of suggestions of the Mandal Commission, with its advantages and disadvantages, is not something very new but can have its genesis in the hoary past which is meant to extend certain benefits to the subaltern people.

Thus, we find Hinduism has an innate dynamism which gives enough scope for adopting modernism and the changing needs of modernity. There have been several instances when changes have been incorporated because of the requirements of the inner dialectic within its broad spectrum. Questioning has been the hallmark of this tradition and there are a number of developments when we find fresh tenets overtaking the old as we noticed in the case of Upaniṣadism in the place of ritualism, the Vaiṣṇava devotional mode as a revolt against the knowledge paradigm of Vedānta and the like. Due to such constant interaction between different modes of thinking, a noticeable growth has been observed in the history of Hinduism, keeping the future possibilities open for incorporation of pragmatic considerations.

Conclusion

In my tracing the concept of *dharma* from its original form in the traditional literature to its application in the contemporary situation, I have tried to show how Hindu society has been trying to be liberated and liberal in its approach towards the concept of *dharma*. This is one of the key concepts which is very basic to Indian ways of thinking. At the same time it is very comprehensive as it has varied implications. In and through the seeming opposition in practice and inherent contradiction in thinking, a balanced world-view has been emerging in the Hindu world of religion and spirituality which is universal in nature. The ability to adapt to any age and place, to any changing circumstances and customs, had been the hallmark of Hinduism at all times. One more thing to be appreciated is that before the Dharmaśāstras, there was a society in the Vedic and pre-Vedic days in which well-founded customs were prevalent in regulating the individual and society. Hence, the *dharma* is not only liberal in the sense that it has multiple options for social behaviour but is also liberational (*mokṣa*-centric) since it exhorts the person to pursue the highest scheme of *puruṣārtha, mokṣa*.

4

Semantics of Dharma

V. Kutumba Sastry

THE term *dharma* is unique in many ways. It is a word well understood and frequently used aptly by common people and yet found impossible to give a straightforward definition by the scholars. It is a word which signifies the law and force of regulation behind the movement of planets, stars and galaxies and yet signifies duty of any petty professional of this tiny earth. It is a word which is explained as the unseen cause for the behaviour of a barber not to cut the throat of his customer while shaving. It is a word to explain which several hundreds of books of Dharmaśāstras, Purāṇas and Itihāsas were written and yet which remained unintelligible and unclear. It is a word which signified such principles, every one of which, at one time or the other, is clearly violated by people and yet such violation is also cited to be signified by it. It is a word which signified, at one and the same time, the universal principles and the sectarian principles. It is a word which defies any attempt to translate it into any other language, both Indian and non-Indian.

According to the Sanskrit grammar of Pāṇini, the etymology of the word *dharma* is as follows. It is a derivative form from the root *dhr̥ṅ* of *bhvādigaṇa*, meaning either to sustain, or to uphold, or to support or to wear. It is derived by adding the *uṇādi* suffix *man* as per the *Uṇādisūtra* (1-140). Most of the commentators explaining this word show its etymology as a principle which sustains the entire cosmos or a principle upheld by the people at large.[1] It is both in the masculine and neuter gender, though its use in the masculine gender is quite frequent. It is a *a*-ending (*akārānta*) word when it is used independently. However, sometimes when it is used in compounds it is seen as *n*-ending (*nakārānta*) word. In the Vedic literature, however, it is used as a *n*-ending word even when it is used independently. This fact gives us a clue that originally the word *dharma* used to have both *a*-ending forms as well as *n*-ending forms, but in due course of time the *n*-ending forms disappeared from the usage in classical Sanskrit language, retaining them, of course, in the compounds. Anyway, we need not show our concern towards these peculiarities as they do not have any bearing on its semantics.

A thorough understanding of the etymology of the term *dharma* helps us to understand its basic underlying character which runs through several shades of meanings it expresses. The sharp and enlightened intuitive mind of great Indians of yore was able to see an underlying power and principle behind the order and rhythm of the cosmos, seasons, the planets and their movement, the day and the night, the behaviour of the animal kingdom and humans and, for that matter, behind everything in the nature. They understood that it is that power and that principle which sustains and maintains the order and rhythm to continue. They named it *dharma* on the basis of its etymology *dharati lokān iti* (*dharma* because it sustains and holds up the worlds). Seen from this point of view, it appears to be very clear to understand what *dharma* is and what is its nature, etc. But, it eludes definite grasp since it is an abstract idea. Later, the same idea of a principle responsible for the existence and sustenance of each and every minute component of the nature around us is also grasped by them and they named it also as *dharma* for obvious reasons of etymological significance of the term.

To give light and heat is the *dharma* of the sun, to flow and to

1. *dharati lokān, dhriyate vā janaiḥ iti dharmaḥ* — *Sudhā* on the *Amarakośa*.

soak is the *dharma* of water. The principle which sustains, maintains or regulates the human society and its various classes also came to be known as *dharma.* Hence, the *varṇa dharma*s, *āśrama dharma*s, *rāja dharma*s, *manuṣya dharma*s and so on so forth. *Dharma* of the learned persons, *dharma* of the servants, *dharma* of various professionals so on and so forth. It may be noticed and appreciated that in all such cases the basic characteristic of "being a power and principle of sustenance and holding up," which is reflected in the etymology of the term *dharma*, is common. This dynamic principle which sustains the worlds and their order is first termed as *ṛta* in the Vedic literature. Varuṇa is said to be the God of the *ṛta*. He is well known as the Law-giver and as the God of the order of the cosmos and the seasons, etc. Hence, the term *ṛta* meant the order of the worlds in the Vedic literature.

Of course, the intuitive mind of *maharṣi*s did not stop with the apprehension of this dynamic principle *dharma*. It saw yet another basic and still fundamental principle which is unchangeable in its nature because of which the change-able regulative principle (*dharma*) continued its sway. It is termed as *satya*. This is clearly stated in a *mantra* of the *Ṛgveda*.[2]

Satya is the unchangeable, primordial cause of the origina-tion, sustenance and involution of the entire universe, whereas *ṛta* is the changeable, primordial principle which holds up, sustains and regulates the universe. *Satya* is the cause of the universe whereas *ṛta* is the rhythm of it. In the later literature, the term *Brahman* replaced the term *satya* and the term *dharma* replaced the term *ṛta*. However, it may be noted that both the terms *dharma* and *ṛta* are frequently used in the *Ṛgveda*, which is supposed to be the earliest Vedic text. They were used more or less as synonyms in the post-

2. *ṛtaṁ ca satyaṁ cabhīddhāt tapasodhyajayata* । *tato rātryajāyata tatassmudro arṇavaḥ* । *samudrādarṇavādadhi saṁvatsaro ajāyata* । *ahorātrāṇi vidadhadviśvasya miṣato vaśī* । *sūryā candramasau dhātā yathāpūrvamakal payat* । *divaṁ ca pṛthivīṁ cāntarikṣamatho svaḥ* ।।

— *Ṛgveda*, 10.190.1-3.

Ṛgvedic literature too. But, in the post-Vedic literature, i.e., in the Smṛti and Purāṇa texts, use of the term *ṛta* slowly decreased and subsequently disappeared.

Realization of *Brahman* is the liberation (*mokṣa*) whereas rigorous and meticulous observance of *dharma* leads to the orderly well-being of the individual, society and the world at large. Realization of *Brahman*, obviously, is of the nature of *jñāna* whereas observance of *dharma* is of the nature of *karma*. Thus, the entire life, activity and the ends of the individual, society and the world as a whole are placed in between these two higher goals, *dharma* on one side and *mokṣa* on the other. Such life, activity and the ends of the individual, the society and the world as a whole is divided into two categories, namely, *artha* and *kāma*. Thus result four *puruṣārtha*s, four ends of humanity, namely, *dharma, artha, kāma* and *mokṣa*. It may be noticed that *artha* and *kāma* are fixed in between *dharma* and *mokṣa*, thus, making a hint that *artha* and *kāma* are *puruṣārtha*s so long only as they do not violate the principles of *dharma* and remain congenial to *mokṣa*. Thus, Bhagavān Śrīkṛṣṇa says that he is of the nature of such *kāma* which does not violate *dharma*.[3] Thus, the life is put in between *karman* and *Brahman*.

Though the understanding of the nature of *dharma* appears to be very clear and simple on the basis of understanding the etymology of the term *dharma*, it is too complicated and elusive on account of the fact that it cannot be uniform and single but countlessly varied. Though it is one and uniform in its essential nature, it is countless and varied in its details. That is why *dharma* is the concept which was discussed at length in Indian thought. Radhakrishnan says, "Next to the category of reality, that of *dharma* is the most important concept in Indian thought."[4]

---

3. *dharmāviruddho bhūteṣu kāmosmi bharatarṣabha* — *Bhagavad-Gītā*, 7.11.
4. S. Radhakrishnan, *Indian Philosophy*, George Allen & Unwin, London, 1923-27, vol. I, p. 52.

On account of varied nature of the principle *dharma* the term came to have several meanings. The meanings are so varied and diverse in their nature that they could not be brought under any single classification, and hence the difficulty of defining the term. P.T. Raju in his glossary of Indian philosophical terms identifies the following meanings of the term: "*Dharma*, law, nature, rule, ideal, norm, quality, entity, truth, element, category."[5] K.V. Rangaswamy Iyengar writes, "*Dharma* is used in so many senses that it eludes definition. It stands for nature, intrinsic quality, civil and moral law, justice virtue, merit, duty and morality."[6] J.A.B. van Buitenen writes, "It is as difficult to define *dharma* in terms of western thought as it is to define 'culture' in Sanskrit, and for the same reason both are all-comprising terms including institutions, a way of thinking and living, accomplishments, characteristic of people."[7] Heinrich Zimmer opines that the term *dharma* "comprises the whole context of religious and moral duties, but considerable misunderstanding results from the frequent rendering of *dharma* simply as religion."[8] Paul Masson comments, "The distinction of religion and law can be justified only from the European point of view, the two notions are one in the Indian *dharma*."[9]

Apart from the etymology, we have yet another source to grasp the meaning of the term *dharma*. For our great advantage, the term is frequently used in all the divisions of Sanskrit literature starting from the earliest work *Ṛgveda*. By analysing the contextual meaning

---

5. P.T. Raju, *Idealistic Thought of India*, Harvard University Press, Cambridge, 1953, p. 445.
6. K.V. Rangaswami Aiyangar, *Some Aspects of the Hindu View of Life According to Dharmaśāstra*, Oriental Institute, Baroda, 1952, p. 63.
7. J.A.B. van Buitenen, "Dharma and Mokṣa," *Philosophy East and West* 7, 1957, pp. 33-40.
8. Heinrich Zimmer, *Philosophies of India*, ed. Joseph Campbell, Pantheon Books, New York, 1951, p. 40.
9. Paul Masson-Oursel, *Ancient India and Indian Civilization*, Kegan Pual, Trench, Trubner & Co. London, 1934, p. 71.

where it is used, we can grasp its meaning in a better way. P.V. Kane, the doyen of the studies in Dharmaśāstra, has used this method. According to him,[10] the term *dharma* is used:

1. In the sense of "upholder or supporter or sustainer" in the *Ṛgveda* (I.187.1 and X.92.2).
2. It is used in the sense of "religious ordinances and rites" in the *Ṛgveda* (I.22.18, V.26.6, VIII.43.24, IX.64.1) and also in the refrain, *tāni dharmāṇi prathamānyāsan* in the *Ṛgveda* (I.164.43-50, and X.90.16). He also identifies significant combination of words, such as *prathama-dharma* in the sense of the primeval or first ordinances in the *Ṛgveda* (III.17.1 and X.56.3), *sanatā dharmāṇi* in the sense of ancient ordinances in the *Ṛgveda* (III.3.1).
3. In the *Ṛgveda* (IV.53.3, V.63.7, VI.70.1, and VII.89.5) the term *dharma* is used not in the sense of "religious rites" but in the sense of "fixed principles or rules of conduct."
4. In the *Atharvaveda* (XI.9.17) it is used in the sense of "merit acquired by the performance of religious rites."
5. In the *Aitareya Brāhmaṇa* (VII.17) it is used in an abstract sense, viz., "the whole body of religious (and moral?) duties."
6. In the *Chāndogya Upaniṣad* it is used in the sense of *āśrama dharmas*. It states, "there are three branches of *dharma*, one is (consitituted by) sacrifice, study and charity (i.e., the stage of house-holder); the second is (constituted by) austerities (i.e., the stage of being a hermit); the third is the *brahmacārin* dwelling in the house of his teacher and making himself stay with the family of his teacher till the last, all these attain to the worlds of meritorious men; One who abides firmly in *Brahman*, attains immortality."

---

10. P.V. Kane, *History of Dharmaśāstra*, Bhandarkar Oriental Research Institute, Poona, 1930, pp. 1-4.

P.V. Kane concludes with these remarks:

> The foregoing brief discussion establishes how the word *dharma* passed through several transitions of meaning and how ultimately its most prominent significance came to be "the privileges, duties and obligations of a man, his standard of conduct as a member of the Aryan community, as member of one of the castes, as a person in a particular stage of life."[11]

It is in this sense that the word seems to be used in the well-known exhortation to the pupil contained in the *Taittirīyopaniṣad* (1.11) "speak truth, practice *dharma*," etc. It is in the same sense that the *Bhagavad-Gīta* uses the word *dharma* in the oft-quoted verse.[12] The word is employed in this sense in the Dharmaśāstra literature. The *Manu-Smṛti* (I.2) tells us that the sages requested Manu to impart instruction in the *dharma*s of all the *varṇa*s. The *Yājñavalkaya-Smṛti* (I.1) employs it in the same sense. In the *Tantravārttika* also we are told that all the Dharmasūtras are concerned with imparting instruction in the *dharma*s of *varṇa*s and *āśrama*s.[13] Medhātithi commenting on Manu says that the expounders of Smṛtis dilate upon *dharma* as five-fold, e.g., *varṇa dharma, āśrama dharma, varṇāśrama dharma, naimittika dharma* (such as *prāyaścitta*) and *guṇa dharma* (the duty of crowned king, whether kṣatriya or not, is to protect).[14]

Apart from the analysis of the contextual meaning of the term *dharma*, as understood from its usage, we have yet another source to understand the meaning of the term on the basis of various

11. P.V. Kane, *History of Dharmaśāstra*, Bhandarkar Oriental Research Institute, Poona, 1930, pp. 1-4.

12. *svadharme nidhanaṁ śreyaḥ paradharmo bhayāvahaḥ*
— *Bhagavad-Gītā*, 3.35.

13. *sarvadharmasūtrāṇāṁ varṇāśramadharmopadeśitvāt*
— *Tantravārttika*, p. 237. As quoted by P.V. Kane.

14. See P.V. Kane, *History of Dharmaśāstra*, Bhandarkar Oriental Research Institute, Poona, 1930, pp. 1-4.

definitions of it. For example, Jaiminī defines *dharma* as "a desirable goal or result that is indicated by injunctive (Vedic) passages."[15] The word *dharma* would mean such rites as are conducive to happiness and are enjoined by the Vedic passages, *iṣṭasādhanatā*, in the meaning of injunctive suffix. Kaṇāda defines the term as "that from which results happiness and final beatitude."[16] Hārīta defines it as *śrutipramāṇaka* (based on revelation).[17] Śabara says, "whatever is means to the well-being of humanity and the world at large is *dharma*."[18] The same is said in the *Bhaviṣya Purāṇa*.[19] The *Taittirīyaśruti* says, "*dharma* is the sustainer of entire universe, people approach a person who is set in *dharma*. By *dharma* one washes away the sin."[20] Viśvāmitra defines *dharma* as follows:

> *Dharma* is that performance which is appreciated by the learned and proficient in the *āgamas*. *Adharma* is that which is condemned by them.[21]

There are several other, more or less one-sided, definitions of *dharma* such as *ahiṁsā paramo dharmaḥ* (Anuśāsanaparvan, 115.1), *ānṛśaṁsyaṁ paro dharmaḥ* (Vanaparvan, 373.76) *ācāraḥ paramo dharmaḥ* (*Manu*, I.108).

In the Buddhist tradition, the term *dharma* stands for "the whole

---

15. *codanālakṣaṇortho dharmaḥ* — *Mimāṁsādarśanam*, 1.12.
16. *athāto dharmaṁ vyākhyāsyāmaḥ* I *yatobhyudayaniśśreyasasiddhiḥ sa dharmaḥ* — *Vaiśeṣikadarśanam*, 1.1.1-2.
17. *athāto dharmaṅ vyākhyāsyāmaḥ* I *śrutipramāṇako dharmaḥ* I *śrutiśca dvidhā vaidikī tāntrikī ca* I — quoted by Kullūka from *Manu-Smṛti*, 2.1.
18. *ya eva śreyaskaraḥ sa eva dharmaśabdenocyate* I — *Mīmāṁsādarśanam* with *Śābarabhāṣyam*, vol. 1, Anandasrama Press, Poona, 1976, p. 20.
19. *dharmaḥ śreyaḥ samuddiṣṭam śreyobhyudayasādhanam*
    — *Bhaviṣya-purāṇam*. As quoted in the *Vācaspatyam*.
20. *dharmo viśvasya jagataḥ pratiṣṭhā* I *loke dhrmiṣṭhaṁ prajāḥ upasarpanti* I *dharmeṇa pāpamapanudati* I As quoted in the *Vācaspatyam*.
21. *yamāryāḥ kriyamāṇaṁ hi śaṁsantyāgamavedinaḥ* I *sa dharmoyaṁ, vigarhanti tamadharmaṁ pracakṣate* — As quoted in the *Vācaspatyam*.

teaching of Buddha" (*B.B.E.*, vol. X, p. XXXIII) and for "an element of existence, i.e., of matter, mind and forces."[22]

In most of the regional languages of India, two expressions are very common in the usage of common people. Whenever any petty quarrel takes place on account of cheating, one usually says to the other "does it appeal as *dharma* to you?" Similarly, at an advanced stage of the quarrel quite often one says to the other, "do whatever you consider it to be *dharma*." Such popular usages of the term *dharma* are in abundance. They too help as to develop an insight into the nuances of the usage of the term *dharma*.

Thus, the above analysis of etymology, usage and definitions of the term *dharma*, only confirms our view that though it is easy to comprehend, it is very difficult to define it. The vast varieties of its meaning cannot be brought under one umbrella. Mackenzie Brown says, "*dharma* is more than laws for it is what underlies law and creates law in the universe. Basic to *dharma* is this view of order or law pervasive in the universe."[23] Betty Heimann[24] isolates five meanings of *dharma* centering around a concept of fixed position. There are: (1) fixed position of duty, (2) right, (3) religious observance, (4) secular law or one's legal status in the community, and (5) a general principle or law of nature. The underlying concept she finds to be everything which is fixed and to which an individual is bound. van Buitenen says:

> . . . *dharma* is all that activity that a man, if he is to live fittingly, is required to contribute to the fixed order of things, to the norm of the universe, which is good and should not be altered.[25]

---

22. Vide Stekerbatsky's monograph on The Central Conception of Buddhism, 1923, p. 73.

23. Donald Mackenzie Brown, *The White Umbrella : Indian Political Thought from Manu to Gandhi*, University of California Press, Berkeley & Los Angeles, 1953, p. 15.

24. Betty Heimann, *Indian and Western Philosophy : A Study in Contrasts*, George Allen & Unwin, London, 1937, p. 68.

25. J.A.B. van Buitenen, "Dharma and Mokṣa," *Philosophy East and West* 7, 1957, p. 36.

Another interesting aspect of *dharma* is that it is divided into several divisions, such as *sādhāraṇa dharma* (general *dharma*) and *viśeṣa dharma* (particular *dharma*), *sanātana dharma* (eternal *dharma*), *apavāda dharma* including *āpad dharma* (emergency *dharma*) so on and so forth. On account of this, what is *dharma* under one division is perceived not to be so under another division. Non-injury (*ahiṁsā*) which is one of the important components of *sanātana dharma* is quite often violated by the kṣatriyas and others under various circumstances. Yet, such violation also came to be recognized as *dharma*. Thus, the entire exercise of the *Bhagavad-Gītā* is to induce Arjuna to wage a war which is considered to be the highest *dharma*.

Therefore, *ahiṁsā* which is supposed to be a very basic *dharma* is also a relative concept, not applicable to all living beings in a single manner. That is why we have the saying, *ahiṁsā paramo dharmaḥ* on one hand and on the other hand another saying in contradiction, *jīvo jīvasya jīvanam*.

In fact, the etymological sense of the term *dharma* gets violated if we perceive *ahiṁsā* as an absolute *dharma* because, it is not possible for the animals to sustain themselves without *hiṁsā*. It is so to a large extent with humans too. To prepare life saving medicines and conduct research in biological sciences, untold *hiṁsā* on rats and rabbits is unavoidable. For Arjuna also, *hiṁsā* was unavoidable in the battle of Kurukṣetra, after every effort for peaceful co-existence having failed, as narrated in the previous five *parvans*. Therefore, in these cases, the *hiṁsā* is considered not as *hiṁsā*.

Another important *sādhāraṇa dharma* or *sanātana dharma* is to speak truth, *satyam vada*, says the Upaniṣad. There are several illustrations in our Purāṇas and Itihāsas glorifying the act of speaking the truth. Even with regard to such a fundamental *dharma* there are several exceptions which are very obvious for all of us.

> *satyam brūyāt priyam brūyāt na brūyāt satyam priyam* ।
> *priyam ca nānṛtam brūyāt eṣa dharmassanātanaḥ* ॥

> One should speak the truth. One should speak about such things which are pleasant to hear. One should not speak the truth which is not pleasant. Neither should one speak lie which is pleasant.

This dictum is captioned at the end as *sanātana dharma*.

Hence, *dharma* is neither uniform nor absolute nor static according to the Hindu tradition. It varies from situation to situation, age to age, caste to caste, so on and so forth. That is why it is ought to be judged very carefully. Several books such as the *Mahābhārata*, the *Rāmāyaṇa* and hordes of Purāṇas came into being precisely to explain the complexity of *dharma*. They declared that the ways of *dharma* are, indeed, hard to comprehend (*dharmasya tattvaṁ nihitaṁ guhāyām*).

However, it is interesting to note that the etymological meaning of the term holds good, in each and every minute shade of the meaning of the term *dharma*. *Sanātana dharma*s and *sādhāraṇa dharma*s are *dharma*s on account of their role in sustaining the humanity and its values. Caste *dharma*s and *āśrama dharma*s are also perceived as the upholding principles to sustain that particular caste or *āśrama*. The *apavāda dharma*, which often appears to be a violation of *dharma*, is also aimed at sustaining the community or humanity when it is closely observed. Thus, a common definition to all sorts of *dharma*s is possible only on the basis of its etymology, however loose such definition may be. Hence, it is said, that *dharma* is called *dharma* because it sustains and upholds the individual, society and the world at large (*dhāraṇāt dharma ityāhuḥ dharmo dhārayate prajāḥ*).

Now, I look back at the apparent dichotomy between the *sādhāraṇa dharma*s and the *viśeṣa dharma*s and make a few observations which I consider to be of greater relevance. It is usually said "there is an exception for every law." It holds good with regard to *dharma* also. Humanity is so large and complex in nature that no universal law can be made to bring an order into it. Hence, it is necessary to identify certain values of life to be values of very high order and universally applicable at all given points of time. Surely, *ahiṁsā* (non-injury), *satya* (truth), *asteya* (non-stealing), etc., are such *dharmas* that no one would contend their position and relevance at any given time. But, within the framework consisting of such principles, we have to make provision for their violation also, so as to suit to the exigencies of context. Such provisions are called *viśeṣa dharmas*. For example, *hiṁsā* is unavoidable for fisherman, for butchers, for kṣatriyas, and for brāhmaṇas also during sacrifices. For all of these, to fulfil their occupational obligation, *hiṁsā* becomes unavoidable. Hence, *viśeṣa dharma* prevails over the *sādhāraṇa dharma*. Further, if *viśeṣa dharma* does not prevail over *sādhāraṇa dharma*, it looses its application in all cases, and as a consequence, it looses its significance being codified as *dharma*.

In my humble opinion, the *Mahābhārata* story and various episodes in it will be better understood if we consider them to be *viśeṣa dharmas*. However, in several of its discourses, it deals with the *sādhāraṇa dharmas* too. Violation of principles like *ahiṁsā*, compassion and considerations of being teachers, grandfathers, kith and kin are held to be *dharma* in the context of the Kurukṣetra war. This is clearly one of the main teachings of the *Bhagavad-Gītā*.

Coming to the point of *varṇa dharmas*, we should understand them also as a kind of *viśeṣa dharmas* prevailing over the *sādhāraṇa dharmas*. That is why, it is accepted that butcher does not violate the principle of *ahiṁsā* as long as he kills animals for his occupational obligations. At the same time, he is considered to have violated the principle of *ahiṁsā*, if he murders a human being. Therefore, killing as such is neither *hiṁsā* nor *ahiṁsā*, but it is assessed to be *hiṁsā* or *ahiṁsā* on the basis of its context. Unless we maintain this position, we cannot explain the wars of liberation, and capital punishments. Nor our Marxist-extremist friends can justify their killings of bourgeois. Nor, the discriminatory punishment given by the judges to the murderers who committed the crime under different circumstances.

Just as ethics is classified into various categories, such as, ethics of doctors and other professionals, ethics of businessmen, ethics of politics, etc., *dharma* is also classified as *varṇa dharmas*, *āśrama dharmas*, etc. We should be very clear that all these *dharma*s of *varṇa* (caste), *āśrama*, etc., are mere arrangements (*vyavasthā*) to bring an order into the society and to protect the interests of all the castes. They are like the different parts of a single piece of land well bifurcated by the farmer into small boundaries so that water would wet them equally and nourish them equally. It is obvious that in the absence of such internal boundaries, entire water will swiftly flow down into the lowest part of the land. As a consequence of it, only the plants in that lowest part get norishment while the rest are deprived of it.

An interesting feature of *varṇa dharma*s is that the more one community or caste holds the responsibility towards the society, greater are sanctions of *dharma* towards it. Thus, in the Dharmaśāstras, the highest number of sanctions of do's and don'ts are prescribed towards brāhmaṇa community. Next comes the case of kṣatriyas, followed by vaiśyas. Among all the *varṇas*, lowest number of do's and don'ts are prescribed for śūdras. The greater number of prescriptions for women in the Smṛti texts should also be construed similarly. Likewise, *brahmacārin*s have lesser number of sanctions against all other *āśrama*s. Whereas *gṛhastha*s are the worst hit by them. This is the textual position. One should not be carried away by the happenings that take place now and then. They only point towards the weakness of humanity rather than the in-built fallacy of the system. The whites' perception of native Americans, hardly a century ago after the dawn of modernity and tremendous scientific advancement, is the best pointer of human weaknesses. In fact, India never exhibited such an obnoxious and brutal attitude towards any community whatsoever at any given point of time. Indian women never sat at the guillotine, knitting the wool and watching the human heads rolling down from the guillotine. India had wisdom all through her history, despite instances of shameful atrocities committed now and then. Various movements of *bhakti* and preachings of hundreds and hundreds of saints, *gurus*, and *svāmījī*s have continuously made successful attempts to rectify the social evils in India throughout the centuries.

Therefore, arrangements towards social order (*vyavasthā*s) keep on changing according to the necessities of the society. If we carefully study the texts of Dharmaśāstras from historical perspective, we would find that these details of *varṇa dharma*s went on changing from time to time. In the light of the spirit of the Dharmaśāstras, there is every scope for throwing out the existing *vyavasthā*, and for bringing in a new one, provided such new *vyavasthā* should satisfy the etymological sense of the term *dharma* and should result in sustaining the society and social order. We should not forget the fact that we require people who are totally distinterested and detached from the bondage of the society, who keep themselves away from the society, who have in-depth vision of humanity and its welfare, whose minds do not get influenced by the temporary contextual exigencies of socio-politico-economical issues and who are, in short, *jīvanmukta*s and comparable to our *maharṣi*s who wrote the Dharmaśāstras as architects to build such new *vyavasthā*.

How many such people are there in and around us? This question deserves to be pondered over.

5

Dharma and Mokṣa
Conflict, Continuity, and Identity

Mahesh M. Mehta

THE two terms, *dharma* and *mokṣa*, are among the most substantive terms in the Hindu religious tradition, that at once illumine its all-encompassing concern for the mundane and the supra-mundane aspects of human existence. However, their juxtaposition has also triggered a serious controversial issue, whether they are mutually at variance or they form an integrated whole.

These concepts constitute the two most important components of the Hindu scheme of Four Goals (*caturvarga*) called *puruṣārtha*s or ends of life sought after by humans. The other two aims behind human actions are *artha* (wealth) and *kāma* (sensual pleasure). The system of four *puruṣārtha*s and its cognate system of four *āśrama*s (stages), insightfully formulated by the authors of the Dharmaśāstras envisage a human person in totality, in their entire gamut of prehuman, human and superhuman needs and aspirations. A person is an epitome of *prakṛti* or Nature, representing basic animalistic tendencies, sophisticated human propensities, as well as spiritual or divine capabilities. The *dharma*-thinkers have recognized and made provision for the multi-dimensional constitution of a human being. They have endeavoured to order and organize, to regulate and refine the composite and complex human disposition, so that while legitimizing the lower and primitive wants of persons they also charge them with a higher and nobler purpose of life, seeking to bring about their ultimate divinity, thus offering a balanced and comprehensive view of human life.

The four objects of human pursuit are arranged in an ascending order as *artha, kāma, dharma* and *mokṣa* or Final Freedom. *Dharma* is placed before *artha* and *kāma* not only to indicate that *dharma* is their hedge and limit, but also that it has priority and central importance in human life. The pursuits of *artha* and *kāma,* even though they are mentioned first, are to be understood as operating within the boundaries of *dharma,* without transgressing *dharma* (*dharma-aviruddha, Gītā,* VII.11). Thus, the order would be like this:

Dharmāviruddha Artha

|

Dharmāviruddha Kāma

|

Dharma

|

Mokṣa

Dharma bridges *artha-kāma* designating a material life of self-aggrandizement and self-indulgence, and *mokṣa,* the spiritual life of emancipation from self. All together they comprehend both the realms, the terrestrial (*aihika*) and the transcendent (*ātyantika*); it is a *lokadvaya-rasāyaṇa*. This ancient Indian concept finds its correspondence in the modern Western concept of "the hierarchy of needs" advanced by Abraham Maslow.

The purpose of this article is not to dilate upon the well-known meaning and structure of *artha-kāma* and their status in relation to *dharma* or even to expound the individual natures of *dharma* and *mokṣa* as such. It is the interrelationship of *dharma* and *mokṣa,* or specifically the problem whether they are opposed to or compatible with each other, that is the theme of the present discussion.

Some scholars of Hinduism are prone to speak in terms of a tension between *dharma* and *mokṣa*. R.C. Zaehner in his *Hinduism* says,

> . . . it is true to say that there is and — has always been a tension within the Hindu religion — the striving after liberation from this world which all admit to be the final goal of man on the one hand and man's obligation to do what is right in this world on the other, the tension between Mokṣa and Dharma.[1]

Thus, for Zaehner, *dharma* and *mokṣa* are exclusive and irreconcilable.

David Kinsley's *Hinduism*[2] written in a very pleasant style maintains the existence of "a lively tension" between *dharma* and *mokṣa*. Actually, to argue this position seems to be his major concern in writing the book. He says,

> The ability to encompass and cherish both points of view, the temporal and the eternal, without surrendering entirely to one or the other, characterizes the distinctive genius of the Hindu tradition (p. 91).

In the Preface he writes,

> The essence of the Hindu vision of reality is located in the persistent tension between dharma, social duty, and moksha, release from the material and social world. Throughout the book these two emphases are treated side by side; and at several points it is shown how they tend to conflict with one another, giving rise to a creative tension that is the heart of the Hindu tradition . . . the book takes examples from both strands — the world-supporting realm of dharma and the world-denying realm of moksha — in order to show how the Hindu tradition insists upon both tendencies as essential in fulfilling human destiny.

---

1. R.C. Zaehner, *Hinduism*, Oxford University Press, New York, 1966, p. 7.
2. David R. Kinsley, *Hinduism, A Cultural Perspective*, Prentice-Hall, N.J. 1982.

And on p. 145 he goes on to add

> The distinctive nature of Hinduism resides in its simultaneous affirmation that people have an obligation to uphold the world, on the one hand, and to transcend the world, on the other hand. Although traditional Hinduism has formulated solutions to this double emphasis, the essence of Hinduism lies not so much in these compromises as in the clear demand that both obligations are absolute. Over the centuries Hinduism has been characterized more by a desire to push each obligation to its limit than by the desire to reconcile the two and risk compromising either of them. It is the tension between dharma and moksha, then, that characterizes Hinduism and lends it special appeal.

The divergent characteristics of *dharma* and *mokṣa* have, as animadverted by these writers, given rise to a tussle between them. According to them, the Hindu religious tradition is a drama of the push-and-pull of these two demands, the secular and the transcendent, and its religious literature, the *Mahābhārata* and the Purāṇas, contain many instances of such a conflict felt by the religious personages of yore. They are both asserted as parallel, as absolute, and no genuine reconciliation is found within the tradition. *Dharma* and *mokṣa* are polar opposites. *Dharma* is temporal, *mokṣa* is eternal; one implies relation to the world, the other means release from the world; one belongs to the world and seeks to preserve it, the other supersedes and relinquishes it. The main distinction, according to these scholars, consists in the attitudes the two goals of life bear towards the world. *Dharma* affirms the world, while *mokṣa* abjures the world. Such a mutually exclusive differentiation of *dharma* and *mokṣa* made by these scholars constitutes the crux.

It must be said to the credit of Kinsley that he has adduced several stories from the *Mahābhārata* and the Purāṇas to demonstrate his thesis. These stories illustrate, according to him, the conflict between *dharma* and *mokṣa*. In chapter two he has narrated the post-war episode of Yudhiṣṭhira's *viṣāda* or grief occurring in Book XII, the famous Śāntiparvan. After the catastrophic war Yudhiṣṭhira, extremely overwhelmed by sorrow, expresses his desire to renounce the kingdom and the world. He is finally persuaded to remain in the world and discharge his kingly duties during that second stage of his life and eventually leave the world at an appropriate time. In this story the tension between *dharma* and *saṁnyāsa* (renunciation) is resolved in favour of the former. And a similar tension is found in the story of Jaratkāru (p. 146) and in the superb story of Indra and the Divine Boy occurring in the *Kṛṣṇa-janma-khaṇḍa* (4.47.50-161) of the *Brahmavaivartta Purāṇa* (beautifully retold by Heinrich Zimmer as "The Parade of Ants" in his *Myths and Symbols in Indian Art and Civilization*. In all these incidents the conflict is settled establishing the superiority of *dharma* vs. renunciation. In the story of Mudgala (p. 147), however, the latter wins). The real issue, therefore, is *dharma* vs. *saṁnyāsa*, and not *dharma* vs. *mokṣa* (on p. 36, Kinsley himself calls Yudhiṣṭhira's dilemma "a tension between *dharma* and renunciation!") The problem lies unwittingly in equating *saṁnyāsa* with *mokṣa* (the first line of p. 146). The misperception of opposition between *dharma* and *mokṣa* arises from the scholars' misidentification of *saṁnyāsa-mārga* exclusively as *mokṣa-mārga*. Hence, their confusion causes the conflict between *dharma* and *saṁnyāsa* as the conflict between *dharma* and *mokṣa*. In the case of *dharma* and *saṁnyāsa* the opposition *seems* to be clear. *Dharma*, as the observance of familial and social obligations and rituals, operates within society and *saṁnyāsa* outside society.

Further, the conflict is presented, but the definite resolution of the conflict is also offered. Therefore, Kinsley is not right in saying that there is "simultaneous affirmation" or that "both obligations are absolute" (p. 145)[3]. In every case one of the ways is arrived at

3. Kinsley's ambivalence is seen at the end of the book. He says ". . . one is constantly reminded that one is both a social animal with worldly duties and an eternal sojourner in an infinite drama whose goal is ultimate release" (p. 153), and, ". . . the essence of human being is to affirm the fundamental importance of dharma while not losing sight of moksha" (p. 154). Both these passages show that *dharma* and *mokṣa* are compatible and not conflicting.

as more cogent or valid than the other, and it is the *dharma* that is largely upheld in contrast to *saṁnyāsa*, if sought to be undertaken at an *improper time-period* of one's life, then it would be disruptive of the order and functioning of the society. This statement refers to the four *āśramas*.

The two values of life, *dharma* and *mokṣa*, are deftly reconciled and their conflict obviated in the scheme of four stages or ages of life, which clearly corresponds to the four aims of life. It means that the *mokṣa*-ideal is to be pursued in the third and fourth stages of reclusion and mendicancy, which are a continuation of the householder's stage, during which *dharma* and *artha-kāma* have had their play. They envisage a well-rounded human life that responds to both the mundane and the trans-mundane dispositions of the human mind, which are to be respected and attended to at proper periods of one's life.

The *Mahābhārata* and the Purāṇas strikingly exhibit secular concerns of a social and political nature. Unlike the Upaniṣads, they are not solely concerned with the metaphysical and transcendent realities, namely *Brahman* and *ātman*. Consequently, they stress the importance of secular *dharma* or familial and social duties to be performed in the *gṛhastha-āśrama*. They naturally resolve the conflict between *dharma* and the *untimely* renunciation of the world during the second stage of life without adequately discharging its responsibilities, in favour of *dharma*. They support the observing of all four stages, the *āśrama-vyavasthā*, in their proper sequence. So, the real conflict is *not* even between *dharma* and *saṁnyāsa*, but between *dharma* and *premature saṁnyāsa*.

The theory of *caturāśrama* was a prudent arrangement to arrest a growing tendency among youths towards a quick, emotional exit from the society to find their salvation. To correct the social imbalance created by such relinquishment of social and familial responsibilities, the thinkers created a synthesis of both dimensions and demands of human life, social and spiritual. Thus, renunciation is included and accommodated in the complete programme in the later part of life, that is, in the third and fourth stages, and since it comes after the fulfilment of *dharma* in the householder's stage, it is not in conflict with *dharma*. The vast majority of Hindus prefer to remain in the society throughout and are engaged in the worldly life involving its comforts and pleasures as well as its manifold obligations of the family and community. One can hardly imagine a whole mass of people promptly quitting the world in the beginning of the third stage in compliance with the recommendation of their law-givers. Although such a state of affairs appears to ignore the last two renunciatory stages of life, it does not however point to any conflict between *dharma* and *mokṣa*, since most Hindus in their old age are indeed concerned a good deal with the "other" aspect of life, and as such are considerably involved in devotion to God and related religious practices and activities.

Now, the question arises whether *even dharma* and *saṁnyāsa* are really opposed. It is rather simplistic and superficial to assume that renunciation is necessarily world-denying and amounts to an abandoning of social concerns, just because it involves a physical withdrawal. True *saṁnyāsa* is not motivated by an intention to shirk or discard personal and social duties. It sets aside such personal *dharma* only for a positive spiritual purpose, for the sake of a *higher dharma*, so to speak. It does not stem from any attitude of aversion or devaluation towards the world, as contact with the society continues to be maintained, though marginally. Genuine *saṁnyāsin*s are not given to any negative, unwholesome or delinquent outlook. They forego a limited, narrow life of personal affections and obligations (*preyas*) for the sake of a more meaningful life of spiritual and social good (*śreyas*). Life is a ladder of values, a series of choices. One sacrifices the lower for the higher. *Saṁnyāsa* is not world-denying, it is only self-denying.[4] It is not inimical to *dharma* in its

4. "When the Hindu thinkers ask us to adopt sannyasa or relinquishment of home and possessions, . . . they point to self-denial as the root of spiritual life. Spirit of renunciation does not mean →

larger meaning. The Buddha and Jina are the classic examples of renunciation.

In fact, giving up of usual attachments is essentially involved in all serious, life-committing undertakings of any kind — academic, artistic, scientific or spiritual. It provides a necessary seclusion in a monastery, for instance, for an undistracted pursuit of one's deeper purpose through study, reflection and contemplation. It is temporary withdrawal for later participation. Affirmation and negation, abandonment and acceptance, *dharma* and *saṁnyāsa*, such a neat rigid compartmentalization of categories does not hold water.

Notwithstanding such a *rationale* behind renunciation, in actual practice, however, some people drop out of society for all sorts of motives. They leave the world out of a tepid attitude towards the world thinking it is all illusory, or out of disgust, despair, or disillusionment, or due to initial excitement and enthusiasm, or out of a desire for social power and authority or plainly out of irresponsibility.[5] The *āśrama*-order counteracts such pseudo-*saṁnyāsa* and its negative tendencies and seeks to foster a balance between *dharma* and *saṁnyāsa*.

In conclusion, it must be said that within the Hindu religious tradition no rivalry between *dharma* and *saṁnyāsa* is discernible. A

→ neglect of social duties. Sannyasa does not mean that we owe no duties to the world, we free ourselves only from ritualistic duties." S. Radhakrishnan, *The Principal Upaniṣads*, Oxford University Press, p. 106.

5. "The word renunciation has a negative ring, and India's frequent use of it has been one of the factors in earning for it the reputation of being a life-denying spoilsport. But renunciation has two faces. It can stem from disillusionment and despair, the feeling that it's not worthwhile to extend oneself; but equally it can signal the suspicion that life holds more than one is now experiencing. . . . If renunciation always entails the sacrifice of a trivial now for a more promising yet-to-be, religious renunciation is like that of athletes who resist indulgences that could deflect them from their all-consuming goal." Huston Smith, *The World's Religions*, Harper, 1991, p. 17.

very significant portion of the Hindu religious literature, such as the Epics, Purāṇas, Dharmaśāstras, stress worldliness and social duty, while upholding *mokṣa* as the *summum bonum* of human life.

It must be clarified that the scholars in question have erred in regarding renunciation as the *only mokṣa-mārga*, and thus squarely identifying it with *mokṣa*. *Mokṣa* does not out of necessity entail *saṁnyāsa* of *jñāna-yoga*, which is only *one* of the *mokṣa-mārga*s, while the others are *bhakti-yoga* and *karma-yoga*, which are both world-based.[6] *Bhakti* and *karma* do not ask one to shun one's *dharma*, since one is stationed in the society and is yet able to pursue one's liberation from the bondage of the world. *Mokṣa*, through the paths of *karma* and *bhakti*, is perfectly compatible with *dharma* or fulfilment of personal and social duties. The *Bhagavad-Gītā*, which is a part of the *Mahābhārata*, strikes a splendid synthesis of *dharma* to be performed in the world and *saṁnyāsa* to be executed out of the world. It propounds a unique concept of *karma-phala-saṁnyāsa*, a blending of performance of action and renunciation of self (*niṣkāma-karma, anāsakti-yoga*). It is *nivṛtti* in *pravṛtti* and *pravṛtti* in *nivṛtti*. If the Dharmaśāstras as social treatises have achieved a reconciliation of *dharma* and *saṁnyāsa* by ordering an individual's worldly life and non-wordly life, the *Gītā* as a religious classic has accomplished a truly spiritual integration of action and renunciation *within* the world. It dispenses with *saṁnyāsa*. The *Gītā* teaches acceptance of life without attachment to self, and non-attachment to self without denial of life.

The universal presence of *bhakti* in India is a most significant feature of the Hindu tradition. The *bhakti* tradition is far more dominant both in extensiveness and strength than the *saṁnyāsa* tradition. To regard the tension between *dharma* and *saṁnyāsa* as a

6. Kinsley himself admits both to be the ways to *mokṣa*. "Although the path of knowledge usually is pursued outside society, in a monastery or in isolated meditation, the paths of works and devotion are often said to be appropriate to life in the world, that is, appropriate to the realm of *dharmic* order." p. 90.

chief characteristic of Hinduism is to ignore the massive impact of *bhakti-yoga* on India's culture.

It is now worthwhile to focus on the exact relationship of *dharma* and *mokṣa*. The definition of *dharma* runs like this: *yato abhyudaya-niḥśreyasa-siddhiḥ saḥ dharmaḥ* (that which is the source of material well-being and transcendent good is *dharma*). One may see opposition or disparity between *artha, kāma* and *mokṣa*, because they are sought after for the gratification of selfish desires, whereas *mokṣa* is elimination of self. *Dharma* acts as a bridge; it touches both ends. *Dharma* is not to be viewed as merely performing a regulatory function in relation to the previous pursuits of wealth and pleasure and as such being conducive to material prosperity and enjoyment in the world. *Dharma*, no doubt, has an application and relevance to the secular world. But for that matter *dharma* itself is not purely secular. *Dharma* arises from a higher consciousness of order, interrelatedness, complementarity, harmony and unity. The true practice of *dharma* involves self-attenuation and amelioration of social conditions through the performance of one's duties and through the practice of higher virtues. Thus, dhārmic life becomes indispensably instrumental (*sādhana*) to the supreme spiritual ideal of *mokṣa*, which is complete freedom from the thraldom of self. It leads to a gradual cultivation of selflessness and thus purifies the mind (*sattva-śuddhi*). Moral discipline and mental purification aid spiritual practices such as *jñāna, dhāyana, bhakti*, which eventually find their fruition in *mokṣa* (*sādhya*). In this regard, Patañjali's five *yama*s and *niyama*s placed in the beginning of his eight-membered *Yoga* system, and the principles of conduct (*śīla*) in the Fourth Noble Truth or the Eightfold Path of Buddha may be alluded to. Thus, *dharma* and *mokṣa* reveal a consistency and continuity. They are both made of the same stuff, self-abnegation.

At this juncture, we must consider the criticism of some scholars, who demur the conformity of *dharma* and *mokṣa*. To them there is an intrinsic conceptual and factual diametricity of *dharma* and *mokṣa*. These critics argue that *dharma* and *mokṣa* are discontinuous and disparate. *Dharma* is located in the world, *mokṣa* transcends the world. *Dharma* has a positively social significance, *mokṣa* is socially non-functional and exclusively individualistic.[7] There is thus a sharp cleavage between them; their spheres of operation are totally distinct. *Mokṣa* means personal release and has no social reference. It is not concerned with the maintenance of social order and is confined to one's own blissful existence. This criticism is obviously based upon the implicit notion that *mokṣa* is tied up with renunciation and world-denial. The question lingers on!

Surprisingly, the same criticism is still being directed against *mokṣa vis-a-vis dharma,* as that levelled by Albert Schweitzer long ago (1936) in his *Indian Thought and Its Development*. Schweitzer contended that Indian thought and culture is life and world negating, as opposed to the Western-Christian which are life and world affirming. Indian outlook is negative, because it is oriented to the abandonment of the world for personal salvific benefit, and eschews "all activity, which aims at an improvement of the conditions of life in this world," or removing the miseries and sufferings of the fellow beings.

To reply to these objections, *mokṣa* or *Brahman*-realization is not transcendence or rejection of the world as such, but only of worldliness, of the false, deluded, self-bound attitude toward the world. It is a *mental* shift, a radical transformation of one's erstwhile preception (*dṛṣṭi*) and a termination of one's personal attachments

7. "*Moksa* is intrinsic and not functional; it is personalistic and not social; . . . *Moksa* thus forms a sharp dichotomy with the other three *purusarthas*, particularly with *dharma*. While *dharma* aims at the maintenance of the world-order, *moksa* deliberately rejects it. *Moksa* signifies release from the entire realm governed by *dharma*; essentially it purports to be the negation of *dharma*." R.N. Dandekar, "The Theory of Purusarthas: A Rethinking," *R.G. Bhandarkar 150th Birth-Anniversary Volume*, June, 1987, p. 667. Also, Y. Krishnan, "The Meaning of the Purusarthas in the Mahabharata," *Moral Dilemmas in the Mahabharata*, ed. B.K. Matilal, Shimla, 1989, pp. 63, 67.

and aversions toward the world and its accoutrements. It actually designates freedom from egocentricity, which seeks to appropriate the world exclusively for itself. The achievement of individual freedom does not imply leaving the world behind. The world remains, and appears in a new light.

A realized or liberated person is still situated in the world and is acutely aware of the *vaiṣamya* and *nairghṛṇya* (inequality and cruelty) rampant in the world. Such a person acts and acts in accordance with *dharma*, in fact the loftiest *dharma* of loving kindness, *agape* and active service of all. He/she has only gone beyond his/her specific social duties and does not abandon rendering larger social good. They are not only personalistic, but on the contrary, intensely socialistic, humanistic and altruistic. A free person cannot toss *dharma* out of their life in the way one may drop a ladder, a raft or a medicine after one has climbed, crossed or is cured. One's personal mental freedom simply provides a fearless and congenial frame of mind to bring about the weal of all. The goal is not individual salvation, but the liberation of all. Individual redemption is but one of the most important catalyst in that direction.

In the state of *jīvan-mukti*, the *dharma* returns and reasserts itself. A *jīvanmukta*, or any advanced renunciant whole-heartedly engages in *loka-saṅgraha* or world welfare (*Gītā*, III.25, IV.23) and indefatigably acts in the world for the deliverance of all creatures from *duḥkha*. It is *dharma* in its most comprehensive meaning of *karuṇā*. Like a full-blown lotus risen above the surface but still rooted in the water, a *jīvanmukta* remains unsullied by the world but still belongs to it, and strives for the universal well-being in spontaneous sympathy and selfless service (*sarvabhūtahite ratāḥ*, *Gītā*, XII.4).

Mokṣa does not and cannot abrogate *dharma*. Without *dharma*, *mokṣa* will cancel itself out. For indifference and inaction in the face of large-scale suffering and pain in the world would *ipso facto* amount to stark selfishness, and forfeit any possibility of having earned *mokṣa* at all. No true realization could be said to have occurred in view of such an attitude. *Mokṣa* obviously accrues to a particular person. It is an individual event no doubt, but it is not individualistic or self-centered. It is not a pursuit for a personal gain like an olympic medal. Selfish salvation is a contradiction in terms. Therefore, to say that the way of *mokṣa* is followed solely for the good of one's own soul and not for the good of others as well, or to regard the attainment of *mokṣa* as autocentric is a serious conceptual blunder and a sad lack of the understanding of the meaning and dynamics of spiritual freedom. Spiritual perfection and social good are concurrent (*ātmaśreyase jagat-hitāya ca*).

Such a criticism will remind one of an old issue in the development of the Buddhist tradition, which actually became the main basis of schism between Hīnayāna or Theravāda and Mahāyāna. The Mahāyāna liberals in their initial zeal accused their predecessor monks of striving for their private *nirvāṇa* and of keeping it to themselves after attaining it, without caring to enlighten or uplift others. They are called *arhat* (worthy saint) and *pratyekabuddha* or the solitary Buddha. However, such a criticism, though inspired by a benevolent motive, is logically untenable. A *pratyekabuddha* is a self-contradiction (*vadato vyāghāta*). By the same token, Schweitzer's view that the Indian renunciants are interested in perfecting themselves and are apathetic and inactive with regard to their neighbhour's plight, is a theoretical impossibility. However, in actual practice within the society, misguided monks, ascetics, *sādhus* may miss their orientation and become involved in purely personal religious and spiritual practices and not be concerned with the community at large.[8] In the history of religious traditions, we do encounter a certain degeneration in institutionalized monasticism, which tends to become individualistic, self-absorbed

8. In *Bhāgavata*, VII.9.44, Prahlāda refers to those who are desirous of their own release (*sva-nivṛttikāmaḥ*) without conducing to others' interests (*na parārtha-niṣṭhāḥ*).

and exclusive in the course of time. The Hindu tradition being conspicuously renunciatory and ascetic in relation to other cultures has incurred the charge of being life and world denying. This question of the Hindu "other-worldliness" is to be dealt with separately.

Finally, let us ascend to a new and unorthodox level of understanding *dharma*. *Dharma* is so far viewed as an ancillary to *mokṣa*, as it serves to bring about *sattva-saṁśuddhi* or mental purification necessary for the spiritual practices which directly lead to liberation. However, it is not necessary that *dharma* must always figure as subservient to the other paths meant for an *inner* spiritual-mystical union with the Divine. In fact, *dharma* or virtue of the highest order, as identified not simply with the discharge of familial duties and social obligations and rules of basic morality, but also identified with the dynamic love and compassion devoted to the solidarity and sustenance of the world (*loka-saṅgraha*) and derived from the perception of the inner unity of all beings, should be capable of yielding the perfection of freedom or *mokṣa* (*Gītā*, III.19, 20, VI.29, 30).

Dharma in preponderance is *constitutive* of *mokṣa*.[9] *Dharma* is the commencement and cultivation of *mokṣa*, and *mokṣa* is the culmination and consummation of *dharma*. As stated earlier, *dharma* and *mokṣa* belong to the same genre; *dharma* is akin to *mokṣa*. Both

---

9. This view is in contradistinction to the view expressed by T.M.P. Mahadevan. "While it is admitted that *moksa*, and not *dharma*, is the supreme end, the sole intrinsic value, . . ." (p. 479) or, "one should not stop with being moral, morality is but the stepping-stone to spiritual perfection" (p. 493).

   Indian philosophy generally holds the sound view, "that morality is not a realm which is self-sufficient and self-complete, that one has to go beyond ethics in order to reach the final goal which is *moksa*, and that it is only in the plenary experience of spiritual freedom that all contradictions and all problems are resolved" (p. 483). "Indian Ethics and Social Practice," *Philosophy and Culture*: *East and West*, ed. Charles A. Moore, University of Hawaii Press, 1968.

involve self-transcendence. Every dhārmic act is an act of *mokṣa*. It progressively brings one closer to the realization of one's true self or *ātman*, which is universal in nature (*bhūmā*). *Dharma-yoga* or the practice of *dharma* most fully refined and accentuated, is identical with *mokṣa*.

And such universalistic *dharma*, in its most chaste and inspired moment, manifests itself to be even trans-mokṣic (not included in the title), as in the touching words of Rantideva and Prahlāda,[10] and in the concept of a *bodhisattva* in Mahāyāna. *Mokṣa* (or *nirvāṇa*) is superseded here by *dharma* consisting in boundless sensitivity and compassion toward all sentient beings and their agonies. One's own uniting with the Ultimate Reality is indefinitely deferred until all beings are finally redeemed (*sarva-mukti, mahā-parinirvāṇa*).

---

10. The noblest of sentiments is expressed in the famous verse ascribed to King Rantideva in the *Bhāgavata* (IX.21.12). The benevolent royal devotee of Viṣṇu is not only not interested in universal sovereignty or in various *siddhis*, but also not in *mokṣa* or non-return to *saṁsāra*, considered to be the state of highest beatitude, which in his case would be the most blessed divine abode of Viṣṇu, his Lord (Vaikuṇṭha). Indeed, all he wishes for is the alleviation of the afflictions of all suffering beings in the world by dwelling in their hearts and taking on their pain. Prahlāda also voices the same feeling in the verse referred to above.

6

Mahatma Gandhi's Notion of Dharma
An Explication

Pushraj Jain

The importance of *dharma* in the Indian thought is highlighted by the following *śloka* of *Mahābhārata:*

> *na dharmo'stiti manvanaḥ śucīnavahasanniva* |
> *aśraddhānaśca bhaved vinaśamupagachati* ||

That is, he who believes that *dharma* has no purpose and makes fun of it as well as of its followers invariably perishes. It is further highlighted by Manu thus:

> *dharma eva hato hanti dharmo rakṣati rakṣitaḥ* |
> *tasmād dharmo na hantavyoḥ ma no dharmo hato'vadhīt* ||

That is, if you transgress *dharma* then it will destroy you, but if you follow it then it shall protect you; that is why one should never transgress *dharma* lest it harms you.

Dharma, as we all know, is one of the most complex, intricate and most discussed concepts of Indian Philosophy. The term is so complex that it defies translation. That is why there is no synonym for this Sanskrit term in any other languages. It has been used in a variety of ways and has many connotations. Broadly speaking, *dhrama* has been used in the following senses:

1. In its most primary sense *dharma* is used to signify the harmonious order of the cosmos.

2. The Buddhists, especially the early Buddhists, sometimes use it to refer to the ultimate element of things and the later Buddhists use it to denote the essential function of things.

3. The Jains understand the term in a unique way. According to them *dharma* and *adharma* are material atoms that enter the soul. They are the principles of motion and rest respectively. The Jains hold that *vastu svabhāvo dharmaḥ* that is the nature of the *jīva* (soul) is *dharma*.

4. At times, *dharma* refers to the ethical and moral duties, and at other times it refers to the laws. This complicates further the problem of explicating the nature of *dharma*.

My purpose in this paper is to explicate the concept of *dharma* as enunciated by Mahatma Gandhi. Since Gandhi's explication is nothing but an elucidation of the traditional Indian concept, I shall first survey the concept of *dharma* as discussed in the Indian tradition and its different schools of Philosophy.

The earliest used term for *dharma* in the Vedas is *ṛta*. The term *ṛta* in its primary sense means cosmic order. *Ṛta*, in the *Ṛgveda* (1.24, 7.8.10, 7.87.1.2), has been used in three senses. In the first sense it represents the universal law according to which the whole (*brahmāṇḍa*) is organized and its parts (*piṇḍa*s) function and partake in the whole. In the second sense it represents the moral and ethical rules according to which persons interact with each other in the given society. In the third sense it refers to the laws governing the do's and don'ts in the sphere of religious norms and practices.

As a result everything, every event, every activity in the universe that is *bhūr, bhuvaḥ, svaḥ* — the three *loka*s — the three worlds — is governed by *ṛta*. This principle is not a principle which can be invented by human beings or any other agency, but is something which like the laws of nature can only be discovered. This does not mean that the concept of *ṛta* or its consequent *satya*

(Truth) and *dharma* are taken as static concepts. These concepts are dynamic and evolutionary in nature and keep changing according to the needs of the times. They are not context neutral but are context specific. That is why the Indians over a long period of their existence have interpreted not only the contents — *do's* and *don'ts* of these principles and laws, their underlying truth and falsity, in a rigid manner but have interpreted them differently to suit the needs of their own times. What *dharma* is in one society is different in a different society, nay it is different for the same society in a different era. *Mahābhārata* explicitly states this everchanging nature of *dharma* in the following *śloka:*

> *anye kr̥tayuge dharmastretāyam dvāpare pare* ।
> *anye kaliyuge dharma yathāśakti kr̥ta iva* ।।

That is, in *satyayuga* the *dharma*s are different from the *dharma*s in the *dvāparayuga;* and the *dharma*s prescribed for the *dvāparayuga* are different from the ones in the *kaliyuga.*

Apparently the *dharma*s for each age are determined by the seers on the basis of the needs, aspirations and capacities of the individuals living in that age.

Dharma, therefore, keeps changing in accordance with the place and time. With the passage of time and change of conditions — material or otherwise, the prevalent *dharma*s go into oblivion and new *dharma*s take their place. There is no sanctity attached to the old or ancient in the Indian tradition. Kālidāsa's saying, *purāṇamityeva na sādhu sarvam* — a thing or principle does not become good or acceptable just by virtue of its antiquity, and *santaḥ parīkṣyanyatarad bhajante* — the learned persons accept only that to be good which has an intrinsic merit, supports this view. That is why terms like *dharmaglāni* or *dharmalopa* are much in vogue in Indian philosophical and other literature. These terms according to the sages of India refer to the fact that the *deśa* and *kāla* — place, time and context have changed and there is a need for reinterpretation of the concept of *dharma* itself to meet the needs of the individual and society. This is supported by the following *śloka* of *Bhagvada-Gītā* (IV.vii):

> *yadā yadā hī dharmasya glānirbhavati bhārata* ।
> *abhyutthānamadharmasya tadātmanam sṛjāmyaham* ।।

That is, "Oh Arjuna! Whenever there is a decline of virtue and increase of vice, then do I manifest Myself." This manifestation is to reinterpret and re-establish the *dharma* which is a means of achieving prosperity and liberation for the human beings.

A glance at the remote and the near past of India shows that the notion of *dharma* has been interpreted, reinterpreted and re-reinterpreted over the ages. The *Rāmāyaṇa*, the *Mahābhārata* and the Purāṇic literature are nothing but attempts at interpreting the *dharma*s as contained in the Vedas. Kundakundācārya, Samantabhadra, Akalaṅkadeva, Swami Kārttikeya, Somadeva Sūri and others in the Jaina tradition, Aśvaghoṣa, Vasubandhu, Dharmakīrti and others in the Buddhist tradition, Śaṅkara, Rāmānuja, Madhva, Nimbārka and others in the Vaiṣṇava tradition have given an interpretation to *dharma* in accordance with their own times and age. Kauṭilya interpreted it for Chandragupta, Hemacandrācārya interpreted it for Kumārapāla, Patañjali interpreted it for Puṣyamitra, Vidyāraṇya Swāmī interpreted it for the rulers of the Vijayanagar empire, Samarth Rāmdāsa interpreted it for Śivājī. Tulsī, Kabīra, Mīrā, Śūrdās, Nānak, Subrahmaṇyam Bhāratī, Nāmdeva, Tukārāma and others interpreted *dharma* according to their times for the common man. In the modern times Maharshi Dayanand, Ramakrishna Paramahansa, Vivekananda, Raman Maharshi, Shri Aurobindo, Shrimad Rajcandra, Acharya Tulsi, Acharya Vidyasagara, the Daḷai lamas, the Brahmosamajists explained it anew in the context and vocabulary of their times. Their interpretations have a freshness which directly appeal to the hearts and souls of the masses and the intellectuals alike because these interpretations are relevant to our times and use the current idiom and terminology. They directly confront the problems faced by us in our work-a-day life and offer their contemporary solutions.

In keeping with this tradition Mahatma Gandhi whose aim in the political and social sphere was establishment of *Rāmarājya* — "the kingdom of God on earth"(*Harijana*, 5.5.1946), "sovereignty of the people based on pure moral authority"(*Harijana*, 2.1.1937), and whose aim in the spiritual sphere was attainment of *mokṣa* not only for himself but also for all human beings, in line with the Buddha and Mahāvīra, interpreted *dharma* in accordance with his time and goals. His interpretation is unique in the sense that it synthesized the ideal and abstract with the practical. He made *dharma* a part of his theory and practical action for getting freedom for India. He not only dissolved the distinction between the *rājadharma* (political) and *devadharma* (the ethical and the religious *dharma*), rather he synthesized the political with the moral and religious. According to him,

> I consider it to be man's achievement to harmonise *dharma* and the ultimate aim of life, truth and *swaraj*: *swaraj* and government by all, the welfare of the country and the welfare of all, that alone is the path that leads to *moksha*, that alone is what interests me. Whosoever wishes to share that interest is welcome to do so. None of my activities are carried on with any other end in view.[1]

Gandhi, therefore, does not understand and explain the notion of *dharma* in a limited sense. He positively, does not take the term to mean religion. Religion implies a society, a group of individuals sharing the same ideology or principles. It has a strong social and communitarian aspect added to it. But *dharma* does not necessarily have a social dimension. According to Gandhi "one's *dharma* is a personal possession. One is oneself responsible for preserving it." He categorically adds that "what can be defended in and through a group is not *dharma*, it is a dogma."[2] In fact, highlighting this

---

1. *Collected Works of Mahatma Gandhi* (hereafter *CW*), vol. XLI, p. 211.
2. *CW*, XXI, pp. 202-03.

distinction between religion and *dharma* he in very strong terms asserts that no organized religion is a special repository of *dharma*. It is not from any religion, exclusive or otherwise, that we learn our *dharma*. We can "get it whether from India or Arabia."[3] So Gandhi by one fell swoop lays down the criterion for making a distinction between the concept of religion and the concept of *dharma*.

Dharma is that which is primarily individual in character and the responsibility of carrying it out lies with the individual. The individual alone is the crusader for it. The dictates of a religion on the other hand are to be carried out by a group or a society which has entered into its folds, voluntarily or otherwise. Gandhi does not use the term 'religion' to connote such individual religions or faiths. According to him, "By religion, I do not mean formal religion, or customary religion, but that religion which underlies all religions, which brings us face to face with our Maker."[4] Describing his use of the term 'religion' further he says that religion is that "which transcends" the limits of any particular religion and "which changes one's very nature, which binds one indissolubly to the truth within and which ever purifies. It is permanent element in human nature which counts no cost too great in order to find full expression and which leaves the soul utterly restless until it has found itself, known its Maker and appreciated the true correspondence between the Maker and itself."[5] That Gandhi does not regard religion or being religious or following of a religious order or creed as something external, some kind of a "job" or "profession" is abundantly clear when Gandhi categorically asserts that, "I do not conceive religion as one of the many activities of mankind." The main reason for this is that "the same activity may be governed by the spirit either of religion or of irreligion." On the contrary he

3. *CW*, XXXII, p.11.
4. Quoted in *The Mind of Mahatma Gandhi*, ed. R.K. Prabhu and U.R. Rao, Navjivan Publishing House, 1967, p. 64.
5. *Ibid.*

regards being religious as something inherent to mankind. Religion, in fact, inheres in all our activities. Therefore, he concludes, "For me every, tiniest, activity is governed by what I consider to be my religion."[6] He could say this because all our actions, irrespective of any value judgement that can be passed on it prospectively, are governed by *dharma*. It is *dharma* which underlies all our actions and activities. Gandhi accepted it as the guiding principle for all his actions. He very explicitly admits this fact when he says, "This is the maxim of life which I have accepted, namely, that no work done by any man, no matter how great he is, will really prosper unless he has a religious backing."[7] From this it is very clear that Gandhi made a distinction between a creed and *dharma*. His usage of the English term does not refer to a faith or any particular creed or religion but to *dharma*. It is *dharma* which underlies all religions, all creeds and all faiths.

Defining *dharma*, negatively, Gandhi says, "Dharma does not mean any particular creed or dogma. Nor does it mean reading or learning by rote books known as *shastra*s (sacred texts) or even believing all that they say."[8] Speaking positively Gandhi adds, *dharma* is a "quality of the soul" present in every individual. He goes on to say, "through it we know our duty in human life and our true relation with other souls." He regards *dharma* as "the means (*sādhanā*) by which we can know ourselves."[9] However from this one should not conclude that Gandhi meant by *dharma* only a metaphysical or spiritual category. He made it amply clear that the nature of *dharma* is not exhausted by these categories. He adds moral dimension to *dharma* and says, "In my opinion *dharma* means morality. I do not know any *dharma* which is opposed to, or goes beyond morality. *Dharma* is morality practised to its ultimate

6. *The Diary of Mahadev Desai*, Navjivan, vol. I.
7. *Speeches and Writings of Mahatma Gandhi*, GA Natesan and Co., 1933, p. 377-78.
8. *Ibid*.
9. *Ibid*.

limits." By saying this he adds a social dimension to *dharma*, because morality is primarily a social virtue. Explaining his notion of 'moral' or 'ethical' Gandhi goes on to say, "Morality in its turn means truth and non-violence. While the end is truth, non-violence is the means of attaining it." Elaborating the relationship between means and ends he says, "in such matters, however, the means cannot be separated from the ends, hence I have written that truth and non-violence are two sides of the same coin."[10] *Dharma*, therefore, for Gandhi is the means for knowing the truth and establishment of a non-violent, peaceful world order.

Gandhi adopted the definition of *Dharma* as given in *Manu-Smṛti* which says:

> *vidvadbhi sevitaḥ sadbhir nityamadveṣarāgibhih* ।
> *hṛdayenābhyanujñāto yo dharmastam nibodhata* ।।

Gandhi translated it as, "that is *dharma* which is enjoined by the holy books, followed by the sages, interpreted by the learned and which appealed to the heart." Accordingly, there are four components of *dharma* or a dhārmic precept. The first is that it should be advocated by a *śāstra* or a holy book. The second is that it should be practised by the saints — men of virtue and men well versed in the worldly and spiritual affairs. The third is that in case of any doubt or conflict, *āptapurūṣa*, that is those who are free from *rāga, moha, lobha* — attachment, avarice and greed, and *dveṣa* — hatred and ill-will, alone are the arbiters. This condition is also highlighted in the *Mahābhārata* when it says: *mahājano yena gataḥ sa panthaḥ*. The above is a definition of a *mahājana*. The fourth condition to be fulfilled by a dhārmic precept is that it should appeal to the person who is going to act on it. That is to say, it should satisfy him about its efficacy. However, Gandhi believes that the fourth condition is subservient to the first three. According to him, "the first three conditions must be fulfilled before the fourth comes into operation." This stipulation differentiates a dhārmic precept from

10. *CW*, XLI, p. 209.

any other arbitrary precept. It also protects the sanctity of *dharma* as it lays down that not just a personal subjective appeal to the heart or what pleases one, can be *dharma*. *Dharma* is that which is objective, which is accepted by the conscientious. It is because of this objective trait that "one has no right to follow the precepts of an ignorant man or a rascal even though they commend themselves to one. Rigorous observance of harmlessness, non-enmity and renunciation are the first requisites for a person to entitle him to lay down the law, i.e., *dharma*."[11]

Gandhi makes a distinction between absolute or ideal *dharma* on one hand and practical or relative *dharma* on the other. Though he does not discuss the distinction with respect to the notion of *dharma* he explains this in the context of the concept of morality. It would be right to presume that what he says about the relativeness of morality is *mutatis mutandis* applicable to *dharma* too. Talking about the relation between the concepts of morality he says, "there is no such thing as absolute morality for all times. But there is relative morality *which is absolute enough* for imperfect mortals that we are."[12] This notion of "absolute enough" shows that Gandhi is not an idealist, armchair philosopher or theoretician but a man rooted in ground reality of human condition and predicament. Unlike Kant he never loses sight of the real complex "lived" situations that human beings face in their day-to-day life. Like Kant he does not advocate imperatives which are categorical and admit of no exception but pleads for imperatives which are *categorical enough* for mortals like us whose life is not just in black and white but bears many hues of gray. This according to Radhakrishnan is because Gandhi "knows that life at best is a long second best, a perpetual compromise between the ideal and the possible. The kingdom of God knows no compromise, no practical limitations. But here on earth there are the pitiless laws of nature. We have to

11. *Harijan*, 17.11, 1946.

12. *Ibid.*, 23.12., 1939, emphasis added.

build an ordered cosmos on the basis of human passions. Through effort and difficulty ideals struggle to realization."[13]

In the case of *dharma* too he makes a distinction between ideal *dharma* and practical *dharma*. By ideal *dharma*, it would not be wrong to construe, he means "ideal enough" in the given human situation. It is something that every conscientious being would follow who finds himself in the identical predicament. It is an action enjoined by those whom we have earlier in the paper described as *mahājana*s. This can be illustrated by taking the example of *ahiṁsā*, non-violence. Though Gandhi prescribes the principle of *ahiṁsā* as the ideal of everyone, he *does not* admit of no exceptions to this maxim. He admits that there can be situations in which a person may have to use force. Gandhi is fully aware that "life is not entirely governed by logic."[14] That is why he does not go into the detailed discussion of the notion of ideal or perfect *dharma*. Instead he concentrates on its practical aspects.

In fact, being a man grounded in human reality, he like the existentialists does not think of "ideal" or "perfect" as categories applicable to the concrete human situation. He admits that like a mirage we constantly strive to achieve the ideal and perfection but due to our limitations, physical or otherwise, they always delude us. He says, "Perfect non-violence is impossible so long as we exist physically, for we would want some space at least to occupy. Perfect non-violence whilst you are inhabiting the body is only a theory like Euclid's point or straight line but we have to endeavor every moment of our life."[15] An ideal or perfect *dharma* for him would be like the Euclid's point or a straight line.

---

13. "Foreward," *The Mind of Mahatma Gandhi*, *op. cit*., p. xi.
14. *Harijana*, 28.9., 1934.
15. *Selections from Gandhi*, Nirmal Kumar Bose, Navjivan, p. 147.

7

India, Europe, and Modernity

Saranindranath Tagore

Introduction

IN this paper, I am interested in disclosing a concept of modernity that is Indian in its conception and development. I will apply the strategy of using the contemporary postmodern construction of modernity to facilitate the task at hand. A salient ramification of my thesis will be that the Indian conception of the modern differs in significant ways from the postmodern formulations of European modernity. Therefore, alternative conceptions of modernity need to be considered by the postmodern theorist. The trajectory of my remarks, basing itself on the claims of postmodernism, then, will run in two directions: on one side, I propose to sketch out an Indian conception of the modern that is distinguishable from European modernity; and on the other side, as a consequence of the earlier point, I will claim that the postmodern theorist cannot translate the criticism of European modernity to a criticism of modernity in general.

Postmodernism, elaborating a novel metaphysics of fragmentation, raises a challenge to the universally enfolding movement of an influential strand of European thought that begins with Parmenides and Plato, and is nourished in sequence by Descartes, Kant, and Hegel, and finds its most recent champions in the transcendental phenomenology of Husserl and in the thinking of the early Wittgenstein. Foundationalism of any species (metaphysical or epistemological) that jettisons the possibility of plurality emerges as the central object of postmodern critique. My remarks will be hermeneutically motivated by a registry of issues that have been raised by the thinkers of European postmodernism; and these notions will be used to disclose the space of modernity in which the more recent episodes of Indian thought are anchored. The period that interests me roughly spans the careers of Rammohun Roy to Rabindranath Tagore. Just as philosophers influenced by the Enlightenment, especially Hegel, are pivotal to the postmodern articulation of European modernity, in the same manner, I argue, the Indian conception of modernity was founded by Roy and was developed during the later part of India's colonial experience.

The analysis will be registered between two philosophical tropes: the foundational and the plural. European modernity is foundational and anti-plural, European postmodernity is anti-foundational and plural. The European conceptions of modernity and postmodernity, it is hoped, through their incommensurate postures towards each other, will open up a rich philosophical space in which an Indian conception of modernity as foundational and plural can be hermeneutically enunciated.

At the outset, three points of clarification are in order. First, my concern in this paper will be weighted more towards conceptual issues, and less on textual analysis. Secondly, though the modern and the postmodern can be used as marking off chronological matrices, I will, in consonance with the postmodern literature, use these notions primarily as indexing a set of philosophical positions. Thirdly, the intention is not to reduce all the narratives of Indian modernity to a singularity; but, rather, the remarks are to be taken in terms of one possible way of articulating the Indian conception of the modern. Therefore, it will be taken for granted that there are figures in the period under discussion who would reject the conception presented here.

Lyotard and Postmodern Plurality

Thinkers who camp under the banner of postmodernism do not constitute a monolithic group, but exhibit an astonishingly wide range of concerns. Defining the postmodern is a difficult task, and will not be taken up here. Fortunately, however, all postmodern theorists are signatories to a philosophical (and metaphilosophical) enterprise of being "incredulous" toward the unifying functions of metaphysical and epistemic foundations. From such a perspective, the entire history of Western thought can open up to a postmodern reading in which, for instance, the accent of value is placed on the Sophists rather than on Plato, on Nietzsche rather on Hegel, on the Kant of the "Dialectic" rather than on the Kant of the "Analytic." Similarly, within the textual corpus of postmodernism, the genealogies and archaeology of Foucault or the rhizomatizm of Deleuze are insistent on the shattering of all possible frames of foundations and unities. As all postmodern theorists cannot be fruitfully discussed within the confines of this paper, I propose to briefly discuss some fragments of Jean-Francois Lyotard's theory in order to frame the hermeneutical tropes of the foundational and the plural that will be of concern later in my remarks.

Rejecting the correspondence theory of truth in his account of textuality, Lyotard writes:

> What is important in a text is not what it means, but what it does and incites to do. What it does: the charge of affect it contains and transmits. What it incites to do: the metamorphoses of this potential energy into other things — other texts, but also paintings, photographs, film sequences, political actions, decisions, erotic inspirations, acts of insubordination, economic initiatives, etc.[1]

Such a view of textuality, questioning the transcendent referentiality of language as the source of meaning, challenges the

1. J.F. Lyotard, *Driftworks*, New York, 1984, pp. 9-10.

ontologically motivated discourses of modernity that presume to provide an absolute access into the Real. The severing of the ties between the implications of language and the structures of the Real — a connection that informs all projects of modernity — partially retrieves Kant's dialectical formulation of the transcendental ideas, and explicitly scorns the Hegelian inscription of historical and constituting content in the Kantian formal unity of reason.

Hegel's metaphysics of Spirit with its attendant account of historical and cultural constitution provides for Lyotard a primary example of what he calls a grand narrative of modernity. Indeed Lyotard defines the modern in terms of such grand narratives. In a famous passage, Lyotard writes that by the 'modern' he means:

> Any science that legitimates itself with reference to a metadiscourse . . . making an explicit appeal to some grand narrative, such as the dialectics of Spirit, the hermeneutics of meaning, the emancipation of the rational or working subject, or the creation of wealth.[2]

Lyotard defines the postmodern, in contrast, as "incredulity towards metanarratives."[3] Shattering the foundational frames of modern discourses of legitimation, Lyotard opts for the viability of what he calls little narratives. Such narratives, inspired by the later Wittgensteinian offering of language games and complementing Kuhn's paradigm-driven account of scientific revolutions, are discursive structures that are not legitimated by meta-figurations of normative codes, but are consolidated by interior rules. Consequently, discourses in general and cultural discourses in particular constitute a narrative universe that, by jettisoning the unifying trope of foundation, valorizes dissensus over consensus, heterogeneity over homogeneity, and the incommensurable over universal legitimation.

---

2. J.F. Lyotard, *The Postmodern Condition*, Minneapolis, 1993, p. xxiii.
3. *Ibid.*, p. xxiv.

Deleuze and Guattari, constituting together another significant voice in the postmodern literature, trace the curvature of Lyotard's account when they endeavour to capture the movement of modernity in the image of a tree. Modernity generates a system of discourses that are rooted in a founded matrix in order to make possible a unified, centered, and hierarchial system. Plato's account of the Forms, or Hegel's postulate of Spirit serve as root-systems that allow for the privileged presentation of particular discursive and cultural platforms. Lyotardian grand narratives have much in common with the arborescent account of modernity. The figure of the rhizome, like the notion of little narratives, is designed to interrupt the congealment of all unities that foundational postures construct. The rhizome, rejecting all metaphysics of substance and unity, invests its capital in the primacy of the ever-becoming logic of desire; and thus celebrates the multiple both in the self-constitution of individuals (schizophrenia) and in the creation of cultural spheres (plurality).[4]

Postmodern theory reverses the tropes of modernity by rejecting foundations in order to secure plurality. This postmodern move is in part motivated by a concern for a politics of demarginalization. Grand narratives, plotting out universal-ized normative prescriptions, construct a hierarchical space in which cultural configurations are situated. Hegel's philosophy of history, for instance, anchored in a teleological foundation, centres the Euro-German cultural ethos, and decentres other cultural formations such as those of India and China. Postmodernism renders a non-hierarchical space where plurality can be championed. Lyotard, explicitly appealing to the Kantian irreconcilability of the "concept of reason" and the "sensible manifold," attacks Hegelian unities that lead to terror.[5] The counter-Kantian proposal of "supplying reality" to the formal texture of the concept of reason forges a transcendental illusion, but such a move for Lyotard is also terrorist

4. Deleuze and Guattari, *A Thousand Plateaus*, Minneapolis, 1998.

5. Lyotard, *The Postmodern Condition*, pp. 81-82.

and hegemonic because by terror is meant the dictum "adapt your aspirations to our ends — or else."[6] Lyotard's distinction between the differend and litigation will illuminate the notion further:

> As distinguished from a litigation, a differend would be a case of conflict, between (at least) two parties, that cannot be equitably resolved for lack of a rule of judgement applicable to both arguments. One side's legitimacy does not imply the other's lack of legitimacy. However, applying a single rule of judgement to both in order to settle their differend as though it were merely a litigation would wrong (at least) one of them (and both of them if neither side admits this rule).[7]

Litigious comportments of modernity are foundationally anchored and by countering the postmodern differend violates the plural and constitutes terror. The twentieth century, Lyotard points out, has given us as much terror as we can take; for the postmodern, terror is a concept that can map the terrains of a politics of extermination.

Lyotard has been used as an example of a postmodern theorist in order to disclose the way in which European postmodernity stands in relation to European modernity. This relation limns the tropes of the foundational and plural which will now be used in sketching out an alternative account of modernity that originates in India.

Rammohun Roy, Rabindranath Tagore and the Contours of Modernity

If European modernity is taken to have the Enlightenment as its source, Indian modernity may be seen as emerging out of the early phases of the Indian Renaissance. I will consider Rammohun Roy's career (1774-1883) to be at the beginning of the Renaissance period, and further I will contend that his concerns may be used as a pivot

6. Lyotard, *The Postmodern Condition*, pp. 63-64.
7. Lyotard, *The Differend*, Minneapolis, 1988, p. xi.

in the task of disclosing the contours of an Indian conception of modernity. In order to facilitate the task of comparing the two constructions of modernity (European and Indian), the tropes of such a disclosure will again concern the foundational and the plural.

Rammohun's formative years were spent in the interstitial space between the horizons of Indian and European cultural matrices that made him equally conversant with the classical traditions of India and the most recent utilitarian developments in English moral theory. He was also steeped in the tradition of Islam which in the nineteenth century with a history of some 800 years constituted a significant religious minority. Through the study of medieval Islamic metaphysics, Rammohun also became acquainted with the edifice of Greek philosophy, especially Aristotle. With a remarkably internationalized intellect, Rammohun proceeded to give shape to the concerns of Indian modernity.

Given the postmodern hermeneutic of modernity, first it will be noted that the trope of the foundational anchors Rammohun's thought. This point can be shown by considering his religious position. Foundationalism posits an immutable conceptual grid that reduces a field of difference to a singularity. Consequently, various forms of thought can exhibit foundational features. Rammohun's philosophy of religion, articulating an essentially Advaitic posture, develops a metaphysics that is ontologically foundational. It is well known that Rammohun argued that the Upaniṣadic notion of *Brahman* should play a pivotal role in a refiguration of the Hindu religious ethos. From the perspective of Vedānta, *Brahman* may be interpreted in various ways. Rammohun's formulation of *Brahman* is quasi-Avaitic. On the one hand, *Brahman* is formless which in the grammar of Vedānta would mean that ultimate reality is *nirguṇa*. Indeed, the Brahmo Samāj names *Brahman* as *nirākāra* which may be taken as a translation of *nirguṇa*. Rammohun, in the *Trust Deed of the Brahmo Samaj*, explicitly claims that no representation of the holy transcendent may be allowed into a Brahmo Samāj temple of *upāsanā*.[8] By making such a move, Rammohun is rendering illegitimate Śaṅkara's sublatable but sacred category of *Īśvara* that can signify any of the deities of *bhakti* in Hinduism. He thus performs a philosophical move that absolutely privileges the unpresentalbility of *Brahman*. Rammohun's enterprise cannot be seen as completely Advaitic because *brahmopāsanā* is an act of *bhakti* and he characterized his position as monotheistic rather than monistic.

Within the discourse of modernity, Rammohun's quasi-Advaitic religious ontology is foundationally motivated. The nature of this foundationalism must now be discussed. *Brahman* is singular, transcendent, and unpresentable. For Rammohun, the sigularity of *Brahman*, within the context of polytheistic Brāhmaṇical practices, effects an ontological reduction of the Many to the One. Just as the Cartesian centering of subjectivity is modern by virtue of its foundationalizing and unifying comportments, Rammohun's anti-Purāṇic insistence on the singularity of the transcendent field enshrines what is essentially a modernist ethos. It is a modernity, however, that shares the trope of the foundational with its European counterpart, but Rammohun and Hegel have precious little in common concerning their views on plurality.

Rammohun, intellectually steeped in multiple religious traditions, is arguably the first comparative religious theorist, and one of the very first thinkers to endorse, what in more recent parlance can be called, religious pluralism. Though not explicitly formulated by Rammohun, a philosophical connection can be drawn between his account of *Brahman* and his religious pluralism. Somewhat reminiscent of Kant's transcendental-theological idea of the first *Critique*, the *nirākāra* conception of *Brahman* is free of conceptual content. Consequently, without the possibility of valorizing any one determination of the transcendent field over another, all conceptual presentations anchored in particular

8. See Rammohun Roy, *Rammohun Rochonaboli*, Calcutta, 1973, pp. 536-43.

religious traditions emerge with identical values. Here Lyotard's point may be recalled that the terror of European modernity is inaugurated by Hegel when he constructs and deploys the transcendental illusion by providing teleological and historical flesh to Kant's purely formal ground of reason. *Brahman* as a conceptually empty ground of Being constructs a foundational narrative that allows for plurality in Rammohun's construction of modernity. This view is entailed by the *nirākāra* account of *Brahman* that is a cornerstone of the Brahmo conception of ultimate reality. Does this view, however, contradict Rammohun's anti-pluralist injunctions against Brāhmaṇical polytheism? The contradiction is resolved if a distinction is drawn between the philosophical and praxial dimensions of the religious experience. Philosophically, as Śaṅkara demonstrates by formulating with consistency the *nirguṇa Brahman* and *Īśvara*, Rammohun need not view his conception of ultimate reality as logically militating against the worshipping of images. On the other hand, a praxial consistency must be preserved, thus the hermeneutic urgency of the unpresentability of *Brahman* is encoded by Rammohun in his caution against the enshrining of an image in the Brahmo temple.

A programme that renders impossible privileged representation secures plurality and cleaves hegemony at the roots. Rammohun inspired a modern ethos that was not culturally reductionistic but championed the virtues of plurality. Respect for plurality, articulated so forcefully by Rammohun, was channelled into the anti-colonial politics of nationalism. In postmodern — especially in Lyotardian — formulations, nationalism as a political agenda would be mounted on a platform of a master narrative. Nationalism, then, in virtue of being a political narrative grounded in constructions of nationality, would erase the space of a micro-politics of difference. Nationalism is a narrative of modernity. When the nation becomes a monolithic construction, then indeed nationalism would flaunt fascist colours. A national politics that is inspired by the continuously privileging comportments of a teleologically conditioned historicism would generate a fascist nationalism. However, if the very construction of the nation is culturally non-reductionistic, and if its singular motivation is anti-coloniality, then the national and the plural can be consistently developed in a politics of nationalism.

Rabindranath Tagore's great lectures on internationalism delivered in the world-theaters of nationalism repeatedly connect the nation with the erasure of plurality:

> During the evolution of the Nation the moral culture of brotherhood was limited by geographical boundaries, because at that time those boundaries were true. Now they have become imaginary lines of tradition divested of the qualities of real obstacles. So the time has come when man's moral nature must deal with this great fact with all seriousness or perish.[9]

Therefore, Rabindranath continues by claiming that human beings:

> . . . will have to exert all his power of love and clarity of vision to make another great moral adjustment which will comprehend the whole world of men and not merely the fractional groups of nationality.[10]

Rabindranath's rejection of the nation and nationalism differs from the postmodern rationale. The postmodern valorization of nomadism and little narratives is unable to account for a politics of liberation. This is in part the reason why Cornel West has dubbed postmodernism as a "kind of European navel-gazing." Rabindranath argues that the nation always translates into self-contained nationalities, incommensurate little narratives in the idiolect of Lyotard. Thus, the construction of nationality is to be rejected. Such a point is just the opposite of the postmodern contention that would claim that nationalism being a master narrative is to be critiqued because it advocates a totalizing politics.

9. Rabindranath Tagore, *Nationalism*, New Delhi, 1976, p. 61.
10. Rabindranath Tagore, *Nationalism*, New Delhi, p. 61.

Rabindranath is arguing, echoing a long tradition that includes figures like Aśoka, Akbar, and Rammohun, for a politics of inclusion and a narrative of tolerance resonating within the frames of a cultural internationalism. Rabindranath's rejection of nationalism is a modern move. Yet, in another sense, Rabindranath is a nationalist. He is a nationalist as an anti-colonialist.

Gyanendra Pandey has described anti-colonial nationalism in the Indian context as plural by contrasting it with communalism:

> just as the new nationalism . . . was defined largely in opposition to a growing politics of communalism, so communalism . . . was defined in opposition to what was now conceived as nationalism. Communalism became in this view a part of a "pre-modern" (if not "pre-political") world that was shored up by the colonial regime in its own interests. Nationalism was all that was forward-looking, progressive, "modern" in Indian politics.[11]

Such a view of nationalism, Rabindranath forcefully argued within a carefully constructed internationalist ethos, can harbour a pluralist vision that feeds a politics of liberation and not a fascist politics of extermination. For Rabindranath, again in consonance with the thinking of his mentor Rammohun, liberation includes but is not confined to an anti-colonial agenda; and it incorporates a wider set of transcendencies from all artificially generated chauvinisms. In Rabindranath and in Rammohun before him, one encounters a richly nuanced pluralism that is not arrived at through a postmodern politics of fragmentation, but through macro-political concerns like the liberation of women, the possibility of cross-cultural communication, the issue of racial harmony.

The tropes of the foundational and the plural simultaneously weave the vision of modernity that I am limning through this brief excursion on Rammohun and Rabindranath. The issue of modernity in the Indian context, gradually congealed against the horizon of a revivifying national culture with anti-colonial comportments, was

11. Gyanendra Pandey, *The Construction of Communalism in Colonial North India*, New Delhi, 1990, p. 241.

by necessity textured by macro-political concerns. These concerns, according to a postmodern hermeneutic, signify the modern because they gather legitimation from foundationally moored notions of culture and nation. However, and this is crucial, modernity in the Indian context does not perform an anti-plural reduction by privileging one cultural representation over another. Ramakrishna's and Vivekananda's religious pluralism, Gandhi's efforts at fuelling the process of social demarginalization, Aurobindo's and Iqbal's appropriations of European philosophy, Jyotirindranath Tagore's pioneering translations of French literature, Radhakrishnan's enterprise of comparative philosophy, Ustad Alauddin Khan's experimentation with European orchestral techniques, Keshub Chandra Sen's ecumenical views, the remarkable international visual idiom of Rabindranath Tagore's art, the cinema of Satyajit Ray, are in part and in a variegated sphere of activities defining moments of a national culture that does not see plurality in terms of postmodern isolationist fragmentation, and does not see the need of representing a national culture in the grammar of pure reductionism.

India, Europe and Modernity

Arborescent master narratives dominantly inform the course of European intellectual history. Even if we take into account the move of defining cultural modernity in terms of the fractured and autonomous zones of science, art and morality, we have to grant the Lyotardian point that each of these zones are modern in virtue of being populated by totalizing narratives. Jürgen Habermas, though in essential disagreement with postmodernism, agrees with the Lyotardian formulation of modernity when he writes that:

> . . . the project of modernity formulated in the eighteenth century by the philosophers of the Enlightenment consisted in their efforts to develop objective science, universal morality and law, and autonomous art, according to their inner logic.[12]

12. J. Habermas, "Modernity and Postmodernity," *New German Critique*, 22, pp. 3-14.

Habermas further contends that thinkers of modernity like Condorcet wished to understand the world and self, promote moral progress, develop just institutions, and facilitate happiness in human beings. The writings of the twentieth century, Habermas has shattered this optimism. The postmodern agrees with the Habermasian analysis. However, while Habermas wishes to resurrect the project of modernity in a general theory of communicative rationality, Lyotard and Deleuze among other postmodern theorists wish to theorize a counter-modern collage of metaphysical and epistemic fragmentation. Given the horrors of totalization from Auschwitz to Amritsar witnessed in the present century, Habermas acknowledges that a totalizing overextension of a narrative would construct a "terroristic rationality," but he wishes nonetheless to develop a modern theory that would be able to disconnect terror from reason.

The problem of "terroristic rationality," emerging out of foundational, representational, and universalizing thinking, and theoretically shaping the modern Habermas and the postmodern Lyotard albeit in opposite ways, is a problem in and for the European conception of modernity and not the Indian conception. In other words, the two conceptions of modernity are structurally independent of each other.

The postmodern invocation of absolute heterogeneity and fragmentation is to be conceived in terms of a resistance to the dangers of totalization. This point is conceptual and is historically real in the blood-drenched spaces of imperialisms and nationalisms that rest on legitimating foundations. In the Indian context, modernity constructs its legitimating discourse also in terms of a resistance embodied in the efforts of demarginalizing a rich tradition captured in the violence of colonializing and orientalizing forces. Liberating and dominating discourses, though militating against each other, are both Lyotardian master narratives because they are founded on universalizing, macro-political concerns. In the colony — a construction of European modernity — the modernity of Europe with its narrative of domination confronted Indian modernity with its narrative of liberation.

The ontological structures of imperialist, colonial, and totalitarian discourses emanate from what Habermas has called terroristic rationality in virtue of their continuous deployment of the rhetoric of marginalization. Indeed, in the twentieth century, in Nazi Germany, in Stalinist Russia, and in Maoist China, the line between marginalization and extermination had been obliterated. A cultural and political discourse of liberation, on the other hand, need not efface the trope of plurality as its ontological structure emanates from a rationality of resistance. Terror cannot accommodate the plural, resistance, however, can. In the global movement of modernity, India had produced a cultural norm in which a foundational and legitimating discourse did not eschew the trope of the plural.

In the European tradition the dominating narrative has been modern. Though Plato acknowledged the Heraclitean many in the positing of the phenomenal world, he ontologically privileged the Parmenidean One. The relegation of the Sophists to the margins of the European thought attests to the arrogation of primacy to master narratives. In the religious history of the West, the Judaeo-Christian (and later Islamic) representations of Ultimate Reality as singular replaced the pluralized pantheon of classical Greece and Rome. The modernity of Descartes was preceded by arborescent discourses of the medievals all founded on the unifying ground of monotheism. Cartesian modernity shifted the pivot of discourse from the divine presence to a centred and representing account of subjectivity. The empiricist and the rationalist traditions, though disagreeing on the mechanics of knowledge, with the possible exception of Hume, agreed on the founding presence of subjectivity. Hegel's dialectical historicization of Kant's transcendental unity of apperception philosophically introduced Judaeo-Christian teleology to the constitution of history and cultures. These are merely examples — and they can be multiplied — to profile the importance of legitimating grand narratives in the course of European thought. European postmodernity is not a period at the end of the modern but a moment of rupture within the modern to bear witness to the terrors of totalization. Lyotard lends resonance to this theme when he defines his notion of "the jews":

> The expression "the jews" refer to all those who, wherever they are, seek to remember and to bear witness to something that is constitutively forgotten, not only in each individual mind, but in the very thought of the West. And it refers to all those who assume this anamnesis and this witnessing as an obligation, a responsibility, or a debt, not only toward thought, but toward justice.[13]

Postmodernism wishes to create a space within modernity where memory can present itself.

If Platonism broadly construed is the backdrop of European postmodernism, the horizon against which Indian modernity as inaugurated by Rammohun takes shape is the plurality of classical Indian religious thought. The cosmic bafflement of the Ṛgvedic hymn of origins, the trans-conceptual formulation of *Brahman* in the Upaniṣads, the Buddha's critique of speculative discourse in general, the Jaina doctrine of Anekāntavāda and Syādvāda, the flexiblity of the Hindu pantheon, Sikh syncretism, exemplify elements of a pluralist episteme. Indian modernity never challenges the trope of cultural plurality even when it is engaged in formulating master narratives of nationalism and anti-colonialism. Indian modernity creates a space within a pluralist ethos in order to challenge the hegemony of European modernity. It is precisely for this reason that post-colonial India must continue to respect plurality if it is to be consistent with its own modernity.

Now the comparative thesis can be formulated. The hermeneutic of postmodern thought allows for the following claim

---

13. Lyotard, "Heidegger and the "jews,"" *Political Writings*, Minneapolis, 1993, p. 141.

concerning the two conceptions of modernity: the European conception of modernity is foundational and anti-plural, whereas the Indian conception of modernity is foundational and plural. In terms of the two tropes that were deployed in the analysis, the Indian conception of modernity slides into a position between European modernity and European postmodernity. Conceptually, it shares the trope of the foundational with European modernity, and shares the trope of the plural with European postmodernity. Such a formulation has ramifications that need to be mapped.

Modernity and India's Cultural Ethos

Indian modernity, given the colonial context, generated a decolonizing nationalism that was culturally non-reductionistic. Lyotard's valorization of little narratives, and Deleuze/Guattari's nomadism articulates a position that connects master-narratives of European nationalism with terror. Partha Chatterjee has pointed out that a cultural view of nationalism is hermeneutically more powerful than conventional histories in which the story of nationalism begins with the contest for political power. Chatterjee writes that in the 'inner' domain of national culture:

> Nationalism launches its most powerful, creative, and historically significant project: to fashion a "modern" national culture that is nevertheless not Western . . . in this, its true and essential domain, the nation is already sovereign, even when the state is in the hands of the colonial power.[14]

The postmodern "incredulity" toward the master-narratives of European modernity provides the tools to disclose the point that the contestation between the two forms of culture runs deeper than the formations of alternative cultural discourses. A comparative archaeology reveals that the very conception of modernity that informs the 'modern' opens up to the field of contestation.

---

14. Partha Chatterjee, *The Nation and its Fragments*, Princeton, 1993, p. 6.

Cornel West develops a theme that is particularly salient for the present concern:

> The current "postmodernism" debate is first and foremost a product of significant First World reflections upon the decentering of Europe that take such forms as the demystification of European cultural predominance and the deconstruction of European philosophical edifices. . . . Ironically, most First World reflections on "postmodernism" remain rather parochial and provincial — that is, narrowly Eurocentric. Jean-Francois Lyotard's well-known characterization of the postmodern condition, with its increasing incredulity toward master-narratives . . . is an interesting but insulated Eurocentric view.[15]

This estimation of ironic Eurocentrism of postmodern discourse is astutely profiled by West. It appears that for the postmoderns there is only one modernity to consider. The multiplicities of modernities that can be excavated ought to be a project of postmodernism. It is the monoglossic nature of the postmodern construction of modernity that makes postmodernism in a gesture of irony, "narrowly Euro-centric." The critique of modernity through the trope of the plural can stand only if different cultural senses of modernity are Eurocentrically collapsed.

If both European modernity and postmodernity are Eurocentric, Indian modernity is, though nationalist, not Indo-centric. Such a theme can be understood in terms of, what Dipesh Chakravarty has called, provincializing 'Europe' — "the 'Europe' that modern imperialism and (third-world) nationalism have, by their collaborative venture and violence, made universal."[16] The self-representation of Indian modernity has just such a provincializing comportment. The provincializing of 'Europe,' that

---

15. Cornel West, "Black Culture and Postmodernism," *A Postmodern Reader*, Albany, 1993, pp. 390-97.
16. Dipesh Chakravarti, "Postcoloniality and the Artifice of History: Who speaks for India's Past?," *Representations*, 37, pp. 1-26.

was underway in the later part of the colonial experience, concerned at the deepest levels with the construction of modern narratives of plurality. Self-representation of a culture need not be an isolationist project. The allowing of the full play of other cultural products in the presentation of one's own cultural narrative is still an episode of self-representation. The provincialization of 'Europe' that is affected by India's contribution to the global conversation of modernity is not motivated by marginalizations as encrypted in the provincialization of the 'Orient,' but is encoded in the determina-tions of a counter-European account of modernity. The full-scale textual defense of this conclusion must await another occasion.

The Indian and the European conceptions of modernity are not identical formulations. It is, then, perhaps a mistake to confuse European modernity with modernity in general. The postmodern accounts of modernity can transcend its ironic Eurocentrism, and perhaps correct its ironic over- extensions if it considers alternative formations of modernity. Pluralism, postmodern or otherwise, demands such encounters.

8

Imperial Identities

The Construction of Britain and India in Children's Literature 1890-1940

Kathryn Castle

IF one wishes to influence the thoughts and minds of the people, it is essential to catch them in their formative years. For the introduction of ideas about identity, individual and national, the schoolage child is fertile ground for instilling beliefs and images which will stand the test of time. What we teach in our schools and encourage our children to read or view at home, may offer important indicators of the social attitudes and behavioural norms they will carry into their adult lives.

For at least the half century from the 1890s the socialization of British youth was into a world infused with the imperial ethos, where citizenship and adulthood carried with them an awareness and support of Great Britain. In the process of creating model citizens for the Empire, ideal subjects also emerged, amongst whom stood the "imperial Indian." As a means of establishing identity — incorporating Britishness and distancing the other — it was an extraordinarily self-serving indoctrination of children, mirroring Edward Said's description of textual dominance — "by which one voice becomes a whole history."[1] It was an activity in which both the image of the colonizer and the colonized were shaped, and which had an impact beyond the time and place of initial encounter,

1. E. Said, *Orientalism*, London, 1991 edn., p. 243.

living on into the post-colonial world of Great Britain and India. In both countries, 50 years on from the end of colonial rule, the consideration of a redefinition and reassertion of identity, beyond the imperial constructs, clearly remains on the agenda. In the country where I live, although not of my birth, the "invisible Empire" of distorted and damaging imagery helps to build the obstacles to realizing the potential of a multi-cultural society at home and international understanding abroad. This legacy of the imperial identity as a contemporary issue added urgency to my search for its origins in the imperial age.

In the world of children's reading it is important to examine what was delivered as received wisdom and what was offered as entertainment, although without doubt the boundaries were blurred. Images of self and other carried across the materials, to youth confined in the classroom and relaxing in out of school hours. Older children who had left school also continued to read the juvenile papers into young adulthood. While there is little evidence that the reader was encouraged to debate or doubt the wisdom of Britain's imperial mission, one must not give into the temptation to claim that the interaction was as one-dimensional as the message: it was not just the Manichean opposition of light and darkness, heroes and villains, powerful and weak, good and evil, although there were strong doses of just such dynamics in children literature. Indeed, one of the lines of enquiry which I shall follow here is the assertion that the relations were complex, with ambivalent notions of British national identity, and a variety of relations with a disparate cast of Indian characters, who suffer from stereotypical distortions, but also suggest the unresolved tensions of identity formation in the imperial discourse.[2]

Concern about national character and British relations with her imperial subjects gave rise to a divisive public mind in the late

2. H. Bhaba, "Difference, discrimination and the discourse of colonialism," in F. Barber, ed., *The Politics of Thoery*, Colchester, 1983; P. Brantlinger, *The Rule of Darkness*, Ithaca, 1988.

nineteenth century. To a certain degree the search for 'identity' represented a retreat into conventional certainties which would stand against the forces of change in English society. The decades before the First World War were anxious ones for traditional elites in Great Britain, who felt the stirrings of class discontent, challenges to sexual moralities, and uncertainties about the physical and moral fibre of the nation. As is often the case an aggressive nationalism masks and seeks to disarm real divisions within the social consensus.

Anxiety and confidence mingled in the response of interest groups to changes in the relations of youth and society. No longer was the imperial message to be confined only to the offspring of the upper orders. By law children were now staying longer in the classroom, including those who in earlier decades would have been found in the ranks of the labouring poor. Increased literacy and an expanding franchise meant a wider net needed to be cast for securing these smaller fish into the imperial basket. At the same time history was becoming more important in the school curriculum, an invaluable medium for transmitting patriotism and national identity.[3]

From the 1880s, the publishers of children's magazines recognized the profits which could be realized, and flooded the market with out of school reading. Youth organizations like the Boy Scouts and Girl Guides also targetted the swelling ranks of schoolchildren. Lord Meath, the guiding hand behind the "Duty and Discipline Movement" captured the uncertainty of the age — meeting the challenges of the future, while linking the maintenance of Empire with the quality of the British character.

> In former years the burdens of Empire or of the State fell on the shoulders of a few — now the humblest child to be found on the

3. Board of Education, *Suggestions for Teachers*, London, 1905; F. Adkins, "Significant History for the Upper Standards," *History*, vol. 1, no. 1, 1912; R. Aldrich, "Imperialism in the Study and Teaching of History," in J. Mangan, *Benefits Bestowed*, Manchester, 1988.

> benches of a primary school will in a few years time be called upon to influence the destinies of not only 54 millions of white, but also 350 millions of coloured men and women . . . such overwhelming responsibilities have never before in the history of this world fallen upon any people. If the white men and women of the British Empire are idle, soft, selfish, hysterical and undisciplined, are they likely to rule well ?[4]

For the rising generation of young Englishmen and women, history in the classroom and the reading in their leisure hours became important contributors to knowledge, beliefs and attitudes, and arguably conditioned their actions and reactions. The vast majority of children would have no first hand experience of Empire, and no opportunity to challenge these received impressions by personal interaction with India and its people. Many of those who did have an experience of 'real' colonial childhood, like Rudyard Kipling, carried through their lives unresolved contradictions between imperial dogma and the individual encounters. Getting too close to the subject undeniably complicated the imperial case for control and intervention.[5]

The propagating and popularizing of imperial Britain brought home the message to the young readership: part of the sense of being British was to accept and uphold the duties and responsibilities of an overseas Empire. Perhaps the most important audience for imperial advocates to reach was the young, the rising generations, from all sectors of society, who would need convincing that the colonies were worth preserving for the forseeable future. In their history textbooks and popular magazines, where I sought the images of Empire, it soon became apparent that much more was happening than the teaching of history and extra curricular entertainment. Both history and the popular press had recognized and responded to the nationalist priorities of their time, and

4. Lord Meath, *Essays on Duty and Discipline*, London, 1911, no. 6, p. 59.
5. Kipling, see A. Nandy, *The Intimate Enemy*, Delhi, 1983, pp. 64-85.

consequently were playing an important role in instilling ideas of self, nation, and the colonial other in the consciousness of the young.[6]

How better for an imperial democracy to ensure loyalty and public consent than through encouraging children into an appreciation of the heroic past? Guidelines from the Board of Education suggested the usefulness of history in child development, and as a vehicle for social cohesion.

> Without laboured exhortation they will feel the splendor of heroism, the worth of unselfishness and loyalty to an ideal, and the meaning of cruelty and cowardice. The influence of their lessons in history will be at work long after the information imparted in them has been forgotten.[7]

Here were lessons for both leaders and followers, images of unity and national purpose to counter the divisions of British society. Where better to find "the wonderful development of the Anglo-Saxon race" than in the history of imperial expansion, and particularly in the story of its crowning acheivement, British India.[8]

While history textbooks responded to the need to bring Empire to the masses in the schoolroom, publishers in the field of juvenile publications rushed to maximize profits and support the cause. *Boys of the Empire*, one of the 150 titles launched between 1890 and 1918, set its course to "nurture and strengthen a spirit of patriotism and loyalty." Prospective members of the Boys Empire League, backed by the popular papers, were expected to demonstrate that

---

6. H.E. Cooper, "British Education Public and Private and the British Empire, 1850-1930," unpubl. Ph.D., Edinburgh, 1979; J. Mackenzie, *Propaganda and Empire*, Manchester, 1984, chaps. 7, 8.
7. Board of Education, *Suggestions for Teachers*, 1904; p. 5.
8. Anglo-Saxon, see T. Livesey & B. Besonthorp, *MacMillan History Readers*, London, 1891-5, p. 224; R. Walker & G. Carter, *Local Examination History of England*, London, 1905, p. 103.

the strength of British character was never compromised, whether at home or abroad.

> Every member promised to treat all foreigners with Christian courtesy, and in the spirit of noblesse oblige to try to do nothing that would lower his country in their eyes. . . .[9]

The juvenile press recognized the popularity of imperial subject-matter among both the parents, who sought wholesome alternatives to gutter comics, and children who were attracted by the heroics of conflict and the mysteries of alien worlds. The Indian Mutiny in particular "had taken the firmest hold on the public imagination."

> The events of the time seemed to provide every element of romance that could be desired in a story-valour and heroism, cruelty and treachery, sharp agony and long endurance, satiated vengeance and blood-thirsty hatred.[10]

In the memoirs of Ralph Rollington, publisher of the *Boys World*, one finds his description of how an editor found a "good story." A Mr. Holloway wandered into the office.

> Mr. H. : I have spent so many years in India, served in the ranks throughout the defence of Lucknow, and witnessed such terrible sights during the Mutiny — my dear wife being murdered by the Sepoys, that it will be quite a relief to be able to sit down quietly and do a little literary work. I've never got over the shock.
>
> Mr. R. : Here's an idea! Write it up, it would make a grand boys' story.[11]

More and more children in Britain were learning about this distant dominion of British India. In their primary readers and textbooks,

9. *Boys of the Empire*, vol. 1, no. 1, London, 1900, pp. 1, 19.
10. "The Indian Mutiny in India," *Blackwoods Magazine*, vol. CLXI, 1897, p. 219.
11. R. Rollington, *The Old Boys Book*, Leicester, 1913, pp. 44-45.

in state and public schools, India became the best example of successful British expansion. Popular magazines led by Harmsworth's Amalgamated Press and later DC Thompson, featured India in both their non-fiction instructive articles and in the increasingly popular adventure fiction. This pattern would hold true for a large part of the twentieth century, notwithstanding the changed realities of Britain's relations with the subcontinent.[12]

Over these years those who came of age in Britain carried with them images of an India filtered through the lens of Empire. By internalizing these images the young reader was initiated into the imperial camp, and its accompanying mythologies. Unity was forged around racial and national identity, and in the process the young were also persuaded of a conservative domestic agenda. There are many interesting questions still to explore on the relationship between the ideology of Empire and the construction of class and gender identities. It became clear in these materials that negotiations were in progress on all these fronts.

It was the British historian J.H. Plumb who observed that "where the service of the past has been urgently needed, truth has ever been at a discount."[13] Whatever one might think about the uses of history, there can be no doubt that excessive nationalism was rampant in the majority of school textbooks used in English schools and exported abroad during the High Noon of Empire. The best instincts of the historian, to open the mind of youth to the diversity and multiplicity of the past, to encourage critical thinking and debate, were rarely exercised in the school histories of this era. The tone of the narrative on British India was set by S.R. Gardiner in his influential *Students History of England*,[14] successively reprinted from 1892. It was his intention to "explore the peace and civilization which was the glory of British statesmen to introduce

12. K. Drotner, *English Children and their Magazines, 1751-1945*, New Haven, 1988, chap. 13.

13. J.H. Plumb, *The Death of the Past*, London, 1969, p. 32.

14. S.R. Gardiner, *Students History of England*, London 1892, p. 859.

into India." The history of the British in India had a clear function — to show the student how a small island nation had managed to gain control of vast territories and diverse peoples and export, with significant success, British values and institutions. Textbooks of the 1930s were still praising the "amazing work in setting things straight" which servants of Empire had carried out in the East.[15]

In surveying the history textbook's treatment of British India from the 1890s to the eve of World War II, certain assumptions about the Indian past and the historical relationship between Britain and India appear repeatedly. The image of India and its peoples emerged from what was included in the text and also through what was omitted, from general observations on the "condition" of India and the assessment of individual figures, and finally through the comparisons which were inevitably drawn between English actions and character and those of the other.

To discover what contribution the exposure to these facts might have made to the reader's understanding of both British and Indian identity, some of the most common and long lived examples of "textbook India" can be selected. These fall into three general categories — representations of India before the arrival of the European imperialists, the expansion and consolidation of British control to 1857 and the post-Mutiny Raj. Not all texts devoted an equal amount of space in the narrative to each sub-section, indeed many concentrated their efforts on the "winning of India" between the mid-eighteenth and late nineteenth centuries.

One of the most revealing comments on British views towards India, and the attitude of textbook historians toward ancient civilizations is the scant attention paid to India before its "discovery" by the West.[16] As was the case in writing of China in

15. G. Warner & C.H.K. Marten, *Groundwork of British History*, London, 1932, p. 69.

16. S.R. Gardiner, p. 859; F. York Powell & T. Tout, *History of England*, London, 1900, p. 898; F. Glendinning, "School History Textbooks and Racial Attitudes," *Journal of Educational Administration and History*, vol. 5, no. 3, 1973.

the same textbooks, there was a tendency to view these Eastern powers as in decline, from a Golden Age as remote to the readers imagination as the classical city states of Rome and Greece. Since India was now conceived to be in a degenerate state, and also because it did not sit comfortably with the rationale for British rule to introduce any questions around accepted hierarchies of nations and races, the young Briton was left with only rather vague impressions of pre-colonial India. What historians did include was clearly contingent upon its relevance to understanding how and why the British became involved in India's affairs. There is a strong sense of justification in the descriptions of India on the eve of Empire. Nearly all the textbooks across the period stress the anarchy, disorder and confusion which characterized the end of the Mughal Empire, making the point as did Warner and Marten in 1912 that "it was the condition of India itself which made interference inevitable."

George Carter's description was of "a state with an entire absence of anything like patriotism and unity," indeed not a nation at all by European standards. Intervention was clearly justified if a population did not meet the Western definition of the nation state. Diversity was viewed not as a rich cultural asset, but as a riot of competing linguistic and religious affiliations. Osmund Airy further distanced India from the Western model by asserting that "our Empire in India had been possible because the inhabitants were not one race, but many races."[17]

From this "vast mass of different elements" a stationary civilization had emerged where "no cohesion or unity was possible." Caste and religion were viewed as insuperable obstacles to progress. Young Britons must have felt a great distance from

17. G. Warner & C.H.K. Marten, *Groundwork of British History*, London, 1912, p. 466; G. Carter, *History of England*, London, 1899, p. 84; O. Airy, *Textbook of English History*, London, 1893, p. 496; M. Keatinge & N. Frazer, *A History of England for Schools*, London, 1911, p. 506. I am indebted to Jim Shaffer and Diane Lichtenstein for new interpretations of the early archaeological record.

"the Hindus of 3,000 castes, the worship of innumerable gods, and endless diversity of ritual" in history texts which celebrated the orderly emergence of the British nation state with its Anglo-Saxon identity, its Protestant ascendancy, and its comprehensible class divisions. These representations of India in the period before British rule demonstrate the close interrelationship in the materials between a validation of British national identity and the unacceptable difference of the soon to be colonized people and state. If Britain represents the forces of order and progress in the modern nation state, then disorder and stasis must give way, just as the young reader was aware that the state of childhood must be displaced by the rules and obligations of the adult world. In a sense both the schoolchild and India were required to recognize the superior qualities of British nationalism, one in the promise of empowered adulthood, the other as a child of Empire.[18]

The assertion of British character at the expense of the colonial subject comes through particularly strongly in the treatment of servants of Empire during the pre-Mutiny period. Here was an opportunity for the reader to compare the character of the British abroad with local rulers. The emphasis on the heroic individual in history was a commonplace in both the primary readers and the more senior texts, as well as providing real life models for the adventure fiction in the popular press. Martin Green's book, *Dreams of Adventure, Deeds of Empire*,[19] did an excellent job of examining the "energizing" myths of imperial England, in particular their movement between history and fiction for the young. Juxtaposing the Indian character with the exploits of these heroes of Empire was another common feature of history textbooks, and another example of the close correlation between building British identity and that of the imperial Indian.

18. Warner & Marten, *Groundwork*, 1912, p. 466, *Avon Historical Readers*, London, 1895, p. 85, York Powell & Tout, pp. 785, 995. Also see M.E. Chamberlain, *Britain and India*, Newton Abbot, 1974; P. Mason, *Patterns of Dominance*, London, 1970.

19. M. Green, *Dreams of Adventure, Deeds of Empire*, London, 1980.

The incorporation of Robert Clive and Warren Hastings into the story of Empire presented some difficulty for historians following the guidelines of the Board of Education's *Suggestions for Teachers*.

> The teacher should place in relief those actions of his heroes and heroines which exhibit their highest qualities but should take care not to raise them too far by omission of their faults and shortcomings.[20]

In texts for the younger pupils the need for simplicity and compression tended to reduce descriptions to a few words or phrases. Clive became "England's champion," her "deliverer," or simply her "hero," closely identified with victory at Plassey and "avenging" the Black Hole of Calcutta. Hastings was accorded the praise of "glorious service," a man whose impact on events meant "that after a century . . . Indian mothers still hush their infants with the name of Warren Hastings." These brief and uncritical references suggested a "mastery" over local affairs. Their relations with India became arguably more complex, however, in senior texts, which introduced the older pupil to the controversy surrounding both Men's careers. What is notable over the entire period under review is the manner in which the authors of the texts explain the errors of their ways.[21]

Few authors offer a defence of the East India Company, acknowledging the uneasy mix of profit and good government, and both Clive and Hastings are credited with recognizing the need to move towards direct rule. However, when dealing with the possibility of corruption and irresponsibility in the Englishmen's careers, India was apportioned a large share of the blame. Both

---

20. Board of Education, *Suggestions for Teachers* London, 1914, p. 9.
21. A. Hassall, *The Making of the British Empire*, London, 1896, p. 52; J.C. Curtis, *Outlines of English History*, London, 1901, p. 58; G. Bosworth, *A History of the British Empire*, London, 905, p. 228; R.S. Rait, *School History of England*, Oxford, 1911, p. 95.

Clive and Hastings, in this version of events, paid a heavy price for their long periods of service abroad — infection with the immorality and venality endemic in the nature of India. Clive was brought down by "the oriental falsity and treachery to which he stooped," while Hastings questionable behaviour was attributed to close association with native princes. Innes' *History of England* summed up his fatal flaw.[22]

> He unfortunately allowed methods to be employed which were a matter of course in oriental warfare and oriental courts, but were thoroughly repugnant to European ideas. The lesson had not yet been learned that in dealing with peoples whose moral standards are different from those of Europe, the white man must hold to the white standard that is not only the right course, but the course that pays best in the long run.[23]

The texts clearly could not allow the reader to draw his/her own conclusions from questionable actions of those who helped to create the Empire in India. Any blemish on the reputation of British actors in the course of imperial consolidation was interpreted as the result of overly close encounters with Indian values and customs — a confusion of identity. The best defence was to retain a distance from the dangers of India, which became a basic tenet of those who administered the Empire. Letting one's guard down invited in the infection of the oriental world, and with it a threat to the high standards expected of British nationals.[24]

That the behaviour of Indian rulers contrasted unfavourably with British norms of conduct became even clearer when Siraj-ud-Daula entered the narrative in close proximity to the discussion of

22. J.M.D. Meiklejohn & J.M.C. Meiklejohn, *A School History of England*, London, 1901, p. 379; Warner & Marten, *Groundwork . . .*, p. 469; J.R. Green, *A Short History of the English People*, p. 1648; Gardiner, p. 802.
23. Gardiner, p. 802; Innes, *History of England*, p. 400.
24. P. Mudford, *Birds of a Different Plumage*, London, 1974, p. 153; Mason, *Patterns of Dominance*, p. 95; Chamberlain, *Britain and India*, p. 101.

Robert Clive. It was the perceived outrage of the Black Hole which led to Clive's advance on Calcutta and his revenge at the Battle of Plassey in 1757. The textbook descriptions of the young Bengali ruler brought forth adjectives which would appear repeatedly to indicate the poor quality of native leadership. He was seen as "weak," "cruel," "debauched," "effeminate," "despotic," "stormy," "treacherous," "vicious" and "monstrous."[25] The decision to seize Fort William and confine its British residents was given little explanation beyond the desire of "a cruel young man who hated the British" to "pick a quarrel by seizing British property." Again, in this instance, one can see the way in which character became a determining factor in historical development, obscuring a consideration of the political or economic factors which may have prompted action against the British presence. For the historian as well as the popular press, British loss of life at Fort William became further proof of the sacrifice involved in promoting British influence abroad, finding in Siraj-ud-Daula the forces of "darkness" and "savagery" which must be displaced. That children remembered the details of the Black Hole of Calcutta and its perpetrator can be deduced from an interesting source. Examiners of the Oxford and Cambridge Local Exams in the early 1900s commented that it would be better if candidates knew more of British policy in India and less of the "grisly details" of Siraj and the Black Hole.[26]

In *Britannia's Children* I devoted a section to the textbook discussions of the Indian Mutiny, and signs that the attitudes toward the mutineers hardened in the narrative between the 1890s

---

25. *Avon Historical Readers*, p. 77; Rait, *School History of England*, 95; Warner and Marten, *Groundwork of British History*, p. 471; M.O. Davis, *The Story of England*, Oxford, 1912, p. 283; Livesey & Besonthorp, *Macmillans History Readers*, p. 54; Carter, *History of England*, p. 86; J.P. Bright, *A History of England for Public Schools*, London, 1901, p. 1118; C. Oman & M. Oman, *A Junior History of England*, London, 1904, p. 253.

26. Oxford and Cambridge Local Examiners Reports, Oxford, Cambridge, 1895-1914.

and the First World War. By 1914 the *Oxford Survey of the British Empire* was suggesting that a concentration on the "heroism of the British" rather than the cause of the mutineers, ensured that a study of the Mutiny "added to rather than diminished British prestige." This is a fairly clear statement of the role that the school history was expected to play in the maintenance of patriotism and national confidence, in this case on the eve of the First World War. In terms of presenting the case of those who rebelled against the British in 1857, there is no doubt that, just as in the case of Clive and Hastings, the character of India was tried and found wanting. Whereas in the early 1890s there had been some willingness to acknowledge British errors of judgement and policy in both junior and senior texts, by 1900 the tone was becoming harsher. Grievances, previously seen as justified, were more often explained by the operations of suspect characters and misunderstandings. Dissent became sedition, and the unscrupulous agitators preyed upon the "weak mind" of the sepoy. In the revised version, Britain's "good intentions" for India before the uprising had been deliberately misrepresented, and details of British reprisals in the aftermath disappeared from the narrative. There was to be no suggestion that the English soldier had ever been "out of control" or had deviated from an honourable military tradition.[27]

History was closing ranks around the imperial cause, setting clear boundaries between colonizer and subject. The overriding concern was to safeguard British interests, which appeared particularly vulnerable as war loomed in Europe. This left little space to open up any historical debate around the Mutiny or any other episode in the expansion of British power abroad. These same texts which denied a rational case to the discontented of the mid-nineteenth century would also discount the rise of nationalist movements 50 years later, dismissing both as the trouble-making

27. E. Hawke, *The British Empire and its History*, London, 1911, p. 3; J. Herbertson & O.J. Howarth, *Oxford Survey of the British Empire*, Oxford, 1914, p. 173.

of a minority seditious element, uninterested in the welfare of the masses.[28]

The school history of post-Mutiny India presented a period of peace and progress, with an emphasis on the community of interest forged with the ruling elites and confirmed by the gratitude of the masses. Reforms, it was claimed, were beginning to affect all areas of traditional Indian life, bringing an end to the "stationary stage of civilization" which had prevailed before Western intervention. The British were credited with gradually "turning a geographical expression into a nation," although there was a significant sense of unease about the extension of local democracy. The textbooks did not ignore signs of unrest, although it was generally attributed to a "half educated" middle class, and balanced against the "loyal, Westernized" princes and a conservative peasantry.[29]

By the 1930s the British Empire in India was older and wiser, and even in the school textbooks there was an air of uncertainty about what the future might bring, and a half acknowledged duty to prepare the pupil for the loss of "The Jewel in the Crown." The same ambivalence and anxiety which had produced such excessive nationalism and flag waving in the imperial accounts of the pre-war textbooks was now expressed more openly. This might have provided an opportunity for the textbook historians to provide a less partial view of the subcontinent, as both colonizer and colonized moved toward a new relationship. However, textbooks between the wars acknowledged that the forces of traditional religion and caste relations had remained somewhat resistant to British influence despite the "noble work of civilization." While Southgate in his widely read text of 1936 writes of the "very great

---

28. Airy, *Textbook of English History*, p. 498; Gardiner, *A Students History*, p. 952; Oman & Oman, *Junior History*, p. 244.

29. Meiklejohn & Meiklejohn, *A School History*, p. 449; Bright, *A School History*, p. 233; Herbertson & Howarth, *Oxford Survey*, p. 305; Hawke, *The British Empire*, p. 315; Hassall, *The Making of the British Empire*, p. 593.

benefits" brought about by the British administration since the Mutiny, in particular the greater safety of life and property; he reminds the reader that continued vigilance is needed to "suppress the inhuman practices associated with the religion of the Hindus." The progress of Western ideas about cleanliness and sanitation has been hindered, he claims, because "the Indian peasant is fatalistic in this as in other directions, and is disinclined to cooperate with his rulers in bringing about a change for the better." Despite these concerns, there was a consensus in the texts around the positive role of the British in the administration of the country. The impatience of the independence movements was contrasted with the measured pace of constitutional reform under British rule, suggesting the caution of a wise guardian in the face of impetuous and somewhat irresponsible demands.[30] As one junior history suggested in 1940.

> . . . conflict was still raging between the British government and Indian leaders . . . they determined to have independence, the British government determined that the Indians were not yet fit to manage their own affairs.[31]

Rayner and Airy in 1938 listed the obstacles to European style democracy in India, explaining to the student why the British had adopted a gradualist approach, "meeting discontent by the largest practicable grant of self-government." The characteristics of Indian society which mitigated against democratic self-rule were "dozens of distinct races," "hundreds of distinct languages," "religious jealousies," "the caste system," and the vast majority of illiterates." It is ironic that little seemed to have changed in the picture of India, despite the British claims to progress since the pre-colonial era, when the same aspects of the subcontinent had invited British intervention. In the face of such resistance, however, the British had shown a great "vigour," and a "healing influence" in the wake

30. G. Southgate, *The British Empire*, London, 1936, pp. 175-234; Rayner & Airy, *A Concise History of Great Britain*, London, 1938.

31. *Mayflower Histories*, London, 1940, p. 267.

of the wounds of Mutiny. A.P. Newton, Rhodes Professor of Imperial History at the University of London, wrote a textbook for senior students in the late 1920s which set out to rectify the "inadequacy" in history textbooks of British Empire. The service of history to nationalism was, however, still endorsed.

> History gives lie to the belief that British Imperialism connotes selfishness and tyranny. In India British officals promote the welfare of their charges . . . a just orderly government . . . social reforms . . . public works . . . all raise the conditions of the masses.[32]

The first sentence is most revealing. One aspect of the study which I have not discussed here is the notable absence in the history textbooks for all ages and standards of the economic motive for expansion — the "selfishness" to which Newton refers. One could claim that geography texts were dealing with the practical elements of colonial trade, but it is revealing that there is almost no mention of the economic Empire in school history. Was this too close to acknowledging the role of profit and loss in the equation, or to awakening youth to the harsher realities of power? Arguably, yes, but it also reflects history's desire to deal only with issues of a higher order, constitutional and political, while leaving the history of the ledger books to minor disciplines. There was also little mention of the role of Christianity in the spread of British influence overseas. Only in the most general of references was the attention of the reader drawn to missionary activity in India, although judgements passed on Indian religious and cultural practices, carried the weight of Christian conviction as well as secular interests.[33]

---

32. A. Newton, *The British Empire since 1783*, London, 1929, p. 116; also Rayner & Airy, p. 569.

33. Mackenzie, *Propaganda and Empire*, pp. 186-88; P. Murrell, "The Imperial Idea in Childrens Literature, 1840-1902," unpubl. Ph.D., Swansea, 1975; M. Green, *Dreams of Adventure, Deeds of Empire*, pp. 25, 31.

These are only a few examples of the textbook treatment of British India in a period which spans 50 years. One could find many more to illustrate how history's version of the "colonial Indian" helped to reinforce a patriotic reading of the past, a commitment of the rising generation to maintaining Britain's overseas dominions, and the connections between these successes and racial/national identity. The student who read these texts, which remained on school shelves for many years, and were exported to assist in colonial education as well, was left with few doubts about history's view of the imperial enterprise. The way in which the teaching of British imperial history to schoolchildren concerned itself with protecting the Empire from the dangers of debate and free thinking, provides a clear cautionary tale about looking to history to construct or maintain national identity. The legacy shows the damage such abuse of history can leave in the minds of both colonized and colonizer. Young Britons were offered one-dimensional, stereotypical views of India and her peoples, imbued with the legitimacy of historical "evidence" and social consensus. These were not ideas which would serve well the post-colonial realities of a multicultural Britain. The arrogance and intolerance of this school encounter with the wider world fed into a "Little Englander" mentality which has been very hard to overcome. History continues to have a role to play in determining identity, but one must exercise caution that the need to recover the hidden past does not just replace one self-serving interpretation with another.

Today debate continues within the English educational establishment on the appropriate balance between the English and the 'other' histories in the syllabus for schools. Traditionalists argue that knowledge of home history remains a prerequisite for good citizenship and the maintenance of social values. There is, however, a growing movement for separate instruction among ethnic minorities wishing to preserve their own cultural identity. History is a discipline claimed by all parties, and this points to the difficult balance between the demands of unity and diversity. Can we tolerate multiple histories and multiple identities within the nation state and still maintain "British" institutions or character?[34]

In a wider sense the world of education for any child must be expanded to include what they choose to read outside the schoolroom. In Great Britain there was a surge of publications for the youth market at the turn of the century. There were titles to cater for all classes in society, from the respectable *Public School Magazine, Captain, Boys and Girls Own Annual, Young England and Chums*, to the half penny weeklies sold on streetcorners — *Gem, Magnet, Marvel, Wizard, Hotspur* and many more. Editors declared their determination to exterminate the "gutter literature" which they claimed had contributed to national decline. The new publications which flooded the market were extremely popular, and the competition fierce. Editors recognized that imperial features and serial stories which offered exotic characters and locations brought in the pennies of the schoolchildren and satisfied their guardians that this was relatively wholesome fare.[35]

There are far too many images to deal with in a short space, but it will suffice to choose a few which illustrate the twin imperatives at work again in these materials — the building of national/self-identity and that of the "imperial Indian": firstly, service in the Imperial context, which brings girls into what is overwhelmingly a boys empire, secondly, relations between the British and the Indian within Britain, and, finally, the mutineer/

34. R. Preiswerk, ed., *The Slant of the Pen*, Geneva, 1980; R. Dixon, *Catching them Young*, London, 1977; G. Klein, *Reading into Racism*, London, 1985; "History men battle over Britain's future," *The Times*, 9 May, 1994; Christopher Hill, "Lies about Crimes," *The Guardian*, 29 May, 1989; J.A. Mangan, *The Imperial Curriculum*, London, 1993; J. Gundara, C. Jones, K. Kimberly, *Racism, Diversity and Education*, London, 1986.

35. J. Richards, *Imperialism and Juvenile Literature*, Manchester, 1989, P. Dunae "Boys Literature and the Idea of Empire," *Victorian Studies*, vol. 24, 1980; G. Avery, *Childhood's Pattern*, London, 1975, Mackenzie, *Propaganda and Empire*, chap. 8.

babu character and his relations with the British. These were aspects of the relationship with India which were replayed in many forms across the variety of magazines, in both non-fiction and fiction, and maintained their presence through the years of this study.

One of the strongest components of the imperial ethos was the idea of service, popularly associated with the "White Man's Burden." The claims which imperial advocates made to a benevolent presence in the colonized areas rested upon a belief in the sacrifice of self-denying imperial servants. Particularly in the post-Mutiny Empire, where the textbook claims that peace and progress were universal, did the popular press find examples of disinterested duty and the civilizing mission. (Proof of the benefits of Empire could also include examples of Indian service, as imperial troops, "coolie labour," or loyal servants, but these articles usually concentrated their attention on the qualities of British masters to guide their subjects into worthwhile endeavours. Disinterested duty as an intrinsic quality of the colonizer was more highly valued than learned behaviour or mimicry.)[36]

Service was the activity which dominated the Girl's Empire. Although girl's magazines tended to concentrate on domestic affairs, they do offer important images of those who volunteered to serve abroad. The roles of ordinary English-women in India were mainly those of medical missionaries and teachers, a transference of traditional social roles into the imperial orbit. In the accounts of their labours, the native population became the victims of "dirt, squalor, ignorance and indifference." This was fertile ground for the good works of women like Emily Kinnaird, who recounted her experience and sought new recruits to the Loving Service League in the *Girls Own Annual* of 1891. For the sensibilities of girl readers, India was fashioned into a powerless, dependent community of

36. "The Indian Camel Corps," *Boys Own Annual*, vol. XXXVII, 1914-15, p. 416; "Shall I go out to the Colonies," *Young England*, vol. XXI, Sept. 1899, pp. 40-43 "Sugar and Milk: an incident in a frontier siege," *Boys Own Empire*, vol. 1, no. 11, Jan 1901, pp. 256-57.

schoolchildren and infirmary patients. In addition, excluded from the male world of offical power in relations to the subcontinent, women could allow themselves the romantic view of the landscape. Mrs. Kinnaird often took her sketch-book and recorded the "picturesque beings" in her time away from the hospital.[37]

Although women might appreciate the spirit of place, as befitted those who did not carry the burdens of governance, softer sensibilities often had to be abandoned in the fulfilment of everyday tasks. Mrs. Kinnaird's duties in the "urban squalor" of India involved the transformation of "urchins" into "happy children in English garments," as well as restoring health to the "passive and apathetic" poor. India for her was a country immobilized by poverty and ignorace, awaiting the energy and resolve of mothering England to alleviate its suffering. Girls of England were therefore incorporated into the British Empire on the basis of traditional gender roles, while carrying a large part of the humanitarian spirit of the imperial encounter. While the men of Empire engaged with military matters and affairs of state, trade or labour relations, women maintained the 'civilizing' mission. There was no question of young women assuming a liberated position within the Empire, even if they were beginning to claim it at home. Arguably the attempts to draw women toward the selfless service of missions abroad can be seen as a counterweight to forces of modernity on the home front, which were challenging both class and gender roles. The magazines for girls of this period were keen to persuade young women that it was more useful and productive to join in a civilizing and caring vocation in the colonies, rather than engage in unwomanly pursuit of the vote at home. An identity for women within the Empire retained the Victorian idea of separate spheres of activity, inferior to their male counterparts, but superior to the

---

37. E. Kinnaird, "In India with medical missionaries," *Girls Own Annual*, vol XIII, 1891, p. 687; N. Chaudhuri & M. Stroebel, eds., *Western Women and Imperialism*, Indiana University Press, 1992.

needy masses of India. Here, as elsewhere in the popular press, the image of India and the imperial ethos more generally was used to endorse a conservative social outlook.[38]

The negotiation of identity within the imperial discourse did become more problematic when dealing with girls' roles (a good reason, perhaps, for keeping them out of the "serious business"). The clear distinctions between the actions and character of Empire boys and the imperial Indian became more difficult to sustain when women entered the text. The conservative consensus which supported the Empire needed to include women in the ranks of imperial advocates, but could not allow them to stand on an equal footing in other respects with British men. (The same issues arose in class relations.) Stories set in India which feature heroines show the tension that could be created if women were empowered in the colonial setting. Mrs. Grimwood, "The Heroine of Manipur," had enjoyed the life of Resident's wife until her husband was "murdered by execution in the palace yard." Thrust into the role of defending "her race," "true character" emerges in the "courage and constancy" she displays in temporarily holding the fort until relief arrives. She is rescued by an English officer, and sent home to recover from her ordeal.[39]

Because Mrs. Grimwood shares the "Anglo-Saxon inheritance" of her countrymen, in an emergency she can summon the strength of character which underpins the survival of Empire in India. National identity can be brought to the fore and supplant temporarily the traditional, gentler role of 'Residency wife.' Her extraordinary heroism is contrasted favourably with the cowardice of the treacherous royals who had been her friends. In the crisis,

38. P. Barr, *The Memsahibs*, London, 1976, pp. 178-80; J. Trollope, *Brittannias Daughters*, London, 1983, p. 86-92; V. Ware, *Beyond the Pale*, London, 1992.

39. "Mrs. Grimwood, the Heroine of Manipur," *Girls School Magazine*, vol. 1, no. 1, 2, March, April, 1892.

womanly characteristics move away from Mrs. Grimwood and are used to discredit the "unmanly" conspirators, a common variant on the "effete," androgynous image of the Indian male.[40] The Empire, however, did not want a rising of its women any more than it wanted native rebellion in Manipur. Once the crisis is past, Mrs. Grimwood returns to her natural domestic sphere and leaves the "real men" in charge.

Any notion that there might be a community of interest between women's liberation and colonial rebellion against a "man's Empire" was effectively discounted in the roles offered to girls in the popular press. Mrs. Grimwood and Mrs. Kinnaird are typical of the women of Empire before the First World War. In the girl's magazines published after 1918, when young women were roving the world with greater freedom and had a more liberated outlook, they still carried the attitudes toward colonial subjects of their sisters before the war, essentially fashioned by the power relations of men. The maintenance of national power through colonial dependencies required that both boys and girls continue to recognize a national and racial identity which remained intact even when gender relations began to change. This prevented a separate negotiation of identity between British and Indian women in the juvenile publications — the needs of Empire always intervened.

In terms of the legacy which these images of imperial relations left for post-colonial relations, it is important to examine encounters between the English and the Indian on British soil. Here the young were being offered what the textbooks could not supply, models of interaction with subject peoples in familiar settings. The "imperial Indian" most often encountered within England appeared in school stories, a very popular genre of the nineteenth and twentieth centuries children's papers. By the 1890s these serial stories often featured a "dusky chum." Frank Richards created the

40. K. Ballhatchet, *Race, Sex and Class under the Raj*, London, 1980, chap. 4; M. Sinha, *Colonial Masculinity*, Manchester University Press, *1996*, p. 34-35.

world of Greyfriars School and the memorable figure of Hurree Jamset Ram Singh, who appeared regularly between 1908 and 1940. In his autobiography, the author explained his reasons for the high profile of the young Indian prince.

> By making an Indian boy a comrade on equal terms with English schoolboys, Frank felt he was contributing a mite toward the unity of the commonwealth, and helping rid the mind of colour prejudice.[41]

As a permanent member of the "Famous Five" Hurree shared endless adventures with Bunter, Bulstrode, Wharton and Nugent, and became arguably the Indian character best remembered by generations of young readers. The stories clearly bring out the differences between the young Indian and his chums while claiming his acceptance rested on equal terms. When Hurree arrives at the school, in the company of other foreigners, French and German boys, he is quick to assure the Greyfriars lads that he belongs to the "English party," and consistently sides with them in the first fights between "alien camps." While Hurree proclaims his loyalty to British values, Wharton reminds the reader that the identities are not so easily transferable.

> . . . a complexion of the deepest, richest olive showed him to be native of an oriental clime, and though he was clad in the ordinary Eton garb of the schoolboy, there was a grace and suppleness about his figure that betrayed the Hindu.[42]

The British sense of fair play brings Wharton to the defence of the Indian when overt racism enters the story, and he thrashes those who address his friend as "nigger." Wharton's reward is leadership within the school, Hurree's undying gratitude, and a large diamond produced from the prince's pocket. No imperial power could ask for more.

---

41. F. Richards, *Autobiography*, London, 1952, p. 38
42. F. Richards, "Aliens at Greyfriars," *Magnet*, vol. 1, no. 6, 21 March, 1908.

While Hurree was not just a crude stereotype, and his place within the stories was not a simple replay of colonial relations, his claims for acceptance within the English community were frequently discounted by his chums.

> He had never lost the beautiful variety of English his Bengal instructor had imparted to him. His good nature was as boundless as the floweriness of his language and the fact that he received a fabulous sum of pocket money did not diminish his growing popularity.[43]

Hurree's use of inappropriate English phrases was a key part of the humour in the Greyfriars stories and a standard device in distancing those who laid claim to joining the dominant culture. The Indian prince joins the English boys in mocking the pretensions of his own "native education," and clearly his acceptance at the school involved a complex negotiation of his own identity. He claims to be English, but the boys' descriptions of him emphasize his "Indian-ness." He is the only character for whom wealth plays a part in sustaining his position. Once inside the world of the English boarding school, Hurree could only stay there by accepting certain rules of engagement, set by his English friends. Bunter and Co. would have scoffed at the idea that they were waving the flag or representing the best of imperial boyhood, yet they implicitly endorse a distance and difference between themselves and the Prince, which reflects the mixture of tolerance and prejudice in the imperial relations of colonizer and Westernized Indian ally. Hurree and other young Indians who appeared in stories based in Britain were welcomed as temporary visitors, recognized as useful allies for their loyalty and financial offerings, tolerated as long as they observed British rules, and were clearly preferred to those who opposed the imperial connection. When undesirable Indians appeared in England, as criminals or political trouble-makers, they

---

43. F. Richards, "Aliens at Greyfriars," *Magnet*, vol. 1, no. 6, 21 March, 1908.

were quickly disarmed and returned to the subcontinent by young British heroes.[44]

The place for Britian's Indian subjects was primarily at home, and the young were clearly being sent a message that only in extraordinary circumstances, or the closed world of the public school, would the realities of Empire intrude on British society. The young were not offered any positive images of Indians living within English society, only those transients whose presence endorsed approval of British institutions or fit the stereotype of troublemaker. Rozina Visram's excellent book, *Ayahs, Lascars and Princes,* shows the variety and complexity of the Indian experience in Britain from 1700-1947, and demonstrates how far the reality was from the stereotypical images. Indian culture, dress, language or religious beliefs were at best of no interest in the school stories, and more often they were the butt of humour and deprecating comments. This did not betray the English characters as intolerant, but fair, flexible and good humoured. All the boys in the story accepted the superiority of British customs and traditions, with the exception of haughty Europeans like the French or Germans. They would not compromise their own national identity for the sake of pleasing the British boys, and there was a sneaking respect for those who were prepared to fight, rather than concede.[45]

The most dangerous Indians in the juvenile popular press were villains familiar from the pages of history. The mutineer and the *babu* figure carried strong messages to the young about the need for control and vigorous defence of the Empire. Both highlighted the heroic aspects of British character, which complemented the tolerant ethos of the public school stories. Just as images of the masses of India justified humanitarian intervention, and Hurree's

44. "England's glory," *Boys Comic Journal,* vol. XXVII, no. 724, Jan 1897; "Why Revel stole the image," *Chums*, vol. XV, no. 732, 1906; "The Green Diamond," *Chums*, vol. XIX, no. 965, March 1911.

45. R. Visram, *Ayahs, Lascars and Princes*, London, 1986; J. Bristow, *Empire Boys,* London, 1991.

gratitude and loyalty proved the value of exposure to Western education, so the fear and disorder caused by the rebellious and hostile Indians supported the need for Britain's military and civil controls.[46]

The casting of malign influences in the imperial landscape drew upon characterizations alive in the popular imagination and the textbook histories. Stories of "famous defences" made good reading, and India provided many examples for the children's papers. At the turn of the century, *Young England* ran a series of articles whose subject-matter and style of writing give the flavour of history recycled in the popular press. For a patriotic adventure, the years of Mutiny were eminently suitable, and the narrative style revealed a desire to appeal to the sensibilities of a young audience. One such account was written from the perspective of college boys caught up in the siege of Lucknow.

> We think no end of our own troops and feel quite certain that they will be able to beat back every assualt . . . but the strain of the ceaseless vigilance and the awful sense of responsibility were telling on us all.[47]

Having ensured that the readers' sympathies were firmly aligned with the defenders, the Indian rebels appeared to supply all that was menacing and evil in the grim story. As the siege progressed the image of India as a contemptible adversary became stronger. There were long periods of waiting and watching for the faceless enemy to show himself, while the landscape seemed infused with a sense of nameless terror. Slowly, while the tension built, there were signs and sounds of burrowing under the walls. Children could easily identify with the emotions felt by the young boys trapped inside. While fears mounted, the narrative explained how far this situation was from a model of heroic combat, the fair fight

46. E. Said, *Culture and Imperialism*, London, 1993, pp. 247-49.
47. H. Groser, "How the British held Lucknow," *Young England*, vol. XXI, 1899, p. 8.

so favoured by the British. The British lion was facing subterranean, sly creatures, snakes and vermin afraid to emerge into the light of day.[48]

In the magazine encounters with mutineers, the "treacherous" opponents of the textbook Mutiny became more fully realized. Details of "glinting eyes" and "cruel smiles" were added, while some of the most lurid detail found in the juvenile press attached to this characterization.

> With smiles on their faces and black treachery in their hearts, they lured innocent men to death . . . all were alike, not one of them but his hands were dyed in innocent blood. No mercy must be shown to such stuff.[49]

The extremity of the language and the harshness of the imagery was all too common in the historical fiction of the periodicals. The long-harboured bitterness of "betrayal" in India found expression in papers where the editors encouraged writers to enthral and horrify the readers with details of the indescribable events hinted at by the history textbooks.

Bloodthirsty details were built upon the foundations of folk memory and school lessons to call readers to the ranks of battling British boyhood. One author referred to the "great, grim game" in progress, where unfortunately a "just encounter" had lost its meaning. The masses of India in rebellion presented a fearful sight, uncontrolled and nameless, the nightmare experience of Empire. Here was India reduced to a primitive savagery, activated only by

---

48. *Ibid.*, also "The beleaguered garrison," *Pluck*, vol. 2, no. 30, 1895; "The fight for the Residency," *Young England*, vol. 52, 1940; J. Mackenzie, "Hunting and the natural world in jubenile literature," in J. Richards, ed., *Imperialism and Juvenile Literature*, Manchester, 1989, pp. 169-70.

49. "Terror from the East," *Chums*, vol. XII, no. 944-60, Sept. 1910- Feb. 1911, p. 34.

a desire to wreak havoc on the interloper, and providing a clear contrast to the restraint and discipline of the British forces.[50]

Another, perhaps even more threatening, aspect of India was the individual whose contact with Western values had produced not incorporation, like Hurree, but explosive instability. There had been some mention of the subversive educated classes in the textbooks, but the tone had been generally confident that their demands could be met within the framework of imperial administration. In the popular press, however, children met the *babu* figure as an undeniable adversary, often crudely drawn and denounced for "mixed parentage" and "cunning intelligence." Their skill in disguise and subterfuge might initially fool the British protagonist into believing them allies, but such an impression could be quickly abandoned. In "The Snake Charmer's Secret," the young Jack Hinton exposes the "wily Sudoo."

> They no longer wondered at their unwilling host's intelligent and sane appearance . . . snake charming was but a blind to cover his true trade . . . writer and printer of the seditious papers that permeate so mysteriously through India, keeping the natives in a ferment with the cunningly fanned flames of suppositious wrongs.[51]

When the Collingwood boys encountered a "leering" *babu* in another story, they observed that his arrival "removed all traces of the heroic" from the narrative. The reader was repeatedly reminded that the brothers particularly despised this Indian for mocking their concern with heroism and romanticism. The *babu*'s mimicry of British language and behaviour was especially galling.

---

50. A. Leigh, "Adventures of Jack Alderson VC.," *Boys Own Annual*, vol. XXVII, 1905-06; "For Queen and Country," *Pluck*, vol. 2, no. 130, 1895; "The Boy Garrison," *Chums*, vol. 1, no. 2, 1895.
51. "The Snake Charmers secret," *Chums*, vol. 1, no. 2, 1895, p. 14.

> "Hello, you chaps," began the babu familiarly, "this is what I call a bully find for us, eh, what."[52]

The marked disdain felt for this character was partly a reaction to the transgressed boundaries of his identity, which challenged the basic assumptions of "Englishness" and the right to rule. In the stories he also frequently challenged the norms of behaviour. George Orwell expressed this dilemma well.

> It is a condition of his rule that he shall spend his life in trying to impress the natives and so in every crisis he has got to do what the natives expect of him . . . my whole life, every white man's life in the East, is one long struggle not to be laughed at.[53]

Between two worlds, the *babu* was presented as a charlatan in both, criminally misleading his fellow Indian while perverting the message of the British ruler. Unlike the good natured prince at English public school, these characters showed no gratitude toward their "benefactors," using their education as a weapon to sow discontent and reap rebellion. Brave only on the printed page, in direct confrontation with young English heroes the subversive was unmasked as both coward and liar, characteristics directly counter to those encouraged in British youth. By drawing this character as one particularly unappealing to youth (intellectual pretensions, a mocking demeanour, cowardice and cringeing duplicity), the popular papers ensured that the rising imperialist would feel little sympathy for his position, indeed would endorse the sentiment that these "troublemakers" deserved stern punishment.

It was the *babu* who represented the most troubling aspect of India for those who sought distance and difference in the construction of national identity. Having stressed to the younger generation that they should identify strongly with inherited characteristics and recognize the role of British education in

52. "Terror from the East," p. 176.

53. G. Orwell, "Shooting the Elephant," *Selected Essays*, London, 1957.

transmitting primary values, it became rather difficult to turn their full fury on those who had acquired either or both. Here character came into play, and it was made clear to the reader that the *babu* had only acquired a superficial knowledge of British ways, proved by his ulimate disloyalty to the pursuit of peace and progress in India. This was a dangerous example for youth, if left unchallenged, for the *babu* turned the lessons of his British education against the Empire, a direct antithesis of the desired outcome for British boys and girls. The contempt shown for him reflected the fear that here rested the greatest challenge to imperial control, and the clearest negation of the simplistic ideas of identity carried to children in this era.[54]

In Britain's imperial era the issues of national identity took on an urgency allied with the preservation of the Empire. At the end of the nineteenth century great concern was voiced within the circle of imperial advocates and society at large about the possible decline, physically and morally, of the population. Conservative, powerful elites expressed anxiety about the spectre of sexual liberation, changes in gender roles, class conflict, urban decay, untutored youth, and the suitability of the newly enfranchised to assume the responsibilities of greater England. The maintenance of national strength and resolve was felt necessary both to meet challenges in Europe and to consolidate British interests in the wider world. Civilizations were known to rise and fall, and one of the commonly held beliefs about national decay was the initial loss of national unity and purpose. It was not coincidental that one of the fictional genres which became popular in the era was the "invasion story," in which an unwary and complacent England became prey to the energy and vigour of rising empires from the East.

---

54. F. Anstey, *Baboo Jabberjee, B.A.*, London, 1897; V. Chirol, *Indian Unrest*, London, 1910, pp. 15-16; E. Said, *Culture and Imperialism*, London, 1993, pp. 247-49; V.G. Kiernan, *The Lords of Human Kind*, London, 1969, pp. 50-51.

A principal point of national unity before the Second World War was the imperial ethos and the patriotism which could be engendered from testing ones national institutions and military strength in foreign adventures. The superiority of British character and standards, expressed in civil administration, the military, religious beliefs, and social relations could be demonstrated by contact and conflict with "inferior" races and nations. The British experience in India, although clearly not the only example, was seen as the most successful export of British rule beyond her national borders, and was therefore summoned to validate the character of the colonizer and the policies of the Empire.

The most important target for this renewal of national purpose was the rising generation. In the early years of the century, for all children, a rather sober middle-class Victorian morality was the order of the day. This would be directed both at the allegedly soft traditional elites, and at the rougher elements who were staying on at school for the first time after the 1880s. There was a clear desire in the materials to ensure that the working class also identified with the imperial agenda, a way of drawing together sections of the community who would naturally divide on economic and social grounds. The interaction with India, in so far as it sold the imperial ideal, was used to still both women and workers. The discourse of progress, the scientific underpinnings of racial hierarchies, the improving impact of "muscular Christianity," the definitive role of character — were all carried as messages in the childrens image of India.[55]

The imperial age was an age of both arrogance and insecurity. The need to construct and transmit nationalist propaganda in the history and popular readings of British schoolchildren betrays the

---

55. J. Mangan & J. Walvin, *Manliness and Morality*, Manchester, 1987; J. Springhall, *Youth, Empire and Society*, London, 1977; J. Gillis, *Youth and History*, London, 1981; J.A. Mangan "Noble Specimens of Manhood" in J. Richards, *Imperialism and Juvenile Literature*, Manchester, 1989.

operation of both factors. It was hoped that by exposing children to the dynamics of the imperial encounter they would identify with the most positive aspects of British identity. A crucial part of this process was the parallel construction of the "imperial Indian." It was this figure, as ally and enemy, who threw "Britishness" into starkest contrast with another way of being. The identity of India which was built in these materials was an essential element in the process of British self-definition. Yet the outline of the imperial Indian is a composite of stereotypes and formulaic characterizations which reduced a complex negotiation of identity on both sides into re-assuring messages of control and natural superiority.

For the needs of imperial Britain, an invisible Empire was constructed in the minds and imagination of the young. It was peopled with characters with whom children were expected to identify — heroes from history, fearless and fair-minded British boys, caring and compassionate British girls who understood how to deal with the ordering and uplifting of colonial subjects. Alongside these role models were the cast of 'others,' who despite their one-dimensional and dehumanized portrayal came to represent much that British children knew of the peoples of the Empire. It could be a very satisfying set of encounters for the child seeking both a sense of self and a national identity. By assuming the case for Empire and the relations which history and the press suggested were the reality for an imperial youth, the rewards included the joining of the forces of good over evil, of progress and action over the darkness of the uncivilized, befriending a "dusky chum," and enjoying a joke at the expense of another "funny foreigner."[56]

In reality two sets of false identity were being constructed, and the legacy of both can be acknowledged. Providing the youth of

---

56. D. Milner, *Children and Race*, London 1983; J. Walvin, *A Childrens World*, London, 1982; J.S. Bratton, *The Impact of Victorian Children's Fiction*, London, 1981; J. Field, *Toward a Programme of Imperial Life*, London, 1982.

Britain with a national identity closely tied in with the image of Empire continued well into the 1950s, when the reality of Empire was clearly contracting. While the physical control of British India had gone, the internalized relationship with the Indian was not displaced. It becomes less difficult to understand the problems of England's multicultural society when one acknowledges the residual imperial imagery obstructing the impulse toward equity and tolerance. The way in which both school history and popular reading associated national and individual identity with racial superiority has been a most pernicious legacy of the imperial ethos.

The imposition of a false one-dimensional and stereo-typical identity on the Indian also needs to be recognized and discarded by the Asian community. It is one strand of the negotiation of post-colonial identity which takes place in a variety of arenas. The conference in July of 1997 at Shimla brought the international academic community together to consider the elements of contemporary "Indianness." At the same time, within Britain, young Asian youth angrily denied the traditional imagery of a cowardly or passive response to harassment. The outbreak of violence between Muslim and Hindu youth in the British suburbs only begins to suggest the complexity involved in all identity negotiations, and raises again the difficult question of whether the assertion of one identity inevitably involves the negation of another.

9

The Goals of Medicine: Setting New Priorities

A Hindu Perspective

Cromwell Crawford

BEFORE we begin to discuss new priorities, it is instructive to know what the conventional ones are, and why it is that we find them wanting.

About the time when the project, "The Ends of Medicine," was launched, the National Institute of Health (NIH) announced its own project to research the following areas:

- The use of acupuncture to treat depression.
- Biofeedback as a treatment for pain control and diabetes.
- Āyurvedic medicine to treat Parkinson's disease.
- The benefits of hypnosis in healing broken bones.
- Indian (South Asian) music therapy for people with brain injuries.
- Massage therapy for patients with the AIDS virus, post-surgical patients, and people with bone-marrow transplants.
- Yoga for heroin addiction and obsessive-compulsive disorder.

These research grants and others are administered by the NIH's recently established *Office of Alternative Medicine*. The grants are monetarily small ($30,000 a piece), but symbolically they are major.

Slowly, reluctantly and with considerable trepidation, the American medical establishment is taking its first steps toward understanding the diverse forms of alternative medicine it has heretofore only scoffed.

The move has been strategic. In 1993 the *New England Journal of Medicine* (*NEJM*) published a survey, indicating that millions of Americans were by that time using unconventional medicine. A watershed study appearing in the *NEJM* (January 1993) by David Eisenberg, an internist at Harvard Medical School, defined unconventional therapies as "commonly used interventions neither taught widely in the U.S. medical schools nor generally available in the U.S. hospitals."

Following this definition, the study found that a third of Americans surveyed had used at least one unconventional therapy in the past year, and estimated that Americans spent almost 14-billion dollars on those therapies in 1990. To be sure, the sum was only a minuscule part of the national healthcare bill that exceeded $700 billion that year, but it was significant inasmuch as most that the $14 billion came out of the patient's pockets; the costs not being covered by insurance.

The phenomenon of alternative medicine, now a growth industry exceeding $27 billion a year (1991), is more than just another American fad: it reflects a gaping dissatisfaction with conventional medicine. Notwithstanding all of its miraculous achievements — the polio vaccine, penicillin, transplant surgery, crisis intervention, pain relief, reproductive technology, physical rehabilitation, life expectancy, gene therapy — conventional medicine has some vulnerable areas. Prominent among these weak spots are: impersonal doctor-patient relationships, health maintenance, management of chronic and degenerative disease of ageing, combating infectious disease now making a comeback, downplaying interactions of mind and body, its materialistic philosophy and prohibitive costs of healthcare.

Thus, modern medicine is a casualty of its own success. In the words of Arthur Kleinman, Harvard professor of medical anthropology:

> The general feeling is that as science has gotten better, the quality of interaction between doctors and patients has gotten worse. People find that medicine doesn't help much with the psychological and moral dimensions of suffering. These are problems for which a technological fix is not available, for which a magic bullet will not work.[1]

Against this background, the aim of this essay is to present a cluster of ideas, insights, principles and practices of *Āyurveda* which can be forged into new goals for medicine. Our presentation is carried out with reference to the designated list of crucial topics and issues set forth by the Hastings Center for discussion by a team of scholars from 14 countries. The consensus reached by this international group was that there should be four goals of medicine.

These goals are:

1. The prevention of disease and injury and promotion and maintenance of health.
2. The relief of pain and suffering caused by maladies.
3. The care and cure of those with a malady, and the care of those who cannot be cured.
4. The avoidance of premature death and the pursuit of a peaceful death.[2]

Though India was not one of the countries that participated in the Hastings project, it is all the more significant that key ideas of its medical system resonate with the goals that have been enunciated above.

---

1. *Harvard Magazine*, September-October, 1989, p. 28.
2. *The Goals of Medicine: The International Project of the Hastings Center*, The Hastings Center Report, Special Supplement, November-December, 1996.

Āyurveda means "the science of (living to a ripe) age." It has an ancient history with roots in the Vedic literature (1500-1000 BC). Over this long haul of time it was never considered an "alternative way of medicine" in its native land. But today, even in that capacity of Alternative medicine, it is gaining popularity across the globe let alone India. The classical texts of *Āyurveda* are the *Caraka Saṁhitā*, the *Suśruta Saṁhitā* and the *Vāgbhaṭṭa Saṁhitā*. Their dates are uncertain, but scholars generally assign *Caraka* and *Suśruta Saṁhitā*s (collections) to the first and second century, respectively, and *Vāgbhaṭṭa* is placed in the seventh or eighth century CE.

The Primacy of the Person

Āyurveda is a system of medicine in which, both in theory and in practice, the person is accorded a primacy that is in keeping with human dignity. The patient is always perceived as a person; not as a case. In the final analysis, all interven-tions of the doctor have a single goal, the care and cure of persons. Caraka begins his treatise with the words, "Now I shall expound the chapter on longevity."[3]

Long life with health is prized because it is "the best source of virtue, wealth, gratification and emancipation while diseases are destroyers of this (source), welfare, and life itself."[4]

Life is viewed as "a tripod" of body, mind and spirit. All levels of life constitute a unified whole. For the purpose of concentration and specialization one may speak of parts but parts have no independent status.

The body, like the rest of nature, is seen as a product of evolution, following the emergence of the five generic essences of physical energy (Ether, Air, Fire, Water and Earth) gross matter manifested in variegated forms. The subsequent evolution of the world, including the human constitution, is from these five

3. Priyavrat Sharma (ed. & tr.), *Caraka Saṁhitā*, vol. 1, Delhi: Chaukhamba Orientalia, 1981, *Sūtrasthānam* I 1.1.

4. *Ibid*, I.4.

elementary principles. The five elements enter the body and become reconstituted in the physiology and anatomy of the individual. As with the rest of nature, the body is in a continuous state of transformation. Death is the final act by which the organism is returned to its original state.

These five elements have three operative principles: *vāta, pitta* and *kapha* which must be maintained in their optimal level; otherwise they become blemishes or *doṣa*s. Hence, they are called *tridoṣa*s. The five elements along with blood, sustain the body and regulate all organic and psychic functions. Without them, the body cannot exist. When they are in a state of dynamic equilibrium, the body enjoys health and well-being; but when there is a loss of balance, disease results.

The five generic essences, also called "the *mahābhūta*s," are present in the seven elements known as *dhātus*. As the basic tissue elements, the *dhātu*s constitute the body and support and sustain it. Of special importance is their role in the body's immunological system. They comprise the body's fluids and its hard and soft parts. These seven elements are: blood, flesh, fat, bone, marrow, semen and oestrum. All of them are directly regulated by the *tridoṣa*s, which permeate the entire organism.

The final excellence of all these elements together is known as *ojas,* meaning effulgence. It gives vitality to all the tissues and is found throughout the body. In a healthy state, *ojas* gives firmness to the body, a shining colour to the skin, and energizes the internal and external organs. In the event it is diminished by hunger, injury, exhaustion or anxiety, the individual's complexion changes, and he or she complains of fatigue and loss of strength. There are three degrees in the diminution of *ojas,* the last terminates in death.

Health and healing in the Āyurvedic system is intimately connected to food and its proper digestion and assimilation. This explains the pivotal function of the *agni*s. *Agni*s are the biologic fires that act as enzymes in the digestion and absorption of food.

In the event that the digestive and metabolic functions of the *agni*s are impeded, the unprocessed food accumulates as *āma* in the intestines and proceeds to decompose. This undigested and unassimilated substance is a major factor in the production of indigenous diseases. It blocks the digestive tracts, and when it is chemically transformed into toxins, it enters the blood-stream, causing injury to the internal organs.

Finally, there are the three *mala*s: secretions that are counted among the constituents of the body — urine, faeces and perspiration. The *mala*s are waste products, following the process of digestion; but in the Āyurvedic conception these excretions are not exactly waste; it is their non-formation that is pathological.

The second leg of the tripod is the mind (*manas*). Along with intellect (*buddhi*) and egoism (*ahaṅkāra*), mind constitutes one aspect of the psychic apparatus of the person. Caraka describes the mind as the sixth sense (*ṣaḍ-indrīya*). He ascribes to it a transcending capacity (*atīndrīya*) for three reasons: (a) mind is both the cause of knowledge of the external world, as with other senses; (b) but it is also the subject of internal perception; and (c) whereas the five senses are grasped by the mind, the mind is not grasped by the senses; and it is the mind that oversees the senses.

The important functions of the mind are its capacities to perceive, think, remember and imagine. As the controller of all cognitive and conative organs, the mind is the controlling factor of the body. It is the direct cause of pain and pleasure in the body and is the seat of conscious, subconscious and unconscious activity in the body. Mind serves as a bridge between the physical body and the spirit. *Manas* is a dynamic agent, and though it is incomprehensive to the senses, its reality is essential for life.

These great and ancient medical manuals lay great emphasis on the psyche/soma identity. A state of reciprocal influence exists between the three operative principles (*tridoṣa*s) and the mind. In addition, the *manas* is governed by three 'qualities' (*guṇa*s) of purity (*sattva*), activity (*rajas*) and inertia (*tamas*). If *rajas* is on the ascendancy it forces one to a perpetual state of restlessness. The reason why the mind becomes agitated is because of the psychological forces of desire and repulsion, i.e., of *rajas*. The basis for the relative preponderance of one of the three qualities in a person, e.g., an overindulgence in *tamas* which makes one essentially dull and negative; could be set in a previous existence. To make the connection between the past and the present, Indian philosophy has had recourse to the notion of the subtle body which is the bearer of one's personal identity amidst the many cycles of rebirth.

The third leg of the tripod is the self or spirit. It is the transcendental element. Bodies perish but the spirit living in the body is not subject to death. Human beings occupy a unique position in nature, for the realization of the spirit, because of their endowment of intellect, memory, judgement, skill and action. The human species can rise above the life of mere instinct of an animal and live spiritually motivated lives. Like the mind, the spirit cannot be grasped by the senses, but its reality is equally essential for understanding all aspects of the human being. The goal of life is to realize the reality of the spirit by personal experience, and the ultimate mission of medicine is to create the most favourable conditions for this possibility. This relationship of means and ends between medicine and human wholeness (body, mind, spirit) elevates all medical art and science to a high calling and renders the pursuit of human well-being as a primary human obligation, both for the individual and for society.

Goals of Medicine

THE PREVENTION OF DISEASE AND THE PROMOTION OF HEALTH

First we outline the meaning of health and disease in the Indian medical texts. The words health (*ārogya*) and happiness (*sukha*) are rather synonymous. This points to a concept of health which is undivided, comprising all aspects of the person — physical, mental and spiritual.

Health in *Āyurveda* may be defined as a state of being in which the vital forces of the body, i.e., its three operative principles (*doṣa*s) are in balance; in which the digestion and metabolism (*agni*) are in order; in which the tissues (*dhātu*s) and excretions (*mala*s) are nomal; and in which the person is physically and mentally happy. The individual in whom this state exists can be designated a normal, healthy person, capable of living to a ripe old age. In contrast to Western medical systems, in *Āyurveda* health is not just a function of the body, but is inclusive of mind and spirit. The task of Indian medicine was therefore to keep all components of life in a state of optimum health and vitality.

Special attention is paid to the balance of three primary principles in the body: *vāta, pitta* and *kapha*. When these vital factors function in balance, health ensues. Health is therefore described as *sāmya* or balance. The value of this condition is gauged by its precarious quality. The fact is that the *doṣa*s are never static, but are constantly subject to change, due to the provocation of external and internal forces. *Doṣa*s function as blockers: when provocations arise, they may neutralize the disturbance or pass it on to the *dhātu*s and *mala*s.

Health is also an individualized matter. Each individual's constitution is uniquely shaped by the relative dominance of the three principles. Since constitutions differ from person to person, the notions of normality in health or normal health must be calibrated to these differences.

The constitution of each person is determined at its conception. When the sperm and ovum unite in the uterus to form a zygote, the *doṣa*s present in them produce specific features called *prakṛti*. If all of the *doṣa*s are in equilibrium, a healthy life is assured. Should the *doṣa*s be in a disturbed state, the condition either prevents conception or produces birth defects. If however, one or two of the *doṣa*s are moderately in excess, they give rise to a particular type of physical constitution and psychic temperament. However the constitution is shaped, it remains unchanged throughout life. Accordingly, Hindus make much of the state of health of partners in marriage, and the quality of the 'seed,' based on hereditary lines.

If health is synonymous with happiness, then disease (*vyādhi*) is the equivalent of misery (*duḥkha*). All physical and emotional states, ranging from pain to passion, are included under *vyādhi*. Similarly, if health is balance (*sāmya*), then disease is imbalance (*vaiṣamya*).

The immediate cause of all diseases is that when one of the operative principles becomes disproportionate *vis-a-vis* the others, due to some internal or external disturbance, and this agitation causes it to disturb the *dhātu*s and the *mala*s, thus producing various diseases. *Vāta* is primarily involved in the process of pathogenesis. Its location in the nervous system lays the basis for the psychosomatic progression of disease. The general theory is that these principles of action become disturbed by excessive use, deficient use, or misuse with reference to —

1. the objects of the senses;
2. the actions of speech, mind and body; and
3. the changing seasons.

Diseases are classified according to their therapies — surgical or medical; their prognosis — curable, incurable and mitigatable; their site — psychic, somatic; their etiology — genetic, congenital, constitutional, traumatic and organic.

Āyurveda acknowledges on the one hand that health and disease are conditioned by hereditary and genetic factors, in addition to the legacy of the individual's own past *karma*s, good or bad; on the other hand, it does not abdicate human responsibility. *Āyurveda* insists that health and disease are not predetermined and that life may be lengthened by human effort, notwithstanding all of the preconditioning factors.

This brings us to the topic of the maintenance of health and the prevention of disease. Suśruta capsulizes the purpose of his medical manual in the first chapter:

> To cure the diseases of the sick, to protect the healthy, to prolong life.[5]

Caraka admonishes:

> As a [mayor] is cautious in the duties of the city and a charioteer in those of the chariot, a wise person should be cautious in duties, relating to his own body.[6]

By contrast, "The fool does not realize till he is afflicted," and only then requests friends and family to bring him a physician, at the cost of all of his possessions even; but this urgency of anxiety is unable to do any good to him, because the patient is now "devoid of life, weak, afflicted, emaciated. . . . Thus not finding a saviour, that fool leaves his life like an iguana with her tail bound and dragged by a strong person. Hence, one who wishes happiness should counteract disturb-ances with medicines before the illness itself is produced i.e., when it is newly risen."[7]

It is clear. The aims of *Āyurveda* are not only curative, but promotive and preventive. The philosophic basis for preventive medicine proceeds from three basic human desires: desire for the preservation of life; desire for wealth and desire for a blessed state hereafter. The first desire, based on the instinct for self-preservation, is of pivotal importance, because without it nothing is possible. Therefore, to achieve all of life's desires, we must wish to preserve life.

5. Kaviraj Kunjalal Bhishagratna (ed. & tr.), *Suśruta Saṁhitā*, vol. 1, Delhi: Chaukhamba Orientalia, 1991, *Sūtrasthānam* I.12.

6. *Op cit., Caraka*, Su. V.103.

7. *Ibid.*, Su. XI, 56-63.

The threat to human well-being comes from diseases that are located in the body and the mind.

Somatic diseases must be prevented by maintaining equilibrium of the operative principles, order in digestion and metabolism, normalcy in tissues and waste products, and keeping the person physically and mentally happy.[8]

To achieve these objectives of physical health, *Āyurveda* lays down a regimen of personal hygiene (*svāstha vṛtta*). Specific routines are itemized for practice during day and night. The ingestion of food is given primary importance in respect to quantity, quality and time of day. To maintain good vision, the application of collyrium is recommended. To keep the head clear and all air passages free and without odour, medicated smoking is prescribed. For oral hygiene, teeth should be cleaned with twigs that are astringent and pungent; the tongue scraped and special leaves, seeds and fruits should be kept in the mouth for clarity, relish and fragrance. The body should be kept clean, well toned and smelling fresh through the use of baths, oil massage and adornment with fresh flowers, perfumes, ornaments and fine apparel. No natural urges must be suppressed. Anti-social behaviour that causes pain to others, such as adultery, theft, lies and violence should be checked in its initial impulse. Physical exercise, laughter, speech, travel on foot, sexual intercourse and nocturnal parties are good when engaged in with moderation:

> But one who indulges excessively in these or similar other activities perishes suddenly like a lion dragging an elephant.

All of these daily and nightly routines are subject to modification with each changing season. *Āyurveda* describes different regimens in respect to food, lifestyle, etc., to conform to the requirements of the six seasons of the year. The physiological basis for these seasonal recommendations is the theory that the *tridoṣa*s are significantly

8. *Op cit., Caraka,* vide Su. VII.

impacted by climatic changes. For instance, *vāta* is sensitive to the rainy season, *pitta* increases during the summer, and *kapha* augments in the autumn. All of these changes affect the type of diet one must adopt in order to prevent partaking of foods which do not fit the season.

In addition to personal hygiene, *Āyurveda* employs two other preventive therapies: *rasāyana* (rejuvenating) and *vājikaraṇa* (aphrodisiacs).

Caraka defines *rasāyana* as a promotive treatment that rejuvenates the body and mind, that enhances natural resistance to disease, and that adds vitality and mental agility to long life. For instance, he claimed of one formula of *rasāyana* that it:

> provides health, sustains (youthful) age, removes sleep, drowsiness, exhaustion, lassitude and debility, restores equilibrium of *vāta, kapha* and *pitta,* brings stability, alleviates laxity of muscles, kindles internal fire (digestion) and produces excellent lustre, complexion and voice.[9]

The third form of preventive medicine in *Āyurveda* is *vājikaraṇa.* The two-fold purpose of this aphrodisiac therapy is to promote virility and fertility. By the administration of various medications, it is claimed that the seminal secretions and physical stamina are increased even in males who are sexually impaired and aged, thus imparting physical and mental pleasure. The medical manuals eulogize the woman as "the foremost aphordisiac."[10] She is "like a noose for all the senses, due to her excellent qualities." The man who is left without progeny, "looks like a tree having only one branch, shadeless, fruitless."

Diverse potions are prescribed for such an individual with claims that:

---

9. *Op cit., Caraka,* vol. 11, *Cikitsāsthānam* I.3.
10. *Ibid.,* II.4-7.

> . . . by proper use of these formulations one becomes endowed with good physique, potency, strength and complexion and sexually exhilarated and potent for women like an eight year old horse.[11]

In addition to the physical modes of preventive medicine we have just reviewed, there is also a mental regimen called *sadvṛtta.* Basically, this measure comprises rules of good conduct in order to maintain psychosomatic equilibrium. As previously stated, the mind is governed by the three essential qualities: *sattva, rajas* and *tamas*. When they are in a state of disequilibrium, disease ensues.

Caraka points out that in the exogenous diseases, errors of the intellect play a role:

> Psychological disorders like envy, grief, fear, anger, vanity, aversion, etc., are also said to be caused by intellectual error.[12]

The code of Good Conduct is "the way shown for prevention of exogenous diseases," because it eliminates irrational thought and alleviates stress. To reinforce one's own efforts toward the maintenance of psychosomatic equilibrium, emphasis is laid upon keeping the wholesome company of those endowed with wisdom, learning, age, good conduct, memory and balanced mind."[13]

Commenting on the social underpinning of the Rules of Good Conduct, Dubey comments that:

> . . . propounders of *Āyurveda* were aware of the fact that abnormal interpersonal relationships produce psychosocial stress, which is responsible for psychosomatic disorders.[14]

---

11. *Op cit., Caraka,* vol. 11, *Cikitsāsthānam* I.3, *Sūtrasthānam* VII.38-41.
12. *Ibid.,* VII.51-52.
13. *Op cit., Caraka,* vol. 11, *Cikitsāsthānam* I.3, VII.60.
14. G.P. Dubey, *Preventive Medicine and Personal Hygiene, in Science and Philosophy of Indian Medicine,* eds. K.N. Udupa, R.H. Singh, Varanasi: Banaras, Hindu University, 1990, p. 99.

Convinced that personal errors of judgement in all the areas of life are responsible for the disease producing stress, the Āyurvedic physicians made much of proper socialization through a schedule of good conduct. Dubey adds:

> To achieve this end, an improved mode of living has been described, so that individuals can prevent themselves from psychosocial stress caused by wrong action. The basic idea of a good life is that it should be so regulated that the body and mind may be free from physical and mental disorders.[15]

The above discussion of health and disease should make it clear that the prevention of disease and the maintenance of health are as much the accredited goals of *Āyurveda* as curative interventions.

THE RELIEF OF PAIN AND SUFFERING CAUSED BY MALADIES

Before we discuss the relief of pain and suffering, a distinction must be made between the two. Though both follow parallel paths, their tracks are not identical. The fact is that you can have pain without suffering and suffering without pain. A woman who has a successful mastectomy because of breast cancer is no longer in pain from the original malady; but she does suffer due to the loss of her sense of femininity and personal identity. The locus of her suffering is not the body, because the body cannot entertain the ideas, beliefs, and fantasies which are the stuff of which suffering is begotten. Only humans have hopes and fears, and therefore only humans suffer.

This brings us to a definition of suffering developed by Eric J. Cassell, M.D. in clinical experience. He says:

> Suffering is a state of severe distress induced by the loss of the intactness of person, or by a threat that the person believes will

15. G.P. Dubey, *Preventive Medicine and Personal Hygiene, in Science and Philosophy of Indian Medicine*, eds. K.N. Udupa, R.H. Singh, Varanasi: Banaras, Hindu University, 1990, p. 100.

result in the loss of his or her intactness.[16]

The person is at the centre of Cassell's definition of suffering. Yet contemporary pain research finds it difficult to deal with the concept of person. As a result, it reduces the person to physical phenomena and relegates all ideas of personhood to psychology, philosophy or religion. The thinking at work is that the physical is the real and that the psychological is not real. However, the fact remains that the person is not just a body or a mind. The person is a whole that cannot be reduced to any of its parts. It is in his wholeness that a person experiences suffering with reference to the full spectrum of his personhood. For instance, disease may prevent a person from performing a professional role with which he very much identifies, and this inability produces acute suffering. This is why most physicians make the worst patients. Similarly, membership in a family having a particular medical history, or membership in a cultural group with specific mores about the public display of emotions, positively affect the way such individuals suffer. The point is that we all suffer as persons who have beliefs, memories and visions of the future. A person who has just learnt that he or she is afflicted with Alzheimer's disease may be free of all symptoms, but he or she looks down the road and envisions himself or herself in a shape and form that renders present existence unbearable, and hence may contemplate ending it all. That type of pre-emptive response is only possible for a person for whom the future is now. Unfortunately, the doctor who views the patient in terms of his or her body parts is quick to dismiss such reports of suffering as being "only in the head" and "unreal" and therefore medically unimportant — the priest can deal with that.

---

16. Eric J. Cassell, *The Relationship between Pain and Suffering, in Advances in Pain Research Therapy,* vol. 1, eds. C.S. Hill, W. Fields, New York: Raven Press, 1989, p. 63.

As with suffering, there are equal misconceptions about the relationship of pain to the person. Cassell explains how pain is related to the person.

> Certain kinds of stimuli elicit the sensory response of nociception. . . . The sensory response is perceived. . . . As such, the sensory response is an event for the perceiver. All events are assigned meaning. That is to say, all events must be integrated into the experience of the perceiver — they cannot . . . float free and unexplained. A percept, of which we are speaking, is a percept of something. Pain is not a something unless it is the pain of something.[17]

When meaning is assigned to an event, it can either be deemed unimportant, as upon the discovery that the sting on my heel is that of an ant, or it can be very important, as when I learn that I have been bitten by a poisonous snake. In either case, the meaning influences the perception and predicts the future. In the case of the ant, the pain is quickly suppressed when the source is identified; in the case of the snake bite, the pain is intensified. Similarly, prediction of some future outcome also influences the perception. In the case of the Alzheimer's patient, anticipation of what is going to happen in the next few years directly impacts initial states of discomfort.

For a time a person may be able to tolerate pain, but when the stage is reached that the pain is making one go to pieces and there is a loss of personal intactness, it is then that the person begins to suffer. Suffering ensues when the individual believes that the pain is destroying his integrity and human dignity.

The upshot of Cassell's study is that the phenomena of pain and suffering are incomprehensible to the extent that the body and mind are viewed as separate. In his words:

---

17. Eric J. Cassell, *The Relationship between pain and suffering, in Advances in pain research therapy,* vol. 1, eds. C.S. Hill, W. Fields, New York: Raven Press, 1989, p. 67.

> From the point of view of a classic concept of science, the inability of researchers to hold pain in their hands as an object separable from the person who has the pain is an overwhelming disadvantage. It makes the truly scientific study of pain impossible — not difficult, but impossible. Until now, recognition of this difficulty seemingly has not been accepted by pain researchers. Mostly they have attempted to force pain back into the classic scientific mold by blinding themselves to the individual nature of pain sensation and by acting as if nociception and pain were the same thing. It makes no sense to keep denying the fundamental nature of the pain experience in an attempt to force it and its study into the reductionist paradigm. It makes no more sense to attempt to force its understanding or research into psychologistic ways of thought as if pain were a "mental" or psychological phenomenon in the narrow meanings of those terms. To force it into these boxes is to lose the great opportunity for understanding the human condition that the investigation of pain and suffering offer.[18]

Āyurveda resonates fully with the concerns that are being expressed by Cassell and like-minded doctors. As a holistic system, it resists being placed into any one box, be it physical or mental. The basis of its holism lies in its original under-standing of the person as a dynamic combination of body, mind and spirit, in which the separate parts have no independent status.

The psychosomatic approach of Indian medicine is not restricted to the pathogenesis of a disease, as is often the case in Western medicine, but is an integral component of all considerations — anatomical, physiological, pharmacological, aetiopathological and therapeutic. All of its major notions show the psychosomatic structure of *Āyurveda*. We have shown that the word for health (*ārogya*) is a synonym for happiness; just as the word for disease (*vyādhi*) is synonymous with misery (*duḥkha*).

18. Eric J. Cassell, *The Relationship between pain and suffering, in Advances in pain research therapy*, vol. 1, eds. C.S. Hill, W. Fields, New York: Raven Press, 1989, p. 68.

Health is more than a physical state or a mental state, or a combination of the two; it is also a function of the spirit. To be healthy one must be fit on all levels of one's being. We have observed that the three principles of the body (*tridoṣas*) and the three qualities of the mind (*guṇas*) constantly influence one another. In the discussion of preventive medicine, the two completely different regimens, *svāsthavṛtta* (Personal Hygiene) and *sadvṛtta* (Code of Conduct), were integrated toward a common goal. Furthermore, practitioners of *yoga* who cultivate the life of the spirit through the combined engagement of body and mind, are known to live longer, happier and healthier lives. All this is to say that *Āyurveda* is essentially dialogical:

> . . . body and mind make up a whole simultaneously, not sequentially, each being of equal value (with no claim to superiority). In the ultimate analysis, there is no such thing as "physical" and "mental" illness; there is only illness.[19]

Thus, by virtue of its holistic understanding of the person and its psychosomatic approach, *Āyurveda* presents an alternate model for both, an understanding of the nature of pain and suffering, and for their relief. This model must replace the current biological model of classical medicine, because though the relief of pain and suffering is the traditional goal of medicine; "contemporary medicine throughout the world often does not adequately meet that goal."[20]

Equipped with the effective pharmacological and yogic approaches to pain, *Āyurveda* can help advance the cause of palliative care, on the one hand; and on the other hand, its rich philosophical insights and power to evoke empathy can relieve the mental and emotional suffering that accompany life-threatening disease.

---

19. Sudhir Kakar, *Health and Medicine in the Living Traditions of Hinduism, in Healing and Restoring*, ed. L.E. Sullivan, New York: Macmillan, 1989, p. 120.
20. *Op. cit.*, Hastings, p. S 11.

THE CARE AND CURE OF THOSE WITH A MALADY, AND THE CARE OF THOSE WHO CANNOT BE CURED

The priorities of allopathic medicine in respect to care and cure are clearly set in favour of cure. In part, this is explainable through modern medicine's heavy reliance on —

1. technology,
2. its preoccupation with acute cases,
3. its concentration on disease,
4. its belief that the causes and cures of disease lie on the outside, and
5. its pragmatic philosophy which reasons that once a cure is found, care is redundant.

All of the above factors form a common syndrome. Since modern medicine locates the cause and cure of maladies on the outside, it tends to elevate exclusively the use of surgery, high-tech treatments, and potent pharmaceutical drugs, notwithstanding their toxic side-effects. This view of the etiology of disease in modern medicine also explains its obsessive quest for the 'magic bullet' — specific cures for specific pathologies. Magic bullets, like penicilin, have worked wonders by killing certain types of bacteria and by dramatically arresting infection, but the magic bullet model loses some of its splendour when it begins to dominate the medical research agenda and inform all dialogue about treatment. The model is also weakened by its logic that to destroy a deadly disease you must employ a deadly drug. If a drug is non-toxic, it is assumed by this logic that it cannot be very effective. As a result, allopathic medicine has an armory filled with drugs that ravage the body's immune system. Often the lethal drug or surgery succeeds, as in the case of a surgically removed ulcer or blocked coronary artery. But while there may be immediate, short-term gains for this system of radical cure, long-term consequences are less certain. The fact is that you can remove a stomach ulcer, or part of the stomach which secretes acid, but you cannot thereby remove the underlying cause of the ulcer, which makes it keep coming back. Similarly, you can bypass the coronary artery only so many times, but its blockage recurs because the source of the problem within the person is left untouched.

The Indian system of medicine reverses the priorities of allopathic medicine. The two main goals of *Āyurveda* are:

1. To preserve the health of the healthy (Prevention/Care); and
2. To alleviate the disorders of the diseased (Curing/Healing).[21]

Here preventive medicine, which is the initial step of care, is given the first position, thus demonstrating where the priority of the Indian physician lies.

Āyurvedic therapeutics is a quartet of ". . . physician, drug, attendant and patient."[22] The patient is expected to provide important input about the disorder, with clear recall; he must not be afraid, and must carry out all instructions.

The medical attendant should have the qualities of loyalty and cleanliness, and must be knowledgeable and dexterous.

Drugs are of animal, plant and earth origin.[23] They should be adequately available, efficacious, of various pharmaceutical forms, and of normal composition. A drug that is unknown "is (fatal) like poison," but a drug that is tested "is (vitalizing) like nectar."[24] Administration is all important:

> A sharp poison also becomes the best drug by proper administration, (on the contrary) even the (best) drug is reduced to sharp poison, if administered badly.[25]

---

21. *Op. cit., Suśruta*, I.I.12.
22. *Op. cit., Caraka*, Su. IX.1.
23. *Ibid*, I.68-73.
24. *Ibid.*, I.124-25.
25. *Op. cit., Caraka*, I.126.

All Āyurvedic drugs have no harmful side-effects when so applied.

The most important member of this therapeutic team is of course the physician himself. Patients are warned against quacks:

> . . . one might survive a direct hit to the head by a thunderbolt, but not the medicine prescribed by an ignorant physician.[26]

Physicians were held to the highest standards, on all counts. In public, the physician must appear well-groomed, healthy, gentle and modest. Professionally the *vaidya* (doctor) must possess the four qualities:

> Excellence in theoretical knowledge, extensive practical experience, dexterity and cleanliness.[27]

The doctor-patient relationship must be marked by a four-fold attitude of friendliness, compassion for the sick, dedication to those whom he can help, and a philosophical attitude toward those whose time has come.[28]

Since faith in the doctor plays such a powerful role in the therapeutic process, the physician must support the trust reposed in him by treating the patient "as his own son."

Aware of the potency of words to harm or heal, the physician, though observing signs of death "should not disclose the approaching death without having been requested for." Even upon request, he should not disclose the condition if, in his judgement, the information is liable to precipitate the patient's death, or to bring "affliction to somebody else." On the other hand, the physician should "certainly tell about the approaching condition of health." At all times the patient's privacy and confidentiality are to be maintained.

---

26. *Op. cit., Caraka,* I.126-33.
27. *Ibid.,* Su. IX.6.
28. *Ibid.,* IX.26.

The medical manuals make a clear division between diseases that are curable and incurable, along with appropriate directives that are relevant to our subject.

Curable diseases are of two types: easily curable and curable with some difficulty. They are also of three grades: low, medium and high. Details are supplied. A physician who acts promptly in such cases, always succeeds with proper treatment. This involves:

1. examination of patient;
2. examination of disease; and
3. examination of drugs.

Examination of the patient must be made by an eight-fold procedure:

1. Pulse;
2. Urine;
3. Stool;
4. Tongue;
5. Voice;
6. Skin;
7. Eyes;
8. General features.

These examinations are always with reference to the individual constitution of the patient. Secondly, the exact nature of the disease must be catalogued by a five-fold diagnosis:

- The cause of the disease
- Premonitory symptoms
- Manifested symptoms
- Exploratory therapy
- Process of manifestation of disease — exogenous, endogenous.

Thirdly, specific medication must be selected, on the basis of:

- The *doṣa*s

- The *dhātus*
- The constitution
- The nature of the disease
- The organ or system which is the site of the disease.

Āyurvedic medicine is administered with reference to such factors as age, season, etc. It is based on the tridoṣic theory in which a disorder is treated with "therapy which is opposite to the causative factor," and is aimed at restoring normal balance.[29] This type of medicine has no deleterious consequences. Medicine that cures in one area and irritates in another area is not considered a cure. This presents a challenge to Western medicine to reconsider its goals if these mean going from the frying-pan into the fire.

The centrepiece of *Āyurveda*'s curative treatment is the five-fold Purification Therapy known as *pañcakarma*. It facilitates a lasting cure and consists of: 1. Emesis; 2. Purgation; 3. Decoction enema; 4. Oily enema; 5. Nasal snuffing.

The immediate effect of *pañcakarma* therapy is to cure tridoṣic imbalance and to cleanse all the channels (*śrotas*). Thereafter, a prescribed diet helps stabilize the cure.

Āyurvedic medicine recognizes that there are limits to curing and the preservation of life. Incurable diseases are of two types: palliable and unmanageable. In the latter type, the physician should take himself off the case. *Āyurveda* discourages resort to heroic medicine and supports the acceptance of a natural process that ends in death.[30] In such instances, there could be no conceivable controversy between a Hindu ethicist and the physician, or between the family and the physician on the issue — "Do not resuscitate."

Caring is administered to the patient who is incurable though palliable. With proper palliation, the patient is able to prolong his days and receive a measure of relief by observing a wholesome

---

29. *Op. cit., Caraka,* X.6.
30. *Ibid.,* XI.21-22.

routine but there is always the danger of the chronic problem flaring up at the slightest provocation.[31]

When all means of medical cure and care are exhausted, a wise physician hands the patient over to the family for care. At this stage, spiritual guides assist the sick one toward his final passage.

THE AVOIDANCE OF PREMATURE DEATH AND THE PURSUIT OF A PEACEFUL DEATH

Death is not a problem for *Āyurveda* — only premature death. This is because in the Hindu tradition death is not the opposite of life, but a gate to another birth,

> In time everyone must go — when the body is worn out and when one has paid one's accumulated debts to the gods, sages, and forefathers. What is seriously mourned is an untimely death. The dead person's age, sex, marital status and place in the hierarchy, the suddenness of death, and the quality of life help to determine responses to the death. Helplessness produced by death or impending death is coped with by the thought of an eternal *atman* or rebirth.[32]

This brings us to the highest goal to which *Āyurveda* aspires — the level of Spirit.

On the physical level, *Āyurveda*'s goal is to delve into all of the matters pertaining to health and disease, along with their causes and cures. On the mental level, the goal of *Āyurveda* is to remove ignorance, to free one from bondage to the senses, and to chart a rational, moral style of life that brings happiness and avoids pain. On the spiritual level, the goal of *Āyurveda* is to supply the person with all powers of body and mind to realize the identity of its individual soul with the universal soul and thus transcend all unhappiness, pain and death. Being medical texts, most of the

---

31. *Op. cit., Caraka,* XI.17-18.
32. Prakash N. Desai, *Health and Medicine in the Hindu Tradition,* New York: Crossroad, 1989, p. 94.

material is devoted to subjects with which the physician is primarily preoccupied; however, it is quite explicit that the preservation of physical and mental health is for the enjoyment of the present life, but ultimately health and longevity are instruments for the attainment of self-realization. The goals of medicine are simultaneously for this world and the next.

By including transcendence as a goal, *Āyurveda* draws on the most powerful resource humans possess to restore the integrity of their personhood, even in the face of death. The experience of transcendence places the individual in a larger reality that gives meaning to death, and the necessary strength to meet it in peace.

Conclusion

Our description of the goals of Indian medicine, based on original texts, demonstrates a curious affinity they share with the four goals, formulated by the international group directed by the Hastings Center. What accounts for this core of values?

The explanation for the above moral consensus lies in the fact that *the point of intersection for both lines of inquiry is the person.* Scholars from many countries have been able to have a meeting of minds with ancient Indian doctors, because all parties have recognized the need for medicine to possess its own "internal compass and abiding values," based on "tradi-tional and largely universal goals."

For *Āyurveda*, the core of these traditional and universal values is the notion that *medicine is made for the person; not the person for medicine.*

Today that relationship of means and ends has been radically reversed: the end has become the means and the means the ends. The reversal of values was engineered in the moment medicine became synonymous with science and technology. Subsequently, medicine has advanced quite apart from the needs and concerns of those who are ill. The latest indicator of this shift is the push toward "medicine for corporate profit." Institutions which have gone commercial might retain their former names, such as "Mercy Hospital," but there is diminishing doubt: *at whose mercy does the patient lie?*

The basis of these critical developments is the reductive philosophy of medical science which is guided by a biological model of the person.

Ironically, it is the same medical technology which has spawned an array of ethical dilemmas, that is now leading us into a new era in which the old model becomes effete and outdated. Ultimately, the beginning-of-life issues, end-of-life issues, and the new reproductive techniques, become gateways to spiritual questions, because in such explorations you are asking fundamental questions about what makes human life human. *Medicine has entered areas in which it is incapable, by itself, to resolve its own dilemmas.* The types of questions that are posed by the problem of suffering can no longer be dismissed as unreal, or passed on to philosophers and theologians to debate. Further, these questions are more than philosophic or theological; they are economic, because we cannot keep paying for more sophisticated technology, endlessly.

One reason medicine has self-consciously avoided questions of spirituality in the medical context, is because of ignorance of what spirituality is, in the first place. In Āyurvedic thought, spirituality means attention to the fact that we are more than our bodies and minds; that we are creatures who find meaning in the world and for whom the world is meaningful. Such thoughts are not just good for the soul; but also in the whole anthropology of *Āyurveda*, they are good for the mind and for the body.

The challenge, therefore, of *Āyurveda* to doctors is to return to medicine's spiritual dimension, because ultimately, this awareness is the true measure of care. This is the pinnacle on which our goals for medicine stand or fall.

To care is to recognize a person in his wholeness. It is the felt need to care for people that initially brings most young persons into medicine. However, at some point, the establishment takes over as much of the economics and organization of health care as a delivery system takes doctors away from caring for people. It is now up to doctors to decide what they wish their goals to be as we enter the twenty-first century.

The care given in a hospice is one model of what medicine can be. It means you go on giving care after there is no hope for curing. This is bitter medicine for physicians to swallow, for whom *medicine is cure.* This is all they have been trained to do. Pill and scalpel are their stock-in-trade, applied equally to acute and chronic disease. In the words of Dean Ornish, "if all you're trained to use is a hammer, the whole world looks like a nail."

On the other hand, palliative care is about comfort, dignity, accepting passages, recognizing the spiritual life. As a bonus, it saves millions of healthcare dollars!

10

The Spiritual Self and Psychopathology

Theoretical Reflections and Clinical Observations

Alan Roland

THE relationship of the spiritual self to psychopathology has had a long and problematic history in psychoanalysis, not to mention at times in various spiritual movements. I shall explore this relationship first by delving into the views of applied psychoanalysis on the subject, including those of Sudhir Kakar and Jeffrey Kripal on major Indian spiritual leaders. Then, I shall formulate my own perspective based on psychoanalytic work with those deeply involved in spiritual practices.

By the spiritual self, I am referring to an underlying ground of being and consciousness in all human beings. This may be experienced by relatively few persons, some referring to it as an immersion in light and/or bliss, or to a far deeper awareness of the underlying relationships in the universe (1994). Others, such as the Buddhists, refer to emptiness, a powerful ground of being underlying the ever-changing flux of the mind. I shall cite clinical experience with those involved over prolonged periods in one or another spiritual discipline, although these may be carried out in a very private way. I have worked over the years psychoanalytically with a few Hindu patients involved in meditation and other spiritual disciplines, with an American Sufi and with American and Indian Christians so involved, as well as with the Hindu, Jewish and Christian artists and writers who consider their art work to be a kind of *sādhanā* or spiritual discipline. By psychopathology I am alluding to those seriously affected by intense, unconscious emotional conflicts and/or deficits in the self that significantly interfere with their everyday relationships, work, and sense of self.

Psychoanalytic Views

Beginning with Freud, psychoanalysis has followed an Enlightenment agenda of rational demystification of religion and spirituality. Freud (1927) was wary of commenting on the spiritual, instead directing his attention to the role of religion within the psyche of the Western common person. He viewed religion as a necessary illusion where images of God are created to compensate and protect humans from the vulnerability of infantile helplessness, and later helplessness in the face of the rigors of nature and civilization.

Romain Rolland, working on a biography of Ramakrishna, wrote to Freud in 1927 agreeing in the main with Freud's analysis of the religion of the common person but asserted that Freud should consider spiritual experiences, or the "oceanic feeling,"[1] in his psychology as the sentiment underlying all religion. Freud responded that he personally had had no such experience himself. Instead, Freud viewed the essential oneness of spiritual experiences, such as Ramakrishna had, as genetically related to the undifferentiated state of the ego in the infant-mother merger experience (Freud 1930, pp. 64-66).

With, but, rare exceptions,[2] Freudian psychoanalysts have continued to reduce spiritual experiences to regressive, symbiotic

1. The oceanic feeling refers to Ramakrishna's description of his spiritual experiences as being like a salt doll that dissolves into the ocean.

2. These exceptions comprise a small handful of highly important Freudian and neo-Freudian psychoanalysts who are no longer living, such as Erik Erikson (1969), Erich Fromm (1970), Karen Horney (1945), and Harold Kelman (1960) in the United States, and Wilfred →

merger experiences from an early childhood developmental stage, to one or another kind of psychopathology. Perhaps most fully exemplifying this approach is the Sanskrit scholar, Jeffrey M. Masson (1976, 1980), who became trained in psychoanalysis. He asserted reductionistic strategies *ad absurdum* in the area of Indian studies by drawing upon the full psychoanalytic armamentarium of psychopathology. His seeming meticulous Sanskrit and psychoanalytic scholarship is unfortunately flawed by his wild methodology of speculating loosely on ancient Indian texts as well as on modern Indian biography, such as on Ramakrishna.

The opprobrium attached by psychoanalysts to mysticism and the spiritual has been so powerful that one of the only Freudian analysts to contribute directly in this area, Marion Milner (1973), delayed publishing her paper on mysticism for a number of years, instead circulating it privately. Another example of this is a two-day conference in 1994, "The Suffering Self: A Dialogue Between Psychoanalysts and Buddhists," in which a few established psychoanalysts involved in Buddhism were highly reluctant to participate unless there were other well recognized analysts on the programme. They were clearly afraid of their reputation in the psychoanalytic field. Moreover, the conference, itself, was sponsored by a small psychoanalytically oriented institute.[3] Most major psychoanalytic institutes would not have touched the subject. Nevertheless, the conference was extremely well-attended, attesting to a change of attitude in many psychoanalysts.

More recently, there are three major books by psycho-analysts that critique Freud's views on religion (Ana-Maria Rizzuto, 1979; W.W. Meissner 1984; and Neville Symington 1994). Rizzuto and Meissner,

→ Bion (1970) and Marion Milner (1973) in England; and several living analysts who are actively involved in one or another form of Buddhist meditation, such as Nina Coltart (1992, 1996) in England, and Paul Cooper (1995), Mark Finn (1992), Jeffrey Rubin (1996), and John Suler 1993) in the United States. (See Roland 1996, p. 146).

3. Metropolitan Institute for Training in Psychoanalytic Psychotherapy.

for instance, contrast Freud's Cartesian dualism of pitting illusion against reality, rational reality being more highly valued, with D.W. Winnicott's view of illusion as central to early childhood development, and to symbolization in all of the realms of culture, including religion. Symington's critique and vision is more far-reaching in his seeing psychoanalysis as a spirituality in the world in its transformation of the inner world of persons from a self-centered, destructive narcissism to more wholesome emotional intimacy relationships, similar to the core values of mature religions. Similar to Freud, they have generally steered away from any detailed considerations of spiritual experiences and spiritual disciplines.

Kakar and Kripal on Mysticism

Writing much more directly on mysticism, Sudhir Kakar over the last 20 years or so has been one of the first psychoanalysts to forthrightly challenge the psychoanalytic dismissal of mysticism,[4] and to assert its validity in major Indian figures such as Vivekananda (1978, pp. 160-81), Gandhi (1989, pp. 85-128), and Ramakrishna (1991). Kakar lays out the Indian understanding of Vivekananda, Gandhi, and Ramakrishna, using an Eriksonian blend of the interaction of the personal biographical, the creative and spiritual talent, and the historical moment and cultural environment. The problem in Kakar's work comes from two directions.

The first is in his psychoanalytic analyses of textual material, either biographical or autobiographical. He fully continues the

4. Both Kakar and Kripal equate mysticism with the spiritual self, which does not seem fully accurate. While the mystic, who is convinced of the existence of a supreme force behind the universe and in oneself, is usually involved in the realization of a spiritual self, others deeply oriented toward the spiritual self may not be so convinced. There are persons such as Jawarhalal Nehru, some scientists and Buddhists, who would fall more into this latter category. (I am indebted to Professor M.N. Srinivas, the noted Indian anthropologist, for this analysis.) The spiritual self is a more inclusive notion than mysticism, and is more psychologically and experientially oriented.

psychoanalytic tradition of reducing spiritual experiences to psychopathology or to early childhood emotional states, in spite of his intentions to the contrary. I shall cite a few examples to illustrate this.

On Vivekananda,

> With the advent of adolescence . . . he found he could not always cope with the claims of archaic grandiosity and the anxiety and guilt associated with its breakthrough. Increasingly, he experienced periods of hypomanic excitement; once . . . when he was fifteen . . . Narendra 'spied a large beehive in the cleft of a giant cliff and suddenly his mind was filled with awe and reverence for the Divine Providence. He lost outer consciousness and lay thus in the cart for a long time.'
>
> — Kakar 1978, pp. 178-79

On Gandhi,

> Economic, social and familial conflicts, besides the perennial erotic one, seem to have spurred Gandhi's travels on the spiritual path. — Kakar 1989, p. 92
>
> . . . from Gandhi's sensuous gaiety stems his ability to rivet masses of men. . . .
>
> — *Ibid.*, p. 102

Kakar reductionistically interprets Gandhi's struggle with celibacy (from his 30s on) — a cornerstone of any fully committed spiritual aspirant in the Hindu and other spiritual traditions — as essentially related to an unconscious fantasy of maintaining an idealized relationship with the maternal body, supposedly the modal fantasy of every Indian man for which Kakar fails to muster any clinical evidence.

> Whereas desexualizing, idealizing, and perceiving only the "milky" mother in the woman is one part of his (Gandhi's) defensive bulwark which helped in preserving the illusion of unity with the maternal body intact, the other part consists of efforts at renouncing the gift of sexual desire, abjuring his own

> masculinity . . . with a wish-for feminization . . . defensive in origin.
>
> — Kakar 1989, pp. 126-27

On Ramakrishna,

> All he yearned for with all his soul, he was to later tell us, was a vision, the personal *darshan* of the Mother. The spiritual thirst, the clinician would observe, was embedded in all the signs of a full-fledged depression. There was a great restlessness of the body, sleepless nights, loss of appetite in which eating was reduced to the bare minimum, eyes that filled up often and suddenly with tears.
>
> — Kakar 1991, p. 13

Discussing *bhāva* and Ramakrishna's visions,

> The affect, so strong that it is experienced as *knowing*, partakes of some of the quality of the symbiotic state in infancy when the child knew the mother through an interchange of their feelings, when affect and cognition were not differentiated from one another
>
> — *Ibid.*, p. 24

> Ramakrishna's longing for the Mother, accompanied by breathlessness of a kind where he feels he is about to die, for instance, is akin to a certain type of asthmatic bodily manifestation of a dammed-up urge for the mother's succor.
>
> — *Ibid.*, p. 25

It is obvious from this handful of Kakar's specific analyses of Vivekananda, Gandhi and Ramakrishna that he continues the very pathologizing and regressive analysis of spiritual aspirations and experiences of other psychoanalysts that he so decries. This stems in good part from the second problem in his work, his theoretical understanding of the spiritual self from a psychoanalytic standpoint.

In the *Inner World*, Kakar states:

> . . . real knowledge is only attainable through direct primary process of thinking and perception . . .
>
> — *Ibid.*, p. 107

> In the Hindu ideal, reality is not primarily mediated through the conscious and preconscious perceptions, unconscious defenses, and logical rational thought processes that make up the ego; it emanates from the deeper and phylogenetically older structural layer of personality — the id, the mental representation of the organism's instinctual drives. Reality, according to Hindu belief, can be apprehended or known only through those archaic, unconscious preverbal processes of sensing and feeling.
>
> — *Ibid.*, p. 20

The primary process, perhaps Freud's most original discovery, constitutes symbolic processes essential to dreams and in various degrees to artistic creativity. Visualization, itself, is sometimes used in spiritual disciplines. But to what extent the primary process constitutes spiritual knowing is highly questionable. It is Kakar's inaccurate use of Freudian psychoanalytic concepts as a Procrustean Bed to encompass psychological processes involved in spiritual realization that results in his reverting to traditional psychoanalytic reduction-ism in his analyses of the spiritual self.

His theoretical understanding of mysticism shifts from the use of the primary process in the *Inner World* to current psychoanalytic relational theories in *The Analyst and the Mystic*. Kakar in this latter work fully accepts the reductionistic psychoanalytic premise that spiritual experiences and motivation are esentially a regression to the preverbal, symbiotic experiences of the mother-child relationship.

> The vicissitudes of separation have been, of course, at the heart of psychoanalytic theorizing on mysticisim. The yearning to be reunited with a perfect, omnipotent being, the longing for the blissful soothing and nursing associated with the mother of

> earliest infancy . . . has been consensually deemed the core of mystical motivation
>
> — Kakar 1991, p. 29

Only Kakar puts a more positive spin on this regression inas much as he sees the mystic as able to effect a deeper regression than that which occurs in psychoanalysis to repair what Kakar deems is the essential depressive core of life; and in Winnicottian terms, the mystic is involved in a creative experiencing through this regression to infancy. Kakar then bends Lacan to support this view by distorting Lacan's concept of the *Real* (pers. com. Paola Mieli, a Lacanian psychoanalyst) (*Ibid.*, p. 27). Thus, although Kakar claims to transcend the classical psychoanalytic model of viewing the spiritual as pathological, defensive or compensatory, he remains fully trapped in a more sophisticated reductionism involving regression to early childhood.

* * * * * *

The latest foray into the investigation of spirituality and psychopathology is Jeffrey Kripal's *Kali's Child: The Mystical and the Erotic in the Life and Teachings of Ramakrishna* (1995). Kripal comes to the subject from the discipline of religion but freely uses psychoanalysis, although acknowledging he has no training in it and is only oriented toward Freud's early work on the drives. Similar to Kakar, he abjures the psychoanalytic tradition of psychopathologizing mysticism while remaining fully within it in his actual analyses of Ramakrishna's motivation.

Kripal in hermeneutical textual analyses of what was written about Ramakrishna by his devotees advances two major thesis that he interweaves through dialectical thinking. The first is that Ramakrishna was far more of a tāntric than his disciples publicized to the world. The second is his assertion of Ramakrishna's homosexual conflicts — including sexual abuse from his *gurus* and others, and his trying to sexually abuse his teenage male disciples — that he tried to alleviate through worship of Kālī and tāntric practices, and that both structured and constituted his mystic experiences.

> In short, I will argue that Ramakrishna was a conflicted, unwilling, homoerotic *Tāntrika* who was as skilled at refashioning and realizing the meanings of the Hindu Tantra as he was uncomfortable in its symbolic world.
>
> — Kripal 1995, p. 3

In the Conclusion, Kripal asserts,

> These homoerotic energies, in other words, not only shaped the symbolism of Ramakrishna's mysticism; they were his mysticism. Let me be very clear: without the conflicted energies of the saint's homosexual desires, there would have been no Kali's sword, no unconscious Handmaid, no conflict between the Mother and the Lover, no child, no Radha, no living *lingam*, no naked *paramahaṁsa* boys, no Jesus state, no love-body, no ecstatically extended feet, no closing and opening doors, no symbolic visions, no *bhāva*, and no *samādhi*. In effect, there would have been no "Ramakrishna." The erotic, then *was* Ramakrishna.
>
> — *Ibid.*, p. 322

There is much that is plausible in Kripal's first thesis that Ramakrishna was much more of a tāntric than his devotees and disciples publicized to the world. It would have been helpful putting this in a socio-historical context that Swami Vivekananda and other disciples might well have downplayed Ramakrishna's involvement in Tantra and advanced Advaita Vedānta monism to counter the British colonial/missionary denigration of Hinduism in general and of Tantra in particular as the epitome of depravity.

Kripal's adamant assertion of Ramakrishna's overriding homoerotic and homosexual conflict is far more problematic. What happens in Kripal's actual analyses of the texts? I shall address three basic problems in Kripal's thinking and approach from a psychoanalytic viewpoint and leave his religious analysis, which comprises the greater part of the book, to others more competent.

The first is a facile decoding of the unconscious from textual sources, together with an equally facile use of primary process of symbolization of culturally imbued symbols, such as Kālī's sword and Kṛṣṇa's flute. Although facile decoding has been the bane of applied psychoanalysis, Kripal seems unaware of just how highly speculative and inconclusive such an approach is. Throughout the book, speculative decoding readily becomes strong assertions of fact, and these assertions soon become adamant conviction.

I shall cite one simple example out of many of Kripal's facile decoding of Ramakrishna's unconscious, where Kripal interpretively privileges regression and psychopathology over spiritual aspirations. Kripal discusses Ramakrishna becoming intensely involved in the worship of Kālī after his older brother's death, who had been a father-figure to him after his father's earlier demise.

> It was at this time that Ramakrishna turned to Kālī, the divine mother, and sought her 'vision' (*darśana*). He could not eat. He could not sleep. . . . He could barely breathe, so great was his desire.

Kripal then cites Datta,

> His state at this time was like that of a boy nursing at its mother's breasts. When one looked at Ramakrishna, one immediately thought of an infant who cannot see its mother and so cries 'Ma! Ma!' and will not be consoled.
>
> — pp. 61-62

Kripal then interprets Ramakrishna as regressing to infancy because of having been denied a father-figure with his brother's death. A psychoanalyst could just as easily interpret that with the death of Ramakrishna's older brother, Ramakrishna was now much freer to be completely involved in his intense worship of Kālī without interference from his brother, as had previously occurred. Or that confronted with death, from a Rankian perspective, he became even more motivated in his spiritual search; or from a self-psychological one, he sought a more enduring self-object. Psychoanalytically, these follow from an appreciation of issues of the self, especially a self-driven by intense spiritual yearnings, rather than seeing all motivation as deriving from unconscious psychic conflict, in this case, anxiety and depression. However, all of these interpretations remain highly speculative. Nevertheless, Kripal always authoritatively asserts the regressive and psychopathological over any other motivation.

The second problem in Kripal's theorizing is his easily conflating *samādhi*,[5] ecstacy, and other spiritual states with unconsicous dissociated states involving repressed homoerotic feelings. This results from Kripal viewing both spiritual states of heightened consciousness and unconscious conflicts as deriving from a more general unconscious. This he simply defines as "a secret dimension . . . of the human person of which he or she is not aware" (p. 43). This does not really encompass psychoanalytic definitions of the unconscious, which usually involve both a repressed, conflictual dimension in which defensive functions predominate and primary process mechanisms of symbolization, such as in dreams, the two often being interrelated. Nor does it cover spiritual states of consciousness, where those experiencing them are usually quite self-aware. The joining together of spiritual states and unconscious conflicts is a highly speculative leap on Kripal's part.

Moreover, Kripal always privileges motivations stemming from the psychoanalytic repressed unconscious over those for spiritual realization; that is, the spiritual becomes deconstructed to unconscious motivation of a defensive nature, always centred around drive theory. All later models of psychoanalysis are conspicuous by their absence. Thus, Kripal sees Ramakrishna going

5. *Samādhi* is considered by Hindus to be the highest state of spiritual consciousness.

into an ecstatic trance as a defense against a supposed homosexual approach by his patron; or gaining a vision of the goddess, Kālī, as a defensive way of avoiding supposed conflicted homosexual feelings. Kripal does not invalidate Ramakrishna's spiritual experiences. In this he differs from the psychoanalytic tradition. He just sees Ramakrishna as attaining such experience through an avoidance of unconscious erotic conflicts.

The third problem in Kripal's use of psychoanalysis is his psychopathologizing the homoerotic, and then facilely equating the homoerotic with homosexuality. Kripal clearly does not understand the psychology of Indian men, especially the homoerotic. Homoerotic feelings in both Indian men and women are far more developed and accepted with much greater emotional and physical intimacy, and are much less conflicted and laden with anxiety and shame, than in most Euro-American men. Developmentally, Indian men have a much greater maternal-feminine identification than most Westerners because of prolonged symbiotic mothering from the mother and other women of the extended family.

Kripal bases his analysis of Ramakrishna's spiritual experiences as defending against deeply conflicted homoerotic feelings primarily on Ramakrishna's anxious dual desire for Kālī and later for his male disciples. Kripal sees the desire for the latter as being imbued with intense homoerotic feelings which are then seen as homosexual (pp. 79-82). He concludes that Ramakrishna's longing for a vision of Kālī must by textual connection be defensively motivated by conflicted homoerotic desires, or homosexuality. In Kripal's analysis, Ramakrishna threatens suicide with Kālī's sword as an unconscious self-castration to defend against his homosexuality, and which then leads to a much longed for spiritual vision of Kālī. Yet, Kripal offers no evidence that Ramakrishna was in the least conflicted over his yearning for male disciples, or had any anxiety or shame when these gifted teenage boys came to him as a *guru*. It is understood within the Hindu religious tradition that a spiritual person of Ramakrishna's stature would intensely seek and need committed disciples to carry on his teachings (personal communication from Owen Lynch, a South Asian anthropologist). To chalk this up as conflicted homoerotic longings, or homosexuality, on Ramakrishna's part is once again to speculatively privilege the psychoanalytic unconscious over the spiritual.

Ramakrishna's identifying with Radha[6] in his devotion to Kṛṣṇa has been cited as an another piece of evidence of Ramakrishna's homoeroticism and homosexuality by Kripal. Yet, this is a common practice of thousands of Hindu men over the last few centuries. They draw upon their strong identification with the maternal/feminine for this kind of spiritual devotional practice. Again, the spiritual is deconstructed to a pathologizing unconscious motivation. Conjectures, innuendos and intimations of Ramakrishna's homosexuality being cited without any real evidence are all too common throughout the book.

In conclusion, Kripal's promise of a fertile dialectic between psychoanalysis and the spiritual cultures of Ramakrishna is largely vitiated by his continuously following an old narrative of psychoanalytic reductionism. Perhaps the greatest contribution of the book is the central question it raises over the relationship of the spiritual self to psychopathology, recognizing both to be valid in their own right.

Theoretical Reflections and Clinical Observations

Until very recently, psychoanalytic work on the spiritual self and psychopathology has originated almost entirely in the field of applied psychoanalysis, that is, from textual analyses such as Kakar and Kripal have made. Within the last 10 years or so, other work

---

6. Rādhā, a female cowherd, stands for the individual soul who is passionately in love with Kṛṣṇa, the Godhead. The two are depicted together in the Purāṇas, and in a great deal of Indian devotional art, dance, song and drama.

has emerged on patients in psychoanalytic therapy who are deeply involved in spiritual practices (Roland 1988, 1996; Rubin 1996), and on psychoanalysts and psycho-analytic therapists who are themselves involved in Buddhist meditation (Coltart 1992, 1996; Cooper 1996, 1997; Finn 1992; Rubin 1996; and Suler 1993). It is now possible to comment much more directly on the relationship of the spiritual self to psychopathology from clinical and personal observations.

I shall state my own point-of-view on this subject from observations both clinically and socially, I see the spiritual self and psychopathology as being on two separate continua that can intersect and interact with each other in complex ways. One can posit that everyone has an underlying spiritual self with an everyday phenomenological self. The continuum of the phenomenological self has persons ranging from severe forms of psychopathology on one end, who can make a shambles of their life, or at the very least, make life difficult for those around them, to mature, sensible and sensitive, persons on the other end who function well in their relationships and work, and who have a good sense of self. Persons who have completed a successful psychoanalysis have often moved into this latter category. The great majority of persons are somewhere in the middle, often functioning relatively well in everyday life but with emotional problems that can sometimes significantly affect themselves and others. This range of normality-psychopathology has been the domain of psychoanalysis in its understanding of the complexities of the everyday, phenomenological self, with its dialectic between conscious and unconscious functioning and motivation. How emotional problems surface and what their nature is can vary considerably from one culture to another, as do ideals of mature functioning.

The other continuum ranges from persons who are not in the least interested in any spiritual quest, indeed having little if any awareness of their spiritual self, probably a great majority of humankind; to the other end of the continuum where there are great spiritual figures, such as Gandhi, Ramakrishna and Swami Vivekananda, who have been previously discussed. In this continuum there is a minority of persons interested in the possibility of realizing their spiritual self, and a still smaller number seriously involved in spiritual practices. Here, too, culture plays a major role in the extent to which great spiritual figures are esteemed, and in what ways everyday life can be lived so as to enhance the spiritual development from grosser to finer qualities.

How do these two continua intersect and interact with each other? Obviously, there are spiritually evolved persons who are also mature and sensible; and there are self-aware, mentally healthy persons who are involved in spiritual pursuits. But not necessarily. There are many mature, mentally healthy persons I have known who are not in the least interested in any spiritual search. Perhaps one can say that they have finer qualities that are closer to the spiritual. But they seem to have little or no interest in realizing their spiritual self.

By the same token, there are those deeply involved and committed to spiritual disciplines, some with very intense spiritual experiences, who may have serious, unresolved emotional problems that adversely affect their relationships with others. I can state this with some certitude from having several such patients, both Indian and Euro-American. This is also confirmed by studies of major Buddhist teachers in the United States from both the Zen Buddhist and Tibetan Buddhist traditions, as well as an occasional Indian *svāmī*. A few have evinced clear emotional disturbance ranging from alcoholism and drug abuse to sexually seducing disciples to absconding with monies.

It makes considerable sense that spiritual persons can have unresolved emotional problems. They, too, have a phenomeno-logical self, one that psychoanalysis has clearly shown to be deeply influenced by the vicissitudes of familial relationships. As even the greatest spiritual figures have physical illnesses and eventually die, they also have grown up in a family and can be adversely affected by disturbed familial relationships. It is interesting to note that in a discussion with two Indian psychiatrists, both psychotherapists who are very deeply involved in their own spiritual practices, they found the notion of spiritually evolved persons having their own emotional problems to be totally compatible (personal communication from Dr. S. Ravi Kapur and Dr. Usha Sundaram, now Swami Dharmakeerti).

To consider further the interface of the spiritual self and psychopathology, one has to differentiate how this takes place in cultures as different as India and the United States. In a culture of individualism in the North American societies, compared to India and other Asian countries, the person is much more on one's own, has to create one's own identity and actualize one's individuality in the social and work world, has to be self-directed in making a plethora of major and minor decisions, and has to be verbally expressive and assertive in implementing one's choices; conversely, the person is far less embedded and emotionally enmeshed in extended family and/or work group hierarchical relationships with their well-defined social etiquette and obligations as is true of those from Asian societies.[7] As a result, personal psychopathology makes a much greater difference in one's life in the United States, and must be taken much more into account in order to function well in life. It is no wonder that there are a plethora of psychotherapists in the United States for large numbers of people to aid them in the task of living.

In India, for instance, my impression is that the extended family tries to contain the psychopathology of any given member, while still being affected by that person. Thus, whatever psychopathology a given *guru* may have in India may count far less since it will often be contained within a well-ordered social etiquette. It may

7. While there are important gender differences in all of these societies, I believe this broad cross-cultural outline still holds up.

well be that the Asian spiritual teachers who then come to the United States are sometimes adversely affected by living in social relationships much freer and less supportive with different value systems and ways of relating than in their own societies.

A profound bifurcation in modern societies must also be taken into account that refuses to address the spiritual self and psychopathology simultaneously. As discussed above, an enlightenment legacy in Euro-American cultures demystifies religion and spirituality, and as inherited in psychoanalysis, relegates them to regressive experiences or psychopathology. In psychoanalysis, psychopathologizing patients involved in a spiritual quest can easily lead the latter in Western societies to a disavowal of the spiritual (Cooper 1996), or in India to keeping their spiritual practices and experiences secret from the therapist (Roland 1988, p. 158).

On the other hand, there has been a long-standing denigration and dismissal of psychoanalysis and other psycho-therapies by Asian spiritual teachers, and some North American ones in the Asian traditions, as not dealing with fundamental spiritual issues. More recently, there are exceptions to this in North America of spiritual teachers, some from Vedānta, others from Buddhist and Sufism, who have sent troubled aspirants for therapy while still continuing their spiritual practices. Thus, from both sides of the divide, there seems to be a beginning coming together where both the spiritual self and psychopathology are simultaneously addressed.

Interface of Spiritual Practices and Psychopathology

An important question arises as to what extent the spiritual practices and experiences can mitigate or resolve unconscious conflicts and deficits. Current observations are that the ongoing involvement in various forms of meditation, prayer, rituals and other spiritual practices can certainly have a calming effect, making a person more self-aware even to the point of realizing some conflicts that have been unconscious, and in general have a centering, stabilizing influence. However, from my own observations with Indian and Euro-American high functioning patients involved in spiritual disciplines (Roland 1988, 1966), and supported by other psychoanalysts in the field (Coltart 1992; Cooper 1998; and Rubin 1996), long standing unconscious conflicts and/or deficits in the self cannot be really resolved by spiritual practices although they may be ameliorated. Coltart (1992) notes that a number of Westerners with significant emotional problems gravitate toward meditation when psychoanalytic therapy would be more to the point, at least in resolving these problems. Rubin cites persons who in part use Buddhist meditation in a variety of defensive ways, although he fully acknowledges that it can be helpful as well.

In what specific ways the spiritual practices can be used in defensive ways to avoid or cope with personal problems, and in what way it may have a healing effect, will depend a great deal on the particular psychology of the person involved. For example, one patient, John, with a strong tendency toward a schizoid flight from emotional intimacy to cope with a highly disturbed mother and a distant father, in earlier stages of a psychoanalysis used meditation in part as a way of avoiding personal relationships. Later on, as he began resolving difficult schizoid defenses, his meditation was helpful in facing this.

It has also been my observation, as well as that of others, that the unresolved psychopathology can seriously interfere with a person's involvement in their spiritual practices. I have cited Shakuntala's lack of discipline in her spiritual devotional practices because of psychological issues related to a depressed mother and an overly permissive father (Roland 1988, pp. 154-74); and Ashis's intense inner conflict over writing, which he considered his *sādhanā* or spiritual discipline, because of a highly problematic relationship with a deceased father (Roland 1988, pp. 25-47). For both my Indian and Euro-American patients, as they worked out their problems in psychoanalytic therapy or psychoanalysis, they became much more, not less involved in their spiritual practices. After not seeing Shakuntala for some 11 years, I asked her if her lack of discipline was still a problem in her frequency of spiritual practices, which she had earlier complained about. She replied that her *mantra* is now with her constantly, that she experiences God as light, at times more intense than the Sun. Coltart (1996) sees the necessity for a strong self to be necessary for those who are seriously involved in meditation. For those with severe psycho-pathology, there is a possibility of a mental breakdown or an aggravation of their emotional disturbance.

I have sometimes seen the spiritual self and psychopathology co-exist in complex ways in patients seen in psychoanalytic work. A Catholic nun, Margaret, had on rare occasions what seemed to be genuine, intense spiritual experiences. On the other hand, by the time she came to see me for long-term psychoanalytic therapy, she had developed intensely antagonistic relationships with some important nuns, who severely marginalized her in the Order. These relationships were gradually understood to be transference and repetitions of rejecting childhood relationships with sadistic older siblings and her mother. As we carefully analysed in what ways she had unconsciously contributed to this debacle with the other nuns, some of whom seemed truly disturbed in their own right, her spiritual practices proceeded unabated, and in fact seemed to deepen. As she resolved more of her knotty emotional problems and ways of alienating others, her retreats and pilgrimages became far better attended, and she was eventually elected to be one of the leaders of the Order.

In another complex interaction of the spiritual and the psychopathological, Alice from a conventional Protestant, Mid-Western American family, had gravitated to the *āśrama* of an Indian *guru* known both for his spirituality and for sexual licentiousness in his *āśrama*. By the time Alice saw me in psychoanalytic therapy, she had long since left the *āśrama*, but was still involved in her spiritual practices. We gradually understood that because of a childhood background of prolonged sexual abuse from an uncle who lived with the family, she had unconsciously gravitated to an *āśrama* where sexual abuse to her could and did occur. Again, this is not to negate her spiritual aspirations, or even what the *guru* and the *āśrama* had positively contributed to her; but rather to see how the *āśrama* experience became intertwined with the unconscious repetition of a childhood relationship involving sexual abuse.

Then there was an Indian patient, Pradeep, with profound problems many of which originated in a dysfunctional family where his mother went far beyond normal Indian symbiotic mothering to have him totally enmeshed with her. Intense transference reactions of rage in part enabled him to individuate himself and not feel so controlled by me in the transference. But his gradual involvement in meditation also helped this individuation process.

Psychoanalysts, involved in spiritual disciplines such as meditation report greater intuitive awareness and clearer perceptions of what they sense, are more in touch with subtle affects and attitudes of patients and with subtle induced counter-transference reactions in themselves, resonate more empathically than before with patients, and are more spontaneous in sessions. Cooper (1999) views some of the process of psychoanalysis as similar to Buddhist analytic meditation in focusing on a patient's and/or the analyst's affect states and staying with the experience. The end goal is different inasmuch as the analyst does this to understand what is unconsciously motivating the patient; whereas the Buddhist meditators focus on their affect states to gradually understand that all such states are transitory. Still another psychoanalytic stance similar to meditation is Bion's (1970) concepts of being and listening to patients, without preconceptions, memory of what has previously taken place in sessions, or any desire for change. In other words, it is to dwell fully in the moment. Others such as Rubin (1996) have related psychoanalyst's evenly hovering attention to the Buddhist mindfulness. Thus, there is an increasing effort to relate meditation and its self-transformation to the actual work of the psychoanalyst in the psychoanalytic process.

Summary

Those who have laboured in the field of applied psychoanalysis have continued to the present to follow in the same furrows of classic psychoanalytic reductionism in grounding spiritual experiences and aspirations as regressive and/or psychopathological. This continues to be true of the work of Sudhir Kakar and to a great extent of Jeffrey Kripal on major Indian spiritual figures, however much they decry the psychoanalytic tradition on this issue. New work is now emerging in the area of the spiritual self and psychopathology from clinical observations of patients in psychoanalytic work who are involved in a longterm practice of one or another spiritual discipline, and from a few psychoanalysts involved in Buddhist meditation. It is from this group that the complex interaction of the spiritual self and psychopathology is first beginning to be written about, differing substantially from the speculative analyses of textual material in applied psychoanalysis.

References

Bion, W., 1970, *Attention and Interpretation*, New York: Basic Books.

Coltart, N., 1992, "The Practice of Psychoanalysis and Buddhism," in *Slouching toward Bethlehem*, pp. 164-75, New York and London: Guilford Press.

———, 1996, "Buddhism and Psychoanalysis Revisited," in *The baby and the Bathwater*, pp. 125-40, London: H. Karnac Ltd., New York: International Universities Press.

Cooper, P., 1998, The disavowal of the Spirit; Integration and Wholeness in Buddhism and Psychoanalysis. In: *The Couch and the Tree: Dialogues in Psychoanalysis and Buddhism*, ed. A. Molino, New York: North Point Press, pp. 231-46.

———, 1999, Buddhist Meditation and Counter Transference: A Case Study, *American Journal of Psychoanalysis*, 59: 71-86.

Erikson, E., 1969, *Gandhi's Truth*, New York: W.W. Norton.

Finn, M., 1992, "Transitional space and Tibetan Buddhism: The object relations of meditation," in *Object relations theory and religious experience*, ed. M. Finn and J. Gartner, New York: Praeger.

Freud, S., 1927, *The future of an illusion*, Standard Edition, 21: 5-56, London: Hogarth Press.

———, 1930, *Civilization and its discontents*, Standard Edition, 21: 64-145, London: Hogarth Press.

Fromm, E., D.T. Suzuki, and R. DeMartino, 1960, *Zen Buddhism and psychoanalysis*, New York: Harper and Row.

Horney, K., 1945, *Our inner conflicts*, New York: W.W. Norton.

Kakar, S., 1978, *The inner world: A psychoanalytic study of childhood and society in India*, Delhi: Oxford University Press.

———, 1989, *Intimate relations: Exploring Indian Sexuality*, Chicago: University of Chicago Press.

———, 1991, *The analyst and the mystic: Psychoanalytic Reflections on Religion and mysticism*, New Delhi: Viking by Penguin Books India.

Kelman, H., 1960, "Psychoanalytic thought and Eastern wisdom," in *The history of psychotherapy*, ed. J. Ehrenwald, pp. 328-33, New York: Jeason Aronson.

Kripal, J., 1995, *Kali's child: The mystical and the erotic in the life and teachings of Ramakrishna*, Chicago: University of Chicago Press.

Masson, J.M., 1976, "The psychology of the ascetic," *Journal Asian Studies*, 35: 611-25.

———, 1980, *The oceanic feeling: The origins of religious sentiment in ancient India*, Dordrecht, Holland: D. Reidel.

Meissner, W.W., 1984, *Psychoanalysis and religious experience*, New Haven and London: Yale University Press.

Milner, M., 1973, "Some notes on psychoanalytic ideas about mysticism," in *The suppressed madness of sane men*, 1987, London: Tavistock Publications.

Rizzuto, A., 1979, *The birth of the living God: A psychoanalytic study*, Chicago: University of Chicago Press.

Roland, A., 1988, *In search of self in India and Japan: Toward a cross-cultural psychology*, Princeton: Princeton University Press.

———, 1996, *Cultural pluralism and psychoanalysis: The Asian and North American experience*, New York and London: Routledge.

Rubin, J., 1996, *Psychotherapy and Buddhism: Toward an Integration*, New York and London: Plenum Press.

Sudarshan, G., 1994, *Science as saksi bhava*, Keynote Address, Fifth International Conference on Vedanta, Miami University, Oxford, Ohio.

Suler, J., 1993, *Contemporary psychoanalysis and Eastern thought*, Albany, New York: State University of New York Press.

Symington, N., 1994, *Emotion and spirit: Questioning the claims of psychoanalysis and religion*, London: Cassell.

11

Recontextualizing Indian History
A Hermeneutic of Saṁskṛtikaraṇa

Shrinivas Tilak

I

Introduction

THIS paper has a two-fold objective: firstly, it introduces a new mode of historiography that is securely rooted in the cultural and hermeneutic tradition of India. This step is warranted because even today, in independent India, historiography continues to be dictated by orientations to history that are essentially discontinuous with the culture and tradition of India. The central paradox of human existence according to the Indian tradition is this: on the cosmic scale the duration of life is insignificant. Yet this brief passage of time marked by human existence is the source of all reflection of any significance. The disparity between the lived time and cosmic time is the source of all human pain and suffering. Yet, it is also the very foundation of all religious and philosophical thought that seeks relief from pain and suffering. The solution to this paradox is offered in the Indian tradition's view of history and the role it is expected to play in the affairs of humans. History divests cosmic time of its terror and tyranny and thereby redeems and humanizes it.

Yet, as a conquered and colonized civilization, India and Indians have had to acquiesce to the invader's sense and meaning of history which was essentially centred on power relations between the victors and the vanquished which are carefully preserved in official documents. It narrated what took place on the battlefield and in the succession of dynasties that occupied the throne at Delhi or elsewhere. These documents signalled a dividing line between history and fiction. The record of what Indians themselves thought or felt to have taken place was deemed to be an ornate narrative in much the same way that metaphor is regarded as an ornament of poetic discourse. The ways in which the feelings, perceptions and narratives of Indians influenced or were influenced by the catastrophic events they experienced are largely absent from extant versions of Indian history.

Secondly, this paper outlines a hermeneutic abstracted from indigenous cognitive categories with a view to facilitate Indianization and humanization of history by recontextualizing it to the culture and tradition of India so that history can fulfil its traditionally assigned role: an instrument of *dharma*. According to N.A. Nikam the maxim that is universalized as a categorical imperative in Indian culture is "Be" which, in practice, means "Become." He paraphrases it to mean, "So be that the Universal Law acts through you" (Nikam 1973: 25-26). Indian culture recommends *dharma* (Universal Law) as a foundational categorial imperative to fulfil the ultimate goal of life (*mokṣa*). History (*itihāsa*) has traditionally been regarded as one instrument of knowing *dharma*, and through it, accomplishing *mokṣa*.

This perspective, however, need not preclude us from seeking common ground on which Indian and Western views of history can be understood as commensurable, even though their cultural contexts are different. A Russian proverb quoted by Solzhenitsyn in the *Gulag Archipelago* would be useful to remember in this context:

> Dwell on the past and you will lose one eye . . . forget the past and you'll lose both eyes.

There is thus an urgent need to determine and recover whatever is worthwhile in India's own cultural heritage so that vision in at least one eye is saved. Second, the vision to the other eye can be restored by selectively incorporating insights from non-Indian sources to foster a composite tradition that is free from distortions (deliberate or accidental) and meaninglessness. Since the principal task of hermeneutics is to discover what is common even in what is different, Paul Ricoeur's reflections on narrative and history will be extended to determine a proper role and meaning of history in the Indian tradition. The central intuition of Paul Ricoeur's philosophical anthropology is that human existence as being is meaningful. In direct contrast to Sartre, his philosophy is characterized by hope and a positive attitude toward life. Human being *is* possibility and human existence is "forward-oriented," i.e., constantly projecting itself toward a possible way of being. Possibility is thus intimately connected to creative imagination which projects it, and to time, specifically the modality of future. This dimension of human existence is brought out in language (particularly in metaphor and narrative) and in action. Ricoeur's philosophy seeks to understand human being by answering the question "what does it mean to be human?" and thereby to achieve self-understanding (Who am I?). But the meaning of human being is gained only through interpretation of human action which attests to human existence. My existential possibility is guided by the ways of living and being (learnt from one's tradition, i.e., history, literature, myths) (Vanhoozer 1990: 7).

It is also essential to remember in this context that this paper is a product of the confrontation with the history of India as it is available now with this interpreter's own horizon of meaning, which again, is defined jointly by his nurturing and enculturation by the Indian heritage and his academic career shaped by over forty years of residence in Canada. No interpreter approaches his/her subject-matter as a *tabula rasa*; a certain horizon of expectations — of beliefs, practices, and norms comprise one's life-world. My personal horizon has been shaped by a conviction that as India stands on the threshold of the beginning of the third millennium, there is an urgent need to launch a historically significant project of creating a unified cultural identity anchored in common history and tradition.

II

Extant History of India: Imperial, Secular, and Subaltern Versions

The nearest equivalent term for history in India's composite culture is *itihāsa*, which expresses the sense of "thus it was" or "so it has been." Additionally, it also incorporates the sense of legend and myth. The purpose of compiling *itihāsa* is to reinterpret the exploits of great heroes and other significant events of the past in such a manner as would relate them to contemporary goals and purposes. To that extent writing and studying history is perceived to be a legitimate hermeneutic enterprise for overcoming cultural alienation and distanciation. This traditional perspective and understanding of history is absent from the various extant "official" versions of the history of India that began to be sponsored and written by the invading victors from the beginning of the second millennium. It is, therefore, not surprising to find that the status of history as an academic discipline is ranked relatively low in today's India. The majority of the Indian population today, in fact, is led to believe that their tradition does not have historical consciousness worth speaking. Consequently, Indians on the whole feel alienated from their culture and heritage.

Motivated by the dream of building an empire and holding on to it, British colonial adminstration generated a version of the history of India to suit its own colonial agenda. In the process, Indian history was totally decontextualized and discontinued from its tradition. Even though the positivistic assumptions appear to be dying a natural death among today's historians, empiricism was strong during the heyday of the British Empire when much of the history of India was formalized and was given a concrete shape and respectability. The empiricist understanding of history was based on the scientific notion of time as a straight line. It was constituted by succession of abstract "nows," and by distinguishing the intervals between them. These two sets of relations were sufficient for defining *when* something happened, for deciding what came *earlier* or *later* and *how long* this or that dynasty lasted.

Another deficiency of this historiography was that it took into account neither the centrality of the present as an *actual now* nor the primacy of the future as the main orientation of human desire. The fundamental capacity of recollecting the past in the present was also ignored. Most scholars felt at home with the task of sifting "documents" of history rather than "works," i.e., repositories of contextual information and insights that inevitably coalesce around documents. The empiricist outlook produced a major dichotomy by distinguishing history from fiction; i.e., between "documents" which are *true* because they are empirically verifiable or falsifiable and fiction whose claims cannot be corroborated by hard facts and evidence. The prevailing notion of a single or unique history of nation states further complicated the matter. Until the eighteenth century, even in the West, the concept of history was a plural one; one referred to "histories" not history with a capital *H* (Valdes 1991: 476).

Nationalist leaders and thinkers, eager to throw off the yoke of colonialism, commissioned or edited their own versions of history to glorify the past of India and her achievements to prove that India deserved to be free and that she was able to manage her own affairs. This version of historiography is similar to Nietzsche's "Monumental history," which stems from learned culture. Even if it is written by enlightened minds, claimed Nietzsche, monumental history is addressed to men and women of action and strength, to combatants in search of models, teachers and comforters that cannot be found among their associates or contemporaries (the volumes edited by R.C. Majumdar is one example). The secret vice of monumental history is that it misleads through the force of analogy by equalizing differences and by dispersing disparities (cited in Ricoeur 1988 3: 237). By giving primacy to the past, according to the canons of historiography established by their former colonial rulers, the nationalist historians in pre-Independent India failed to recognize that the retrospection towards the past can also be carried forward to the future as a project.

Nietzsche therefore makes a case for a third kind of history to serve life: critical history. Historiography in independent India, indeed, is concerned with critical history. Unfortunately, this concern has been coloured by secular and subaltern interests whose avowed purpose is to dislodge the hold of entrenched elitist groups on the history of India. In early decades of the twentieth century, Darwin's theory of evolution through natural selection and Marx's theory of evolution through class conflict had provided the impetus for rewriting history informed by these new insights. Intellectual roots of secular and subaltern scholarship may be traced to these insights.

Methodologically, modern Indian historiography has become a trendy and unwieldy mixture of Critical Social Scientific, Post-Structuralist, Anthropological and Linguistic approaches informed by insights of Habermas, Foucault, and Gramsci. Beginning in 1982, for instance, eleven volumes of articles have appeared under the series title *Subaltern Studies* edited by Ranjit Guha. The general thrust of these volumes is that there were two elite groups firmly entrenched in colonial India: (1) the European elites, comprised mostly of British capitalists, industrialists, plantation managers, financiers, merchants, the civil service, and missionaries; and (2) their subordinate Indian counterparts in these fields. According to Guha (1983), there was a third group which was recruited by the British and Indian elites to act as their henchmen at the local level in village India. This third group originally came from disenfranchized population but gradually managed to occupy a relatively elitist position and status. All others, according to Guha, could legitimately be identified as subalterns.

Gerald Larson finds the subaltern approach to be hampered by the old problem of self-referential paradox. "Western bourgeois thought" is challenged using the instruments of "rational Western scholarship." Their analysis depends upon the very paradigm they are attacking leading them into a *cul-de-sac* intellectually (1995: 307, n. 98). The same can be said of the secular approach. Notwithstanding their internal methodological differences, both secular and subaltern historians, however, join hands in roundly condemning historiography in modern India that aspires to remain continuous with the tradition by making use of the traditional myths and symbols as a product of "Hindu fundamentalism."

How can a distinct Indian historiography, that is not "fundamentalist" yet is *continuous* with tradition and employs indigenous cognitive categories, be developed and projected today? How can the voice of the subjugated and subaltern find legitimate expression in India's history? Potentialities have long existed both in the learned thought and in the perceptual and cognitive categories of everyday life and discourse in the Indian languages and world. But they have been neglected for centuries as competing intellectual theories of history and its interpretation were imposed by the colonial authority or were uncritically appropriated from the Western scholarship by modern Indian intellectuals who cannot yet shake off "orientalizing discourse." Madhav Deshpande, for instance, accepts an essentially orientalist characterization of *dharma* as timeless and ahistorical:

> Thus there was no history in a real sense. . . . We certainly do not know the real cause of Manu's failure to take note of the facts of Indian history as our modern historians perceive it. However, the historical impact of this "unhistoric history" has been quite significant. . . .
>
> The synchronic feeling of socio-religious unity was more important than the historical fact of diverse origins, and therefore, to serve a synchronic purpose, the synchronic unity had to be

projected back into history to the first acts of creation.

— cited in Larson 1995: 157.

But Deshpande does not clarify (1) what is "history in a real sense" and (2) how could Manu be conscious of what history means to "our modern historians?" The problem is, as a philosophical discipline of rational interpretation, hermeneutics of history has been firmly established in the West. But no comparable development has taken place with reference to India as Deshpande's comments reveal. One popular explanation accounts for this lacuna by suggesting that Indian history writing is somehow non-rational, non-textual, and mystical and hence devoid of the rigors of discriminating history from myth. Carl Jung's widely quoted article, "The Psychology of Eastern Meditation," may be taken as an illustration to delineate the bias and unavowed colonial stance, which was implicit in the nineteenth century Western scholarly encounters with the culture and historiography of India. Jung's logic seems to operate through the three stages:

(1) xenophobia tinged with xenophilia upon recognizing a virtue or merit in the native [Other] civilization and conceding some authority and recognition to it.

(2) appropriation of recognized virtue or quality to self and reclaiming ceded authority and recognition from the native's [Other's] civilization.

(3) categorically asserting differences from the native's (Other's) civilization and the mode of thinking and forging distance from it.

Similar operation is discernible in the motives, assumptions, interpretive devices and legacies of scholarly paradigms produced by the nineteenth and twentieth centuries' 'pioneering' historians of Indian art. Thus, Vincent Smith, Aurel Stein and Alfred Foucher aggrandized the significance of Greek and Roman influences on [Indian]-Buddhist art so that it came up [or down?] to a level of aesthetics acceptable to Western standards. It took Ananda

Coomaraswamy to admonish these scholars that Buddhist art cannot be understood unless approached within the context of [Indian]-Buddhist culture, intuitions and spiritual quests.[1]

In the last decade or two this situation has changed somewhat with the appearance of a number of edited monographs on the history or the tradition of hermeneutics in "South Asia." Contributors to a volume edited by Jefferey Timm (1992) acknowledge that in the past the Western scholars and academics tended to arrogate to themselves license for the ultimate act of cultural and exegetical imperialism, denying the right of interpretation to non-Western cultures and societies using their own cognitive categories. They imputed a static definition of non-Eastern traditions thereby implying that the traditional exegesis is nothing more than naïve, superficial and formulaic encounters with their own traditions. Often a text is called "apocryphal" not so much in virtue of its being so regarded within the tradition it is found but, rather, in virtue of the scholar's judgement (Kapstein 1989: 219).

Overlooking or ignoring instances of history and hermeneutics, the Indian tradition provides modern scholarship with the necessary rationale and space to develop "exegesis" (*lege* = agenda) of its own to engage in exegetical imperialism. There is certainly nothing wrong with this practice as long as it is acknowledged as such, and not portrayed either as *the* unique reading or as the 'official' views of the Indian tradition. In an insightful introduction Timm demands that the dubious practices and inherited presupposition that the Other is like us, must be removed. Western academics must stop valorizing their own methodological approaches and listen, instead, to the voice of indigenous exegetical traditions through in-depth analysis. We need to attend to the dynamics of relations that people have had with their texts in the

1. This line of interpretation was suggested by John Holt's (1997) review of *Curators of the Buddha: The Study of Buddhism under Colonialism* ed. Donald Lopez (1995). The reference particularly concerns the article by Luis Gomez in that collection.

context of their overall socio-cultural projects. The centrality of oral tradition and of recitation in its performative and aesthetic dimensions cannot be overemphasized in the Indian context (Timm 1992: 1-13). This approach is also echoed in Nikam's quotation (1973: 4) from Ananda Coomaraswamy:

> A faithful account of Hinduism might well be given in the form of a categorical denial of most of the statements that have been made about it, alike by European scholars and by Indians trained in our modern sceptical and evolutionary modes of thought.

III

Hermeneutics: Bridge between History and Fiction

Hermeneutics is a valuable aid in working out and understanding the intertextual relations that historians often overlook. Devising complementary hermeneutic strategies for appropriating history for the benefit of Indians using mainly Indian cognitive categories but supported by insights from the Western notions of hermeneutics and history, therefore, is a necessary task. But it is not enough or useful merely to draw on Western hermeneutic theory to supplement the Indian sources. It is necessary to plumb and probe into the very concept of hermeneutics as a bridge of discourse. The metaphor of bridge acts as a linking function which, among other things, brings together elements that are different — spatially or in other ways. The bridge is not a stable habitat, you are not expected to stand or stay on it for long periods. It is rather, "being on the way" (*unterwegs*) from somewhere to somewhere — a transport or a transition. It connects the past with the present and the future. It is passing from an old place to a new one or vice versa. The hermeneute's responsibility, Silverman (1994: 238-39) reminds us, is to be a *bridge*, to link ideas, concepts, points of view, and practices. The bridge can show how and why this or that terminus, and what they may represent, are different and why.

The purpose behind the bringing together of the historically unrelated ideas in a critical dialogue is to find a common ground on which the Indian and Western views of history can be reconciled. If the encounter between something alien and unfamiliar is that from where hermeneutics starts, then the enrichment of experience and knowledge in a mutual engagement of the Self and the Other, or what Hans Georg Gadamer calls "fusion of horizons," is the final destination it will lead to. The process of understanding is also a process of learning or self-development (*buildung*), in which the unfamiliar becomes familiar, adding to the repertory of our knowledge, and the alien is absorbed till it becomes part of ourselves (Longxi 1992: xiv). The form of hermeneutics of history that is proposed here need not be construed as of interest and value only as a refutation of the Western ethno-hermeneutic's claim to universality. A more fully developed Indian hermeneutics must take its place beside the Western hermeneutics. Together with the ethno-sciences of interpretations of other lands, Indian hermeneutics may provide better bases for the future claim of an expanded, multicultural set of interpretations to have that *universal* significance and value.

Interpretation is a key methodological tool of hermeneutics. This latter is an art of extending, stretching and enlarging the meanings of a tradition's core values preserved through its symbol system. Interpretation is indispensable to hermeneutics because the temporal gap often obscures or even distorts the meaning of the tradition by producing a chasm between a community and its heritage. The golden rule of all hermenutics, therefore, is that the interpreted object — whether action, phenomenon or reality — must be reflected in the interpretation. This implies that interpretation is mediation between the understanding of the interpreted reality and the understanding realized by the interpreter (Panikkar 1979: 10).[2] The challenge of hermeneutics is to transpose the message from its original historical context into

2. It is interesting to note that the *pres, pretis* of interpretation comes from the Sanskrit root *prath* (*prathati/prathate*) meaning to spread, stretch, scatter, extend, increase, enlarge (Panikkar 1979: 105).

the context of present-day readers or hearers so as to produce a similar impact on their selves as well as on their lives as it presumably did on the original hearers or readers. One of the aims of hermeneutics is to struggle against cultural distance. It is a struggle against the estrangement of meaning itself from the system of values in which that culture is founded.

Ricoeur on Narrative Forms: History and Fiction

The foregoing suggests that hermeneutics has an important role to play in the field of historical inter-subjectivity since it enables us to understand the relationships with our predecessors (past), contemporaries (present), and successors (future). A given tradition or historical transmission is normally mediated by the documents and monuments in which it has become fixated as left traces. A trace is a vestige left by the passage of a human being or an institution. It remains as a double status reminding us of the two levels of meaning of time: On the physical level, the trace is a mark that exists in the present. The historian can work on the "traces" of the past, a past that is now absent and inaccessible. However, when such documents and monuments have been destroyed by ravages of time or by wars of aggression and invasions and no trace or mark remains, hermeneutics must recruit the second, noetic level of meaning. This type of trace or mark is preserved in songs, narratives, myths, and legends.

The contemporary position in hermeneutics that lives up to this challenge and addresses it creatively is that of Paul Ricoeur. Taking his cue from Gadamer's *Truth and Method* (262-64), Ricoeur emphasizes that hermeneutics is essentially concerned with the vicissitudes of rival traditions to which we belong in a pluralistic society and culture strangeness. It must address their internal crises, their interruptions, their dramatic reinterpretations, and their schisms that introduce into the tradition as one instance of truth a "polarity of familiarity." Hermeneutics makes use of historiographical objectivity as a means for sifting through dead traditions or what may be taken as deviations from those traditions in which we no longer recognize ourselves. Here, a question is not of understanding better. It is enough, insists Ricoeur, to say that we understand in a different way, if we understand at all (Ricoeur 1988 3: 224).

Ricoeur's writings on history have continued to develop from his early essays compiled in the *History and Truth* up to the *Time and Narrative* (1984-88; 3 vols). The objects of history are the past actions that were recorded or that we can infer based on records and reports. The history we write is the history of those actions whose projects or results can be seen as akin to our own action. Like saga, all history is a narrative of events in which human thought and action play a dominant part. However, the traditional understanding of historical reference as correspondence to what happened in the past, believes Ricoeur, is ill-suited to the mediation of true claims of history and fiction. As Kevin Vanhoozer has observed, fiction cannot compete in the truth game if the real is defined in terms of correspondence to what once was, or to what actually happened. Histories and fictions do not correspond to, describe or 'imitate' human action. They remake or redescribe it by acting as interpretive grids through which to view human action (Vanhoozer 1990: 192).

In the *Time and Narrative* Ricoeur deals with the treatment of human time and the historicity of human existence in the form of narrative, which he considers the form of creative language par excellence. It also demonstrates a connection between the theory of the text, the theory of action, and the theory of history. A large part of volume three of *Time and Narrative* is concerned with developing the inter-connections observed between history and fiction as hermeneutic modes of narrative. It is also concerned to respond, "in what way is the ordinary experience of time, borne by daily acting and suffering, refashioned by its passage through the grid of narrative?" In response, Ricoeur brings together two problematics that are not usually connected: the epistemology of the narrative function and the phenomenology of time experience. The former takes for granted that narrative occurs in time, i.e., within a given temporal framework, and uncritically identifies it with the ordinary representation of time as a linear succession of abstract "nows."

The phenomenology of time-experience on the other hand overlooks the fact that the narrative activity provides a privileged access to the way we articulate our experience of time (human time). History attempts to reconcile lived time with cosmic time by fashioning two key inventions. The first "invention" is the use of the calendar. By relating days and events to the movements of the sun, the calendar integrates human actions into cosmic order and rhythms. Such mediation is creative in that history, both "cosmologizes" lived time and "humanizes" cosmic time. The second strategy is the use of the "traces" of the past. Because it belongs both to the empirical and existential order, the trace becomes the ultimate connector of cosmic time and lived time (Ricoeur 1988 3: 109-16). Narratives, on their part, present concrete possibilities for action bridging the two imaginative modes of history and fiction both individually and collectively. Ricoeur hopes that though operating under peculiar and particular constraints, such an interweaving of fiction and history can provide the possibility of refiguring time in human dimensions (Ricoeur 1988 3: 181).

Ricoeur next argues that both history and narrative fall under the genus of 'story.' A major presupposition of a 'poetics' of historical discourse is that fiction and history belong to the same class as regards their narrative structure. Writing is constitutive of the historical mode of understanding. History is intrinsically historiography. Citing Hayden White, Ricoeur defines history in a deliberately provocative way: a literary artefact (Ricoeur 1984 1: 162). As a general synonym for "imaginary configuration," fiction is an operation that is common to history and to the fictional narrative. Every configuration is feigned, i.e., not given in the materials arranged by the narrative. Fiction is similarly understood as the antithesis it forms with respect to true narrative (Ricoeur 1984 1: 267 fn.1). During the second half of the eighteenth century in Germany, points out Ricoeur, the term *Historie* gave way to *Geschichte*, which has the double connotation of (1) a sequence of events taking place and (2) the relating of events done or undergone, in other words, a two fold sense of actual history and told history (Ricoeur 1988 3: 209). "History," therefore, means both a particular discursive discipline (historiography) and that which this discipline is about (i.e., "history," actual happenings). It is significant that in French too, *une histoire* can mean either a supposedly factual account of past events or a mere fanciful tale. Telling history and being in history belong together. "We belong to history before telling stories or writing histories" (Ricoeur 1981: 294). History and fiction have a common referential aim: our "belonging to" history.

By revealing and emphasizing its narrative thrust, Ricoeur hopes to retrieve a temporal dimension in history by linking it with fiction as one genre of story. By linking fiction to history, on the other hand, he tries to rescue narrative from its understanding in chronic terms in the manner made fashionable by a structuralist like Levi-Strauss. By reclassifying history in this manner, Ricoeur seeks to break the grip of philosophers like Karl Gustave Hempel (1959) on it. Ricoeur is particularly opposed to the positivist version of history wherein the concepts of law, cause and explanation overlap and which also mark the triumph of the document over the monument. This is discernible in the central thesis of Hempel's article: "general laws" have quite analogous functions in history and in the natural sciences.

The fact is, Ricoeur points out, history is not a fully developed science. He introduces narrative criticism as a challenge to historical criticism in order to suggest that while the two methods understand authors and readers in different ways, both methods actually use the same author-text-reader model of communication. Results of the narrative critical method, believes Ricoeur, can be fruitfully incorporated into a historical-critical agenda although narrative criticism cannot ultimately evade historical inquiry and considerations. Narrativity is the mode of discourse through which the mode of being (Ricoeur calls it temporality after Heidegger) is brought to language. The temporality of the narrative is particularly discernible, argues Ricoeur, in the plot, which is defined as the deliberate structure (intelligible whole) that governs a succession of events in a story. Emplacement is a craftsmanship by which events and a succession of event are crafted by the narrator into a pattern to form a whole. Since the reader must 'follow' the story, it must possess 'followability.' The reader must understand the sequence and must experience the events narrated, by reacting to them and their challenges. They must pass through the story and follow it to its conclusion for it to be meaningful and to be understood.

Fictionalization of History

Ricoeur's thesis that history is a species of the genus of story is borne out by the fact that all traits attached to the story: (1) emplotment; (2) the configuration applied to the events and to the sequence of events; and (3) the sense of ending are applicable to the realm of history. The only distinction that one might draw between history and fiction is based on their referential quality. The most realistic hypothesis about history is that it reinscribes the time of narrative within the time of the universe. This is a 'realist' thesis in the sense that history locates its chronology on the scale of time common to what is called the 'history' of the earth, the 'history' of the living species, and the 'history' of the solar system (Ricoeur 1988 3: 181-82). While history claims to represent actual occurrences or what was once possible, fiction deals with what might be possible. As the narrative matrix, plot provides a common structure for both history and fiction. Just as novels choose a certain plot (intrigue) to fashion and order their material into a narrative sequence, so too the historians order or re-enact the events of the past guided by the ideology they adhere to. The historian seeks to place and think him/herself into a past action in order to discern the thought of the agent. All history, therefore, is the re-enactment of past thought in the historian's own mind.

In the contemporary Indian context such a procedure is evident in the "subaltern" rereading of history according to the Marxist model of the class struggle which champions the cause of the subalterns commonly described as the oppressed. Many secular historians of modern India also endorse this line of approach. The imaginary character of the activities that mediate and schematize the "trace" is evident in the intellectual works that accompany the historian's interpretation of remains, fossils, ruins, museum pieces or monuments. But Ricoeur cautions that once it is realized that the writing of history is not something added from outside to historical knowledge but is one with it, nothing prevents us from admitting as well that history imitates in its own writing the types of emplotment handed down by the literary tradition. If fused with history, fiction can carry history back to their common origin in the epic. More precisely, what the epic did in the sphere of the admirable, the story of victims does in the sphere of the horrible. Fiction, thus, is placed in the service of the unforgettables, which permits historiography to live up to the task of memory (Ricoeur 1983 3: 185).

Fictionalization of history is necessary, according to Ricoeur, because there are crimes that must not be forgotten, and there are victims whose suffering cries less for vengeance than for narration. In support of this thesis, Ricoeur refers to Hannah Arendt's fine analysis carried out in *The Human Condition* (1958) on the relation between narrative and action. In the face of fragility of all things human, narrative (1) uncovers the "who" of action; (2) exposes the agent in the public sphere; (3) confers a coherence deserving to be recounted; and (4) finally assures the immortality of reputation. Ricoeur, however, is careful to point out that Arendt does not separate those who suffer history from those who make it. She begins her chapter on action with a line from Isak Dinesen: "All sorrows can be borne, if you put them into a story or tell a story about them" (Ricoeur 1988 3: 320-21 fn 8).

Historicization of Fiction

On its part, fiction, too, offers features that are conducive to its historicization. Recounting something is like recounting as if it were past. Here, grammatical tense forms provide an infinitely more complex literary system to the narrator than the linear representation of time would suggest. Ricoeur accordingly argues that as narrative forms history and fiction mediate; they need each other. Each can accomplish its aim only by borrowing from the other because each must refigure time to make history meaningful.

It is because of its quasi-historical character that fiction can exercise its liberating function with respect to possible elements in the actual past which otherwise would remain hidden. Unfortunately, verisimilitude in fiction is often confused with a mode of resemblance to the real placing fiction on the same plane as history, which Ricoeur rejects. It is not when the novel has a direct historical or sociological role that it poses a problem with its verisimilitude. The true mimesis of action is to be found in the works of art least concerned with mirroring their times. The quasi-past of the narrative voice is then entirely different from the past of historical consciousness. It is identified with the probable in the sense of what might have been. What "could have taken place," is the object of poetry as opposed to history according to Aristotle. What "might have been" (the possible in Aristotle's terms) includes both the potentialities of the "real" past and the 'unreal' possibilities of pure fiction (Ricoeur 1988 3: 192).[3]

3. Sydney Hook has observed that we are more alive to the chances of the future because they are still before us. But the past too, even though it is over, is an exciting story of chances missed. If we seek understanding and not salvation from the past pages of history, we will not fail to recognize the might-have-beens of the past. Some of them may turn out as relevant to the chances of the future as a recognize mistake is to the successful action that follows it (Hook 1965: 134).

Historians, on their part, can determine the significance of various causes by imagining what would have happened if an event had not occurred. Both history and fiction have the potential and capacity to fuse the potentialities of the "real" past and the "not yet real" possibilities of the future. It is therefore only in the intersection of history and fiction (in the refiguration of time) that we discover or invent what Ricoeur calls "human time." It is that fragile mix where the representing of the past of history and the imaginative fiction can be joined against a background of the aporias of time (Ricoeur 1988 3: 189-91).

Historical consciousness can thus find its outward expression in a narrative mode: whether fictional or historical. History brings it to expression through documents, memoirs, letters, etc. The fictional narrative, on its part, brings potential and possible reality to expression by means of the reference (as the term is understood in Ricoeur's works). Historicity is created, as mentioned above, to the extent that we tell both stories and histories. Both history and fiction refer to *Geschehen* i.e., to "making history" by means of narrativity. What expresses itself in the form of the fiction and history as narrative is human existence and time as historicality, which then adds a new dimension (an original, equiprimordial dimension) to temporality.

Hermeneutic of Historical Consciousness

Ricoeur's reflections on history as presented above precipitate a paradox similar to that referred to in the beginning of the article: on the cosmic scale the duration of our life is insignificant, yet this brief lapse of time where we appear on the scene of the world is the very place from which proceeds every question of significance. All philosophical reflections on time only serve to deepen this paradox. The discontinuity between 'lived' time and 'cosmic' time is perceived and felt as the misery or terror of life. Humans, as a species are 'historical' in a unique sense. Only persons, argues Ricoeur, are conscious of past and future, memory and hope.

Without such historical consciousness, there would be no human being, no passion for the possible.

Ricoeur's proposed solution to this paradox is to "redeem the time" by making it human by gaining a historical consciousness. Ricoeur holds that expectations (future) and memories (past) are always criss-crossing and affecting the present. We thereby gain an awareness that the present is now a time "to do" something and to create a "historical present." For Ricoeur, to be conscious historically, explains Vanhoozer, is to be aware of being affected by the past but also of "making history." Ricoeur characterizes the historical present by the term "begin." The concept of beginning or doing implies that the world is not totally actualized, the world includes something "to be done by me." Finally, in giving us a historical consciousness, the narrative bestows an identity as well. Indeed, personal identity is inherently narrative in nature. Though the self is affected by history, it yet remains itself (Vanhoozer 1990: 103). Thus interpreted, Ricoeur's views on the narrative forms of history and fiction and the relationship between them would seem to facilitate a better understanding of the traditional Indian notion of *itihāsa* and *saṁskṛti*.

IV

Sanskrit and Prakrit: Building Blocks of Civilization

Ricoeur links historicality to narrativity by the notion of culture and heritage perserved textually in language. In his introduction to the collection of articles on the relationship between cultures and time edited by him, Ricoeur points out that most of the writers recognize that the sense of time and culture in a given tradition is conditioned by the language(s) and linguistic conventions operating in that tradition.[4] The manner in which a tradition internalizes modalities of its collective existence as well as its

4. *Les cultures et le temps*, Paris, Payot, 1975.

perceived limitations (as reflected in its behaviour patterns) is determined by its language/s. Here, grammarians play a decisive mediating role between language and tradition. Ricoeur observes that Sanskrit grammar and the system of its verb tenses, for instance, have been far more decisive in India's sense of time [and of history, we might add] than the Sanskrit vocabulary designating time. Sanskrit grammarians (Bhartṛhari, for instance) quite early acknowledged the reflexive nature and potential of language and the role it can play in the analysis of time on the basis of verbal tense structure of Sanskrit. Citing Raimundo Panikkar, Ricoeur points out that these features of Sanskrit grammar also played a unique role in India's spiritual preoccupation with trans-cending time (Ricoeur 1975: 21).

One can draw upon something that is transmitted from the past only in word and work. The resource of the tradition is drawn by going back into the past, by repeating the past, and by drawing on one's existential possibilities that were articulated in the past. But whereas Heidegger conceptualizes such repeated gleanings from the past (*wiederholung*) at the individual level, Ricoeur believes that this exercise is collective and is preserved culturally in a given civilization's symbols, metaphors, and myths. The historian gleans from the past what needs to be remembered, i.e., the cultural values that guide actions, the life of institutions, and the social struggles. Historiography turns this recovered cultural source material into critical inquiry using the power of language, narrative, and hermeneutics. What follows below, accordingly, develops the connection between Indian civilization and its dominant linguistic streams.

Noam Chomsky views language as a truly *natural* phenomenon, i.e., as an endowment "from nature." Language is a physical organ that is purported to be as innate as our ability to use our eyes. The speech faculty is determined by a set of "universal principles" present in the brain since birth with an inbuilt neurological generator of language structures that are subjected to culturally-specific "parameters" during infancy. Mind is abstract machine that continually manufactures strings of linguistic symbols on the basis of neurologically determined rules. The mind is programmed by nature to manipulate formal symbols which take on the structure of propositions in discourse or thinking and so generates thoughts. Cumulatively they constitute the brain's universal grammar — a neural system that manipulates symbols without considering what they might mean (Danesi 1994: 84-86).

The relation of thought and language is the fundamental premise for defining the nature of interpretation. Indian tradition sees language as playing a crucial role in human cognition and the structure of empirical knowledge. It is discernible in the theory of linguistic relativity formulated by Bhartr̥hari (*ca.* 500 CE), the foremost philosopher of language and grammar. "What does it mean to communicate through language?" Bhartr̥hari's answer is:

> There is no cognition in the world in which the word does not figure. . . . If this eternal identity of knowledge and the word were to disappear, knowledge would cease to be knowledge. . . . It is this [identity] which is the basis of all the sciences, crafts and arts.
>
> — *Vākyapadīyam* I: 123-25

Bhartr̥hari here is referring to creative linguistic potentialities and mediative abilities of language. Hermeneutics is involved in attempts to detect and describe these resources. One early attempt is to be found in the *R̥gveda* where the ultimate reality is alternatively conceptualized in linguistic terms as a productive principle and force of energy expressed as speech and is often personified as goddess (10:125; Vāc). For Bhartr̥hari, the phenomenal world and its operations are expressive of the primordial reality as word (*śabdabrahman*) — and the Veda is impregnated with it. Intertwined with word and language (*vāc*), consciousness (*caitanya*) is refracted in the fifty-two phonemes making it the primal linguistic matrix and model (*ādiprakr̥ti*) of both, the *devavāṇī* (language of addressing gods and a vehicle of spiritual quest) and the *lokavāṇī* (people's language of secular communication and exchange).[5] These two language streams are comparable to the two physical eyes with *vāc* acting as the "third eye."[6]

In course of time the two language streams blossomed into Sanskrit and Prakrit respectively (Deshpande 1971: 83). Like modern languages of computer science and artifical intelligence, Sanskrit was created and promoted deliberately to serve two *ad hoc* and practical purposes: (1) a spiritual and ritual *lingua franca*, a pure vehicle of communication with the world of gods and goddesses; and (2) a useful vehicle of communication as well as a bridge of discourse to speakers of Prakrit. As it evolved, Sanskrit was destined to act as the basis of India's collective identification. Prakrit, on the other hand, metamorphosed naturally and spontaneously into a variety of regional languages, which today are divided (quite arbitrarily) into "Indo-Āryan" and "Draviḍian" language families said to be prevalent in north and south India respectively. As opposed to Sanskrit, these languages are natural in that they are acquired and used instinctively and as a matter of course by hundreds of millions of Indians.

Aśvaghoṣa (*c.* 100 CE) was perhaps the first and most important figure in consciously promoting Sanskrit as a spiritual and cultural *lingua franca* in the ancient Indic world which then stretched from Afghanistan to Vietnam in the East and to Sri Lanka in the south. Early Buddhist scriptures were composed and preserved in Pāli and other Prakrit languages. Soon texts were also being composed

---

5. *na so'sti pratyayo loke yaḥ śabdānugamād ṛte*
anuviddham iva jñānam sarvam śabdena bhāsate
— Cited in Gachter 1983: 5 fn 7

6. In explaining an expression from the *Ṛgveda* (I.164.45 *catvāri vāc parimitā padāni*), Yāska observes that *vāc* is of four types — *ṛcaḥ, yajūṁṣī, sāmānī* and *vyāvahārikā* (*Nirukta* 13:9). Of these, first three are divine (*devatābhidhāna*) and the last human (*manuṣyābhidhāna*
— Cited in Deshpande 1971: 34-36

in what is known as "hybrid Sanskrit." With Aśvaghoṣa began the trend and practice of using elegant, Pāṇinian Sanskrit as a medium of both verbal and written communication. In the process Aśvaghoṣa changed the destiny of both Sanskrit and Buddhism by initiating a socializing process of enculturation which, centuries later, was labelled Sanskritization (obviously with considerable modifications, see below). Aśvaghoṣa's project shows how language is *inventive* despite the objective limits of grammar and codes which govern it. His masterful handling of the metaphorical and narrative resources of Sanskrit demonstrated how a language can always be rejuvenated for the benefit of all forms of linguistic usage. By the time of Kālidāsa (*c.* 600 CE) Sanskrit had become a dominant language that was studied and mastered consciously by the literati for the dual purposes for which it was intended. It, therefore, never was a dead language. It is living, as Coulson (1986: xix-xx) points out, because Indians have continued to choose it to formulate their ideas and ideals in it in preference to some other language. After Śaṅkarācārya (*c.* 700 CE) onward, though it remained an artificial and refined language, Sanskrit nevertheless flourished as a *living* language of inter-regional communication and understanding before being eclipsed first by Persian and then by English after the political conquest of India.[7]

Taking their cue from Bishop Caldwell, most modern Indologists and scholars erroneously identify only the so- called "north Indian languages" (Bengālī, Gujarātī, Hindī, Marāṭhī, etc.) with the Prakrit group and conclude that they are derived from Sanskrit. This group of languages is thought to be distinct from the so-called Draviḍian group of languages (Kannaḍa, Malayālam, Tamil and Telugu) which today are mostly spoken in the southern region of India. Yet the habit of recognizing two structurally

7. Communicative power of Sanskrit is reflected in the wealth of new terms that can be coined by employing more than twenty prefixes. From the verb *dhā*, for instance, the following words are derived: *vidhāna, nidhāna, samādhāna, paridhāna, ādhāna, vyavadhāna, saṅdhāna*, etc.

separate and independent language families ("north Indian" and "south Indian") disguises the fact that they have originated from one common source (*vāc, prakṛti*). This indigenous understanding receives support from one modern American anthropologist who has argued that most of the languages of India share certain common features which serve to differentiate them from the languages of other geographical areas:

> (M)odern Indo-Aryan languages are more similar to Dravidian languages than they are to other Indo-European languages. (Tyler 1973: 18-20)

Tyler concurs with the observation of a Russian scholar Andronov who contends that the convergence between Draviḍian and Indo-Āryan is the initial step in the formation of a new language family which will be neither Indo-Āryan nor Draviḍian. But there is no need to speculate for such a *new* language family because it already exists in the language family, known as Prakrit. Gumperz (1969) has demonstrated that code-switching among bilingual speakers of Marāṭhī and Kannaḍa involves only the simplest word-for-word translation. For Gumperz long and intimate contact between the speakers of languages originally belonging to different families has gradually eliminated the structural differences between their two languages. Though his observation is valid, Gumperz's premise is contestable. The structural convergence that he sees in Marāṭhī and Kannaḍa may be attributed to the fact that they both belong to the same family group — : [Prakrit] (Tyler 1973: 18-20).

Since the classical period, the relation between the two language streams of India — Sanskrit and Prakrit has remained one of reciprocal exchange and mutual reinforcement. The use of a past participle and a passive construction (more prevalent in Prakrit), for instance, occurs freely and frequently in classical Sanskrit. From popular speech patterns Sanskrit picked the use of various cases to represent certain "abstract" syntactic relationships. Instrumental or ablative case, for instance, is used to explain causality and etiology, dative to indicate purpose or motive, locative to indicate hypothesis, etc. The increasing use of nominal composition, prevalent in Prakrit, is another feature of classical Sanskrit. Because it did not occur to Pāṇini to prohibit usage in this manner, such popular features of Prakrit could be freely incorporated without contravening the rules of Pāṇinian grammar. Pāṇini, thus, could both be obeyed and bypassed in the interest of saving Sanskrit from extinction and thereby also helping to preserve and promote the cultural unity and heritage of India.

Ricoeur is appreciative of such liberties taken by poets and writers against the grammar, laws, and codes of language that regulate it. If the narrative order of language is replete with codes it is also capable, claims Ricoeur, of creatively violating them. The imagination is always working on the basis of already established laws and it is its task to make them function creatively, either by applying them in an original way or by subverting them; or indeed both — what Malraux calls "regulated deformation." The task of hermeneutics is to charter the unexplored resources of the to-be-said on the basis of the already-said (Valdes 1991: 470-71).

V

Saṁsṛtikaraṇa: Contextualizing History to Civilization

The concept of *saṁskṛtikaraṇa* (enculturation, making of civilization) is necessary to break down a pervasive and misleading dichotomy between (1) history and fiction and (2) between elite and popular or subaltern dimensions of culture that is operative in much contemporary scholarship on India. Civilizations constantly face the dilemma of mediating between the internal need for continuity and maintenance and the external threats and pressure to change and accommodate to new situations, which may be a condition for survival. Sometimes this dilemma is resolved through the creation of subcultures or subsects, which siphon off discontented elements into little groups or factions. Though such formations are at variance in certain respects to the mother civilization, they do not necessarily aim at overthrowing it. External aggressions, however, provide an impetus for countercultures to arise which are antagonistic to the mother civilization. It is then forced to fight for survival — a fight which is often successful, but only after major accommodations have been made by the mother civilization. Indian history has documented some of these battles.

Since any civilization strives towards totality it must cover as much of the participating subcultures' world of experience as it can. It is this comprehensiveness which accounts for its invisibility. Since civilization is ubiquitous, members take no notice of it. It really is a case of fish not being aware of water. Civilization constitutes members' total environment and ethos, and so becomes invisible — they cannot get away from it and examine it as the significant Other. The composite Indian cultural ethos and consciousness is grounded in the ongoing process and phenomenon of "enculturation" (*saṁskṛtikaraṇa*) which was and is being driven by the two forces of Sanskritization and Prakritization. In the Indian social scientific and academic milieu, Sanskritization is a much better known and accepted concept (thanks to the works of M.N. Srinivas see below). However, Prakritization, a process corresponding to Sanskritization, is generally not well known or even accepted. In a later work published in 1989, for example, Srinivas acknowledges that Prakritization exists but dismisses it as "parochialization," "de-Sanskritization (1989: 62). The fact is, besides being names of two language groups, both Sanskrit and Prakrit have a wider, more general meaning in the sense of vibrant rhythms of civilization. The emergence of Indian civilization (*saṁskṛti*) was facilitated by a flow of reciprocal influences and inputs among a variety of subcultures and peoples who used Sanskrit and Prakrit as languages of communication and exchange. It would be pertinent to explain and analyse how a hermeneutic of enculturation operates through the process of *saṁskṛtikaraṇa* transforming and appropriating, in the process, disparate cultural strands, whether indigenous to India or introduced there from outside, into a composite whole.

Saṁskṛtikaraṇa is facilitated by a conscious interplay of key culture building themes or blocks: symbols, myths, and narratives operating at the level of both the 'great' and 'little' traditions. Enculturation involves creation of a tradition or ensembling of beliefs, ideas and instituted practices to constitute the common sense, taken-for-granted and, usually not consciously reflected aspects of daily routine action. Tradition may be seen as series of shared, repeated, structured, communicative acts — verbal, gestural, and physical — that form a culture, binding generations together and forming social groups. Tradition shapes and preserves a personal and group identity, an especially important function among new immigrants. The threads that form tradition are individual and group memories, and the process by which the tradition is preserved, adopted and transmitted is analogous to the function of DNA structures. DNA is semi-conservative replication because half of the strands is new material. Tradition is that which provides a syntax of language and action — verbal, ritual and visual — enabling us to continue the conservation of culture and civilization and to maintain a creative thrust toward the future (Williams 1992: 228-29).

In modern times it has become fashionable, both in India and abroad, to concentrate on teaching Sanskrit only as a language. In most Western universities Sanskrit is taught as part of an 'Indo-European' philology. True, Sanskrit is a language of erudition of India; but the word has a wider, more general meaning in the sense of civilization. Etymologically, Sanskrit means 'elaborated,' 'refined,' 'cultured,' or 'civilized.' To that extent, it is distinct from the Prakrit (natural) group of languages, though intimately related to it. The fact is, though employed by the refined and the educated as a language and a means of communication; Sanskrit is also a vehicle of civilization (Gombrich 1978: 22). It is, therefore, not enough to know or study Sanskrit alone. We must also know and study *saṁskṛti* in order to learn and know India and her people through her heritage preserved in Sanskrit (and Prakrit) literature. Sanskrit, as Monier-Williams once remarked, is the very heart of Indic civilization (a relatively modern anonymous expression, *saṁskṛtiḥ sanskṛtāśritā*) makes the same point. Civilization, in anthropological sense, is more comprehensive than culture, more global in outlook and application than the "high culture" or "great tradition." The process of Sanskritization was first promoted by S.K. Chatterjee. M.N. Srinivas who later elaborated it, acknowledges Chatterjee's contribution in a later work:

> The progressive Sanskritization of the various pre-Aryan or non-Aryan peoples in their culture, their outlook and their ways of life forms the keynote of India through the ages and in the course of this "Sanskritization" the affected peoples also brought their own spiritual and material milieus to bear upon Sanskrit and Sanskritic culture which they were adopting and thus helped to modify and to enrich it in their own circles. (Srinivas 1989: 56)

Sanskritization would seem to proceed along two dimensions — cultural and social. Rulers, pilgrim centres and temple complexes have traditionally been the agents of Sanskritization. In modern times, state operated broadcasting agencies, school textbooks, and the film and music industry have emerged as new agents. As a cultural and social process, Sanskritization derives its power and potential from Sanskrit. Raghavan (1956) identified its adaptive strategies to new forces and circumstances. As a profound and many-sided cultural process, the impress of Sanskritization is seen in Indian languages, literature, ideology, music, dance, drama, style of life and ritual. Its influence is not confined to Hindus or India, but is visible even in sects and religious groups outside Hinduism or India. Once information about local or regional cultural traits is recorded and encoded in Sanskrit they became part of *saṁskṛti*. This process is akin to Sanskritization. On the other hand, when elements of *saṁskṛti* are localized and acquire a local flavour, they manifest a distinct regional cultural identity and colour. This process may be grouped under Prakritization. Just as the local cultural elements become incorporated into *saṁskṛti*, the elements of *saṁskṛti* similarly flow into regional cultural units. In a very intriguing and interesting instance provided by V. Raghavan it is possible to see the mutually reinforcing processes of Sanskritization and Prakritization simultaneously at work:

> The shrine [of Naṭarāja at Chidambaram] embodies the Daharvidyā of the Upaniṣads. *Dahara* or *dahra* or *dobhra* means "small" and *dabhra-ākāśa* is the small or microcosmic space, the image of the macrocosmic *ākāśa*, of which the correct Tamil rendering is *Sirrambalam* or *Siruambalam*. But when *ākāśa* was also thought of as embodying *cit*, the principle of consciousness, the name *sirrambalam* by quasi-folk etymology was remade as *cid-ambaram*, a freshly formed Sanskrit name, which still persists. Sanskrit devotional literature was also increased by re-absorbing in Sanskrit garb, material which was originally given to the people in their own local tongues. (cited in Srinivas 1989: 62)

The above clearly suggests that the relationship between Sanskrit and Prakrit is reciprocal and symbiotic. India's civilization operates on a much larger scale, uniting both the great and little traditions. Her civilized society and religions, sharing dominant moral and aesthetic values and norms, has prized Sanskrit [and Prakrit] language as vehicle and transmitter of those values.[8] Pan-Indian

---

8. A popular maxim or saying is usually found expressed both in Sanskrit and Prakrit languages of India. Consider by way of example the following proverb, "On a desolate treeless plateau Castor Oil shrub passes off as tree."

Sanskrit: *nirasta pādape deśe eraṇḍo'pi drumāyate.*

Hindī: *jahān rukh nahin vahān eraṇḍa rukh.*

Marāṭhī: *osāḍ gāvī eraṇḍa baḷī.*

Gujarātī: *ujād gāmamā eraṇḍo pradhān.*

Beṅgālī: *nei deśe eraṇḍ gāch.*

Telugu: *Cetti leni ulalo āmudapu ceṭṭe mahāvṛkṣam.*

Malayālam: *Marāmillā nāṭiṭal āvaṇkku mahāmaram.*

civilization emerged in its present composite form when the two cultural streams reacted upon one another. That it was facilitated by the flow of reciprocal influences between Sanskrit and Prakrit languages has been confirmed by various scholars using festivals and ritual worship offered to deities as "tracers." Several articles in a collection edited by Marriott (1990) delineate the process of Prakritization or downward spread of cultural elements symbolized and preserved in Sanskrit into smaller, regional cultural units represented by different Prakrit languages spoken all across the subcontinent of India. The converse, the process of Sanskritization implies an upward spread and infusion of cultural elements preserved in the Prakrit group of languages into the culture largely preserved in Sanskrit.

The unity of India does not exclusively reside in an exemplary set of norms and scriptures of any one particular religion that arose on her soil. The unity, rather, is to be found in the Indian civilization — the lore and repository of song, dance, play, sculpture, painting, religious narrative. Dimock (1963: 1-5) has suggested that the diversity to be found in Indian subcontinent is limited by patterns which recur throughout the area, so that each region, despite its differences from other regions, expresses the patterns — the structural paradigmatic aspects — of the whole. Each regional culture is therefore to be seen as a structural microcosm of the full system, because the regional variation does not disturb significantly the unified underlying patterning deriving from the larger cultural unit (civilization). David Mandelbaum sees the integrative potential of *saṁskṛti* for India in the practice of pilgrimage (*tīrthayātrā*):

> There is a traditional basis for the larger national identification. It is the idea, mainly engendered by Hindu religion but shared by those of other religions as well, that there is an entity of India to which all inhabitants belong. The Hindu epics and legends, in their manifold versions, teach that the stage for the gods was nothing less than the entire land and that the land remains one religious setting for those who dwell in it. That sense was and is

> continually confirmed through the common practice of pilgrimage.
>
> — 1972: 140

Saṁskṛti, thus, has been a product and a cause of a pan-Indian cultural consciousness that is shared by most Indians whatever their caste, class or gender and is expressed in essential similarities of mental and spiritual outlook and ethos. While the elitist, high culture of the sophisticated urbane population provides *saṁskṛti* with comprehensiveness and refinement; cultural input from the rural masses gives it popularity and pan-Indian outlook. Again, thanks to *saṁskṛti*, the acceptance of 'modernizing' and 'progress' ideologies and thought patterns in modern India does not result in linear forms of social and cultural change. In fact, it ends in incorporating 'modern' innovations into the tradition. It can allow India to be modern without becoming less 'Indian.'

The temple of Mīnākṣī, the cave sculptures and paintings of Ajantā and Ellorā, the giant statue of Gomateśvara of Śravaṇabeḷagolā, the Gol Gumbaz of Bījāpur, the *stūpa* of Sāñcī, the Tajmahal of Agra, the Red Fort of Delhi, and even the Victoria Memorial Complex of Calcutta (now Kolkata) have one thing in common. Underlying the diversity of their architectural plans and designs is to be found the constant and recurring pan-Indic cultural traits and their interplay (*saṁskṛti*). As expressions of dominant ideals or values, the cultural traits are seldom indifferent to one another. The affirmation of one may dictate the repudiation of another; the realization of the latter may demand the acceptance of a third. Different cultural traits may complement each other or they may conflict with each other. Tension or competition may exist among different themes without being incompatible with each other. The value of *mokṣa*, for instance, is not necessarily incompatible with the values of *dharma, artha* and *kāma*. *Dharma* does not logically exclude the other three. They may, however, be in competition with each other, and their competition can create tension. Nevertheless, theirs is the dialectic of compatible or commensurate themes. The conflict between them can be resolved by resort to different hermeneutic strategies.

As a form-producing process, *saṁskṛtikaraṇa* may be said to provide a kaleidoscopic view of a six-fold enculturing process incorporating the processes of Sanskritization and Prakritization:

(1) Enculturation takes place in a specific context involving a physical, psychological, social and ethical environ-ment, roles, and rules.

(2) Enculturation involves agency. Agents of enculturation consciously intervene according to set goals and intentions.

(3) Enculturation is intentional. It is produced by verbal and/or non-verbal action; singly or collectively.

(4) Enculturation is teleological. The meaning of the end-product, *saṁskṛti*, may vary among performers, participants, and outside observers.

(5) Enculturation occurs in real time and history as a twin correlative process of Sanskritization and Prakritization. It has a specific sequential and syntactic structure, i.e., historical consciousness.

(6) Enculturation is transformative of self and self-identity through historical consciousness.

VI

Itihāsa: Record of Significant Actions Rooted in Saṁskṛti

All cultures, in one way or another, recognize that history is a record of significant actions. Great heroes (male and female) are often implicated in such actions and are therefore recognized as 'instruments' of providence, justice or the spirit of times (*Zeitgeist*) destined to accomplish a definite plan and purpose. The hero can be prophet, poet, king or priest according to the kind of world the hero is born into. But heroes cannot influence or make history until the times are ripe for them. Their exploits are kept alive as narratives to be told to successive generations. In the *Heroes and Hero-Worship*, Carlyle outlined one way of conceptualizing history:

> Universal History, the history of what man has accomplished in this world, is at the bottom the history of the Great Men who have worked here.
>
> — cited in Hook 1965: 14

The events to which such exceptional deeds were attributed were determined by the needs of the period in which the hero appeared. A need will be felt for a hero to initiate, organize, and lead a community insofar as alternatives of action are believed to be open. These compelling needs are characterized and catalogued in different cultures as metaphysical or ideal. They may be covered under the general term of 'cultural.'

In the Indian context the historical perspective and consciousness is bound with the recognition that events invariably produce effects and consequences, both external and internal, to the authors and agents of these events and their community. History as a record of meaningful or heroic actions (*nārāśaṁsī*) was already spelled out in the *Śatapatha Brāhmaṇa* (XI.1.6.9; 5.6.8; XIII.4.3.12). The *Mahābhārata* uses the term *itivṛttam* for history and recommends that actual doings of great kings and seers are to be analysed within the parameters of *dharma, artha, kāma* and *mokṣa* (Shendge 1996). In his *Nirukta* (11: 25), Yāska understands the role of *itihāsa* to be the teaching of the philosophy of life. He cites supporting references to relevant traditional narratives (*pāramparika kathā*). *Aitihāsika*s are the persons who elucidate the meaning of Vedic hymns by commenting on them with citations from such narratives. The tradition of Mīmāṁsā, too, refers to the categories of "heroic action" (*parakṛti*)[9] and "record of heroic actions"

---

9. Kṛṣṇa Yajvan defines *parakṛti* as "that corroborative statement which demonstrates that a particular work was done by a great personage." (1987: 70)

→

(*purākalpa*).[10] The Dharmaśāstras and Purāṇas in turn, remind the reader that a proper understanding of history is crucial for fulfilling *dharma* and the other ends of life.[11] History is written and transmitted as a record of actions. According to the theory of *karma*, the forces that energize an action leave their mark on the agent as well as on the world. Within the agent these energizing forces leave a residual effect (*karmāśaya*) that shape and direct future actions, carrying the combined influence (*saṁskāra*s) of past actions, forward into the agent's and along with him/her their tradition's future. Some of the internal effects of actions show up directly in the habits and character of the succeeding generations.[12]

The above understanding of human action is remarkably similar to the hermeneutic of human action developed by Gadamer and Ricoeur. The meaning of a social action is the result of a mutually negotiated understanding between the agent and others immediately or distantly involved with the agent and the particular act. Consider the example of a ceremony in which a public figure

---

→ *pareṇa mahatā puruṣeṇedam karma kṛtamiti pratipādako'rthavādaḥ parakṛtiḥ.*

10. Kṛṣṇa Yajvan defines *purākalpa* ("past incident") as that corroborative statement which demonstrates something that has been narrated by another. Swami Madhavananda's gloss adds that according to Kumārila Bhaṭṭa, and others, both these [*parakṛti, purākalpa*] are narrations of some past event, the former by one person and the later by many persons (1987: 71). As a category *purākalpa*, therefore, comes close to *itihāsa*.

11. One popular verse puts it as follows:

    dharmārthakāmamokṣāṇām upadeśasamanvitam
    purāvṛttam kathārūpam itihāsam pracakṣate

    — Sathe, n.d.: 22

12. According to Panikkar, in the tradition of India, *karma* serves a function similar to that "historical consciousness [or historicity] entrusted within Western philosophy. In the Vedic world as well as in any analysis of human experience, it is usually human or divine action which determines the sense as well as the passage of time.

→

plants a seedling and throws a spadeful of earth and water on it. The preliminary meaning of this act is obviously horticultural. But a general, secondary, and shareable meaning of initiating or commemorating something can emerge only if both the agent and the audience recognize it in terms of a mutually agreed upon and shared symbolism traditionally associated with such an act. The version of history that is written of this episode will depend upon how the writer derived and understood the meaning of that central action. Meaningful action is an object for hermeneutics because the objectification that action undergoes is similar to the fixation of discourse by writing. Action, like text, acquires a delineated pattern which can be interpreted according to its inner traits. A dialectic within the process of transaction enables us to detach the *event* of action from its *meaning*. This is possible because action has the structure of a locutionary act.

Ricoeur argues that action can also be identified according to its illocutionary force (quality) and its noetic structure which may be fixed and detached from the process of interaction. It may thereby become an object to interpret. It is derived by describing the functioning of the verbs of action. For example, the distinction between states, activities, and performances can be made with reference to the tenses employed for the verbs of action. A typology of action following the model of illocutionary acts, therefore, is possible. The propositional content and illocutionary force of action constitute its sense-content which inscribes the 'done' of action, just as writing inscribes the saying as *said*. This event can be

---

→ The law of *karma* rules both the notions of time and history. In the first instance, *karma* designates action, then results (good or bad) of such action and which survive the person in question. *Karma*, finally determines retribution of one's acts and coordinates all actions of beings. As a universal law of retribution, *karma* is not linked to an outer historicity or explanation of events taking place in the world outside. *Karma* rather refers to the inner historical awareness or consciousness [within], which is very subtle and as such invisible (Panikkar 1975: 86-87).

captured in the metaphor of 'trace' or 'marks' that are left by an event or act. The trace suggests the idea of a harder, more durable support than the transitory activity of human beings. It is because humans worked and committed something to stone or baked clay tablet or papyrus that their works outlive their actions and working. While people pass on, their works might remain. To follow a trace is to reason by means of causality about the chain of operations constitutive of the action of those who have passed on (Ricoeur 1988 3: 120).

This is similar to the account provided in the tradition of Mīmāṁsā. An individual action once performed can be detached from its remarkable performer to let it develop legacy and consequences of its own (*parakṛti*). A memorable work or act, so autonomized, comes to be invested with cultural and social dimensions. As a social phenomenon this act can be repeated by others individually or collectively but its consequences cannot always be distinguished or foretold. Similarly, repeated actions may leave repercussions which their agents did/did not necessarily intend. In a simple action the meaning (*noema*) and intent (*noesis*) may overlap or coincide. But in a complex action it is not always possible to assign doership of a given act/s. That is where the need and scope for hermeneutics becomes evident. If heroic actions of great cultural and social consequences leave marks; on what do they leave or imprint them? On time! Because time is not merely evanescent or something that flees. In its socio-cultural aspect, time is the repository of durble effects and of persisting patterns. In leaving marks on events registered or recorded in time, patterns of significant actions become the *documents* of human action for posterity. History itself is a record or register of such human actions — whether of common, subaltern folks or of great heroes, royalty and other remarkable personages. History is a quasi-'thing' imaginatively created around an action which had left a 'trace' or 'mark.' Thanks to the sedimentation in social and cultural time, deeds of remarkable individuals can become 'institutions' or 'traditions.' Their meaning may or may not coincide with the logical intentions of original actors. Over time, the meaning may be 'depsychologized' to the extent that actions become semantically autonomous from their original agents; and as such amenable to objective scrutiny.

Another fundamental trait of great works is their ability to overcome the conditions of their social production. A great work or act does not only mirror its time and place, it also opens up a world of civilization which it bears within itself. When preserved in narrative episodes and transmitted to successive generations, such works and words come to be known as a stream of heritage (*purākalpa*). *Saṁskṛti* is comparable to the sea into which various individual streams flow. As a text, *saṁskṛti* is addressed to an infinite range of possible 'readers.' As an open document its meaning, like text, is floating or 'in suspense.' This is where hermeneutics sets in. Readers of texts are not only contemporaries, but as Hegel said, history itself. All significant events and deeds are, in this way, open to interpretation through hermeneutic *praxis*. The importance of a civilization and tradition so created, can go beyond its *relevance* in the initial situation. A truly significant action develops meanings which can be actualized or fulfilled in situations analogous to or even other than the one in which this action originally occurred. The meaning and significance of an important event thus can exceed, overcome, and/or transcend the social and cultural conditions existing at the time of its initial production. It may be narrated repeatedly or re-enacted in new social conditions, away from the original place or location. The importance of such re-narrated and re-enacted acts is their durable or enduring relevance. This trait of heroic or significant action has obvious implications for the relation between civilization and its social conditions and for preserving them as history and myth.

Itihāsa as Myth and History: Views of Raimundo Panikkar and N.A. Nikam

A balanced perspective on the relationship of time, history and culture is provided by Raimundo Panikkar (1975, 1979) and N.A. Nikam (1973). The vision that a people has of its own history, argues Panikkar, suggests how its tradition understands its past and assimilates it into the present. But a people's attitude to their history is determined less by written interpretations of that past than through their ways of life and in the manner of reliving or revisiting it. India, for instance, has lived her souvenirs and memories of the past more through her myths than through the written records or documents of history. Not that 'hard' history is absent in the Indic ethos and culture. The fact is, India has not assiduously developed discriminating criteria of separating myth from history. The expressions 'mythic history' and 'historical myth' are indistinguishable. In the Indian tradition they come across as *itihāsa* (thus it was) and *purāṇa* (past narrative). The relation between the two is not comparable to the one existing between truth and fiction in the popular Western mind. Such disinterest in historiography can be very frustrating and upsetting to the Western mind. But the same Western mind, retorts Panikkar, fails to see that its own 'myths' precisely are taken as 'history' (Panikkar 1975).

Panikkar then subsumes the categories of myth and history in the following manner: The same horizon of reality which is interpreted or dismissed as 'myth' by someone looking from outside the tradition is defined as 'history' by one looking at it from within. What, in the West, serves the function of history is defined as 'myth' in the Indian context by the Western scholars. In other words, what is called history by the Westerner from the perspective of his/her own tradition, is lived by the Indian as myth. The opposite, too, is true. That is, whatever has a degree of reality to the Westerner, will be recognized as myth by the Indian. To put it differently, what the Indian would recognize as history in the context of India, would be lived as myth in the West. From the

Western standpoint, it is not history that carries weight for the Indian. But, precisely, it is myth which is important in the historical consciousness of a people (Panikkar 1975: 88). It is heroic personages and significant events that profoundly mark and inspire the life of Indians (in Western terms — personages and events carrying greater historical weight) that are transformed into myth in the Indian tradition because whatever has existential 'consistency' is mythicized in India. To the Indian, accordingly, the degree of reality of a myth is higher than that of history. A convincing example of this predilection and approach is to be found in the manner in which a more recent "heroic" event (birth of Bangladesh) is being incorporated into the Indian psyche (see Panikkar 1975: 88-89).

For N.A. Nikam, history is but a 'regressive' perspective of time. However, since a regress into the past is always possible, there is 'history' behind history. The paradox of history, therefore, is that in human culture the beginnings of history are not in history but in 'pre-history' and pre-history merges into the myth. What happens in the myth, therefore, will happen in history. The myth puts in words what never is in time. It gives a beginning to what has no beginning. To what occurred "once upon a time" the myth provides a significance that is at once eternal and contemporary. Myth uses fiction to instruct and bring enlightenment of truth unto humans. But human make history only when they make new history and not merely repeat it. History, therefore, is not memory alone; it is also hope. *Chāndogya Upaniṣad* exhorts humans to 'make' history rather than remain content with repeating it — *āśā vāva smarā bhūyasī* (Nikam 1973: 13-15).

VII

Concluding Observations

If the thesis that Indian "mythic consciousness" corresponds to the Western "historical consciousness" insofar as the functions of preservation and integration of the past into tradition are concerned, is accepted then it must be said that India has not developed a tradition of historical consciousness. Rather, history has been assimilated organically into India's extensive mythology. It is not mere chance or accident that the *Bhagavadgītā* (as part of the *Mahābhārata*, it is *itihāsa*) was 'rediscovered' in modern India with a view to provide a spiritual base to political movements. Because, among other things, it also teaches the path of *karmayoga*. On the battlefield of Kurukṣetra, Kṛṣṇa advises Arjuna to carry out his appointed role in history — to not to abandon his duty assigned according to his intrinsic nature (*svadharma*). Nationalist leaders like Lokmanya Tilak, Mahatma Gandhi and Acharya Vinoba Bhave found in the teaching of the *Gītā* a source of inspiration: One's actions must be purified by renouncing attachment to its results (*karmaphala-tyāga*), which alone, can assure order and justice in the world (*lokasaṁgraha*). They sought to purify their political mission by removing any trace of personal gain from their actions by spiritualizing politics and history (Panikkar 1975: 90).

Indians, accordingly, must stop being overawed by the tall ontological claims of Western academics (from Karl Gustave Hempel to von Ranke) that only historians can describe the past as it actually happened. The fact is, history refers to the past and past events only indirectly. The historian's reconstruction is not a reproduction of the actual course of events. Like metaphor, history is also a matter of *seeing as*. The historian's narrative is a 'model' of the past but Ricoeur reminds us that there is no original given with which to compare the model. In other words, historical narratives are *creative* imitations (Vanhoozer 1990: 95-96). Secondly, historiography in modern India needs to steer clear both of nationalist historians on the one hand, and the secular and subaltern historians on the other and strike a middle position. The manner in which Ricoeur mediates between Gadamer and Habermas (1974) could be extended to mediate between the nationalist historians on the one hand and the secular and subaltern historians on the other in order to create a new mode of historiography suitable to the cultural context of India.

Like Gadamer, the nationalist historians tend to view tradition as an authentic dimension of historical consciousness. Secular and subaltern historians, who often quote Habermas, view tradition as the source of distortion and alienation. The focus of debate between the two antagonists thus concerns the role of the tradition and cultural values. For Gadamer tradition is a dimension of our human historicity. In a hermeneutic of tradition our original belonging to tradition and being has been brought to expression. We can never extricate ourselves from history and its effects. The position of Habermas is that our freedom and knowledge is distorted by prejudice, authority and interests. It is the task of critical social sciences to unblock the distorted communication. For Habermas value comes not from the recovery of past traditions but from the regulative idea of a communication. For Ricoeur this obvious antinomy between Gadamer and Habermas calls for a dialectical approach. Against Gadamer, he suggests that there is a need to interject critical agency in his hermeneutics of reminiscence. Ricoeur assigns this task to the notion of distanciation, which need not be perceived a harmful alienation. By interpreting it positively, Ricoeur creates a useful opening for a critical recuperation of history and past traditions. Against Habermas, Ricoeur argues that the critique of ideology requires a more sympathetic reabsorption of the past traditions. The past, he says, is more than a distortion of communication. Ricoeur, therefore, rejects the claim of Habermas that only the critical social sciences are the praxis and knowledge that bring about emancipation (1974).

Surprisingly, Ricoeur's two major building blocks of historiography — action and time — are, to some extent, anticipated in the *kālasamuddeśa,* which constitutes section nine of *kāṇḍa* three of Bhartr̥hari's *Vākyapadīyam*. According to a tāntric text, *Tripurā Rahasya* (XI.46), space is a limitation of form and time that of action (Panikkar 1992: 28). For Bhartṛhari, though absolute, time appears differentiated and divided as past, present and future because of action (*kriyābhedāt*, *Vākyapadīyam* III.9.32). The very fact that things are remembered at all is proof of the existence of time. The fact that we can anticipate and conceive of events yet to come, is also proof of time's existence. Actions which are complete give the name "past" (*atīta*) to time. Objects produced by action in time going by are preserved (as present) in memory and given the name past. Past actions are remembered and expressed in appropriate words. Past, present and future (like quick and slow, before and after) are the evidence of time's existence but in themselves they do not constitute time (III.9.47). For Panikkar, this relationship between *karma* and *kāla* is the counterpart of that which exists between historicity and time in Western thought. Firstly, time's *raison d'être* is precisely the existence of *karma*. So long as *karma* exists in the world, time will be necessary. *Karma* is, as it were, the intrinsic quality of time. *Karma* gives time substance and entity; and secondly, without time, *karma* would remain in a latent state. Without the collaboration of time, beings would not be able to attain liberation (*mokṣa*) through the performance of assigned duties (*dharma*) for which the consummation of all *karma* is a pre-requisite (Panikkar 1992: 32-33). By so describing the inter-relationship of time and action, Bhartṛhari seems to prepare a way to the explanation of cosmology, the existential concerns of humans, and the very vexing problem of relating "lived time" to the cosmic time.

Again, according to Ricoeur, no action is possible, much less intelligible, apart from a history of actions — both those of one's own and those of others. Hence, Ricoeur speaks of the time of action as historical time. When articulated narratively, historical time becomes human time. Historical time presupposes at least a latent recognition of a fundamental paradox in our experience of time. The wisdom of ages has always known the disproportion between time that we deploy in living and the time that coheres in the world process. On the one hand, we experience the flow of our own brief lives from birth to death, which is lived time. On the other hand, we also experience the time of the cosmos, a seemingly endless succession of undifferentiated moments. There is no way, Ricoeur argues, for us satisfactorily than either to hierarchically order or to make homogeneous these two times. In historical time, human life shows itself to be an open though incomplete interplay of an anticipation of the future, a reception of the past, and a living out of the present. Contrast to cosmic time in historical time (as in lived time) there is a present that enables us to distinguish *qualitatively* between a before as past and an after as future. But in contrast to mere lived time, which could be lived and experienced as both fundamentally detached from and evanescent; the historical time is the time in which we find it possible to develop procedures that link us both to others and to the material cosmos we inhabit. Some of these procedures show up in historiography.

Aided by the insights of Bhartṛhari and Ricoeur, it would be possible to initiate a creative dialogue between the two major opposing schools of historiography in modern India: (1) nationalist and (2) secular/subaltern. The following points might serve a basis for such an encounter:

1. The task of narrative interpretation must be focused at the intersection of history and fiction, that is, neither exclusively with history alone nor fiction alone, but in dialectic encounter between the two.
2. Any attempt to reduce or remove the creative tension obtaining between history and fiction within narrative will impose an arbitrary closure on hermeneutic enterprise of narration. Interpretation must keep in view and maintain this tensional character of the two components of narrative.
3. Any interpretation must bring forward both the historicity and fictionality of Indian civilization preserved in narration so that the interpretive encounter can engage the two spheres of discourse.

4. The interpretation itself must be dialectical and must envisage to disclose truth and reality.

5. The task of narrative interpretation is never completed, for the aim cannot be to deplete or exhaust the tradition or culture of its dynamism.

References

Coulson, Michael, *Sanskrit: An Introduction to the Classical Language*, New York: David McKay Company Inc., 1986.

Danesi, Marcel, *Messages and Meanings: An Introduction to Semiotics*, Toronto: Canadian Scholars' Press, 1993.

Deshapande, G.T., *Indological Papers*, vol. 1, Nagpur: Vidarbha Samshodhan Mandal, 1971.

Dimock, Edward C., *The Thief of Love*, Chicago: University of Chicago Press, 1963.

Gachter, Othmar, *Hermeneutics and Language in Pūrva Mīmāṁsā*, Delhi: Motilal Banarsidass, 1983.

Gombrich, Richard, *On Being Sanskritic: A Plea for Civilized Study and the Study of Civilization*, Oxford: Claredon Press, 1978.

Guha, Ranjit, *Elementary Aspects of Peasant Insurgency in Colonial India*, Delhi: Oxford University Press, 1983.

Guha, Ranjit, *Subaltern Studies: Writings on South Asian History and Society*, 9 vols., Delhi: Oxford University Press, 1982.

Gumperz, John J., "Communication in multilingual societies," in *Cognitive Anthropology*, ed. Stephen A. Tyler, New York: Holt, Reinhart, and winston, 1969.

Hempel, Karl, "The Function of General Laws in History," in *Theories of History*, ed. Patrick Gardiner, pp. 344-56, New York: The Free Press, 1959.

Holt, John Clifford, "Review of Curators of the Buddha: The Study of Buddhism under Colonialism," ed. Donald S. Lopez Jr., Chicago: Chicago University Press, 1995, *Journal of Religion* 97, 1 (Jan. 1997): 180-82.

Hook, Sydney, *The Hero in History: A Study in Limitation and Possibility*, Boston: Beacon Press, 1965 (fifth printing).

Kapstein, Matthew, "The Purificatory Gem and Its Cleansing: A Late Tibetan Polemical Discussion of Apocryphal Texts, *History of Religions*, 28 1989 (3): 217-44.

Larson, Gerald James, *India's Agony Over Religion*, Albany, New York: SUNY Press, 1995.

Longxi, Zhang, *The Tao and the Logos: Literary Hermeneutics, East and West*, Durham, N.C.: Duke University Press, 1992.

Majumdar, R.C., ed., *The History and Culture of the Indian People*, 2 vols., Bombay: Bharatiya Vidya Bhavan, 1984.

Mandelbaum, David, *Society in India*, Bombay: Popular Prakashan, 1972.

Marriott, McKim, ed., *India through Hindu categories*, New Delhi: Sage Publications, 1990.

Mimāṁsā Paribhāṣā of Kṛṣṇa Yajvan, tr. Swami Madhavananda, Calcutta: Advaita Ashrama, 1987.

Nikam, N.A., *Some Concepts of Indian Culture: An Analytical Interpretation*, 2nd ed., Simla: Institute of Advanced Studies, 1973.

Panikkar, Raimundo, "Temps et Historie dans la Tradition de l'Inde," in *les Cultures et le Temps*, ed. Paul Ricoeur, 74-89, Paris: Payot, 1975.

———, *Myth faith and hermeneutics: cross-cultural studies*, New York: Paulist Press, 1979.

———, Time and History in the Tradition of India: Kāla and Karma," in *Time in Indian Philosophy*, ed. Hari Shankar Prasad, 21-46, Delhi: Sri Satguru Publications, 1992.

Prasad, Hari Shankar, ed., *Time in Indian Philosophy*, Delhi: Sri Satguru Publications, 1992.

Ricoeur, Paul, "Ethics and Culture: Habermas and Gadamer in Dialogue," in *Political and Social Essays*, ed. D. Stewart and J. Bien, Athens, Ohio: Ohio University Press, 1974.

———, ed., *les Cultures et le Temps*, Paris: Payot, 1975.

———, *Interpretation Theory: Discourse and the Surplus of Meaning*, Fort Worth: Texas Christian University Press, 1976.

———, *Hermeneutics and the Social Sciences: Essays on Language, Action and Interpretation*, ed., tr. and introduction by J.B. Thompson, Cambridge: Cambridge University Press, 1981.

———, "Narrated Time," *Philosophy Today* 29, no. 4/4 (Winter 1985): 259-72.

———, *Time and Narrative*, 3 vols., Chicago: University of Chicago Press, 1984-88.

———, "The Human Experience of Time and Narrative," rpt. in *A Ricoeur Reader: Reflection and Imagination*, ed. Mario J. Valdes, Toronto: University of Toronto Press, 1991.

Sathe, Sriram, *Bharateeya Historiography*, Hyderabad, India: Bharateeya Itihasa Sankalana Samiti, n.d.

Seung, T.K., *Semiotics and Thematic in Hermeneutics*, New York: Columbia University Press, 1982.

Shendge, Malati J., "The Other Half of the Indo-European Postulate: Early India in a New Perspective," *Annals of the Bhandarkar Oriental Reasearch Institute*, vol. LXXXVII, Pts 1-4 (1996): 179-93.

Silverman Hugh J., *Textualities: Between Hermeneutics and Deconstruction*, New York: Routeledge, 1994.

Singer, Milton, *When a Great Tradition Modernizes: An Anthropological Approach to Indian Civilization*, Chicago: University of Chicago Press, 1972.

Srinivas, M.N., *The Cohesive Role of Sanskritization and Other Essays*, Delhi: Oxford University Press, 1989.

Timm, Jefferey, ed., *Texts in Context: Traditional Hermeneutics in South Asia*, Albany, New York: SUNY Press, 1992.

Tilak, Shrinivas, *Religion and Ageing in the Indian Tradition*, Albany, New York: SUNY Press, 1989.

Tyler, Stephen A., *India: An Anthropological Perspective*, Pacific Palisades, Ca.: Goodyear Publishing Company, Inc., 1973.

Vākaypadīyam [of Bhartṛhari, with the Commentary "*Prakāśa*" by Helārāja]. 2 vols., ed. Bhagiratha Prasada Tripathi, Saraswati Bhavan Granthamala no. 91, Varanasi: Sampurnanada Sanskrit Visvavidyalaya, 1977.

Valdes, Mario J., ed., *A. Ricoeur Reader: Reflection and Imagination*, Toronto: University of Toronto Press, 1991.

Vanhoozer, Kevin, *Biblical narrative in the philosophy of Paul Ricoeur: A study in hermeneutics and theology*, Cambridge: Cambridge University Press, 1990.

Vrat, Satya, "The Concept of Time according to Bhrtṛhari," in *Time in Indian Philosophy*, ed. Hari Shankar Prasad, 221-31, Delhi: Sri Satguru Publications, 1992.

Williams, Raymond Brody, "Sacred Threads of Several Textures," in *A Sacred Thread: Modern Transmissions of Hindu Traditions in India and Abroad*, ed. Raymond Brody Williams, 228-57, Chambersburg Pa.: 1992.

12

Secularism *vs.* Hindu Nationalism
Interrogating the Terms of the Debate

Makrand Paranjape

THIS paper is a reflection on academic pragmatics in contemporary India. More particularly, it examines how the predominantly secularized, Hindu academy has responded to the threat posed by the political upsurge of right-wing, Hindu majoritarianism. It argues that the academy has responded by a peculiar politics of its own, a politics which, by virtue of its apparently oppositional and progressive stance, cheats itself into feeling that it is fighting religious fanaticism, but actually prevents it from doing so. This "false consciousness" prevents it from discharging its larger social and cultural responsibilities, something which it appears so eager to do. In other words, this paper tries to show that much of the counter-communalistic academic discourse is, paradoxically, a distorted reflection of the very thing that it seeks to defeat and destroy. This discourse which has its own paranoias and insecurities, upon closer scrutiny, reveals an uncanny resemblance to Hindu fundamentalism itself. Consequently, the secular academy is not just fearful and aggressive, but also partial and selective in its methods and strategies.[1]

---

1. It is only in retrospect that one realizes how quickly academic writing, especially that which tries to understand contemporary reality, dates. This paper was originally written in April 1996 and then revised for presentation in the seminar on "Dharma: The Categorial Imperative," held at the Indian Institute of Advanced →

Simply speaking, anti-Hindutva academics is born out of the insecurities of the secular Hindu intelligentsia. Alarmed that the very middle-classes, whose vanguard and champion it supposed itself to be, was now deserting it allured by what was so obviously an inferior ideology, it has reacted with predictable anger and bitterness. This secular intelligentsia had almost come to equate Hinduism with its brand of secularism, having been paternalistically tolerant of minority fanaticism, whether Muslim, Sikh, radical, or caste-based. None of these extremisms threatens it in the way Hindutva does. This sort of selective opposition to Hindu political militancy suggests the presence of an inverse communalism at the very core of this discourse. Such implicit tolerance or even support of minoritarian extremism actually lends strength to the insecurity of the majority, thus, perversely abetting militant majoritarianism. Hence, ironically, the academy ends up feeding and energizing the very beast that it wishes to bind and tame.

I am offering this paper not as one who hates or distrusts the academy, but as concerned and committed member who finds himself almost driven to silence or despair at his own loneliness within it. While I fervently hope and wish that I am proven wrong, that the fears and anxieties informing this paper are actually unfounded, I am afraid that I may not be all that mistaken after all. We who have taken upon ourselves the task of interrogating and unmasking Hindutva, need to interrogate and unmask ourselves first. Only then can we face our adversary effectively.

→ Studies, Shimla, in July 1997. This paper was written in the context of some of the shrillest rhetoric unleashed by Indian academics and intellectuals against the pro-Hindutva forces. For about five years, from 1992 to 1997, this tirade continued, almost as a last ditch effort to prevent the BJP from coming to power. Today, in May 1998, after the swearing in of the second BJP government at the centre, the dynamics of the secularist intelligentsia has changed considerably. Hindutva, or at any rate, the more liberal face of it presented by Atal Behari Vajpayee's coalition government has become an acceptable fact of life.

I

Rethinking Secularism and Communalism: The Case for India

I would like to begin this section with a plain statement: India is not a secular country. It is not secular in the sense that it is not irreligious or even non-religious. Furthermore, I believe that India is a communal country, communal in the sense that Indians usually define their identities in terms of the community to which they belong. The above observations, I contend, certainly apply to the Indian people by and large, and, to a lesser extent, to the Indian state.[2]

Hence, it is clear to me that the Hindi equivalent for secularism, *dharmanirpekṣatā*, is a misleading and unfortunate coinage. This is not an *dharmanirpekṣa* country, that is a country which disfavours *dharma*. Instead, we are a *dharmasāpekṣa* country, a country which favours *dharma* but, as our Constitution stresses, does not favour any specific religious sect or tradition — we are not *dharmanirpekṣa* but *sampradāya-nirpekṣa*.[3]

2. The original Indian Constitution, which was adopted formally on 26 November 1949, defined the country as a "Sovereign Democratic Republic." This was substituted by "Sovereign Socialist Secular Democratic Republic" by the 42nd Amendment in 1976 and took effect from 3rd January 1977. However, my assertion that India is not a secular country must not be seen in purely constitutional terms, nor should it be misconstrued to imply that I disregard the Indian Constitution. Rather, it reflects my understanding of Indian culture and civilization. As S. Radhakrishnan, our first President, observed, "Secularism here does not mean irreligion or atheism or even stress on material comforts. It proclaims that it lays stress on spiritual values which may be attained by a variety of ways" (Foreword to *The National Culture of India* by Abid Hussain, Bombay: Asia Publishing House, 1961, p. 8). Even Indira Gandhi said that secularism is not *dharmanirapekṣata* but "*equal alignment with each religion*" (quoted in P.C. Chatterjee, *Secular Values for a Secular India*, New Delhi: Lola Chatterjee, 1984, p. 2).

3. A similar point has been made by Koenraad Elst in the *Ayodhya and* →

Similarly, as has been repeatedly pointed out, secularism in the Indian context does not imply a disregard for religions, but an equal respect for all of them. Mahatma Gandhi used the phrase *sarva-dharma-samabhāva* to describe this position; in recent times, Pandurang Shastri Athavale, the inspiration behind the Svadhyaya movement, has extended it to *sarva- dharma-svīkāra* — an acceptance of all religions.[4]

Finally, we must bear in mind that though India is a religious country, what we do have is a clear separation of religion and state. It is also useful to bear in mind that almost throughout the entire sweep of Indian history up to the Muslim conquest of India, there never was a state religion. Even when there was one, as in the case of Aśoka, there was tolerance for other faiths. Those who invoke

---

After: Issues Before Hindu Society (New Delhi: Voice of India, 1991, p. 156). Elst suggests Lokāyata (in the sense of worldliness) as a better Hindī word for modern secularism. This distinction between *dharmanirapekṣa* and *sampradāyanirapekṣa* has, of course, be seized by the BJP leaders and ideologues, including Atal Behari Vajpayee and Lal Krishna Advani.

4. There is a great deal of literature trying to define the Indian version of secularism. A recent overview is offered in M.M. Sankhder, ed., *Secularism in India: Dilemmas and Challenges* (New Delhi: Deep and Deep, 1992). The secondary literature on secularism and Hindutva is vast and varied, especially after the destruction of the Babri Masjid in 1992. Some clear strands in this debate emerge: first there is the leftist position of attacking Hindutva from a secularist point of view; then there is the liberal defense of secularism which also seeks to expand the frontiers of the term; finally, there is the right-wing, Hindutvavādī attack on secularism itself. There are, of course, several positions which are more complex and which therefore defy such neat categor-ization. Most of these positions interrogate both secularism and the politics of Hindutva. Of these, Ashis Nandy's neo-traditionalist critique of secularism is perhaps the best-known. See "The Politics of Secularism and the Recovery of Religious Tolerance" in *Alternatives*, 13.2: 177-94. T.N. Madan also develops a complex argument questioning the received wisdom on secularism; see *Modern Myths, Locked Minds: Secularism and Fundamentalism in India* (Delhi: Oxford University Press, 1997).

fears of a theocratic state might therefore take solace from the fact that such a system is against the natural genius and inclination of the Indian people.

From such a point of view, the implications of a dhārmic perspective on secularism are clear: while there is a genuine and emancipatory space within the discourse of secularism, such a space cannot be seen as secularism's exclusive preserve. Secularism cannot afford to be intolerant to *dharma*, especially in a country like India, where a majority of people are, or profess to be, both God-fearing and dhārmic.

Secularizing Indian society is therefore not the way to combat religious fanaticism. Instead, secularism will have to define for itself a different *dharma*. What this *dharma* might be, I shall try to spell out at the end of the paper. But the bulk of what follows is devoted to examining a more specific debate that has dominated Indian academics since Ayodhyā, the debate between secularism and Hindu nationalism. It is my contention that this debate, for most part, shows a profound lack of awareness of the issues at stake. Willy-nilly, the debate widens rather than lessens the divide between genuine *dharma* and genuine secularism by positing a mutually exclusive polarity between them. This paper is a plea against the divisive manner in which this debate has been conducted.

II

Hindu Nationalism as a Category

One of the main planks of the secularlist attack on the forces of Hindutva is their use of a rather ambiguous category called "Hindu nationalism." It seems to me that Hindu nationalism — as distinct from Hindutva — is a rather specious and suspect category. It is a category invented by the official champions of resistance as a convenient whipping-boy. It used to be the oppositional categories that were 'nationalism' *vs.* 'separatism,' or, if these nouns needed qualifying adjectives, "Indian," not Hindu nationalism *vs.* 'Muslim,' separatism. It was assumed that Indian nationalism was not necessarily of exclusively Hindu parentage, but that Muslims, Parsis, Christians, Buddhists, Jains, and so on, also championed it and contributed to it. Nationalism, by definition, was not seen as the exclusive property of one class, community, caste, region, or religion, but of the entire country. As opposed to this cooperative and collaborative project, a section of vested interests raised the slogan of Muslim separatism and, with the help of the British, secured an independent country for themselves, using the disguise of Islam to camouflage their political ambitions.

This used to be what we were brought up to believe. It, alas, is no longer good enough for us. With the failure of the project of Nehruvian secularism, we have begun to suspect that what was thought of as Indian nationalism was simply Hindu nationalism, with the token participation of other communities thrown in as window dressing. What was worse, it seemed that all we had to do, was to scratch an Indian and beneath him lurked a Hindu fundamentalist. How else would our secularist intelligentsia explain the rise of the proto-Facistic BJP? For this left-liberal intellectual class, which had grown complacent and secure under state patronage for decades, what could be a greater disaster than the destruction of the Babri Masjid?

This class conveniently forgot that not only were several thousands of temples destroyed during 800 or so years of Muslim rule, but there has been a history of conversions in this country, not only of individuals and communities, but also of places of worship. Thus, there are records of Buddhist *vihāra*s being converted into Hindu temples, of Hindu temples being converted into Jaina shrines, or Śiva temples being transformed into Vaiṣṇava temples, and so on. What is more, these were secular acts, not necessarily religious ones. They were secular because they were sanctioned by the state which by definition always acts in the secular space. These captures and conversions of shrines were fueled by worldly greed and the compulsions of realpolitik, not by motives of spiritual advancement. What is more, there are competing and conflicting versions of such take-overs, crossings and conflicts. Thus, as Shahid Amin has shown us, a site of religious conflict gradually becomes transformed into a site of religious syncretism. Or, the villains and heroes change depending on whose version you're listening to. In the *Periapuranam*, which is a Śaiva text, the Jainas appear to be villainous. If one goes to Sri Lanka, then the Śaivas are portrayed as blood thirsty and treacherous while the Buddhists are ethical and compassionate.

Gandhi wished to down-play majoritarian politics in his vision of democracy. In a Gandhian democracy, the single individual, the absolute minority, was as important as the masses who belonged to any one ethnic or religious group. Of course, the Congress, which ruled continuously for three decades, was always playing the numbers game, dividing and ruling, cobbling together a majority by forming a collective of minorities, each wooed, appeased, and maintained. India, then, has never been a secular state in the Gandhian sense. It has been a state in which the minorities had enjoyed a disproportionate political power because of their capacity to vote *en-block*. The destruction of the Babri Masjid was a signal that the politics of minoritarianism has suffered a serious set-back by the newly emerging majoritarian politics. This was a political and secular crisis, not a religious one.

Threatened with the rising tide of Hindu majoritarianism, our secularist, left-liberal academic community, naturally, panicked. None was buying their histories. Their explanations as well as their prognostications had been falsified. They came together, as never before, to denounce the destruction of the Masjid. That was, of course, a good thing. All thinking people, including several people of faith, also denounced this act of senseless vandalism. Gandhians, spiritualists, sufis, Sai Baba devotees, followers of Sri Ramakrishna, Sri Aurobindo, the Radha Soamis, and several other sects also expressed themselves, both publicly and privately, against the demolition.

This wider, people's displeasure was, of course, underplayed by the secularists. Their agenda was to isolate and corner the Hindutvavādīs, to give them no place to run. So anyone who refused to accept the dominant, secularist terms of discourse was, willy-nilly, branded a Hindu fundamentalist. This led to the absurd situation in Indian academics wherein Hindu fundamentalism became the default mode: the only way to prove you were not one was to declare yourself to be a secularist. If you're not one of us, you must be one of them — was the logic, not very different from the logic, or should one say, illogic of the Cold War. Though more books and collections of critical essays have been published on the Babri Masjid-Rām Janmabhumi issue than on any other single political event since Independence, yet the people, the voters have not been listening. I predict, somewhat cynically, that if the BJP is voted to power in the elections, several of our secularist academics will be singing a different tune. Because, after all, our intellectuals are not so much secularist as statist; there is only a slight difference of shade between the red and the saffron.

My point is that the tendency in recent times to equate communalism with nationalism, to consider both to be invented through similar processes and manipulations, is an example of back-formation, the attempt of the beleagured secular intelligentsia to invent a past for Hindu fundamentalism. What better way to do this than by suggesting that Hindu fundamentalism and Indian nationalism, which seemed to be opposed discourses, are actually co-extensive and overlapping. It is only one more rhetorical step before subsuming the whole of Indian nationalism into the category of Hindu fundamentalism: this way you can kill both the Hindu and the nationalist, two birds of the same feather, with one discursive stone. A brilliant conflation thus turned all Indian nationalists into Hindutvavādīs.

III

The Dhārmic Challenge to Secularism

I have spoken so far about the secular challenge to the religious outlook, particularly the manner in which the category of Hindu nationalism has been deployed to discredit the whole dhārmic impulse behind our quest for *svarāja*.

In fact, it might even be useful to reverse the terms and to talk of the dhārmic challenge to the secularist extremism. Because, the fact is that secularist discourses have begun to wield greater and greater institutional authority. They are backed, to varying degrees, by political and administrative power and have become the officially sanctioned ideologies of our times. This is not to imply that the forces of religiosity and obscurantism no longer operate in India or that they have ceased to oppress the masses. On the contrary, we must remind ourselves that the religious intolerance and fanaticism do exist simultaneously with the unprecedented power and patronage that the secularist academic and non-academic sectors of our intelligentsia enjoy. It would be a dangerous mistake to over-look or deny the power and privileges of one because of the real threat and danger of the other. It is important to recognize that these officially sanctioned discourses, sometimes with unbelievably brutal cynicism, exploit the very oppression of their constituencies to extract greater benefits and privileges for themselves, somewhat in the manner in which our NRI novelists sell the poverty and exoticism of India to avoid Westerners.

The time has come to question not just Hindu nationalism and its hegemonies, but also to interrogate secularist challenges and the counter-hegemonies that these engender. This is not to equate the violence of the oppressed with the violence of the oppressors, but to question the ideology which believes that violence can only be overcome by counter-violence, that means justify the end, that it is better to violate the other than be violated by the other. The real choice is not between the oppressor and the oppressed but between both and neither, between being either oppressor or oppressed and between being neither oppressor nor oppressed.

If so, then sooner or later, not just the so-called Hindu nationalist, but also the Hindutvavādīs, Muslim fundamentalists, tribals, women, *dalit*s, nationalists, critics of nationalism, and all kinds of others will have to find ways of talking to one another, negotiating with one another. But in order to do this, they must all agree on an agenda of minimum cooperation and coexistence. And this will happen only if we abandon the politics of special interests and accept the broader framework of *sarvodaya*, or universal responsibility. Of course, we need not give up our special interests in order to do so, but only align them to everwidening concentric circles of universal human welfare. After all, I must recognize that my interests are not inherently incompatible with the interests of others — true, they may appear to be so, but ultimately they are not. This ought to be my belief. But if, on the other hand, I were to believe that my interests can be secured only by denying or negating the interests of others, then I place myself in a state of continuous warfare and conflict.

IV

Re-aligning Secularism

We need a much greater degree of introspection and self-examination before we can occupy the higher moral and intellectual ground from which to mount an attack on Hindutva. But instead, we find ourselves incapacitated and blinded by the deceptions and distortions of the very secularism which we claim to espouse, having enjoyed several undeserved privileges for decades as its official high priests. Instead of preserving and protecting such a decadent and debilitating secularism, perhaps we need to abandon it in favour of those neglected yet vital religious traditions which still hold the keys to our survival as a civilization.

Or, if we cannot abandon our secularism, we need at least to modify it, purify it, recognize that it can at best be a minority position in a country such as ours, a vast majority of whose denizens are people of faith and *dharma*. If we accept this we shall try not to convert these so-called ignorant and superstitious masses to our superior brand of secularism, but instead align our secularism with those benign and emancipatory dhārmic forces which have both defined and sustained India's unique civilizational orientation for thousands of years. Our secularism cannot afford to be intolerant or insensitive to the religious identities and self-definitions of our fellow-citizens, rather, it needs to strengthen the best of these traditions by configuring itself into them, in a supportive and complimentary role if necessary.[5]

What we need to recognize is that hyper-secularism is also a corruption, just as Hindutva itself is. This secular fundamentalism secularism projects itself as the self-righteous other of Hindutva, the only antidote to the excesses and insecurities of the latter. In fact, secular fundamentalism is a product of the assault of modernity upon our civilization. Such hyper-secularism, which takes us away from ourselves, is appealing to many of us at an early stage in our lives. Later, several of us, invariably return to the faith of our ancestors, finding the whole spiritual terrain of modernity invariably barren and sterile. In fact, the only secularism which survives such a crisis is one which has a strong humanitarian and communitarian component. But the more humanitarian and communitarian it becomes, the more it begins to resemble *dharma*. In fact, I would go so far as to argue that without recourse to the metalanguage of *dharma*, such humanitarian secularism still remains incomplete and flawed.

If we agree that the rise of the forces of Hindutva is an alarming and dangerous trend, then we will have to do better than to knead

5. As Madan, *op cit.*, puts it, "Secularism in India becomes a religious idea: it underscores the importance of religion, and not in private life alone, but also in the public domain" (p. 279).

all its adherents into one ideological dough. That would only betray our need to create a demonology against which we can begin our self-serving intellectual crusades. The room for a dialogue must be created precisely by wedging into the tell-tale divergences not only between larger entities like the Shiva Sena and the BJP, but between the various members and factions of the so-called Sangh Parivar. Unless we recognize the differences between Govindacharya and Ashok Singhal, between Uma Bharati and Sadhvi Ritambhara, we will make a dangerous and costly error.

We shall have to admit that there is a space in India not only for a right-wing party, but also for one which claims to espouse the interests of the Hindus. What we must argue, however, is that the interests of the Hindus are not really different from the interests of the Muslims and of the other minorities because these interests are economic, political, social and cultural. If the BJP tries to claim Gandhi's *svadeshi* for itself, we shall have to remind them that *svadeshi* is for both Hindu and Muslim, that the *desha* belongs alike to all those who live in it. We shall have to remind them that our religion does not condone, let alone encourage, the destruc-tion of the shrines of other religions, that it does not equate temporal power and glory with spiritual upliftment.

In brief, Hindutva can be challenged by showing how un-Hindu it is. We can defeat it not by retreating from Hinduism, leaving its rich and nourishing terrain to be appropriated by Hindutva, but by contesting Hindutva's claims over Hinduism, by disputing them, fighting them, and, ultimately disproving them. Hinduism must not go on the defensive, apologetically seeking refuge in secularism; instead, it must take the fight into the enemy's camp, challenging Hindutva to prove its 'bonafides.' Hindutva can be defeated not by substituting Hinduism with secularism, but by replacing a corrupt and rotten secularism with a genuinely pluralistic and satisfying Hinduism. Or, to put it in another way, Hindutva can be defeated only when a genuine secularism works to support a genuine Hinduism.

Right now, however, what we have is a rotten secularism weakening and undermining an already embattled Hindu tradition by a politics of counter-minoritarianism, which its colonized mind has copied and derived from certain trendy modes of Western scholarship. Such university-bred radicalism cannot survive without a continuous patronage from the West because, ultimately, it derives not only its agenda but its legitimacy from the West. *Dalit*s and women, especially those among them who have reaped the benefits of affirmative action and social reform, and who now share the same privileges for which they attack high-caste Hindus, can make a crucial contribution at this stage by opting out of their pseudo-victim positions, abandoning the politics of special interests, and trying to evolve common causes with caste Hindus. A politics of cooperation and mutual responsibility needs to replace a politics of opposition and mutual hatred. And here, a sensitive and responsive majority looks towards a courageous and unselfish minority to take the lead.

Conclusion

What, then, we might ask, the *dharma* of secularism be? Surely, it would be to continue its fight against forces of religious intolerance and violence, to prevent the politicization of these forces so as to create vote blocks, to prevent political parties which espouse such ideologies of opposition and hatred from assuming power. What is more important, is that such criticism or resistance ought not to be partial and selective, but fair and consistent. But the duty of secularism is much more than this. It is to show tolerance for its Other, which is religious, the spiritual, the dhārmic. Only when secularism displayed a genuine understanding and respect for our dhārmic traditions can it play a useful role in our intellectual and political life. Without such understanding and respect, it will merely mirror what it opposes, its own fanaticism pitted against that of Hindu fanatics. The *dharma* of secularism, at the least, is to show the same kind of tolerance to the religion as religion has shown to it in India. The result is that the best of our intellectuals and sages either demonstrate a dhārmic secularism or a sort of secular *dharma*. Either will do, provided it is sincere and serious. What will not do is either religious or secularist extremism.

13

Hindu Dharma and Indian Funk

K. Dad Prithipaul

ON Sunday 11 June 1997, the Canadian Broadcasting Corporation (CBC) carried a two-hour programme in commemoration of the fiftieth anniversary of the Independence of India. The second hour was taken up with an interview with the three Indian women writers who, in faultless English, articulated their views of the current situation obtaining in their country. One of the three writers attributed to non-resident Indians what she deems to be the undesirable practice of making substantial contributions to the financing of the Bharatiya Janata Party. In her mind such non-resident Indian intervention in Indian politics constitutes a direct, if not a pernicious, way of promoting intolerance and chauvinism in India. In the context of the conversation she seemed to suggest that the rise of Hindu fundamentalism — if, according to a current fad, this be the proper designation for the emergence of traditional Hindu values in Indian national politics — is not a product and an expression of the dynamics agitating the indigenous Indian socio-political realities, but an import from the communities of Indians living abroad. Such a statement from an enlightened, highly educated and independent-minded person demonstrates the confusion that has prevailed in India ever since she obtained independence. The writer interviewed did not seem to be aware of the absurdity of her statement. For, a few moments later, on being asked by the CBC reporter what is taking the place of British culture which "is burning on its own funeral pyre," one of the trio of writers answered coolly that the cultural vacuum is being filled by MTV, Michael Jackson, internet, disco, etc. Further, none of these writers seemed to appreciate the interviewer's expression of surprise caused by his discovering that Bill Gates' dolls are being marketed in India, while such is not the case in North America. His remark triggered a mild laughter as one of the writers volunteered the information that her brother is a manufacturer of these dolls. Nevertheless she blamed the media for blowing the occurrence out of proportion.

In Edmonton (Canada), during a conversation, at a private reception given in the late spring of 1997 in honour of a visiting classical dancer from India, the latter felt no compunction in berating the British-Guyanese Indian community for their adherence to the mother dialect they still speak a century after they had been transported from north India to provide cheap labour for the British plantation owners. Mallika Sarabhai was smugly unconcerned with the incongruity of her using the English language to express her contemptuous comment on the "culture" of Indo-Guyanese before whom she had produced her pretentious, multi-media, one-dimensional, one-hour "V for . . ." show during which, dressed in a dark brown tail-coat, brown slacks with a revolver tucked in her belt, she spewed out at machine-gun speed a text riddled with clichés tied together with the thread of anarchist slogans. After the show, dressed in *shalwār-kamīẓ*, she came on the stage to interact with the audience and claimed that she was bringing the Gandhian message to the people! She showed no awareness of the indifference and neglect which, for five or six generations, the elites in India have manifested towards these poor diaspora communities. The best that India could offer to them in the matter of culture was whatever dripped from the formula-structured films churned by the hundreds in the Bombay studios. Middleclass, educated Indians too easily forget that Mahatma Gandhi spent 21 years in forging the instruments of *satyāgraha* and of *ahiṁsā* while working among a community of deprived diaspora Indians in South Africa. It was the greatest gift which overseas Indians have offered to the mainstream of Indian life in this century. In a different context the small island of Mauritius has, in addition to hosting a World Conference on "Francophonie," sponsored international conferences on Hindi, Tamil, Bhojpuri. These too are gifts which Indian diaspora have presented to the Indian mainstream. It is befitting that such contributions, as vibrant testimonies of loyalty to the presence of an unquestionably glorious heritage, be mentioned as a postulate of the validity of a diaspora concern for the preservation and development of the values that have their roots in what can still be called "Hindu *dharma*." Moreover, it may be borne in mind that Lee Kwan Yew of Singapore has in the past years acquired some eminence as a major spokesman for the relevance and meaningfulness of a renewal of the confucian tradition which he raises as a bulwark against the dehumanization inherent in the triumph of an inexorable Western cultural and ideological domination. In 1993 he was invited as a guest speaker and as a major participant in an international conference on confucianism sponsored by the Communist government in Beijing.

Cultural Decolonization Halted

In this essay, the reflections on *dharma* do, as a matter of course reflect a comparative point of view. The 1950 Constitution of India is widely accepted as a document which enshrines the legal thought that have gone into the Constitutions of several Western democracies. It goes to the credit of India that the Constitution was elaborated and freely accepted as Law by a people exercizing its freedom without any form of pressure exerted by an external authority. At about the same time Japan and Western Germany had democratic constitutions imposed upon them while each of them had an army of occupation based on its territory. The voting of the Indian Constitution was a political act performed by a sovereign nation asserting its will on its own. Regarded as one of the best democratic constitutions in the world today the 1950 Constitution is above all a cause for national pride and may even be viewed as a blessing bequeathed by those who gave so much of themselves in the struggle for Independence from British rule.

Macaulay and the English Language

As a lateral extension of the Constitution, the English language still forms part of the Indian administration and of the medium of communication of the middle class, especially between the people living in the northern Hindi belt and those who live in the southern non-Hindi speaking provinces. In fact, English, or Indo-English as some designate it, has by now acquired a permanent niche in the intellectual space of India. The punch lines of almost every Indian feature film and of the television serials are invariably uttered in English. Despite the fact that India officially recognizes 21 indigenous languages, the hero and the heroine of the average Bombay film must inevitably use the English expression "I love you" as confirmation of their mutual romantic attraction. Gratitude is invariably conveyed by "Thank you very much." Transitive verbs take the form of the English equivalent coupled with the semi-auxiliary verb *karanā* (e.g., *tum mujhko avoid karte ho, kyon*?) ; intransitive verbs are formed by the corresponding English adjective added to the auxiliary *honā* (e.g., *lekin be careful, woh bahut dangerous hai*). The cultural mimicry is best encapsulated by the repulsive expression "Bollywood," popularized by the film magazines and by the more serious print media.

Moreover, a feature film seemingly will not be 'bought' by the Indian middle class unless it has some expensive dance sequences which crudely mimic the gyrations of Michael Jackson. The latter thus provides consumer delectation to a people who, after having given to the world the unique aesthetic conception of Mahādeva Śiva as the Cosmic Dancer, is unable to develop and foster contemporary indigenous choreographic styles for its own entertainment. The plot surrounding a romantic triangle often requires the intervention of the young hero who returns from the U.S.A. and the happy ending rests on the release of tension with one member of the love trio taking a flight back to New York. The popular imagination assumes Indian space and time to be inadequate for the film plot to unfold and run its course.

In his *History of the Urdu Literature*, Mohammed Sadiq observes that Urdu poetry still uses an imagery reminiscent of its Persian environment. Name of flowers, trees, birds, native to Persian soil still recur in descriptions of, and in allusions to, nature. This nomenclature suggests that Urdu has not fully internalized the local Indian colours as it still carries a nostalgic attachment to a foreign land of a distant time. Concomitantly, it would be instructive to make a list of the similes, metaphors and other figures of speech that currently find their place in the editorials of an English weekly like, for example, *India Today*. Almost invariably they refer to Western literature, history, social sciences, and to Western modes of thought. Such a cultural alienation has become an unreflecting feature of Indian middleclass consciousness. One of the regular contributors of *India Today* was at one time a trusted adjunct of the dynastic power ruling the country. One cannot help wondering how such a mind, functioning with a set of references grown on the soil of English culture, could have rightly understood and correctly perceived the problems of a nation still — fortunately — cherishing pertinent forms of thought and of feeling bequeathed by its past.

During the month of September 1967, I spent a few days in New Delhi as the guest of Judge Shiv Manchanda (the author of the book on *Indian Divorce Law*). One day I asked him if the act of witnessing in a court of law is borrowed from British practice. I wanted to know if witnessing to the truth has its historical root in Christian theology, that is, if the witness testifies as if he is in the real presence of a monotheistic deity. Swearing on the *Bhagavad-Gītā* does not have the same connotation of the witness speaking in the presence of a Deity as the Supreme Judge. Judge Manchanda had no immediate reply and promised me he would seek a decisive opinion from his colleagues at the Supreme Court. Actually a few days later he invited me to meet a few senior jurists in the library of the Supreme Court. I found myself in the company of six eminent, elderly jurists, among whom was Deputy Attorney General Setalvad. They graciously explained the mechanism of testimony under oath and they were of the unanimous opinion that the form and substance of witnessing in an Indian law court bore no relation to a Christian ethos, that the act of witnessing is fully Indianized, and is totally independent of any link with Western jurisprudence.

Nevertheless, the romanization of the Indian consciousness finally vindicates the racist dream of Lord Macaulay who argued rightly that the British conquest would rest on firmer ground if the English language served as the vehicle of the settlement of British culture within Indian society. To a large extent the culture of the "Raj" is being preserved and has actually been adopted by the exercise of a free national will. In the mid-1980s a newsletter issued by the Indian High Commission in Ottawa reported that New Delhi had become, after London and New York, the third producer of books in the English language.

Either by consent or by constraint, India accommodates herself to Western demands and pressures. For instance, all international flights entering or leaving India are regulated according to Western timetables. Scientific and business standards are prescribed by the Western institutions. Higher education has to meet criteria set by the Western universities. Women's fashions follow the Western trends. India has to heed the call for the protection of human rights as defined by the Western institutions. Indian politicians are always bending backward to win the approval of Western democracies, like children craving for the tinsel stars distributed by the school teacher. 'Secularist' leaders of, in particular, the Communist and the Congress parties, are often blissfully unaware of their own secularist fundamentalism. How absurd is it that secularist fanaticism have to force a universalist cultural institution like the

Ramakrishna Mission to appeal to, and obtain from, the Supreme Court the diminished status of a sect in order to be entitled to obtain funding for its educational institutions!

Yet the 'secularist' politicians have seized every opportunity to assail those political formations for their reliance on the Hindu traditional forms of thought as being contrary to the letter and spirit of the Indian Constitution. At the same time they have not shied away from seeing virtue in, and seeking merit from, competing against one another in their abject adulation of a semi-literate, fundamentalist Mother Teresa by showering rewards and honours upon her for earning fame and international recognition by marketing the ugliness and inhumanity of Indian poverty and depravation. With independence, the Indian leaders themselves chose to proclaim as national virtue the practice of mimicking Western modes of thinking and behaviour. Against such a sketchy, symbolic background, it is fair and legitimate to discuss the vagaries of Hindu *dharma* in a global context.

In this manner India has become a valley, a flat lowland where the currents of Western technologies and forms of thought, Western realities and appearances, Western artistic and literary expressions, flow and irrigate popular and, in particular, middleclass sensitivities and modes of behaviour. India does not give, or rather has ceased to be a donor, because whatever she still calls her own indigenous culture is strictly endorheic and does not flow outward to other countries and continents. On the contrary, she receives almost everything from abroad and deludes herself by thinking she is again active in the process of synthesizing foreign cultural forms and values in a diachronic process of Indianization.

The English Language and the Delusion of Open-Mindedness: Funk as the Substitute for Puraskāra

The question which immediately comes to mind is why Indians are tormented by the funk of speaking of, and owning, what has been so patiently, so heroically elaborated by the sages of old times. India is the only major country which, while historically and geographically coinciding with her culture and civilization, cultivates a mentality that deems it modern and progressive to promote rejection of her former achievements and of her ancientness as the politics of tolerance and inclusiveness. India is the only example of a major civilization country which, in its capital, does not have a single monument which recalls its past prior to the fifteenth century. India is the only major country where the political leadership sinks into a sort of paralysis, driven by a morbid funk, when the social need arises to refer to her classical philosophers, her architects, her artists, her past exemplars, her monuments, her heritage. Today India does not have a single leader who has the intellectual sagacity of a leader like Lionel Jospin who, in a discussion with financial leaders opposed, for economic reasons, to the admission of Italy to the common currency of the euro argued that the Italy of Dante cannot be left out of the European Monetary Union. Has any Indian leader, during the past half century, ever referred to Vālmīki or to Kālidāsa?

In *The Religion of Man*, Tagore confesses that his family is a confluence of Hindu, Mohammedan and British cultures. His grandfather Dwarkanath was conversant with Arabic and Persian. Rabindranath himself grew up in a family environment enriched with Sanskrit and Persian lore. But what astonishes the reader of Rajmohan Gandhi's biographies of eight eminent Muslim leaders (Sayyid Ahmed Khan, Iqbal, Muhammad Ali, Jinnah, Fazlul Huq, Abdul Kalam Azad, Liaqat Ali Khan, Zakir Husain in *Eight Lives: A study of the Hindu-Muslim Encounter*) is that none of these Muslim social and political leaders seemed to have taken any notice of the existence of the Hindu values, of Hindu philosophical, moral and cultural realities. Hindu culture was invisible to them. They were fascinated by the British culture and were, as a result, eager to return to their Islamic tradition, to adapt, reformulate and strengthen it in accordance with the political and social environment prevailing in the subcontinent.

Yet the greater astonishment stems from the political will of the post-Independence Indian leadership to draw a curtain on the past, to foster a national attitude that flatters itself by rendering the Hindu past invisible. A culture which does boldly translate into wood and stone and stucco the erotic paragraphs of Vātsyāyana's *Kāmasūtra* suddenly, with the advent of independence, develops a cringing bashfulness that views as a political sin any endeavour to reassert a way of life which has been driven underground for centuries by alien forces. This cultural shyness recalls the British puritanical condemnation of Bharata-Nāṭyam as a decadent form of art, till Rukmini Arundale appeared in the 1920s and rose up to rehabilitate and rescue this art form from neglect and decay.

Besides India, the history of the world does not present a more persuasive example of collective funk adopted as national policy. The Indian elites manifest funk with regard to their past. The educated Hindu feels he has to overcome an inner resistance when the occasion requires him to say: "I am a Hindu" — as a noun, or "I am Hindu" — as an adjective. He is afraid to say it, or to own it. The funk which inhabits his consciousness is evident when he hastens to qualify his Hinduness with a "but" when he sets forth the damper: "I am a Hindu, *but* I am an Indian first." In the West one never hears someone say: "I am Christian (or a Christian), but I am a Canadian, or a Frenchman, or an American first." Just as in Canada no one knows what Canadianness means, the educated middleclass Indian does not know what Indianness means. The Indian is a rudderless individual cast in the sea of what is now euphemistically called 'globalization.' For the Indian middle class, represented by the three women writer referred to above, the *rāma-rājya* does not lie on the banks of the Sarayū, but it is found ready-made in Chicago, New York, California, Toronto, Vancouver.

Indeed of the three major Asian nations — Japan, China and India — only the latter unabashedly exhibits such funk with persistent, glorious obstinacy. Nothing expresses this funk of the Hindu tradition as the cliché representation of the Hindu priest in the average B-movies produced in Bombay. For the entertainment of a community, where since times immemorial the family has freely chosen and adopted its own *purohita*, the 'puṇḍit' is always portrayed as an ignorant pot-bellied buffoon, cowardly and mean, lustful and greedy, driven by hate, fanatical. In contrast the Mullah is always a bearded man in his 50s who speaks in an unctuous tone, never stops raising his two hands towards the sky in the midst of an evocation of a benevolent Allah; he is very tolerant, loving, a reservoir of merciful humanity (e.g., Manmohan Krishna in *Sholay*). The Christian priest always moves slowly, is compassionate, understands the young lovers' problems; he is the respected 'Farder,' charitable, forgiving, a haven of peace and understanding for the lovers caught in a crossfire of conflicting social forces (e.g., the priest in *Khamoshi*). While the classical literature describes Nārada as a learned scholar, endowed with a perfect knowledge of the Vedas and the Upaniṣads, of the Dharmaśāstras, of the six *darśanas*, of grammar, of astrology, of music and song, he is nevertheless personified as an ever grinning young man with a mute *vīṇā* hanging from his neck and all his knowledge is condensed into the insane repetition of "Nārāyaṇa, Nārāyaṇa" (e.g., the serial *Hanumān*). He is supposed to provide comic relief, he is the convenient *vidūṣaka* for the film producer and the script writer who betray an unquestioned funk in regard to their own culture as is evident in their inability to do justice to a mythic exemplar of traditional knowledge and spiritual lore.

The Absence of Ideals in the Indian Democracy and the Resulting Funk

The French Revolution was initiated and carried out by individuals inspired by the conquests of reason, by the ideals of the heroes of

Greek and Roman history and literature, by the excitement and passion of carrying the message of Freedom, Equality and Fraternity to all the oppressed peoples of the world. The republican ideals of the French Nation were lucidly enunciated and the elites demonstrated the will to establish the permanent foundation of the presence and relevance of these ideals in new laws and institutions. The instruments fashioned to carry these ideas to the remotest corner of the territory were the reformed jurisprudence, the public school and a scholastic curriculum conforming to the secular institutions deemed to be indispensable to the establishment of a way of life marked by the ideals formulated by Rousseau, Voltaire, the Encyclopaedists and other thinkers of the Enlightenment. Condorcet stands out as a great, innovating philosopher and scientist who, while being an aristocrat, wrote, worked and died for the establishment of the new republican democracy.

But the funk felt in not formulating ideals congruent with the genius, the history and the personality of the Indian people was a decisive factor in the Constituent Assembly elaborating a Constitution and a system of law without any reference to any philosophical or moral determination of the future of the nation. The mind is baffled when it contemplates the Indian elites remaining silent during the past five decades without feeling the slightest anguish over the drift which such a funk was bound to generate. Funk of the need to build up a national language, funk of a common legal system, funk of the imperative to engage a dialogue with Islamic theology, funk of the necessity of articulating the right ideals of a nation which, more than any other, has, in the past, had the courage to define, and the sagacity to establish, a social order on the basis of the highest reach of individual self-fulfilment. While Mahatma Gandhi boldly argued, in his lectures on the *Bhagavad-Gītā*, that for him *svarāja* was synonymous with *mokṣa*, his political heirs, once they held the levers of government in their hands, did not hesitate to scuttle such lofty ideals with their glorification of a jurisprudential knowledge borrowed from traditions of legal thought from beyond the frontiers of India.

India, like China, has rightly, with a sense of justice still insufficiently acknowledged in the West, never in the past four or five millennia, overstepped her national or cultural borders with a desire to enlarge her territory. Yet the irony is that she has done precisely that, once she gained her independence, by ranging across the intellectual spaces of other nations to give to herself a legal system which bears faint organic continuity with her own past history. That such an alienating process would have lasted for so long without tragic consequences deserves to be examined by historians, philosophers, sociologists and by all those who simply care for the importance of India representing in historical imagination what she was and what she can still be. Funk as a bureaucratically enforced virtue would require to be probed and its legitimacy justified or negated.

The 1950 Constitution: Its Inadequacies

It behoves any fair-minded person to defend the pure intention of the jurists who deserve praise for having laboured to write, in good conscience and with love and devotion to a country as multilayered and complex as India has always been, a workable and humane Constitution. But it must be emphasized that while they drew on the most important of the moral contributions of the French Revolution to proclaim the equality of rights for all the citizens of the country, one wished they had also studied the philosophical presuppositions that inspired the declaration of the inalienable rights of man.

For in addition to its juridical sophistication the Indian Constitution ought to have had a Preamble which approved the elimination of inequality among nations, promoted the equality among the citizens of a single nation and, above all, unambiguously declared the need to remove all obstacles to the free striving for, and the practice of, the perfectability of the individual man. Equality cannot be a requirement unless it is buttressed by a genuine possession of rights. Furthermore, equality must coexist with the promotion of public welfare and with the gradual diminution of excessively large fortunes which confer privileges and abuses of power. Perfectability must be accompanied by the material and legal ability of parents to assure the welfare and spiritual uplift of their children, by the judicious use of science and of the arts, to the exculsion of all the possible harm that may arise as a result of their misuse. In short, the Preamble ought to have, in new, virile terms, adapted to the socio-political realities obtaining at the end of the century, proclaimed whatever was optimistic and just in the former *dharma* pronouncements and in harmony with an understanding of a comprehensive history of the world. That would have been a unique gift to the Indian nation and to the world.

But, as the pendulum of *dharma* swung to the West in the minds and hearts of those thinkers who so generously laid down their lives for a better future of all mankind, India chose to measure herself by her funk of all that was exalting and inspiring in her past achievements. The result has been that funk has become the national egg within which lives the Indian nation. Funk compels India to face the future by being burdened with a collective neurosis. Socially the Hindu is and is not; he wants to be a Westerner, but he is not a Westerner; he wants to be an Indian, but he does not know what are the unique relevant ideals or universals which India ought to carry into the future to assert its specific identity as a collaborative offering to the world.

Nehru's Vision and Cultural Amnesia

It is generally acknowledged that the 1950 Constitution consecrates Nehru's will to break away from the Gandhian presuppositions of the Congress party ideology and to usher India into a future defined by his anglo-socialist rationality. Nehru always flaunted what he believed to be a progressive outlook by making fun of brāhmaṇas and ridiculing their attachment to orthodoxy and tradition. He wanted India to have no affinity with her past. The future was to be an entirely new collective experience, pruned from the chaotic undergrowth of tradition, exclusive of the moral precepts of *dharma* and of popular religion. Nehru's recognition of folklore as a vital aspect of rural life was limited to its token representation in the procession of floats illustrating regional folk traditions on the occasion of the 26 January, Republic Day celebrations in New Delhi.

Nehru saluted Bhakhra-Nangal as a new temple and as a place of pilgrimage for the uplift of the new, independent Indians. Built on a patch of land without any association with past culture or tradition, Chandigarh was hailed as the architectural prototype of the new city: it recalled neither the architectural beauties erected according to the prescriptions of ancient *vāstuśāstra*, nor the architectural designs of New Delhi by Lutyens. It was meant to be a concrete symbol of the Nehruvian dream, of what India was hoped to be. The new Constitution represented the affirmation of a still formless, abstract future and a wilful rejection of the past. It was viewed as the political and legal womb which would give birth to a modern India, untainted by the blemishes of the failures that had marked the previous centuries of her history. Cultural amnesia was thus proposed as a political necessity and as the social prerequisite of a blissful future. That was how the notion of *dharma*, hitherto held to be the source of the most vital impulse of Indian polity, as well as of the individual and of family life, came to be driven to the farthest reaches of the collective consciousness.

In classical India the *rājā* (king) never placed himself above *dharma*. Any violation of *dharma* on his part would be immediately known by the common citizens (*prajā*). *Dharma* encompassed the sensitivities of the ruler and of the ruled. It was a multilayered social structure that made allowance for the needs for hierarchies and differences, and provided direction to the life of individuals and of communities. It rested on the weakening of conflicts whenever these broke out. *Dharma* worked in the midst of the population as a set of principles, injunctions and prohibitions, held together by universal consent, without any constraint exercised by a dominant central bureaucracy.

Yet, with unquestioned hypocrisy, the Congress Party, once it took charge of the administration of the country, deliberately set out to infuse new vigour into the rigidities of caste loyalties and to extract all manners of advantages from the mutual exclusivism of castes, in its varying equations of its grab of, and hold on, power. It is ironic that, while proclaiming an abstract egalitarianism, the Congress Party should have failed to implement civic equality by means of a cognate education and of an economy based on social justice. It is ironic that, while rejecting the provisions of the traditional Dharmaśāstras, India should have used the new legal dispensations to protect and promote graft, kleptomania, corruption, abuse of public trust. As a result, the new rulers have in practice succeeded in placing themselves above the Law. The safe-keeping of dishonesty and hypocrisy in their administrative practices reminds one, not of the *dharma*-bound *rājā*, but of the Caliphs of Islamic history who always stood above the law to which they subjected their people.

The Absence of Dharma: A Moral and Cultural Vacuum

Rousseau's influence is felt in the American Constitution in the declaration of its purpose being to promote the happiness of the American people. The iteration of the American dream still resonates as a vital motivating impulse in their collective sensitivities. The citizens of the French Republic still bristle at the slightest indication of a threat to the values and ideals which are still operative in its institutions. Educated Indians are at a loss to answer when queried about the moral and spiritual ideals of the Indian Republic. It has none. And the funk of ideals has prevented the political leadership, especially of the Congress Party, from considering it its duty to formulate the basic values and ideals around which the rich and the poor, the scholar and the rustic, the artist and the craftsman, could identify their existence and the pursuit of their individual goals.

No one ever speaks of the "socialist pattern of democracy" enunciated in the 1950s by Pundit Nehru. With hindsight one has to acknowledge that it was an expression of undiluted funk. All the terms of this expression have their roots in Western political thought, without the slightest bearing on Indian tradition and values. It openly refused to seek out the positive features of the past "*dharma*-inspired" culture and build the future upon them. Nehru's formula is a characteristic example of an anglicization of the mind of the Indian elite that has proved to be insular, unconnected with any political and moral reality, either in relation to the West or still less so to India.

Only funk of the metaphysical imponderables can explain the indifference that has veiled perceptions of the extant British Raj bureaucracy and of the Macaulayan system of education, both of which have lain on the Indian polity like a shroud of lead. India is the only country which has a temple dedicated to herself, as Mother India. Yet popular funk has succeeded in keeping India not as a temple attended by active, faithful devotees, but as a silent museum of its mummified past glories, and as the super market expanding according to a rhythm set by American merchants and entrepreneurs.

Dharma as the Essence of the Hindu Ways

Yet, if there is one value that distinguishes India and marks it off from other nations or cultures, it is the concept of the *dharma*, as an ethos comprising a set of values which regulate individual, family and collective life. It is a comprehensive set of principles and regulations that is based on harmony, on the avoidance of conflict, on the ceaseless pursuit of the ultimate good both as individual and national ends.

Though the texts mention *dharma*, as one of *puruṣārthas*, always in this order: *artha, kāma, dharma, mokṣa*, yet it is worth emphasizing that *dharma* is not exclusive of the other purposes. For instance, there can be no possibility for one to cultivate *dharma* without the assurance of material security. Among the lies that are considered to be morally neutral and not contrary to *dharma* is the one that can be said for the protection of a legitimately acquired wealth in view of the fulfilment of the *dharma* of oneself and of one's family. At the same time *dharma* is postulated as an absolute. In fact, Hindu culture has its foundation in the double Absolute of *dharma* and *mokṣa*. Yudhiṣṭhira tells Draupadī that for him *dharma* is higher than life itself: he would rather renounce Draupadī herself and his four brothers, but he would never renounce *dharma*. It is worth remembering that the four younger Pāṇḍava brothers are each the offspring of a god: Arjuna is the son of Indra, Bhīmasena of Vāyu, the twins Nakula and Sahadeva of the Aśvins. Only Yudhiṣṭhira does not have a divine father, as he is the son of *dharma* who is not a god. *Dharma* is a *yakṣa*. Still the younger brothers defer to the moral authority of Yudhiṣṭhira.

As an absolute *dharma* coincides with *mokṣa*. If the One is all-pervasive and *mokṣa* is the immediate experience of it, personalized in the daily avocations of the individual, then *mokṣa* must be understood and felt as coterminous with the practice of *dharma*. The linguistic enumeration of the *puruṣārthas*, with a comma — especially in the texts written in the Western languages — interspersed between *artha, kāma, dharma* and *mokṣa*, becomes misleading when these are interpreted as successive values, developed in a sequential, linear time. The intention and the direction prescribed by the *dharma* literature requires the insertion of *mokṣa* in the present instant, at all the levels of thought, speech and action. This intention is best expressed in the celebration of the ethos of *aparigraha* (non-obligation) and of *niṣkāma karma* (desireless action): the totality of thought — present and inculsive of the future, of speech as self-expression in refined communication with the Other, of action for and to oneself, and for and to the Other — loses its specific, historical relativism when it becomes a concrete personalized expression of the ineffable, metaphysical reality of *mokṣa.*

The *dharma-mokṣa* nexus defines the particular bent of Hindu Culture which accordingly plunges roots in a metaphysical reality that calls on the individual to seek moral and spiritual perfection in the human condition, as the paramount social goal and end of earthly existence. As the substance of *dharma, mokṣa* impels the individual to a constant striving for his own self-perfecting while enriching and elevating the interrelating community. With this understanding, the intent of *dharma* is to insert *mokṣa* as a dynamic thrust within individual existence, as a sublime precondition for the universal social welfare. The *dharma-mokṣa* nexus shares co-substantiality with the natural wilfulness prevailing in the impulses which strengthen and sustain a joyous acceptance of the certainty of self-perfectability. As such the *mokṣa*-based culture does not forfeit its authority on account of the political failures, nor must it be viewed as being irrelevant to the prospects of a happy collective future.

Despite the rise and fall of empires regulating the rhythm of the course of Western history, the Western elites, nevertheless still, in times of stress and of crisis, seek inspiration in the ideals that distinguished the lives and thoughts of the Greeks of the age of Pericles, or of the Romans of the age of Augustus, and learn from their virtues and foibles as personified by the heroes in the epics of Homer and of Virgil. Only in India, for the first time in history, have the elites spawned by the peaceful struggle for independence prevailed in persuading, certainly in good faith, a meek and submissive people into believing that the uses of the past were an impediment to progress.

Nothing better recalls to mind the funk of the quintessence of the *dharma* tradition as does the absence, in the Preamble of the

1950 Constitution, of the highest ideal that India once prescribed for her citizen. India failed to respond to the call for a tryst with destiny by abstaining from offering to the world the value of absolute freedom (*mokṣa* or *nirvāṇa*) as the goal of national and international politics. *Mokṣa* or *nirvāṇa* were not prescribed as realities to be experienced as heroic solitude in individual isolation, but in constant active interacting with the community. Such an opportunity may never recur during the remainder of the *kaliyuga*.

Manu, Democracy and Demagoguery

Yet Manu, with perfect lucidity, proclaims *mokṣa* as the goal of existence conducted according to the prescriptions of his Smṛti text. Manu placed himself and his co-citizens on a higher ground than did Aristotle who, in the Nicomachean Ethics, considers politics as the supreme art which enables Man to attain his self-fulfilment. Manu proclaimed a human destiny higher than what Rousseau considered to be ideal for Man freed from the shackles laid on him by his past history and culture.

Yet nothing reveals Indian funk so much as the success surrendered to Mayavati in her denunciation of those she abuses as *manuvādins*, with her characteristic alienation from, and ignorance of, all that Hindu *dharma* stands for. It is on account of the political indifference to, and the neglect of, the reform of education, as a requirement for national reconstruction following the accession to independence, that so much ignorance can have become so pervasive in regional and national politics. Otherwise one would not be able to understand the utter ignorance of Indian history, which passes for modernity and progress, on the part of a demagogue like Mayavati in her mindless denunciation of *manuvāda*.

The observer of the Indian political scene cannot resist the painful astonishment at how such public, unabashed dissemination of ignorance can, by constant reiteration over a long period, prevail and become transformed into an ideological doctrine without any institution or individual standing up to refute it. No one in the history of the world has defined freedom with as much nobility of thought as has Manu: "He indeed attains freedom who regards his self as a sacrifice, and sees the Self in all beings and all beings as being established in the Self" (*sarvabhūteṣu cātmānam sarvabhūtāni cātmani samam paśyann ātmayāji svārājyam adhigacchati*). Sacrifice (*yajña*) is a self-denial for the purpose of enhancing life for oneself and for others. It has no common measure with the notion of martyrdom, which postulates a witnessing to truth by means of death. The *dharma* ethos prescribes witnessing to truth in living as *jīvanmukti*, in the search for an end of the succession of births.

Dharma and Education

It has been said above that, following the Revolution of 1789, the French nation set-up a public school system and a corresponding curriculum to foster a culture based on Reason, to the exclusion of all forms of secular and religious fanaticism. This scholastic system still functions to this day after more than 200 years. It must be recalled that the Western Europe and subsequently America borrowed the idea of the public school system and of its promotion of meritocracy from Confucian China. In the eighteenth century it was hailed, and adopted by the Enlightenment thinkers, as an effective instrument for the establishment of democracy and of social equality.

However, in 1947, after nearly a thousand years of India having lived under alien rule, the leaders of the Hindu majority should have understood that what the independent and democratic nation needed most was an educational system as the indispensable instrument required for the corrections of the social deformations that had grown out of the loss of self-governance. Traditional India did not possess an educational system geared to the formation of an egalitarian society. The British system of education — itself a variation of the original Confucian — was the best available for the collective benefit of a democratically governed country. The need of the times consisted in adapting the existing system to the moral and spiritual requirements of the individual and of the community.

It would have been a folly for anyone to return to the rigidities of the past. In fact, P.V. Kane's monumental work, *History of the Dharmaśāstra* provides abundant evidence of the changes and evolution in the application of the laws of the *dharma* over the centuries. Hindu *dharma* bears inherent flexibilities that enable it to conform to emerging social needs. Indeed, a characteristic feature of the Hindu approach to life is the sophisticated ability to bend a rule, as required by a specific need, without emptying the same rule of its permanent validity. An anecdote will illustrate the relationship between the rule and the exception.

One afternoon, in 1958, I called on Professor T.R.V. Murti, at his residence, in Varanasi, in connection with a problem I had encountered in my doctoral research. I saw him sitting alone, with a sad, angry look on his face. He was staring at the newspaper lying on the coffee table in front of him. I glanced at it and the full-page blazing headline read: "Chinese delegation leaves Delhi emptyhanded." The news of the day related to the visit of the Chinese delegation of 64 cartographers, historians and other experts led by Prime Minister Chou En Lai. They had spent four days in New Delhi for discussions with the Nehru government, on the settlement of the borders which the British had unilaterally and arbitrarily marked as the common frontier of the two countries.

After a long moment of silence I rose to leave; I said I would return some other day as it seemed that he was not well. But he motioned to me to stay. Then after another long moment of silence, he burst out: "This Nehru is not a Hindu. He is too much of the B.Sc. from Cambridge. He is too rigid." When I asked him what he meant, he said: "A genuine Hindu never lets a guest leave his house emptyhanded. That is not the way to behave towards the Chinese. They came in good faith, with a lot of good will. They were seeking a peaceful arrangement. Nehru should have given them something to take back home; he ought to have made some concession. Look at our grammarians: to every fundamental rule they have attached a minor exception. The Hindu must know how and when to be flexible. Nehru does not know this."

The absence of *dharma* categories from Nehru's thinking has had one of the most unfortunate consequences for India after Independence. It has resulted in the loss of lives, of territory, of national prestige. The effect is still being felt to this day. Indeed, rigidity is what is fundamentally unbecoming to the Hindu ways of thinking. The paradox is that it is rigidity that distinguishes the insular, fossilized, anglicized mind of the "modern" Hindu "who is first an Indian." He revels in his funk which he fondly takes for broadmindedness. Another example illustrates the argument being here set forth.

Bhakhra-Nangal, the steel plants, Chandigarh, the 1950 Constitution, all still stare the contemporary Indian, or the sympathetic visitor, as the concrete expressions of Nehru's urgent optimism and hasty hope of such a future as to assure the material well-being of the nation. On the other hand, this enthusiasm to race India to a successful, modern state failed when other tasks claimed his imgination.

Dharma and Iconoclasm

The media and a large segment of the Westernized Indian middleclass have unequivocally voiced anger and disapproval over the demolition of the Babri Masjid. This incident was used as a foil to denounce those political formations which were directly responsible for the destruction of the Masjid. The reasoning undergirding such denunciations was that it was wrong to destroy a religious building, it was the manifestation of a fanatical, fundamentalist Hindu attitude; it was described as a fascist action. The Bharatiya Janata Party was particularly maligned for promoting a fascist ideology, though most 'secularist' journalists and political activists were as little informed of the real nature of fascism as an ideology and as a political and military reality. Obversely Stalinists considered Mahatma Gandhi as a bourgeois reactionary. This abstract perception of the BJP is now shared by many academics across North America, especially among the non-Indian American and Canadian scholars specializing in micro-segments of Indian studies. For instance, last year when a south Indian journalist sponsored by the Indian government visited the University of Alberta to speak of the new political forces in India, his lecture was advertised in the academic campus weekly as a criticism of Indian fascism.

The inability on the part of the West to grapple with the emergence of the BJP as a new political reality runs deeper than is often admitted. One afternoon, in the mid 1950s, during a conversation I had with Professor J.L. Mehta — whose writings constitute the best interpretation of Heidegger in the English language — on the topic of the Kashmir issue being then debated at the Security Council, he observed that the hostility of the West towards India was not merely due to the dynamics of realpolitik. "The problem is not political," he said, "it is metaphysical. The West understands Islam with its stark distinction between a Heaven-centred Allah and an Earth-centred Man. But the West cannot understand the fundamental premise of Hinduism which views the entire universe and all that moves and does not move as a manifestation of an all-pervasive Unitive Reality." My experience of teaching the Indian religions and philosophies for 25 years in my Canadian University fully vindicates the insight of Professor Mehta. I have no assurance that any of my students or colleagues did ever fully grasp all that is implied in the belief of a non-dual Absolute Reality.

In recent times certain writers on India still evince a biased perception and interpretation of the dynamics of the essential values of Hindu culture rising to the surface of national politics, after an eclipse that has lasted nearly a thousand years. Their articles address the Hindu question as if Hinduism, with all its aesthetic and moral expressions, exists only in a social vacuum, distinct from its spatial and temporal context, without its specific historical trajectory. Implicit in their writing is a procrustean inclination to cast what they assume Hinduism to be into the mould of a micro-specialization in an abstract segment of academic indology unrelated to the actual national and global context in which live the Hindus with their myriad castes and rituals, tastes and prejudices, aspirations and cynicisms, ambitions and self-denials (cf. Roderick MacFarquhar, *India: Imprint of Empire*, *New York Review of Books*, vol. 44, no. 16 of October 13, 1997; Ian Buruma, *India: the perils of democracy*, NYRB, vol. 44, no. 19, December 4, 1997). During a discussion which I had, in early 1963, at the Sorbonne (Paris University), I told Professor Madeleine Biardeau that the Hinduism she was referring to was not the Hindu tradition of India: it is a "Parisian Hinduism." She replied: "Yes, you are right. It is a Parisian Hinduism." She assumed that "Parisian Hinduism" was more authentic than the Hinduism which is lived by the Hindus. Hinduism remains the Other, for Western academics and writers on India. The Hindu, as the Other, is always maligned and despised for what he (or she) is not. Many in the West shared Churchill's contempt for the "naked fakīr."

However, the incident at Ayodhyā must not be viewed as limited to the demolition of a Masjid. *The issue was and remians one of iconoclasm*. Is iconoclasm good for the Muslim and an evil when practised by the Hindu? Is it good for both Muslim and Hindu? Is it evil for both Muslim and Hindu? Was it necessary and desirable in the past, but has no place in contemporary Indian polity? What do Muslims have to say about the continued iconoclasm as displayed by the disfigured sculptures that one can still see in so many monuments all over the country? There has been little, if any, debate on the merits or sins of iconoclasm. Nor has there been a debate on the reason which would have prompted Hindus to commit an iconoclastic act fifty years after having voluntarily, and in an atmosphere of hope for a more humane, peaceful Indian society, adopted a secular Constitution which, incidentally, got hinged to secularism by Indira Gandhi acting under the authority confered upon her by the Emergency (1975-77).

The Ayodhyā incident ought to have been presented against the backdrop of the zeal of generations of Muslim iconoclasts. Their legacy is such that one cannot today find a single noteworthy Hindu or Buddhist monument across the entire stretch of territory from Peshawar to Calcutta. Architectural gems like the temple of Somnāthpur in Karnataka still bear mute witness of the fury of Islamic iconoclasm. The ruins of Hampī still utter the glory of the art and architecture of Vijayanagar. Throughout the centuries when so much architectural treasure was razed to the ground, the Hindus abstained from any retaliation of the same nature. Maybe the Brāhmaṇical elites were so beaten down, so emasculated, so decisively suppressed that the loss of so much beauty lasting over so many generations was bewailed by nobody.

The history of Indian Islam may legitimately claim the Taj Mahal as one of its accomplishments. But this history also includes the destruction of such famous centres of learning as Taxila, Nālandā, Sārnāth, Vikramaśilā, Vaiśālī. It also views as part of its greatness and glory the genocidal elimination of flourishing Buddhist cultures in Central Asia. The imposition of the *jizya* upon the Hindu 'infidels' and the forced conversion of the latter were practised by a Muslim power that never felt it was acting as a minority. One aspect of the communal hatred which plagues the politics of India has escaped the attention of the sociologists and historians. The worst anti-semites in Europe were the converted Jews and the sons and daughters of converted Jews. Torquemada, perhaps the most notorious of the Spanish Inquisitors, was a converted Jew. The most rabid antagonists of the Hindus in the Island of Mauritius, during the 1920s and 1930s, happened to be the coloured Creoles who were actually converted Hindus. The Hindu community received more consideration, understanding and help from the descendants of the white French settlers. In India too, many members of the Anglo-Indian community always yearned to go 'home,' in England. Much of the hatred which Muslims feel for Hindus stems from their being converted from Hinduism. Jinnah and Zulfiquar Ali Bhutto were only one or two generations away from their Hindu ancestry. Mahatma Gandhi failed to grasp the fact of hatred being generated by conversion when he argued with Jinnah that it would be the first time in history that a minority community of converts would assume the identity of a people entirely distinct and different from the rest of the population.

Nevertheless, one must not forget that tolerance towards Jews, Christians, Zoroastrians and Muslims was the cultural pre-condition of social life during those times when Hindu orthodoxy prevailed. Hindu orthodoxy never sponsored the idea of killing someone for his adhesion to a different creed as a meritorious act. Such an idea is a major contribution of Islam to Indian intellectual history. Nevertheless, the sudden, unparallelled outburst of iconoclasm in the midst of a Hindu environment demands a serious examination of what kind of social alchemy is at work in the Hindu society. Demagogic denunciation of this act as 'fascism' or 'chauvinism' or 'fundamentalism' actually serves as a smoke-screen to hide hard realities and to avoid taking the necessary decisions to bring about genuine harmony and peaceful cohabitation among the diverse religious communities. Any future government in India must view as irreversible the contribution the BJP has made to political discourse: communalism practised by the majority is as baneful as the communalism practised by the minority.

With the Babri Masjid coming down, the Congress leadership adopted an attitude of hurt pride instead of engaging in a dispassionate examination of the dramatic changes occurring within the Hindu society. In fact, the Congress Party has never been able to fashion an ideology of secularism out of the substance of Indian, not Western, history. For *dharma* is not unitive in the same sense as Islam is, though it covers the whole span of what is today dichotomized as religious and secular civic activities. The Allah-ordained *sharia* claims to bind together the secular and religious dimensions of private and civic life. But Islam, with its emphasis on social conformity, has frowned on the development of an intellectual component equivalent to the Greek rationalism, to Socratic Reason as the foundation of Christian theology and subsequently of Enlightenment Science and Philosophy. Along a trajectory different from that of the Greco-Christian, but with a cognate spirit, the *dharma* literature developed in unison, and even gets intertwined, with the sophisticated Reason one encounters in the *darśana*s and in the metaphysical commentaries of the Śrutis. The differences between the Christian, Islamic and Hindu theologies or forms of religious thought are scarcely debated with the result that the arcanes of ideological convergence and difference are not brought out into the open for the public to participate.

Nothing illustrates national funk so much as the paralysis of the Congress Party leadership when confronted by the *fait accompli* of the destruction of the Babri Masjid. It showed itself incapable to engage in a public debate on the religious, moral and political issues raised by that incident. Its inaction reminds one of the American government appealing to the people not to engage in a discussion of the moral or immoral purpose of the war in Vietnam after the debacle in 1975. Instead of boldly challenging the proponents of both the Muslim and the new Hindu exclusivisms to a fruitful, civilized dialogue, the Narasimha Rao government chose to retreat behind the pusillanimity of entrusting the Supreme Court with the task of finding a legal solution to a political problem.

This indeed leaves the Indian public in ignorance of the relation that exists between religious thought and national jurisprudence. Above all, it is an inescapable fact that a religious or philosophical tradition necessarily finds its expression in the politics which it generates. But in India the evidence points to the politicians being themselves ignorant of the subtleties of the co-existing religious ideologies. On the contrary, their ignorance becomes an armour within which they stand, impavid, unfeeling, when suddenly they are confronted by a crisis which they then helplessly allow to run its course and get resolved with violence and destruction of lives and property. The outburst of communal violence almost invariably brings forth mutual recriminations and the facile condemnation of fanaticism as the dominant feature of the religion of the Other. With the public school system eschewing all forms of study of the cultural fabric of the nation, the intellectual vacuum thus generated is erratically filled by arbitrary pronouncements based on convenient simplifications and stereotypes which appeal to the baser sentiments of captive electoral clienteles for the satisfaction of self-interested, greedy power seekers.

Sometimes it can be disconcerting to listen to those university educated diaspora Indian who claim to exude modernity when they ridicule Hindu *dharma* by interpreting it as being nothing more than the closed-soulness which fits the arbitrary dimensions of VHP or BJP slogans. Had they been acquainted at least with the first couplet of the *Īśa Upaniṣad* they would have acquired a valid frame of reference to provide them with a surer grasp of the nature of the new emergent forces in Indian society.

The Hindu ideology advocated by the BJP or the VHP does not exhaust the totality of the *dharma*. When the crowd becomes a nuisance, one must climb to the mountain top. To avoid being buffetted by the storm one must soar to those regions where it is quiet and sunny, above the layers churned by weather. If the BJP is serious in reviving the tenets of Hinduism to refurbish the social fabric of India, then the logic of the task requires it to rest its appeal on the meaning and social implications of the *mahāvākya*s of the Upaniṣads, on the insights of the great *ācārya*s, and on the virtues prescribed by the *dharma* texts for private and public life. That seemingly it does not do so, forces it to project the image of being relevant only in that part of the country where lives the major portion of the Muslim minority.

Throughout the course of her history India has always been revitalized by the accomplishments of thinkers, cultural pioneers moving northward from the south. At a time, during the twelfth and thirteenth centuries, when Islam seemed to have succeeded in totally submerging the Hindu Culture and Hinduism was almost on the verge of extinction, suddenly thinkers like Madhva, Rāmānuja and poets and writers who brought into being the different vernacular languages steeped in the Epics, came forward to assure the *dharma-vijaya* of the Hindu tradition.

Today the BJP seems to offer for the first time the example of a reform movement orginating in the north of India: it bears affinities which place it in the tradition of such movements as the Brahmo Samāj, the Ramakrishna Mission, the Arya Samāj. Its appeal and its ideology are quite different, both in form and in substance, from those of Ādi Śaṅkarācārya, Rāmānuja, and the luminous, dazzling philosophers of the Mahāyāna. The difference lies in the BJP's appearance in the political arena, in independent India. Nevertheless, it teases the mind if one seeks to venture an explanation of its not being able to attract the adhesion of the south Indian population.

Dharma and the Law

The inadequacy of the law prevailing in the face of the enormity of certain types of crimes, leaves the common man with no moral alternative. Instead there is the funk concomitant with a definition of secularism which actually is a surrogate for cultural amnesia.

Clause 14 of the Constitution proclaims the inalienability of equal rights for all the citizens. That is, it asserts a legal egalitarianism, based on the right to own private property, of all Indian citizens. But it does so without those instruments which should have been fashioned to bring freedom to them: freedom from fear, freedom from poverty, freedom from ignorance, freedom from alienation and freedom to resist oppression. The history of the last 50 years has unveiled the hiatus between Independence and

Freedom. It is significant that as soon as Mr. I.K. Gujral was sworn in as Prime Minister, one of his first decisions was to reassure foreign investors of the economic stability of the land. In other words, India still continues to define herself in terms and ways approved by the outsiders. At the same time, when pressed by a reporter to justify his being qualified to serve as the chief executive of the country, despite his having no political base of his own, he lay claim to his having clean hands and to the moral authority of his personal integrity, a statement which *India Today* has already questioned by referring to his role as a close collaborator of Indira Gandhi. Subsequent decisions of his interference with legitimate investigation of corruption on the part of officials in the higher echelons of the administrative hierarchy, waiving a debt owed by the province of Punjab in order to secure a safe electoral seat — do detract from any possible claim of an inexpugnable moral integrity. In contrast, when Sitaram Kesri took over the Congress Party from Narasimha Rao, no one in the Congress Party made a commitment to return morality to politics. To encounter such a commitment on the part of an active politician one has to turn to Lionel Jospin who, during the last campaign for the election of a new parliament in France, promised to restore public confidence in government by bringing back virtue to politics. One does not hear of an Indian politician committing him or herself to a return of *dharma* to politics.

It is in comparing the Indian situation with what obtains in other cultures, in other countries, that one feels one's soul shrinking with the contemplation of so much shabbiness befalling the nation when *dharma* deserts private and public consciousness. At a private dinner party, it was depressing to listen to a young visiting Indian technocrat complaining that the police and the judiciary were wrong to prosecute certain Indian leaders for taking bribes. He argued that even Mahatma Gandhi did so as he accepted money and material conveniences from the rich. He felt it was a wrong done to the country that certain national leaders were being dragged to the courts to answer for financial crimes. He was scarcely scandalized that Indian democracy would elect as its representatives individuals who had committed blood crimes. When highly educated technocrats can display such brazen indifference to moral values, one feels inclined to believe that in India the ethical collapse has become deeply etched into the consciousness of a large segment of the population. Visiting Indians often astonish Canadians by their quiet, smug boasting that, more than in India, immorality in the West is more insidious, more widespread, more resistant to the law.

The Presence of Dharma in the Folk Sensitivity

One Saturday afternoon, in the winter of 1992, in New Delhi, I found myself unable to pay the driver of an auto-rickshaw the required fare as I had only a 50-rupee note. I asked the young *pān*-vendor on the footpath to give the fare to the driver with the promise that I would return him the money. I even gave him a 50-rupee note as a surety and he agreed I could claim it back after changing some travellers cheques at the American Express close by. When I returned some two hours later I was surprised to see the *pān*-vendor still sitting at the same place. With a big smile he returned me the money less the fare which he had earlier given to the driver of the rickshaw. I was quite impressed by his honesty. It would have been so easy for him to move to some other crowded footpath during my absence and decamp with the surety money.

During stay in Varanasi in the late 1960s my family hired a servant to clean the two-room apartment and to bring water from the well available in the compound. He also worked for other tenants who were professors at the Banaras Hindu University. One day I asked him how he knew the difference between right and wrong. He laughed and made it clear that I was asking a silly question. He told me that he learnt it from his parents who learnt it from their parents. And he was teaching his daughters the same lesson. The oral transmission was still active. Shivnath's attitude recalled to my mind how F. Max-Müller extols the truthfulness of the Hindu peasantry as recorded in the writings of the British collectors. One can even proceed further in saying that the Indians fought as bravely as the British in their military encounters and sometimes displayed greater tenacity and courage in facing the superior British military. But in one domain the Indians were tragically defective: the use of reason in the techniques of deceit and machiavellian duplicity, as practised by the British military and political elites.

With the moral imperatives of *dharma* still running through the social life of the Indian and providing direction to his actions, truthfulness had become a handicap for the Indian in his confrontation with the machiavellism of the foreign invader. Fortunately it is this silent, still active oral transmission of a moral culture, continually revitalized, for example, by the folk theatre of the *Rām Līlā*, which Mahatma Gandhi tapped in his enterprise of applying the Vedic values of Truth and Non-Violence to the politics of the Independence movement.

But in contrast to the *pān*-seller and the illiterate water-carrier servant, the four Indian publishers of five of my books never provided me with the royalties due to me, as per the contracts which I had signed with them. I have had to buy copies of these books from other suppliers to establish my credibility in the eyes of my faculty colleagues after I had reported that the books had been accepted for publication. *Dharma* transmitted orally still inhabits the minds of the unlettered folk while the well-established, educated, anglicized publishers of Indological texts failed to honour even a written contract. It is still worth asking if conscience (*antarātmā*) always prompts rectitude to a heart filled with a feeling for *dharma*, and if it remains undisturbed, often in an anglicized mind, in the face of a conscious refusal to abide by the law.

The Dissolution of Dharma

What happened after Independence has been of greater import in the matter of moral dissolution than what the media have made it out to be. I recall a private conversation I had with professor A.K. Narain in the mid-1950s when I was an undergraduate student at the Banaras Hindu University. As a disciple of A.L. Basham he had just returned from London with a Ph.D. in Ancient Indian History and Culture and was considered a star scholar at the College of Indology. Commenting on the situation then obtaining in India he said: "The country is so corrupt that it may even be a patriotic duty to become in turn very corrupt to speed up the process of the rot so that the whole structure can come down quickly under its own weight. Then, perhaps, we could build something new for the good of all." Such a pessimistic statement was made at a time when India was being led by the immediate heirs of Mahatma Gandhi, by such unblemished politicians as Rajendra Prasad, Raja Gopalachari, Jawaharlal Nehru, Pandit Govind Vallabh Pant, T.T. Krishnamachari, Abdul Kalam Azad, Acharya Kripalani, Morarji Desai, Ram Manohar Lohia, S. Radhakrishnan, Vinoba Bhave, Jayprakash Narayan and so many others of like mettle who had earned esteem and respect for their knowledge, their merits and their virtues.

But what they failed to observe was that the Indian working at the low levels of the administration was getting corrupt. Every morning when the office clerk sits down at his desk to begin his daily chore, the *caparāsī* takes out the files from the Godrej steel locker and places the heap in front of the clerk. Before the latter undoes the red tape that binds the top file he sips a cup of tea which the *caparāsī* gently places on the table. In the meantime the office clerk may be persuaded by the *caparāsī* who, faithful to the little bribe he has taken, would coax the clerk into processing the relevant file as the first business of the day, even if it happens to have been placed near the bottom of the heap. This is how the corruption started — from the bottom, and thence slowly over the years, it reached up to the higher echelons of the administration. The little corruptions do not have space in the written and oral media. That is why the corruption of the political elites has become embedded in the public mind as being limited to only those who happen to be in the limelight. The rot, when viewed dispassionately, moved slowly from the lower strata of society upwards. One is left wondering why the very leaders who had been during all the years of their activism so close to the common people would have suddenly become so blind and so insensitive as not to understand that it was their duty to protect the little wageearner against the temptation of sliding into a way of life interspersed with little dishonesties.

The 1950 Constitution: A Dharmicidal Document?

Consequently the real lapse from *dharma* moved and swelled from the ground and ultimately extended across the vertical stretch of the different patterns of government bureaucracies.

Such a moral failure on the part of the governing elites sprang up from their funk of the bureaucracy built by and for British imperialism. The bureaucracy was to imperialism as Karṇa's armour was to his body: the armour was an integral, organic part of his body. Karṇa became vulnerable when in conformity to *dharma* principles he surrendered his armour and his weapons which he cutoff from his body and gave them to Indra who had, disguised as a brāhmaṇa, come to beg for them. The Congress Party never demanded of the bureaucracy that at least it shed its imperial *saṁskāra*s. Above all it displayed, almost unconsciously, a collective funk of the effort necessary for the establishment of a culture of virtue, of a revitalized, operative set of *dhārmika* norms in the fulfilment of civic duties. Thus, was the drift allowed to develop and to become a national policy, as an outcome of the accession to Independence.

In fact, the hiatus between freedom from internal constraints and independence from foreign authority was never perceived by academics, intellectuals and by politicians. With hindsight it seems that in India's engagement with the "tryst with destiny" funk intervened with the result that very quickly the people were led to seek comfort in adopting somnambulism as national culture. There can be no *dharma* without vigilance and tireless effort. But with independence, *dharma* rules and principles were held in abeyance as the intellectual elite chose to escape from honouring its responsibilities by transferring to the popularity of the leaders the confidence that the welfare of the population lay in their safe keeping.

Despite its genuine merits the 1950 Constitution appears like a puny achievement when viewed against, and evaluated by, a consideration of the characteristic achievements which gave to India her unique greatness: the cave temples of Ajantā and Bhaja, the Kailasa Temple at Ellorā; the glories of the Trimūrti of the Elephaṇṭā caves; Tanjore, Koṇārka, Mahābalipuram; the magnificent syntheses of Vasubandhu and Śaṅkara; the epics of Vyāsa and Vālmīki, of Kamban and Tulasīdāsa; the Institutes of Manu — to name but only a few. What distinguishes these achievements was the daring to bring the infinite and the eternal into the affairs of Man and to investigate, find and teach the means to suffuse the decaying *kaliyuga* with the perfection of moral and spiritual purity. In the Hindu and Buddhist cultures the manifestation of the all-pervasive Absolute Reality, of the eternal and the infinite in Time, in daily existence, bears no resemblance to or affinity with the Judeo-Christian notion of a personal, monotheistic divinity interfering in History. Accordingly, it behoves the Indian intellectual today to justify whether a legacy bequeathed by the heroes and visionaires of the past has become irrelevant to the future generations of Indians and of the world at large.

Ibn Khaldun, certainly the most perceptive of the philosophers of culture, enjoins upon the responsible elites of a civilization the duty to preserve its Being (*asala*) while faithfully transmitting it, for the enlightenment and inspiration of successive generations, as a Becoming (*tajjaddud*) conforming to their needs. Unfortunately, Nehru and his companions had no feeling for the metaphysical presupposition of Indian culture. They were not acquainted with the *asala* of Hindu *dharma* and consequently the 1950 Constitution failed to emerge as a *tajjaddud* of the fundamental Being, the pathways to which still rank as the noblest contributions India has made to the understanding and to the experience of Man's spiritual finality. If the Śrutis are the normative exposition of the *asala* of Hindu *dharma*, the Dharmaśāstras, the Smṛti literature, including the epics of Vyāsa and of Vālmīki, the Purāṇas, represent the various forms of *tajaddud*.

The still-born task of preserving the *asala* of *dharma* and assuring its passage through correct expressions of its *tajaddud* acquires tragic proportions with its simultaneous failure to invite the minorities to proclaim their respective *asala* and to publish and affirm its corresponding cycle of *tajaddud*. It is no wonder then that, instead of the transparency of the *dharma* texts and of the activities they prescribe, we now have conflicting reminiscences of past history leading to divergent policies rooted in cultural atrophy and political backwardness. Had this distinction between the *asala* and the *tajaddud* been made, had the perservation of the Being been allowed to flow through the Becoming of national development, and through the Constitution, one may justifiably venture to argue that the vision of Nehru would have been hitched to the vitality of the traditional values still urging and directing the minds and hearts of the voiceless millions living in the villages and small towns. This metaphysical presumption would have served as a solid foundation on which the State, as the provider of moral and material goods, would have stood. For one thing, the Indian Muslims, locked within the narrow psychological confines of a minority — a status conferred upon them by the British authorities, for in the times of their domination the Muslims never felt or acted with the consciousness of being a minority — would have acquired the intellectual tools to provide the *tajaddud* of their Koranic *asala* in conjunction with the *tajaddud* of the Vedic *asala*. Hindu intellecutals of free, independent India have yet to engage, from their Vedic point of view, an in-depth dialogue with Islamic theology, without any fear of antagonizing the religious sensitivities of either community.

That *dharma* became associated with obscurantism and backwardness was unfortunately due to the fact that, by 1950, the voices of Culture had already been stilled. Towards the end of the last, and early in this, century Vivekananda had proclaimed that the fall of India and the loss of her freedom was due to her alienation from the sublime values laid down in the Vedas and the Upaniṣads. Few academic philosophers and political scientists in India have noticed that Vivekananda, without in any way attracting to himself the attribute of a fanatical fundamentalist, advocated Vedānta as a virile political ideology. Rabindranath Tagore died in 1937. Aurobindo's rediscovery of Vedic culture remained limited to a small group of fervent devotees gravitating around his *āśrama*. The voices of Rama Tirtha and of Raman Maharṣi did not reach out to the Congress Party. Rukmini Arundale almost single-handedly revived the Bharata-Nāṭyam and rescued it from near oblivion. Adyar became a centre for the rehabilitation of classical Indian art and of Sanskrit lore. Bhagwan Das spoke and wrote from his standpoint as a theosophist. Despite his philosophical writings S. Radhakrishnan nevertheless reminds one of Prem Chand's chess players who could not see the country being taken over by the invader. The events that altered the state of the nation passed by Radhakrishnan without his perceiving them. We may acknowledge that, with his adoption of the *āśrama* at Wardha as his political base, where he delivered his lectures on the *Bhagavad Gītā*, Mahatma Gandhi was aware of the existence of a still vibrant undertow of *dharma* sensitivity among the vast numbers of rural folk. But his voice was stilled by the bullets of Nathuram Godse and by the subsequent indifference of the Congress Party.

But all these voices raised earlier in defence of culture and *dharma*, and other uttered in unison with them, did not shake the Indian soil and rise to the clouds as did the tumult of Hṛṣikeśa's blowing the conch Pāñcajanya, followed by Arjuna's blowing his conch Devadatta and plucking the string of the bow Gāṇḍīva, just before the great Bhārata war started.

The Rejection of Dharma: A Self-Inflicted Alienation

The alienation of India from her native tradition is the product of an endogenous will and of the style of her administration. A fair comparison may be made with Japan and with China. Japan has maintained its identity, despite the catastrophic defeat suffered in the last war, and has presented to the world a cultural personality on the basis of its achievements, in strict conformity with its past. The maintenance of the Mikado as the symbol of Japanese unity preserves a historical continuity that goes back well into the sixth century before the common era. Despite its adoption of alien Marxist ideology, China too has kept its historical and cultural distinctiveness to the extent that it can reject, with pride and honour, the pressures exerted on it by Western haughtiness. Only India constantly acts out to the Western gallery: she seems to be doing so, not in terms of her history or of her culture, but with the infantile idology of a latter-day Dale Carnegie in her ceaseless, almost grovelling effort to influence Western investors and win friends among the Western chancelleries.

The Isolation of the Indian

Sometimes Indian elites have difficulty in understanding that their use of the English language does not serve as a bridge between them and the West. On the contrary, it seems to extend the psychological distance between the Indian and the Westerner. Indian leaders speaking in English in the West hardly attract the attention of the media. Narasimha Rao's speeches during his last visit to the U.S.A. were reported neither in the print or visual media in North America. One wishes that, even if an Indian leader knew English, he would speak in his vernacular language and have a translator act as a linguistic intermediary between him and the Western audience. Jacques Chirac can speak faultless English. But in his international meetings he never strays from speaking French. So do the Chinese leaders, even if they have an adequate command of the English language. The Canadian media ignored the pronouncements delivered in English, of the South-East Asian heads of state at the recent Pacific Rim conference held in Vancouver. It is an illusion entertained by most Indian leaders, and further strengthened by the print media, that their use of the English language enables their thoughts to reach out to the Western audiences.

The diaspora Indian presence does not pass into the civil life of the West. It is the "But . . ." which predominates: "I am a Hindu, but I am a Canadian/American/Britisher first." The Indian wants to be like his host neighbour in the West. But for that very reason he is mistrusted: of all the minorities living in Canada, the Indian commands the least esteem on the part of the majority host community. He has no moral configuration, derived from his culture and tradition, which identifies his distinctiveness. His film music does not cross the ethnic barrier. Most of the time his public festivals mimic the artificial amusement represented by clichéd film sequences; nothing universal is transmitted by his presence, either as an individual or as a group. After nearly three decades of its activity the Indo-Canadian Shastri Institute has failed to establish Indian Studies in any of the Canadian universities which hold membership in the Institute. After going through a series of meetings and discussions, over a period of more than five years, a group of Indian scholars at the University of Alberta could not collect — literally — even a single dime in view of establishing a chair of Distinguished Professorship in Sanskrit and Indian Culture, despite their having started with the declared intention of garnering a $1.5 million trust fund.

Consequently in his isolation the Indian is left to himself largely because India does not have a cultural policy to support his initiatives. One wonders why India is the only country which has a ministry of Information and Broadcasting. In the French government, for example, two of the most prestigious ministries are those of Culture and of Education. With such a dramatic, urgent need for cultural redress, as was evident in 1947, India did not establish a Ministry of Culture. It still does not have one. After the death of Maulana Abdul Kalam Azad, the Ministry of Education was downgraded to near insignificance.

The egalitarian intention of the 1950 Constitution required a levelling of the caste distinctions and the removal of inequities based on caste prejudices. While the quota system was a tactical dispensation for immediate, economic short-term redress of these inequalities, the long-term solution should have required the use of the school and an appropriately redesigned curriculum to provide substance to the implementation of social justice. Half a century after the advent of independence it is a moot question to ask whether it would not have been a cheaper and more effective means of carrying out the needed reforms by means of an application of *dharma* rules, modified and adjusted to meet contemporary social complexities.

With philosophers, proponents of culture, sociologists, historians, intellectuals exerting at best minimal influence on the debates at the Constituent Assembly, the 1950 Constitution represents the vision of men trained in British jurisprudence. It is this narrow intellectual mould that lies at the base of the collective neurosis in India: it is a neurosis which consists of the tension of what the Indian is in terms of his history and what he ought to be in terms of an abstract legal will, assumed to be a modern impersonal Viśvakarmā capable of generating a utopian future.

Dharma and Virtue

When the sage Nahuṣa asked Yudhiṣṭhira to define a brāhmaṇa, the latter replied that a brāhmaṇa is someone who forgives, who seeks learning and shares it, who is compassionate and restrained, who is at all times a giver, who is truthful, who is never angry, who is non-violent in his thought, speech and behaviour.

Nahuṣa said that such virtues can be found also in śūdras. Yudhiṣṭira replied that if such virtues are to be found in a śūdra, then he is indeed a brāhmaṇa, though the world calls him a śūdra. He went on to emphasize that if these virtues are absent in a brāhmaṇa then he is actually a śūdra though the world considers him to be a brāhmaṇa.

One wonders why such stories are not made the stuff of readers in the elementary school. Had this been done the politicans today would not be accused of the hypocrisy of claiming to be secular while actively promoting caste politics. That it was not done prompts one to ask whether it was out of funk, or was it due to the ignorance of their own tradition that kept the politicians alienated from a correct perception of the social issues that confronted them. Such school instruction could have been easily brought to the mind of the entire nation, if only the educational or cultural will was available in the late 1940s and early 1950s.

A reference to commercial cinema further justifies the validity of the argument. The entire *Mahābhārata* tells stories of sages and kings, of brāhmaṇas and kṣatriyas. But a film like *Kaliyug* and the serials *Andaz* and *Parampara,* for example, tell of stories with parts of the plots borrowed from the leitmotivs of the *Mahābhārata*. These plots are set in the context of warring families of young degenerate, upstart multi-millionnaire businessmen and women driven by sex, vindictiveness and by an arrogant, cynical display of their wealth. Still these are convincing examples of the osmosis which the classical values generate in the Indian society. No one in India has proffered the slightest criticism that it was contrary to tradition for businessmen to don the garb of kṣatriya and brāhmaṇa heroes of the epic. In other words, the classics of the *dharma* literature contain valid, persuasive universal lessons applicable to social problems obtaining at the end of the millennium.

Dharma: Its Relation to Social Justice and to Democracy

There is one important feature of the *dharma* which has been discarded, to the great loss of the country. In the classical period when *dharma* seemed to have provided the moral structure of the society, every citizen, once born, was entitled to own at least the basic necessities of his life. The ethos of the *dharma* was, and is, a negation of what is generally understood to be the Darwinian way of life. *Dharma* further rejects the morality advocated by Saint Paul who avers that only he who works earns the right to eat. The apostle of charity falls short of the notion of the giver as understood by the *dharma* sages who celebrate life as a continuous giving, for the individual himself, not necessarily the Supreme Being, is effectively a cosmic centre of universal good. That independent India would have decided to reject such noble ideals at the very time when she had the opportunity to bring them into the language of international politics just defies comprehension. For there ought to be room for *dharma* imperatives in the elaboration of economic projects to provide jobs for the millions who are being discarded and cast into the margins of society under the pressure of market forces. *Dharma* considerations ought to, and could, be integrated with economic consciousness as a correction of the mythical assumption that market forces act blindly, without the conjuncture of boardroom decisions affecting their direction and purposefulness. Markets are instruments of prosperity and of impoverishment; they are not values. Defined as one of the traditional goals of human existence, *artha* is a value.

Let us take another example. According to *dharma* imperatives a man who deliberately commits a moral crime forfeits the right or the privilege of begging for his material sustenance. One may argue that were the common people aware of the validity of this principle the ordinary individual would not give his vote to someone who is tainted by scandal or by corruption. For even if the law exonerates the corrupt person, the legal innocence does not always coincide with moral purity. In such a case the law of *dharma* would hold and the offender or criminal would be denied access to power. The implementation of such a *dharma* rule would be of direct, substantial service to the cause of democracy. The abuse of bureaucratic political power in thwarting the independence of the judiciary and of the police, resulting from an excessive reliance, as evinced by the high and mighty, on the recourse to law rarely makes it possible to have a full trial of the guilty. Michel Rocard, the former Prime Minister of France, once said during a television interview: "Never tried, always guilty!" In India the situation demands a careful study of whether the Law itself can become a *cause* of corruption, thus deviating from its purpose of acting as a deterent of, and as a protection from, public offence.

The Death of the Dharmātmā

In this century no one in India has earned the distinction of having been honoured as a *dharmātmā*. In any country the law is such as takes into acount the moral principles which have been patiently elaborated and nurtured by the makers of Culture and Civilization. These moral principles are the precondition of the effectiveness and relevance of the Law. The Indian Constitution is no exception. But what are the moral principles which it takes for granted as its historical antecedent? Was the popularity of the leaders in 1950 the only absolute norm which gave sanction to its approval? Was the prestige of the post-1947 political leaders the source and generator of the Constitution? Was it a *de facto sharia* bestowed on the nation by an unchallenged political authority? Or must the Constitution also plunge roots deeper into the past history of the country? Is appeal to secularity of the Constitution merely an aesthetic élan? Or is a *suni generis* moral frame of reference as Indira Gandhi wanted it to be? If it is, then the secularity of the Constitution stands for the complete abrogation of the past history and culture of India.

As the ochre band on the Indian flag indicates, *dharma* implies self-sacrifice: it is not an aesthetic value. It is an absolute, with *mokṣa* pervading it. *Dharma* is a universal; the 1950 Constitution is a specific, contingent reality. *Dharma* is eternal; the Constitution is material, born at a particular moment; it has a beginning, it is consequently imperfect and will in time perish. India made a choice between the eternal and the transient, between the absolute and the relative. She chose the moment, the present, without a lucid, inspiring vision of the future, for there can be no durable expectation of glory in the future when it is assumed that faith in the past is only a return to darkness and ignorance. Indeed, during the Emergency the Indira Gandhi government introduced the 49th Amendment to the Constitution in a bid to restore the category of obligations as a necessary complement to the declaration of the rights of man in Article 14. This Amendment, which has scarcely had an impact on the behaviour of politicians and of the civil service, was a belated recognition that something vital had been left out from the Constitution when it was adopted in 1950.

Dharma and Public Service

Only the virile power wielder can uphold *dharma* and inspire in the citizenry the desire to abide by it. Its goal is *sukha* for all, first for the subjects and last for the leader and his family. *Dharma* is antithetical to kleptocracy.

It exacts from the ruler sweetness and harshness according to the occasion. The *Mahābhārata* repeatedly questions and examines the existential absurdity of Evil being rewarded with success and happiness, while Virtue is scarred by deprivation, banishment, humiliation, suffering, hardship. Yet truth and rectitude, in the midst of tragedy, still orders the thoughts and actions of the strong adherents to *dharma*. The person established in *dharma* is *ārya*, a noble soul. Yudhiṣṭhira tells Bhīma that sovereignty, son, fame, wealth are not worth one-sixteenth of *dharma*. The goal of *dharma* is so difficult (*dharmasya gatim agryām sudurvidām*). It is subtle.

The practice of *dharma* is a *tapas*. Even going on pilgrimages is accompanied by *tapas*. The organizers of *ratha-yātrās* ought to tell the people that such demonstrations ought to be adopted as ways of introspection, not merely as short-cuts to the seats of power and office for the few. The sage Lomasha advises Yudhiṣṭhira that he must never suffer whenever he sees others succeed in *adharma*. Mārkaṇḍeya relates the story of Damayantī to console Draupadī in her ordeal and the story of Rāma to strengthen Yudhiṣṭhira's resolve to abide by *dharma* despite all the suffering and misery that have befallen him. Material power needs to be exercised by the duly elected authorities in conjunction with the power of restraint, of fidelity to *dharma* even in the face of failure, of *tapas* and restraint as the generator of *śakti*. These are the virile components of the governance of civil life.

Dharma and the Individual

As has been hinted above, the centrality of *dharma* consists in its consideration of, not God but, the individual as the centre of the universe. Birth confers on the individual the status of being a *kalyāṇakr̥t*, and his life-long concern extends to the welfare of the entire world community.

Duryodhana's birth was immediately followed by evil omens. Vidura advised Dhr̥tarāṣṭra that it would be best for all and for the kingdom if the child were put to death. He argued that when the need demands it, the individual must die for the family, the family for the town or village, the latter for the country, and the country for the world. The seventeenth-century humanist philosopher Montaigne expresses a similar sentiment in almost identical terms. In the 1920s Mahatma Gandhi wrote an exactly similar paragraph in which he articulated his vision of a future independent India, an India where self-sacrifices, as *yajña*, would be the order of the day for both the citizen and the nation.

Accordingly, no one in India can claim to use reason to argue for the reinstatement of past disparities and injustices as a beneficial return to a past idealized by nostalgia. As Mahatma Gandhi said: Hinduism does not stand or fall on the preservation of the caste system with all its inequalities. Nor ought it to stand and co-exist with slums and to provide a free-for-all in the institutionalization of a kleptocratic dispensation. For, in *dharma* terms, the sources of goodness are: sacrifice, giving, austerity, learning, holding on to the truth, satisfaction, non-violence.

Dharma and the Naked Fakīr

We are wrong to have lost our sense of perception. We have not sufficiently taken the full measure of the epic enterprise of a half-naked *fakīr* who challenged a mighty empire with the weapons of the purest of the values propounded by the *dharma* thinkers: Truth and Non-Violence. It surprises me to encounter many educated Indians who do not grasp the distinction between Peace and Non-Voilence.

In the history of the West peace is construed as a provisional suspension of hostilities. The Romans who, more than anybody in the entire history of humanity, knew all about warfare, gave to the world the famous adage: "If you want peace, prepare for war" (*si vis pacem, para bellum*). The Cold War was not peace as it rested on the threat and fear of assured mutual destruction by weapons that could have obliterated most of mankind. The *Pax Britannica* which I studied in my high school history textbooks was actually a violent period: the reign of Queen Victoria was punctuated by no less than 60 wars. Mahatma Gandhi was right in seeing competition as a form of violence, which resulted in the many man-made famines that characterized the British genocidal domination of India for nearly one and a half centuries, by means of the savage practice of an unbridled economic exploitation.

Indeed, the opposite of war is not peace, it is non-violence; the opposite of peace is not war, it is non-violence. Mahatma Gandhi did not preach *śānti* (peace). He advocated *ahiṁsā* (non-violence). In the Hindu tradition *śānti* stands for experience of oneness with the One, with the Absolute. It may be compared to the Dark Night of the Soul, according to St. John of the Cross, or to Meister Eckhart's experience of the Father begetting the Son in him. But Non-Violence is the application of the mystical *śānti* to public life; it has an incommensurate dimension in regard to peace; it is infinity infused into Time, into History. Such an epic venture is far greater and more heroic than easily Christian resistance to Roman imperial might. The only worthy image that conveys a right comprehension of it is mythopoeic story of Varāha-Viṣṇu retrieving the Earth Goddess (Bhūdevī) from the depths of the ocean. And it is this unprecedented transubstantiation of Politics and of History that has been screened off public imagination by the idolatry of the 1950 Constitution which the nation has been made to accept as the indispensable *mārga* that leads to the establishment of a new *rāma-rājya*. Suddenly the Indian nation became like the oyster which has no eye to see the pearl of its own making when Nature asserted its own logic and resolved to take the Mahatma away on 30 January 1950.

It defies comprehension that India should have failed to introduce Gandhian criticism of competition as a form of violence in international political discourse and to persist in asking for universal disarmament. It is ironical that India should be absent, or should play such a minimal role, in the many peace-keeping missions sponsored by the United Nations. India ought to take note that by the end of the First World War the West controlled 84.6 per cent of the whole planet: no one has as yet provided, at the end of the century, an assurance that it has been for the greater benefit of those held in thrall to Western domination. With two World Wars and others equally bloody originating from its own internal conflicts, the Christian West made the twentieth century the most violent ever in history. Moreover it has quietly, during the last 50 years, transformed the whole world into an armed camp, for the first time in history. It is true that, despite all this violence, values disseminated by the West — democracy, free enterprise, freedom of the press and of religious belief, human rights, technology — have become nearly universal and have been adopted as a way of life in most countries, especially by India. Nevertheless that India should remain indifferent to this violent state of the world and not make her voice heard is difficult to understand. In truth she could still do this despite her having a large army and with her capacity to develop a nuclear weaponry as a response to external threats to her security. But the adoption of such a virile, heroic *puruskāra* presupposes the possession of a moral strength as a national attribute. India has no *dharma* authority to project on the world stage.

A cycle came to an end with the Mahatma's silence. While shouts were resounding from the ramparts of the Red Fort, on 15 August 1947, he spent the day spinning in silence. In the intellectual history of India this is the second great silence, coming some two and a half millennia after Gautama Buddha's silence when he was asked to elucidate the meaning and substance of the imponderables (*avyakta*).

Modernity and Dharma

Instead of the secular Constitution it is the silence of Mahatma Gandhi that ought to be viewed as a new beginning in the process of diverting the course of the perennial values of *dharma* into the socio-political discourse, without fear of its being denounced as reversion to obscurantism and exclusivism. It has been a wrong done, not to India, but to the whole world, that a moral ideology based on Truth and Non-Violence, and set into motion in a century filled with so much totalitarian and imperial violence, came to be treated with the same indifference, as has been done with one of the myriad commission reports, when it got replaced by a dharmicidal Constitution. It is no wonder that India has become a democracy which favours greed and competition over self-sacrifice and mutual sharing, promotes selfishness and exclusiveness to the detriment of giving (*dāna*) and desireless action (*niṣkāma karma*), and builds the future on the foundation of shifting, *ad hoc* sands while leaving behind the structures built by the contemplative heroes, of which the first of the breed happened to be the Mahatma, Aurobindo and Vinoba Bhave.

In the last century the French philosopher Lamennais wrote that trees and nations have this in common that their death begins with the head. When one reads the interviews which Indian leaders give to the newspapers, magazines, television, one is left wondering how despite her glorious history India can afford to be administered by so many inferior, shallow individuals. It seems that intellectual and moral talent has become incompatible with the art of governing India. To the banal questions of the reporters the ministers or leaders invariably answer in monosyllables, or in short cryptic sentences, which read like coded messages, startling on account of their intellectual sterility. Petulance takes the place of profundity. A rebuttal is assumed to stand for innocence. Smugness must be reckoned as responsibility. These are individuals who do not expound their ideas in an article or essay; they do not write a book to describe their experience: their ideals, motivations and political passions are either non-existent or are deliberately kept hidden.

Mahātma Gandhi was a mountain: his totality was visible to all. The political minions who claim to be his heirs are like icebergs, with only their mask being visible on the surface of public life while their reality stays hidden beneath the sparse, minimal prose of non-committal pronouncements. Were one to be ignorant of the history of India and if one tried to take interest in her by reading *India Today* or some other Indian magazine, one would have the impression that India is, on the world stage, as insignificant a prop as Malta, or Fiji or Mauritius. Indeed how can India afford to be led by such mediocrity? What is worse is that there is so much popular acquiescence in it.

Dharma and the Future

The Indian citizen justifiably takes pride in the historian's celebrating the gifts India has made to Greater India, to the cultures of South and South-East Asian countries. Yet any visitor to these places is struck by the intensity of the indifference, if not the hostility, felt towards India. The most impressive monuments dedicated to Buddhism and to Hinduism are to be found outside India: Borobudur in Java and Angkor Vat in Cambodia. These monuments still sing the glory of India as a cultural giver. Besides these monuments Chandigarh gives a real measure of the material smallness which the Nehruvian dream bloated into a giant bubble of hope for the future of the country.

The national bank of Indonesia is called Kubera bank; Indonesia's national airlines bears the name Garuḍa. The folklore of Thailand, Cambodia, Indonesia is largely coloured by Indian themes borrowed from the classical epics. The Theravāda Buddhism of Sri Lanka, Burma and the other South-East Asian countries ought to act as a bridge of friendship and understanding to link up with India. Why is it then that this alienation from India does not seem to preoccupy the framers of the foreign policy of the country? What is lacking in the language of Indian diplomacy?

From what body of knowledge must the elites derive an epistemology which, in conformity with the particularities of Indian culture, will emerge to provide purposeful direction to the Indian masses? Hindu *dharma* cannot be constrained into the narrow space of an exclusive search for power. Yet, without excludig Power — which is always to be used for a higher, nobler finality — *dharma* needs to be reformulated in a way which eschews all forms of Machiavellian thought. For instance, with a policy inspired by the spirit of *dharma* India ought to tell the world that globalization — whatever may this term mean — cannot proceed with the uncontrolled violence of a dehumanizing competition. India's *dharma* still has a contribution to make to the reorganization of international finance, to a humane perception of the conduct of market forces; to the fostering of a humanitarian treatment of the weak and the deprived, of those who are excluded and discarded beyond the pale of profit, of the victims of privilege and of unmitigated appropriation; to the reduction of the lethal self-confidence of those powers which transmute the toil of the many into the prosperity of the few.

The setting into motion of a revised moral code must be seen to rise from the mysterious silence of the Mahātma when he must have been horror-struck on contemplating the death of *dharma* and the abyss of blood-filled chaos growing wider.

The rebirth of *dharma* lies, not in a rejection, but in a responsible, creative negation, that is, in a transcendence of the national funk as represented by its monumental expression in the 1950 Constitution.

For the good of all Indians. For the good of all.

14

Vedic Mythology
An Archetypal Delineation of the Hindu World-View

B. Rambilass

Introduction

My aim in this paper is to examine critically the broad and somewhat prescriptive sweep of Orientalism on the interpretation of the Vedas. From an orientalist perspective the mythology of the *R̥gveda* purveys a world-view no different from the one imposed by modern scholarship upon the Graeco-Roman world. Naturally the Indian scholar is vehemently opposed to such an approach, shaped as it is to such a large extent by the pervasive, if subtle influence of Christian theology.

Notwithstanding the acknowledgement of the grandiose splendour of Greek and Roman civilizations, and the degree to which their institutions influence the ethos of presentday Western civilization, the Christian world rejects entirely any suggestion that Greek and Roman mythology bare vestiges of profound theistic speculation; in short, where religion was concerned, the Greeks and Romans were relegated to the realm of the pagan.

In India, however, Christianity has failed to hold sway; Indian myth has remained a part of the body of Hindu/Vedic literature and the worldview proffered by it still informs modern Indian thought.

At the outset, I must emphasize the special appeal that this conference has for me. My interpretation of the Vedas has been profoundly influenced by Swami Dayananda, whose espousal of a "Return to the Vedas" ideal to revitalize and perpetuate the dynamism of Hinduism needs little justification and explanation. This paper embodies three themes that I have been working with: (1) the use of the seventh chapter of Yāska's *Nirukta* as a guide to the interpretation of the Vedic texts; (2) my study of the *vyāhṛtis vis-a-vis* the cosmography of the three worlds in the *Taittirīya Upaniṣad*, and (3) the tracing of certain myths, specifically the tortoise myth, back from the Purāṇas and *Brāhmaṇa*s to the Vedas. My aim will thus be to illustrate how Indian thought, both religious and philosophical, can be traced to Vedic roots.

Structuralism

Returning to the West, the turn of this century saw the advent of Structuralism which marked a revolutionization in the approach of the interpretation of myth. While structuralism has been superseded by other schools of Literary Theory, it is important to remember that its initial concern was not with literature in general but specifically with the nature of the myth.

Claude Levi Strauss' approach to myth is an attempt to pursue the intellectual quest for order in a world that is apparently in a state of flux and chaos. The prevalence of myth in all ancient civilizations provided him with the opportunity to discover this order by identifying sequences that occurred in them. He was able to represent these recurrent patterns diagramatically and systematize them into an organised nucleus representing an emergent order from apparent chaos.

C. Segal in his book, *Tragady and Civilization — An Interpretation of Sophocles*, makes some important observations that hold true for Indian myth. He refers to Aristotle's definition of man as one who belongs to the city (*polis*). For Aristotle the locus of civilization is the *polis* and whoever cannot share in the *polis* must be either below it or above it, a beast or a God. A man was considered as God among men when through his excellence he became superior to his fellow men. Man's virtue and morality placed him above bestiality and enabled him to aspire to divine status.

The Vedas, too, define man as being above the beast because he lives a life governed by the norms of society. In Greek mythology man had to attain divine and heroic excellence to be God, but in the tradition of the Vedas the mother, father and teacher enjoy the status of being *deva* (God) by mere virtue of the authority vested in them by the social hierarchy. Hence, the many human gods were slowly evolved to divine gods by the extreme reverence with which they were held in. There were also those great seers and sages who aspired to elevated positions through the attainment of knowledge, i.e., by subscribing to the prescribed methods of such a pursuit in terms of the classical traditions prevailing at the time.

While Strauss' methods are controversial, structuralism has been significantly modified by people like J.P. Vernant and is being successfully applied to a number of classical and older literary texts. The techniques of structuralist analysis enable a clarification of the logic that governs the relations among the various expressions of order in the human world and in the literary work that mirrors and transforms the world. The structuralist approach enables an understanding of the systematic relationships among symbols although it contributes little to the unravelling of their real meaning.

Segal affirms the significance of the role of the myth in establishing or maintaining the social order; another important note made by Segal, relevant to the repetitive nature of Vedic hymns and verses, is the effect of redundancy in this process of re-encoding.

Despite the flaws inherent in Structuralism as a school of literary theory, one should not forget that its initial concern was myth, this article therefore regards the structuralist approach as vital to the understanding of the neo-Hindu trends in interpreting the *Ṛgveda*. Of course, commentators like Dayananda have not used the structuralist school of the West; it was not even conceived of at the time. What is fascinating is that a system similar to that of structuralism was advocated by Dayananda in the middle of the nineteenth century and that he used as authority Yāska who is dated at 600 BC.

Jean-Pierre Vernant

Before analysing the deities according to the methods offered above, let us first examine Vernant's employment of the structuralist method in the interpretation of Greek mythology. To appreciate the impact of his observations on the interpretation of the *Ṛgveda*, a brief discussion of Dayananda's approach becomes necessary.

Dayananda uses the method of translation prescribed by Yāska in the seventh chapter of the *Nirkuta* entitled *Daivata Khaṇḍa* — The chapter on Deities. He states that there are three meanings that can be attributed to the ṛks. Let us see how Sūrya can, for example, be interpreted in these three aspects. Sūrya within its context in the verse may be translated in:

(i) the *ādhyātmika* sense as God — the all pervading Light and Destroyer of Darkness;

(ii) the *ādhidaivika* sense as the Sun — element of nature, the source of energy and life; and

(iii) the *ādhibhautika* sense as (a) the physical sun — the ball of fire, and (b) the individual in society who is himself enlightened like Sūrya and enlightens his fellow men with knowledge.

Jean-Pierre Vernant's (1982: 92) comments on the interpretation of Greek mythology are worthy of note. He reminds us that modern scholarship has amply illustrated the dangers inherent in an approach which evaluates different civilizations from a standardized viewpoint, and which disregards certain idiosyncrasies that arise out of the particular ethos of each civilization. The conclusion that in Vedic religion natural forces by virtue of their being inexplicable in terms of the then available knowledge of scientific laws were animated and personified to the extent that every element of nature was seen as the domain of a particular deity would be a blatant denial of any credit to the remarkable insights of the sages evidenced in the Vedic verses.

Vedic theism and its pantheon in terms of the new scholarship are seen as a system of classification, a tangible means of conceptualizing the cosmos, distinguishing between multiple types of force and power operating within it. The pantheon, is thus an organized system implying definite relationship between the various Gods is a particular way of apprehending reality and expressing it in symbolic terms.

Vernant in chapter 5 of his *Myth and Society in Ancient Greece* explains how a wide range of epithets given to a god such as Zeus helps up to glimpse one of the essential functions of the supernatural powers. The various epithets show the power of Zeus is not restricted to just the natural forms, but also work in human activities and social relations. As Zeus Basileus, he is present in the person of the king and as Agamemnon, he is in the sceptre of the king enabling his decisions to be put into force:

> The same dominion that Zeus has over the universe and the king over his subjects is also exercised by the head of each family in his own house. . . . In this way the power of Zeus establishes the connections between various types of human activities, social relations and natural phenomena. It links them together but does not confuse them. The Greeks knew perfectly well that a king was not a force of nature and that a force of nature was not the same as a deity. Nevertheless, he saw them as linked, interdependent, as different aspects of a single divine power.
>
> — 1982: 94

Three-fold Interpretation of the Heavenly Deities

We ought to have then according to this method of translation, three different interpretations of the *devatās*. Satya Prakash Sarasvati and Satyakam Vidyalankar (1977: 83) explain it as follows:

> In the light of these deities, the Vedic verses can be interpreted on multiple planes: social plane, cosmic plane, and mystic plane or spiritual plane. Sometimes we call these inter-pretations as 'Ādhibhautika, Ādhidaivika and Ādhyātmika.' Dayānanda has tried to interpret these verses on the social plane, and thus in his interpretation, 'agni' may stand for a learned person, a leader of the society; 'Indra' would be a king or the officer commander of an army; 'soma' would be a person of tranquillity, or a graduate of a spiritual academy; 'varuṇa' would be a learned preacher or a teacher or a defence minister; 'savitā' would be a teacher or inspirer; 'pūṣan' would be the sustainer of the people and hence, may be the head of an administration; 'ṛbhu' would be an architect, and 'marut' the soldier of an army.
>
> On the cosmic plane the 'devatās' are Nature's bounties; for example 'agni' would mean fire, electricity or the sun: 'Indra' is the sun or electricity or lightning; 'soma' is the medicinal plant or curative principle in any medicinal herb; it may be moon too, 'varuṇa' is water, sea or cosmic plasma; 'mitra' is vital breath; 'savitā' is the sun; 'viṣṇu' is the sun or yajña; 'pūṣan' is the earth; 'ṛbhu' the rays of the sun and 'marut' the atmospheric wind.
>
> On the spiritual or mystic plane, the same devatas will have other connotations. Aurobindo has his own fascinating system of mystic interpretation; on this plane, these terms stand for appellations of one and the same God; sometimes they refer to the soul, and so often to the mental behaviours or to the different states of consciousness. When applied to God, 'agni' is foremost adorable and omniscient Lord; 'Indra' is the resplendent Lord; 'soma' is the Lord worthy of our affection and devotion; 'varuṇa' is our Lord of justice, venerable and acceptable; 'savitā' is the creator Lord; 'viṣṇu' is the omnipresent Lord; 'pūṣan' is the sustainer Lord; and 'marut' is the vital breath.

The need to interpret the deities at the various levels arises out of their operation in different capacities in the different worlds. Indra, god of rain in the firmament, becomes the mortal king ruling over his kingdom on earth. The gods of the heaven and firmament are the elements which also symbolize certain human virtues; on the earth they depict the various social relations. It therefore becomes necessary to look at how Vedic texts define the three worlds and how this definition can be used in the interpretation of the deities on the different planes.

Vyāhṛtis

The classification of the Vedic *devatā*s into the three worlds of the heaven, firmament and earth and the various forms they accordingly assume has its roots in the cosmography of the three worlds as outlined in the Vedic texts. In a paper entitled "Vyāhṛtis and Vedic Cosmography" presented at the Tenth World Sanskrit Conference in Banglore, I examined the three sets of Vedic triads commonly used in the *mantra*s of *havan*. They list the division of the universe into the three worlds *bhūḥ*, *bhuvaḥ* and *svaḥ* and associate them with the elements Agni, Vāyu and Āditya and the vital airs *prāṇa, apāna* and *vyāna* respectively. The gradual progression of the triads and their respective interrelations with one another make for an interesting study.

Earth, Atmosphere and Heaven

Keith (1925: 77), in his introduction to the sixth chapter entitled "Vedic Cosmology," notes that the cosmology of the Vedas is very simple and natural, consisting of *dyāvāpṛthvī* — the heaven and earth, united at first and then parted with the firmament separating the two. This threefold division beomes very popular, as are all Vedic triads; the solar phenomena are assigned to the heaven, and those of lightning, rain and wind to the atmosphere.

In his book *Triads in the Veda*, Gonda (1976: 49ff) explains the world-view of the *Ṛgveda* which in effect serves as the quintessence of the evolution of the triads. The various elements or deities are the "powers governing the universe or presiding over its provinces" and, in the quest for prosperity, the microcosm of human existence had to, through the ritual, be brought into harmony with these natural forces that constitute the macrocosm.

Gonda asserts that among the Vedic triads "none is so frequent as the three regions of the universe, none so characterisitic as the threefold Vedic lore, the triple sacred fire and the many ritual triads." He cites Hopkins (1894: 141) who holds that the simplest and earliest form of a three-fold division (of the universe) is that of earth, air and heaven. Gonda gives a detailed account of how the dual compound (*dvandva samāsa*) denoting the sky and earth has the third region, the atmosphere appended to it, e.g., *dyāvāpṛthvī antarikṣam, rodasī antarikṣam*; thus demonstrating the gradual progression from a bipartite to a tripartite universe.

Yajurveda

The first reference to the cosmography of the Vyāhṛtis are to be found in the *Yajurveda*. In the *Ṛgveda*, e.g., the famous *gāyatrī mantra* (3.62.10) reads *tatsavitur-vareṇyam bhargo devasya dhīmahi dhiyo yo na pracodayāt*; it is in the *Yajurveda* (36.3) that the *vyāhṛti bhūrbhuvaḥsvaḥ* becomes prefixed to it.

Not only are there references to the three worlds *dyauḥ, pṛthvī, antarikṣam,* but these worlds are also associated with their respective elements *vāyu* and *sūrya* (23.43). Although the *vyāhṛtis* do not list the colours of the worlds yet it is interesting to note that in 24.10 the worlds yet are described as *kṛṣṇāḥ bhaumāḥ*, the dark earthly regions *dhūmrā antarikṣāḥ*, the misty or cloudy firmaments and *bṛhantaḥ divyāḥ*, the expansive or brilliant skies.

Verse 39.1 is of particular significance in the progressive evolution of the *vyāhṛtis*. There is a distinct pairing of *pṛthvī* and *agni; antarikṣa* and *vāyu; dyau* and *sūrya*. The ritualistic import of the verse is also relevant to the development of the *vyāhṛtis* in the context of the *yajña* being a microcosmos encapsulating the macrocosmos.

Vyāhṛtis in the Taittirīya Upaniṣad and Āraṇyaka

The source for this particular set of verses is often given in the texts published by the Ārya Samāj adherents as the *Taittirīya Āraṇyaka*. The verses exactly as they appear in the "Saṁskāra Vidhi" are not to be found anywhere in the *Taittirīya Āraṇyaka* or *Taittirīya Upaniṣad*. The *vyāhṛtis* in the *Taittirīya Āraṇyaka* and *Upaniṣad* transcend the ritual and explain the triads of the *vyāhṛti* in a metaphysical sense adding to each of the triads a fourth element which gives it a typically Upaniṣadic flavour.

Monier-Williams (1979: 1039) lists the names of the seven worlds: *bhūr, bhuvar, svar, mahar, janar, tapar, satya,* the mystical utterance of these, as *vyāhṛtis*; and the first three, *bhūrbhuvarsvar* or *bhūrbhuvaḥsvaḥ* as the great *vyāhṛtis*, which are pronounced after *oṁ* by every brāhmaṇa in commencing his daily prayer. The *Taittirīya Upaniṣad* (1.5), however, clearly states that *bhūrbhuvaḥ-svaḥ* are the three *vyāhṛtis*. It further defines the three members of this triad, adding a fourth to each triad, finally resolving that the *vyāhṛtis* are four-fold; the 3 × 3 composition as stipulated in the *Saṁhitās* and *Brāhmaṇas* for the *yajña* becoming a 4 × 4 Upaniṣadic formula leading to the contemplation and realization of Brahmā. Titled "Contemplation the *vyāhṛtis*" the actual text of this fifth lesson (*anuvāka*) illustrates how the Upaniṣads give a metaphysical transformation to earlier Vedic texts (A.M. Sastry 1980: 71 ff).

The *Taittirīya Āraṇyaka* (Sastri and Rangacarya 1985: 125) speaks of the worlds in a similar vein but not as *vyāhṛtis*. It associates the three worlds of *pṛthvī, antarikṣa* and *dyauḥ* with Agni, Vāyu and Sūrya respectively. The fourth world is that of the Quarters (*dikṣu*) and is associated with the Moon (*candramā*) . . . *agniḥ pṛthivyām, vāyurantarikṣa, sūryo divi, candramā dikṣu*. . .

Vyāhṛtis of the Brāhmaṇas

The Upaniṣadic version of the *vyāhṛtis*, as illustrated above, lend a metaphysical character to a set of *mantras* that are meant to make the *yajña* a model of the three worlds of the Vedic cosmocs. The *vyāhṛtis* as they are described in the *mantra* parts of the Vedic texts become unique because they repre-sent a clearly distinguishable effort at establishing a Vedic Cosmography.

The *vyāhṛtis* as they appear in the Upaniṣad and those that are used in the *yajña* make for an interesting comparison. Generally most of the litanies for the *yajña* are regarded as propitiatory and dismissed as chants that supplicate the gods. However, these verses are of particular significance because, while they may have a similar purport, the structure of the verses give a very precise stratification of the universe and further, they offer definitions of the attributes of each of the spheres that comprise the Vedic cosmos.

1. *bhūragnaye prāṇāya svāhā. idamagnaye prāṇāya idanna mama.*
2. *bhuvarvāyave apānāya svāhā. idam vāyave apānāya idanna mama.*
3. *svarādityāya vyānāya svāhā. idamādityāya vyānāya idanna mama.*

The fourth verse lists the three sets of triads that appear in these three verses:

bhūrbhuvaḥ svaragnivāyvādityebhyaḥ prāṇāpānavyānebhyaḥ svāhā. idamagnivāyvādityebhyaḥ prāṇāpānvyānebhyaḥ idanna mama.

The *padas* of the first three verses are three sets of triads. In the fourth verse a vertical grouping of the triads is given. The table below shows the pattern in which the triads appear.

World	*Element*	*Air*
1 *bhūḥ*	1 *agnaye*	1 *prāṇāya*
2 *bhuvaḥ*	2 *vāyave*	2 *apānāya*
3 *svaḥ*	3 *ādityāya*	3 *vyānāya*

The table lists horizontally the triads in the first three verses. Vertically, it presents the triads as grouped in the fourth verse.

In the first three verses, the *pada*s, except for *bhūh, bhuvaḥ, svaḥ,* are in the dative case, singular, where the members of the triads occur singly. In the fourth verse the triads appear collectively as *itaretara samāsa*s in the Dative Case, Plural.

Vedic cosmology divides the universe into three spheres viz., *bhūḥ-pṛthvī,* the earth; *bhuvaḥ-antarikṣa,* the atmosphere and, *svaḥ-dyauh,* the heaven (*Chāndogya Brāhmaṇa* 1.6.31).

The above *vyāhṛti* table, the one specified for the *yajña,* can be compared with the one below which marks the fourth stage of progression in the *Taittirīya Upaniṣad.*

Worlds	*Elements*	*Vedas*	*Airs*
1 *bhūḥ*	1 *agni*	1 *ṛk*	1 *prāṇa*
2 *bhuvaḥ*	2 *vāyu*	2 *sāma*	2 *apāna*
3 *svaḥ*	3 *āditya*	3 *yajus*	3 *vyāna*
4 *mahaḥ*	4 *candramā*	4 *oṁ*	4 *anna*

A detailed study of the triads, the members of each triad, the interrelations represented vertically and horizontally in the table are dealt with in details in the article on the *The Vyāhṛtis and Vedic Cosmography.*

The following table lists the *vyāhṛti*s as they are stipulated in the *Saṁhitā*s and *Brāhmaṇas,* their associations with the elements and vital airs, and demarcates them from the fourth component and the fourfold division that evolves in the *Taittirīya Upaniṣad.*

Worlds	*Elements*	*Air*	*Vedas*
1 *bhūḥ*	2 *agni*	3 *prāṇa*	4 *ṛk*
1 *bhuvaḥ*	2 *vāyu*	3 *apāna*	4 *sāma*
1 *svaḥ*	2 *āditya*	3 *vyāna*	4 *yaju*
1 *mahaḥ*	2 *candramā*	3 *anna*	4 *oṁ*

Triads as Divine Groupings

Gonda (1976: 7) supports and lends greater importance to Hopkin's view that "there are obvious threes all around us: earth, air, and sky. . ." (*Holy Numbers*, p. 145) Gonda goes on to explain:

> . . . the remarkable ancient practice of adding, in stating the numerical value of an entity or concept, the whole to the number of its components. . . . This implies that a number exceeding a given quantity by one summed up and moulded into one complex the entities constituting that quantity. . . . It follows that the number three can often be described as the higher synthesising unity of which the other two — two other entities — are parts or individual aspects.

Kunhan Raja

Kunhan Raja in the Preface to his book, *Poet-Philosophers of the Ṛgveda* (1963: xxii), makes an invaluable comment on the nature of the three worlds.

> We hear much of the three worlds in the Cosmology of the *Ṛgveda*. There are the three worlds of *pṛthvī, antarikṣa* and *dyaus*, the Earth, the atmospheric region and the celestial region. In the *pṛthvī* region, matter predominates, the *antarikṣa* region, activity predomin-ates and in the *dyaus* region, sentience predominates. These are the three layers in the course of evolution on the basis of finesse so far as the matter side is concerned; in the celestial region, matter is least predominant, and as such there is extreme finesse, and in the atmospheric region, there is a greater ratio of matter in relation to the celestial region and that region is grosser than the celestial region. The earthly region is the grossest.

He also goes on to state how the five Elements of the latter day philosophical systems evolved out of this notion of the initial division of Ṛgvedic cosmology into the three worlds:

> The earth and the atmosphere and the heaven are only symbols to denote the three layers. It is these three that developed into

the first three of the Five Elements in the later day philosophical thought pattern. The other two of the Five Elements are represented by the Dark Region (Kṛṣṇa Rajas) and the *Parama Vyoman* in the Ṛgvedic Cosmology. Sound (*Vāk*) is in the highest *Vyoman*. The first impetus for the diversification came from the *Tapas* in the Absolute; this is the impetus represented by *Vāyu* in the later systems of thought. This is what is called *Sparśa* or touch, which is nothing but the impetus from the *Tapas*.

Grouping the Deities into Triads

Gonda (1976: 12, 13) gives a splendid account of how, as a gradual progression from the diad to the triad, the elements/ deities evolved from groups of twos to groups of threes.

> It may be noticed in passing that a dual deity could be amplified so as to constitute a group of three: in a frequency of cases the less well-known Aryaman joins Varuṇa and Mitra. The goddess Sūryā accompanies the typically twin deities, the Aśvins, so that their chariot has three seats; the number three is in the hymns devoted to their praise and oft-repeated characterization of the constituent parts of that vehicle. The co-existence of expressions for a bipartite and a tripartite world and the relations between the twofold and threefold universe (sky and earth; sky, atmosphere and earth). . . . However the mythical accounts handed down in ŚB. 7.1.2.23 may find a place here: at first heaven and earth were together, and when they parted asunder, the space which was between them became the intermediate region, the air.

He also makes the following observation regarding the grouping of the classification of the Vedic deities (1976: 66):

> Dividing the gods into those whose place is the earth, those whose sphere is the atmosphere and those whose place is the firmament Yāska (*Nir*. 7, 5) records that the whole of the deities could traditionally be reduced to these three, Fire, Wind, Sun, the first on earth, the second in the air, the third in the highest region.

In my unpublished Ph.D. thesis "Heavenly Deities of the R̥gveda" (1993), I also base my definition of each of the Heavenly Deities as being a manifestation of the Āditya or the Sun — Viṣṇu, e.g., is the all pervading light of the Sun that covers with three steps the three worlds; Pūṣan is the Sun as the nourisher, etc. In the atmosphere the same Sun becomes the fluid or translucent form of lightning, *vidyut*, which becomes the thunderbolt of Indra. In this world of the firmament the elements assume a form that is Vāyu, aqueous in nature. That Sun/Agni again on the earth is the fire in its flaming or molten form, i.e., its gross form (see Kunhan Raja's quote above).

The Heaven, the Earth and the Tortoise

Having looked at the three worlds and their cosmography as illustrated in the *Taittirīya Āraṇyaka* and *Upaniṣad* and other Vedic texts, in terms of the chronological evolution of these texts, it is appropriate then to examine how the Vedic myths evolve and reflect Indian cosmogony. While the mythical anecdotes of the Purāṇas are attractive by the very nature of their narrative/story, it is the germinal theme of the myth that attracts our attention for in it lies the gradual evolution of the abstract deities of the Veda to the fully blown and clearly distinguishable gods of the Purāṇic pantheon.

A detailed study of the evolution of one such myth has been done by myself and a summary of the paper is given here to illustrate the main thesis of this paper, i.e., the development of Indian thought can be clearly traced in its progressive stages within the body of Vedic literature.

The germ of two other *avatāra*s are found in the *Brāhmaṇa*s. They are the 'fish' and the 'tortoise' incarnations. In the *Śatapatha Brāhmaṇa* the fish, at this stage not connected with Viṣṇu, delivers Manu from the flood (1.8.1.1) and in the Purāṇas, becomes an incarnation of Viṣṇu.

The Tortoise in Ancient Mythology

Tripathi (1981: 368) contends that the myth of the earth resting on the shell of the tortoise is not unique to Indian mythology. Traces of this myth can also be found in Chinese, Japanese and Red Indian folklore. In ancient Tao belief God made, for virtuous souls, a heaven of five islands which were abodes of total bliss. To steady these islands which swayed with the rolling barley fields, three tortoises were appointed to each island to make them firm (*Myths of China and Japan*, Donald & Mackenzie, pp. 111-12, 140, 280). In Almonkin Red Indian lore, the tortoise enjoys a position of importance as the sustainer of the earth and, at places, the earth is even described as the shell of the tortoise (*Der Ursprung der Gottesidee*, W. Schmidt, p. 445).

The Śatapatha Brāhmaṇa and the Tortoise

Tripathi's study of the tortoise incarnation begins with the earliest references to the tortoise in the *Śatapatha Brāhmaṇa*:

> Prajāpati, having assumed the form of a tortoise created this world — *prajā*. It is for the reason of having created the world in this form that the very form itself is called *kurma* i.e. it derives from the root *kṛ* — to do plus the affix *manin*. (*kṛ* + *auṇādika* = *kūr* + *manin* = *kūrma*) Another name for *kūrma* is *kaśyapa*, thus all of humanity is said to be the progeny of Kaśyapa. — 7.5.1.5

The etymological derivation is meant to emphasize the meaning of the root *kṛ* — "to make or do" and the suffix *manin* — "endowed with" so as to bring out the sense of *kūrma* as Creator. In verse 7.5.1.1 of the *Śatapatha Brāhmaṇa*, *kūrma* is said to be very essence — the *rasa* of the three worlds — *raso vai kūrma*; *kūrma* emerged from the etherial waters as the three worlds. Just as the *rasa* is said to be the aggregate of all that constitutes it, similarly *kūrma* is the very soul of the three worlds. Verse 6.1.1.12 deals with a similar idea.

Theriomorphism as Evidenced in the Manifestation of the Tortoise

As stated earlier the comparisons made in the *Ṛgveda* between the element and human or other life forms remain more at the level of poetic simile rather than evolve to a level where they can be strictly classified as anthropomorphism or therio-morphism. In the *Śatapatha Brāhmaṇa*, however, and parti-cularly in the case of the tortoise there is a clear description of the physical form of the tortoise as the embodiment of the three worlds of heaven, earth and the intersphere. The shell of the tortoise which resembles an inverted vessel, *kapāla*, is the sky, the base or floor of the shell is the flat earth and between the two exists the life form, the living substance of the tortoise; just as between the earth and the dome of heaven exist all life forms (7.5.1.2). The *Śatapatha Brāhmaṇa* continues in this vein to make the tortoise the very embodiment of Creation lending to it the heights of grandeur that equal even the Ṛgvedic hymns of Creation. In verse 7.5.1.7, *kūrma* is described as the *prāṇa* — the soul force and the power of consciousness of all sentient beings — *prāṇaḥ vai kūrmaḥ. prāṇo hīmāḥ sarvāḥ prajāḥ karoti.* Tripathi traces very meticulously the progressive evolution of this myth through the *Brāhmaṇas*, *Mahābhārata* and then to the Viṣṇu and other Purāṇas.

The *Taittirīya Āraṇyaka*, in keeping with the philosophical nature of the deliberations continued in this class of literature discusses the primordial nature of *kūrma*. *Kūrma* in a dialogue with Prajāpati, claims to have existed in the form of the eternal waters even before Prajāpati. Here the *kūrma* acquires the status of the thousand-headed and thousand-eyed *puruṣa* of the *Ṛgveda* 1.23.3, 4. Philosophically then *kūrma* as the earliest form of creation derives its basis directly from the *Puruṣa Sūkta* (10.90).

World-Bowls in the Ṛgveda

For the purpose of this paper the theriomorphism embodied in the tortoise in the *Śatapatha Brāhmaṇa* is of great significance. The *Ṛgveda* describes the two worlds of heaven and earth as two hemispheres constituting a globular universe, figuratively, the two world-bowls. It is in the *Śatapatha Brāhmaṇa* that the world-bowl becomes transformed into the shell of the tortoise which becomes, in the Purāṇas, the incarnation of Viṣṇu.

Dyāvāpṛthvī, the Ṛgvedic dual compound, refers to the "twoness" of the *pṛthvī*, earth, and *dyaus*, heaven. These two worlds are portrayed as world halves, the heaven as a dome or the upper inverted vessel and the earth as the lower bowl upon which the heaven rests. Since the word *kapāla* which means a cup, jar or dish is used in the *Śatapatha Brāhmaṇa* to denote the shell of the tortoise, I have looked for the equi-valent of this imagery in the *Ṛgveda*. It may be noted that the *kapāla* was used particularly for the Puroḍāsa or Soma offer-ing in Vedic ritualism.

There are two words *camū* and *dhīṣaṇā* which are used in the *Ṛgveda* in association with Soma. A study of the usage of these words shows that while *camū* clearly denotes a vessel or vessels in which Soma was prepared, collected or drunk from; and *dhīṣaṇā*, the boards between which the Soma was pressed, both words also in certain instances signify the world bowls as does *kapāla* in the *Śatapatha Brāhmaṇa*.

In the paper there is a detailed study of the grammatical use of *camū* and the implications of its various uses for interpretation. While *camū* is used to denote the bowls used to press Soma, it is also used in several instances to depict the world bowls or the hemispheres.

The same applies to *dhīṣanā*; the word is used in the sense of the bowl or vat used for the preparation of Soma, it could mean the Soma itself or it refers to the worlds — two where it is used in the dual and three when it is used in the plural.

In employing the use of these two words, *camū* and *dhīṣaṇā*, the cosmology of *Ṛgveda* uses the simile of a spherical division of the two worlds of heaven and earth as hemispheres. Just as the hemispheres of the earth constitute the globe of the earth, the hemisphere of the earth forms a bowl and the hemisphere of the heaven is a second inverted bowl forming the greater global universe. This simile becomes transformed into a simpler and more poetic image of the tortoise representing the two world halves or hemispheres, i.e., the shell is one hemisphere, the dome of heaven, and the flat bottom of the tortoise is the other hemisphere, the flat earth, the only difference being that the second hemisphere becomes reduced from a spherical dimension to a flat expanse.

It is also interesting to note that the *Atharvaveda Pariśiṣṭa* and Varāhamihira's *Bṛhat Saṁhitā* uses the word *kūrmavibhāga* to mean a division of the globe or semi-globe of the earth. In Varāhamihira's *Yogayātrā*, the word *kūrmāṅga* means the globe of the earth (Monier-Williams 1979: 300). It therefore can, I believe, be safely concluded that the word *kapāla*, meaning a vessel, which in the *Śatapatha Brāhmaṇa* denotes the shell of the tortoise, uses as a basis for this imagery the description of the heaven and earth as world-bowls, expressed by the terms *camū* and *dhīṣaṇā* in the *Ṛgveda*. Insofar as the evolution of the tortoise incarnation is concerned the sequence of its development would be as follows: In the *Ṛgveda* the words *camū* and *dhīṣaṇā* denote the hemispheres of the heaven and earth as world-bowls, these words find a parallel in the *kapāla* of the *Śatapatha Brāhmaṇa* where Creation is described as having emerged from the waters in the form of the tortoise, *kūrma; kapāla* meaning a vessel, being used to describe the shell of the tortoise. In the Purāṇas the *kūrma* which symbolizes the initial form of Creation in the Brāhmaṇa becomes a fully blown *avatāra* of Viṣṇu.

Anthropomorphism/Theriomorphism

In the *Ṛgveda* itself the trend towards the anthropomorphism of divinities is almost totally absent. The ascribing of human or animal features or characteristics to the elements for instance is not to be regarded as evidence for a nascent anthropomorphism but should be viewed in the light of literary conventions and techniques that abound in the poetry of the Vedas. The lack of a clearly defined anthropomorphism in the Vedas has led to the interesting and antithetical stances by scholars in their interpretation of the *Ṛgveda*. For the early school of Indologists such as Macdonell (1974: 2) this lack of anthropomorphism reflects the primitive or rudimentary nature of the poetry of the text. For those like Dayananda (commentary on the *Ṛgveda*) and Aurobindo (*On the Veda*) who argue in favour of a more sophisticated theism in the Vedas the lack of anthropomorphism is rather interestingly used to good advantage. For them, the lack of clearly defined anthropomorphism does not prove that the speculation on the divine was primitive, on the contrary the absence of clearly pronouunced physical attributes serves as proof for the abstract nature of God. Needless to say the debate is an unending one not only for those with deep rooted religious convictions but also for academics who find themselves being confounded by texts such as Yāska's *Nirukta* which make possible a wide range of speculation on the etymologies of Vedic vocable.

A good example of how a deity which has in the Vedas an abstract character, epithets meaning "goodness, auspiciousness, bliss," and later becomes in the Purāṇas a fully evolved mythical god is that of Śiva.

Śiva of the Vedas

In the *Śiva Purāṇa*, the abstract nature of the Vedic Śiva (also) known as Śaṅkara and Śambhu) has evolved into fully blown myths. In the Vedic texts the etymology of the epithets of Śiva can, besides being expounded in the various Vedic *kośa*s, be explained by the Vedic *mantra*s themselves.

> *namah śambhavāya ca mayobhavāya namaḥ śaṅkarāya ca mayaskarāya ca. namaḥ śivāya ca śivatarāya ca.* — *Yaju* 16.41

Śambhavāya is the Dative Case of *śambhu* = *śam* + *bhū* which then becomes *śankarāya* comprising the roots *śam* + *kṛ*. Since in both the epithets the base root is *śam*, the principle notion would be "peace, serenity, calmness" as connoted by this root. The *bhū* appended to it will therefore mean the "embodiment" or "being" of peace. The *bhū* then becomes *kr̥* which marks the transition of the deity from a stage of embodiment of peace to that of an active principle, the doer or generator of peace. We note a similar progression in *mayobhava* which evolves from *māyas* + *bhū* "the embodiment of bliss" to *māyas* + *kr̥* "the generator of bliss".

The next part of the verse gives a third epithet *śiva* presumably from the same root *śam* in the sense of "auspiciousness" or "goodness" and *Śiva* then becomes *śivatara* — "the greater good" where the *tara* is treated as the suffix denoting the comparative degree.

There is a further stage in this progression, from comparative to the superlative, as evidenced in a *mantra* from the *Brāhmaṇa* text. The notion of good and peace here become supreme virtues:

> *āpaḥ śivāh śivatamāḥ śāntāḥ śāntatmās tāste kr̥ṇvantu bheṣajam*
> — *Pāraskaragr̥hyasūtra* 1.8.5

In this *mantra śiva*, which became *śivatara* in the earlier verse, now becomes *śivatama*, the *tama* being used as a suffix to indicate the superlative. The association with *śāntaḥ* is also maintained and with the superlative added to it, the connotations of "peace" and "auspiciousness" can be seen as a parallel evolution of these epithets. Monier-Williams (1979: 1074) also defines *śivatara* and *śivatama* as, respectively, the comparative and superlative of *Śiva*.

The epithets of Śiva can therefore be placed in a sequence according to a progression that systematically unfolds the meaning and the perception of the term in the Vedic texts: Śambhu, Śaṅkara, Śiva, Śivatara, Śivatama.

Such an example not only vindicates but amply illustrates the theory posited by Patañjali and the resulting school of thought that Sanskrit nouns can all be traced to their verbal roots.

Conclusion

It also becomes quite evident that there is within the Vedic texts a means of identifying the various deities and listing their definitions, without our having to resort to any mani-pulation or adaptation of the linguistic laws or schools of literary theory outside that of the Indian texts. The literary approach suggested by Yāska in his *Nirukta,* Patañjali's treatment of words as derivatives of verbal roots and the various other Indian philosophical schools which speak of the nature of language, its eternality, the origins and notions of sound — all these demonstrate that a treatment of the word, the myth and philosophical thought is possible through a systematic study of the Vedic texts themselves, a reaffirmation of the Vedas being *svataḥ-pramāṇaḥ* — valid in themselves. The Vedic myths and the etymology of the names of the deities are the germ of a later more clearly anthropomorphosized mythology, the evolution of which can be easily traced through a chronological study of the Vedic texts. The worldview of the Vedas is vividly enunciated in the early Vedic hymns and myths, it becomes more colourful in the stories of the Purāṇas and finds philosophical perfection in the Upaniṣads.

References

Arya, Dev Narayan, *Sanskara Vidhi* by Maharṣi Dayanand, Triveni Publications, New Delhi, 1995.

Aurobindo, Sri, *On the Veda*, Pondicherry 1964, Sri Aurobindo Ashram.

Chinmayananda, Swami, *Discourses on Taittirīya Upaniṣad*, Central Chinmaya Mission Trust, Bombay, 1983.

Dayananda, Saraswati, *Satyārth Prakāśa*, tr. Chiranjiva Bharadwaja, Sarvadeshik Arya Pratinidhi Sabha, New Delhi, 1984.

Dayananda, Saraswati, Swami, *Introduction to the Commentary on the Vedas*, tr. P.T. Ghasi Ram, Delhi 1958, Sarvadeshik Arya Pratinidhi Sabha.

Eagleton, Terry, *Literary Theory, An Introduction*, Oxford, 1983, Basil Balackwell.

Eggeling, Julius, *Sacred Books of the East*, 5 volumes; on *Śatapatha Brāhmaṇa* (nos. 12, 26, 41, 43, 44), Oxford, 1899.

Filliozat, J., *La doctrine classique de la medecine Indienne*, Paris, 1949.

Gonda, J., *Triads in the Veda*, North-Holland, Publishing Company, Amsterdam, 1976.

Griffith, Ralph T.H., *The Hymns of the Ṛgveda*, ed. J.L. Shastri, Motilal Banarsidass, 1976.

Hillebrandt, Alfred, *Vedic Mythology*, tr. into English by S. Rajeswra Sarma, Motilal Banarsidass, Delhi, 1981.

Hillebrandt, Alfred, *Vedische Mythologie*, 2 vols., Hildesheim, 1965.

Hopkins, E.W., *Holy Numbers*.

Keith, A.B., *The Religion and Philosophy of the Veda and Upaniṣads*, Harvard Oriental Series, ed. Lanman C.R. Harvard University Press, London (Printed by Oxford University Press), 1925.

Levi-Strauss, Claude, *The Raw and the Crooked: Introduction to a Science of Mythology*, tr. J. & D. Weightman, New York, 1969, Harper and Row Levi-Strauss, Claude, *Myth and Meaning*, Toronto, 1978, University of Toronto Press.

Macdonell, A.A., *Vedic Mythology*, Delhi, 1974, Motilal Banarsidass.

Max-Müller, F., *A History of Ancient Sanskrit Literature*, Varanasi, 1968, Chowkhamba Sanskrit Series, vol. 15.

Monier-Willaims, M.A., *Sanskrit-English Dictionary*, Motilal Banarsidass, Delhi, 1979.

Raja, C. Kunhan, *Poet-Philosophers of the Ṛgveda*, Ganesh & Co., Madras 1963.

Rambilass, B., *Heavenly Deities of the Ṛgveda*, Meerut, 1992, Unpublished Doctoral Thesis.

Sarup, Laksman, *The Nighantu and the Nirukta*, Motilal Banarsidass, 1984.

Sastri, Mahadeva A. & Rangacarya, K. (eds.), The *Taittirīya Āraṇyaka* with commentary by Bhaṭṭa Bhāskara Misra, Motilal Banarsidass, 1985.

Selden, Raman, *A Reader's Guide to a Contemporary Theory*, Great Britain 1985, Harvester Press.

Suresvaracharya & Vidyaranya, *The Taittirīya Upaniṣad*, with commentaries by Śaṅkarācārya tr. Alladi Mahadeva Sastry, Samata Books, Madras, 1980.

Tripathi, Gayacharan, *Vaidik Devatā, Udbhav aur Vikās* (Hindi), Delhi, 1981, Bharatiya Prakashan.

Vedalankar, Nardev & Chotai Sukhraj (eds.), *Āryan Prayer*, Veda Niketan, Durban, 1980.

Vernant, Jean-Pirre, *Myth and Society in Ancient Greece* (tr. Janet Lloyd), London, 1982 Metheun & Co. Ltd.

15

Modern Philosophical Fragmentation versus Vedānta and Plato

Bart Gruzalski

In this paper I focus on a compartmentalization within contemporary Western philosophy that results in a loss of ethically relevant content. Compartmentalization that obliterates content results in fragmentation. As Alasdair MacIntyre wrote in *After Virtue*,

> the language and the appearances of morality persist even though the integral substance of morality has to a large degree been fragmented and then in part destroyed.[1]

I will illustrate approaches, both from the East and from the West, that do not exhibit this fragmentation. My theme is that students of contemporary Western philosophy might have much to learn from classical sources in both Western and Eastern philosophy and from modern applications of the ethical directives found in these sources.

The Fragmentation of Modern Western Philosophy

The compartmentalization within Western philosophy is so orthodox that it is almost imperceptible. For example, contemporary philosophy treats epistemology and ethics as

1. Alasdair MacIntyre, *After Virtue*, Notre Dame: University of Notre Dame Press, 1981, p. 5.

autonomous areas of study. In no contemporary discussion of ethics would a philosopher suggest that what one can come to know about the nature of reality is a function of ones moral development. Likewise, epistemology is limited to the field of what can be publicly verified. Hence, the modern epistemological perspective rules out the possibility of knowing a transcendent reality. Although these positions constitute philosophical orthodoxy for journals and universities worldwide, this disengagement of epistemology from ethics has a cost. Part of the cost is that we have no adequate answer to Plato's profound question: Why be moral? The lack of an answer to this question is a good gauge for a failure of contemporary Western philosophy to address fundamental questions that we human beings raise when we think about our lives and about how we should live them.

It is my hypothesis that compartmentalization in contemporary Western philosophy has fragmented philosophy and obliterated important connections between ethics and epistemology that we find in Plato and in the living traditions of Vedānta and Buddhism. In this first section I shall briefly describe three holistic systems.

THE HOLISTIC APPROACH OF VEDĀNTA AND BUDDHISM

According to Vedāntic thought, what one can come to know about the nature of reality is a function of ones moral development. The *Kaṭha Upaniṣad* makes perfectly clear that one has to give up attachment to all externals in order to achieve the highest knowledge. Yama is only willing to teach after his student had renounced "the goal of worldly desire, the glittering objects for which all men long, the celestial pleasures they hope to gain by religious rites, [and] the most sought-after of miraculous powers" (II.11).[2] To be free from desire, to have a heart in which "desire is dead" (V.14), is a precondition for seeing things as they are. In the

2. *The Upaniṣads*, tr. Swami Prabhavananda and Frederick Manchester, Hollywood: Vedanta Society of Southern California, 1948.

Bhagavad Gītā, too, one finds this theme. There the highest knowledge involves union with *Brahman*. To 'attain' this realization one must renounce attachment to things of the world:

> Let him who could climb in meditation to the heights of the highest union with *Brahman* take for his path the *yoga* of action. . . . For, when a man loses attachment to sense-objects and to action, when he renounces lustful anxiety and anxious lust, then he is said to have climbed to the height of union with *Brahman*.
>
> — VI. 3[3]

The loss of attachment is crucial for realization:

> Do your duty, always; but without attachment. That is how a man reaches the ultimate Truth.
>
> — III. 19

We are told of saints that have reached enlightenment following this path:

> Janaka and many others reached enlightenment, simply because they did their duty in this spirit
>
> — III. 20

The point, both according to the *Kaṭha Upaniṣad* and the *Gītā*, is that a person needs to renounce desire to come to realization.

In the *Gītā* and in the *Kaṭha Upaniṣad* we also find clear statements that although one can talk about, write about, and study about *Brahman* and *ātman*, that neither the mere "study of the Vedas" (*Gītā*, XI. 48) nor any other "vain theory" (*Kaṭha*, II. 9) can reveal what is to be realized. What is to be realized is ineffable and not publicly verifiable. Practice is crucial and its aim is the realization of that which cannot successfully be conveyed in words.

We find the same themes in early Buddhism, which have

3. *The Song of God: Bhagavad Gītā*, tr. Swami Prabhavananda and Christopher Isherwood, Hollywood: Vedanta Society of Southern California, 1944.

generally been described as the fifth *yoga* of liberation.[4] The practice of morality or *śīla* is essential to developing the inner condition of tranquillity without which the practitioner cannot realize the way things are and cannot realize that transcendent unborn to which the Buddha refers in the *udāna* (VIII. 1-3).

In summary, in the early texts of Vedānta and Buddhism we find that ethics and epistemology are intimately inter-woven. According to these texts, ethical development is required in order to realize our own nature and the nature of reality. The result is an epistemological (in addition to a prudential) answer to the question: "Why be moral?" We find analogous components of an integrated philosophy in Plato's *Republic*.

PLATO'S REPUBLIC

In the *Republic*, IV. 443, Plato tells us that the moral person is to develop inner tranquillity. The development and maintenance of inner harmony is so central that it determines which external actions a person should perform to be moral:

> In reality morality[5]. . . is not a matter of external behaviour, but of the inward self and of attending to all that is, in the fullest sense, a person's proper concern. The moral person does not allow the several elements in his soul to usurp one another's functions; he is indeed one who sets his house in order, by self-mastery and discipline coming to be at peace with himself. . . . In all these fields [whether it be making money and satisfying bodily wants, or business transactions or affairs of the state] when he speaks of moral and honourable conduct, he will mean the behaviour that helps to produce and to preserve this habit of

4. "Bondage, Liberation, Perfection," Kireet Joshi, presented at a seminar on "Bondage and Liberation," July 14, 1997, at Seminar Hall, Rajendra Bhavan, Deen Dayal Upadhyaya Marg, New Delhi.
5. I am substituting the words "morality" and "moral" for "justice" and "just" since these are better renditions for a contemporary reader of the Greek. I am also substituting the word "person" for the word "man" for similar reasons.

> mind [well-tempered harmony]; and by wisdom he will mean the knowledge which presides over such conduct. Any action which tends to break down his habit will be for him immoral; and the notions governing it he will call ignorance and folly.[6]

Every action is under the scope of this criterion, and every aspect of life is intended to develop this inner quality. Plato asserts in IX. 591:

> Health, strength, and beauty he will value only in so far as they bring soundness of mind, and you will find him keeping his bodily frame in tune always for the sake of the resulting concord in the soul. . . . In adding to or spending his substance, he will, to the best of his power, be guided by watchful care that neither want nor abundance may unsettle the constitution set up in his soul. . . . In accepting power and honours he will keep the same end in view, ready to enjoy any position in public or private life which he thinks will make him a better man, and avoiding any that would break down the established order within him.

Plato ends the main section of the *Republic,* IX. 691-692, with the following emphasis on this inner focus:

> Then [says Glaucon], if that is his chief concern, he will have no wish to take part in politics.
>
> Indeed he will [responds Socrates], in the politics of his own commonwealth, though not perhaps in those of his country, unless some miraculous chance should come about.
>
> I understand, said Glaucon: you mean this commonwealth we have been founding in the realm of discourse; for I think it nowhere exists on earth.
>
> No, Socrates replied; but perhaps there is a pattern set up in the heavens for one who desires to see it and, seeing it, to found one in himself. But whether it exists anywhere or ever will exist is no

---

6. *The Republic of Plato*, tr. Francis MacDonald Cornford, London: Oxford University Press, 1941.

> matter; for this is the only commonwealth in whose politics he can ever take part.[7]

The basic ethical teachings of Plato in the *Republic* emphasize developing an inner harmony or tranquillity, as does the ethical focus in the *Gītā*. In the *Gītā*, however, in addition to being centered on inner harmony or tranquillity, the realized person is "poised in the tranquillity of *ātman*" (III. 18). The approximation of the *Gītā* to Plato is even closer than this quotation from the *Gītā* suggests, since once we realize the ineffability of *ātman*, the only idea remaining that we can convey successfully in words is the idea of inner harmony or tranquillity. When we acknowledge the ineffability of *ātman*, the ethical directive of Plato's *Republic* and the *Gītā* become more analogous.

Plato also makes clear the teleological and epistemological ramifications of his view in his commentary on the Allegory of the Cave. This commentary is remarkably like the epistemological requirement of non-attachment we find both in the *Gītā* and in the *Kaṭha Upaniṣad*. Plato in VII. 518 writes:

> Our own account signifies that the soul of every man does possess the power of learning the truth and the organ to see it with; and that, just as one might have to turn the whole body round in order that the eye should see light instead of darkness, so the entire soul must be turned away from this changing world, until its eye can bear to contemplate reality and that supreme splendour which we have called the Good.

In short, turning away from the things of the world — health, reputation, security, money, happiness, pleasure — is part of the

7. This passage remarks on the impossibility of external "perfection" and in this regard is remarkably similar to a passage in the *Gītā* where the point is made that all external "action is involved in imperfection, like fire in smoke" (XVIII. 48), and so one should simply do what is one's own duty and not be persuaded to try to do the duty of another.

path of the person trying to realize the highest knowledge. These are the same phenomena to which one must be nonattached if one is to develop inner harmony. Plato not only sees desire and attachments to phenomena as an impediment to realization, but also that desires "are the most fruitful source of evils both to individuals and to states" (II. 374).

When we turn to metaphysics, we initially seem to find a significant difference between the *Republic* and the Gītā. In the Gītā one is to realize *ātman*, which is the same as *Brahman*, which is the source of all. In the *Republic* what one is to come to realize is the Good. Yet if we reflect on Plato's Allegory of the Cave, it is obvious that those who are unenlightened and taking shadows to be the whole of reality cannot verbally be told this, for words about shadows would literally make no sense to be prisoners and would not convey to them that they were taking shadows to be all of reality. Plato seems to acknowledge the ineffability of their situation when he has Socrates say that giving an account of the Good is beyond his powers (IV. 506). He does, however in XXIII. 508 give a limited account of what he means by the Good:

> The objects of knowledge . . . derive from the Good not only their power of being known, but their very being and reality; and Goodness is not the same thing as being, but even beyond being, surpassing it in dignity and power.

This is a description of what is clearly beyond words and of what is superlative in every way. We find here, even in Plato, a metaphysical analogue to what we find in the *Gītā* and in the *udāna*.

SUMMARY

This short comparison of the writings of Plato in the *Republic* and the central themes of the *Gītā*, the *Kaṭha Upaniṣad*, and Early Buddhism reveals a striking similarity between the themes of ethics in early Western philosophy and those living ethical traditions that one finds in Vedānta and Buddhism. In particular, we find a clear illustration of a philosophical perspective in which moral development is a condition of full realization. Each points to a practical way of living in which action without attachment is a path to tranquillity and realization. Although feminist epistemologists and some eco-feminists are moving toward less fragmentation in contemporary philosophy, an examination of the living traditions of Vedānta and Buddhism might not only help us in the West to move toward less fragmentation, but in so doing would also help us better appreciate our own philosophical roots.

Practical Applications

When we turn to contemporary applied ethics in the West, we also discover a great deal of compartmentalization. For instance, business ethics, environmental ethics, and distributive justice each refers to an area of application that philosophers typically treat as autonomous. The question to which I now turn is whether the practical applications of the ethical perspectives we find in Vedānta, Buddhism and Plato are less compartmentalized. I will illustrate my discussion with a holistic approach to issues as divergent as poverty, unemployment, community vitality, and environmental degradation. The problems on which I explicitly focus are poverty and ecological destruction.

Although overpopulation and overconsumption are the two central causes of these problems, my focus will be on overconsumption for two reasons. First, for those of us in the socio-economic group that includes university faculty and most university students, our contribution to the problems of poverty and environmental degradation tends to be through overconsumption rather than through overpopulation, and so overconsumption is more relevant to our own lives. Second, even if we could actually solve the population expansion problem by maintaining current population levels, a generalization of US consumption standards across the globe would of itself be ecologically disastrous.[8] It follows that overconsumption is a problem to be addressed in its own right. Hence, while not diminishing the urgency of the overpopulation problem, I shall instead briefly explore one model for dealing with the harms caused by overconsumption.

The practice of Vedānta and of Buddhism provide the basis for this approach. The practice of these *yoga*s of Vedānta and Buddhism "all agree that the state of liberation is impossible without the elimination of desire and egosense."[9] An application of these philosophical traditions to the harms caused by overconsumption suggests that we restrain our consumption in order to not only stop reinforcing desire and ego-sense, but also to stop causing harm to future generations.

This philosophical directive is found not only in Vedānta and Buddhism, but also in Plato's *Republic*.[10] Plato claims the ideal community is one in which individuals eschew luxuries. In the same passage, he cautions that desire is the most significant cause of evil for individuals and for states. Insofar as we are concerned about future generations, Plato's directive affirms that we should not consume resources unnecessarily but so live that our children can live after us in the manner that we lived.

But restraint in consumption is only one factor in any successful approach. If we are to address meaningfully the crises caused by overconsumption, we must live so that others can have a full, meaningful, and comfortable life, including those in future generations. This way of life, therefore, must be sustainable.[11]

---

8. Herman Daly, *Beyond Growth: The Economics of Sustainable Development*, Boston: Beacon Press, 1996, p. 104.

9. Joshi, *op cit*.

10. *Republic*, II.372-74.

11. There are many meanings of the term "sustainable." For the purposes of this paper, I follow John Gowdy in citing three that are central: (1) sustaining intergenerational economic welfare, (2) maximizing

→

Gandhi, applying the principles of Vedānta and the ethics of the *Gītā*, provides one model for dealing with the poverty and ecological degradation caused by overconsumption.[12]

Gandhi saw that full employment was part of a sustainable way of life. His emphasis on full employment led him to what, today, we refer to as appropriate technology. He objected to "the craze is for what they call labour-saving machinery. Men go on 'saving labour' till thousands are without work and thrown on the open streets to die of starvation." He wrote that if the power were in his hands, he "would penalize the manufacture of (labour-saving) machines and protect the industry which manufactures nice ploughs which can be handled by every man."[14] He considered

→ the time of existence of the human species, and (3) sustaining nature and its diversity [John M. Gowdy cites these three primary meanings of sustainability in "Progress and Environmental Sustainability," *Environmental Ethics*, vol. 16, 1994, p. 45]. In this paper my focus is on (2) — maximizing the time of existence of the human species. My rationale for this emphasis is two-fold: first, I think (2) is less controversial than either (1) or (3). Many would theoretically oppose sustaining a level of economic welfare that caused humans to die prematurely because that level of welfare included substantial luxury, convenience and entertainment. Many would also oppose sustaining nature and its diversity at the cost of causing the premature deaths of human beings. While resolving these issues would take us afield, I believe it plausible that (2) and (3) are causally supportive of each other. For those of us who are biocentrists and believe that there are non-human entities that have intrinsic value, the principle of not risking the premature deaths of others, and its implications; can easily be translated to acknowledge these values.

12. The following draws extensively on a longer piece on Gandhi: "Healing the Ills of Unemployment, Societal Breakdown, and Ecological Degradation: Gandhi's Vision for a Sustainable Way of Life," Bart Gruzalski, *Philosophy in the Contemporary World*, vol. 1, no. 3, Fall 1994.

13. *Young India*, 13 November 1924, quoted in *The Mind of Mahatma Gandhi*, ed. R.K. Prabhu and U.R. Rao, Ahmedabad, India: Navajivan Publishing House, 1967, pp. 235-36.

14. *Gandhi: Essential Writings*, ed. V.V. Ramana Murti, New Delhi: Gandhi Peace Foundation 1970, p. 298.

large scale machinery "wholly destructive" because it destroyed jobs, but he was not against machinery that would better the lives of all individuals. "Simple tools and instruments and such machines that save individual labour and lightens the burden of the millions of cottages I should welcome."[15] The goal "is not to produce village articles as cheap as possible; it is to provide the workless villagers with work at a living wage."[16]

Full employment and appropriate technologies were each required, and this, in part, explains Gandhi's great emphasis on decentralized village industries. While the principal village industry is agriculture, Gandhi saw that other village industries supporting agriculture were needed to meet the goals of full employment. Gandhi saw spinning as the perfect cottage industry that could support all of India:

> Agriculturists in no country can live without some industry to supplement agriculture. . . . Even if we have sufficient mills in the country to produce cloth enough for the whole country, we are bound to provide our peasantry, daily being more and more impoverished, with some supplementary industry, and that which can be suitable to crores of people is hand-spinning and hand-weaving. Opposition to mills or machinery is not the point. What suits our country most is the point. . . . I am only concerned with what these machines are meant for.[17]

Gandhi thought that the spread of the practice of spining would empower people as well as liberate them from their dependency on industrial manufacturing:

> It is not merely the wages earned by the spinners that are to be counted but it is the whole reconstruction that follows in the wake of the spinning wheel. The village weaver, the village dyer,

15. *Young India*, 17 June 1926, quoted in *The Mind of Mahatma Gandhi*, p. 237.
16. *Gandhi: Essential Writings*, p. 311.
17. *Gandhi: Essential Writings*, p. 298.

> the village washermen, the village blacksmith, the village carpenter, all and many others will then find themselves reinstated in their ancient dignity, as is already happening wherever the spinning wheel has gained a footing.[18]

The result, according to Gandhi, would not only be full employment, but the rekindling of dignity for people who were not beneficiaries of the industrial society.

Gandhi wanted to replace the emphasis on profits and greed with an emphasis on what makes for a life of dignified community. He believed that:

> God never creates more than what is strictly needed for the moment, with the result that if anyone appropriates more than he really needs, he reduces his neighbour to destitution. The starvation of people in several parts of the world is due to many of us seizing very much more than they need. We may utilize the gifts of nature just we choose, but in her books the debits are always equal to the credits.[19]

Gandhi claimed that we needed "a new outlook" according to which "multiplicity of material wants will not be the aim of life, the aim will be rather their restriction consistently with comfort. We shall cease to think of getting what we can, but we shall decline to receive what all cannot get."[20] The result would be a significant reduction of consumption, for the aim always would be to live in a way that was harmonious with sustainable community. Gandhi offered what he called the "golden rule":

> The golden rule to apply in all such cases is resolutely to refuse to have what millions cannot. This ability to refuse will not descend upon us all of a sudden. The first thing is to cultivate the mental attitude that will not have possessions or facilities

18. *The Essential Gandhi*, ed. Louis Fischer, New York: Random House, 1962, p. 225.
19. *The Mind of Mahatma Gandhi, op. cit.*, p. 199.
20. *Harijan*, 1 February 1942.

> denied to millions, and the next immediate thing is to re-arrange our lives as fast as possible in accordance with that mentality.[21]

The kind of life towards which Gandhi pointed is one of simplicity, non-accumulation, and community-empower-ment consistent with comfort. In the *Republic,* Plato also thought, consistent with Gandhi's vision, that the "ideal" community in "sound health" would be an agrarian community of people living in a "simple way" (II. 372-73).

The changes that Gandhi's model requires, as radical as they may appear, are more than just living a more simple lifestyle and reorganizing our communities. In order to fully live out the Gandhian proposal, we must do the inner work that involves changing and freeing ourselves from conventional attitudes, expectations, and desires.

Gandhi was explicitly aware of the need for more than just external adjustements in our material circumstances. "The reforms required are more from within than from without. A perfect constitution super-imposed upon a rotten internal condition will be like a whited sepulchre."[22] A Northern California environmentalist expresses a contemporary version of this idea as follows:

> People have to get involved, they have to act. It's not enough just to be entertained by all of this. It's the time in the history of the planet when all people have to start picking up their share and cleaning up the mess of sloppy cultures, mindsets and philosophies that have resulted in this massive destruction of the earth. We need to reinstitute spiritual process. Spiritual process in a healthy religion is one that teaches people to be responsible for their emotions. It teaches them to accept pain and suffering rather than running from it. It teaches them to internalize rather than to constantly act in an imperialistic

21. *Young India*, 24 June 1926.

22. *Ibid*.

> manner. Most of the consumption, the consumtion that is destroying our planet, comes from unmet emotional needs. We need to accept responsibility for our emotions, we need to learn to internalize, we need to learn to be in harmony with ourselves so that we are able to be at harmony with all other things. It's basically a spiritual message and a spiritual revolution that has to happen and it begins with every individual, it doesn't begin with overturning the big corporations. The corporations are a symbol, they aren't the cause.[23]

The message that we must take an inner turn that involves non-attachment and the restraint of desire is not new in philosophy or religion. It is an essential message in Vedānta, Buddhism, and in Plato. It is part of a practical approach to the problems of unemployment, poverty, starvation, community breakdown, and ecological degradation. The inner turn is a source of support for the external changes we must make in our own lives and in our communities if we are to address the basic survival needs of current and future generations.

Conclusion

In contemporary philosophy in the West we face fragmentation both in our theoretical discussions of ethics as well as in our approaches to the problems we address under the rubric of applied ethics. By exploring the philosophies of Vedānta, of Buddhism, and of Plato, we discover holistic perspectives that can inform contemporary Western philosophical thinking. Likewise, when we look at the approach of Gandhi to the problems of poverty, unemployment, community vitality and environmental degradation, we see the practicality of a less fragmented and more holistic approach to applied ethics.

---

23. Quoted in "Healing the Ills of Unemployment, Societal Breakdown, and Ecological Degradation: Gandhi's Vision for a Sustainable Way of Life," *op. cit.*, p. 26.

16

The Dhārmic Journey of Svami Vivekananda

From the Apostle of Hinduism Universalism to Hinduism as the Religion Eternal

George M. Williams

As he walked to the stage of Hall of Columbus before four thousand assembled delegates and visitors, Svami Vivekananda personified some surprising tensions which would take a century to unfold. Yet fittingly, he would become the symbol of the parliament itself, its key representative, for most who know about that great event.[1]

Vivekananda came as a monk in the dress of a *rājā*, having received his costume and name from the Maharāja of Khetrī. The combinations of two royal coats, one of bright orange and a second of rich crimson, and two turbans, one lemon and another red, made

1. Two studies on the Parliament make it abundantly clear that the Eastern speakers changed the World's Parliament of Religions from a narrowly Western meeting celebrating Western civilization and/ or Christianity's coming triumph to one where religionists of the East were vying for equality and undertaking.

   Richard Seager, "The World's Parliament of Religions, Chicago, Illinois, 1893: America's Religious Coming of Age." Harvard Dissertation, 1986, p. 286.

   Kenten Druyvesten, "The World's Parliament of Religions," University of Chicago Dissertation, 1976.

him the easiest delegate to identify.[2] He was credentialed as brāhmaṇa *saṁnyāsin* of the Śaṅkarācārya Order from Bombay, although he actually was a kṣatriya and a self-initiated follower of Shri Ramakrishna of Calcutta.[3] He had taken a vow of poverty and yet came to raise money for India.[4] At precisely 30 years of age he was the next of the youngest of some 60 divines on stage (Dharmapala was but 29) and the twentieth of 24 speakers to express words of introduction at the opening ceremony. He joined

---

2. Interview with *Boston Evening Transcript*, September 30, 1893. ". . . the Brahmin monk . . . either a lemon colored or a red turban, and his cassock . . . alternated in a bright orange and rich crimson."

3. John Henry Barrows, ed., *The World's Parliament of Religions : An Illustrated and Popular story of the World's First Parliament of Religions. Held in Chicago in connection with the Columbian Exposition of 1893*, Chicago: The Parliament Publishing Company, 1893, 2 vols. "Opening Remarks" of Vivekananda of Bombay, pp. 101-02.

   Walter R. Houghton, ed., *Neely's History of the Parliament of Religions and Religious Congresses at the World's Columbian Exposition compiled from Original Manuscripts and Stenographic Reports*, (Chicago: F.T. Neely, 1893, 2nd edn., p. 1001), "Most ancient order of monks. Swami Vivekananda of Bombay," p. 64. Opening Comments, pp. 39-40. "Svami Vivekananda of Bombay, India, a monk, responded: It fills my heart with joy unspeakable to rise in response to the warm and cordial welcome which you have given us. I thank you in the name of the most ancient order of monks in the world."

   Marie Louise Burke, *Svami Vivekananda in America: New Discoveries*, Calcutta: Advaita Ashrama, Rev. 2nd ed., 1966, pp. 69-70, discusses some of this problem as "due to expediency" and American ignorance of India, concluding that it "was a careless but forgivable error." [Hereafter, Burke, I].

   Even before the Parliament Vivekananda had given different cities of origin other than Calcutta. Cf., *Daily Saratogian*, Sept 6, 1893, Burke, I.46.

   "A Brainy Gathering Elects Its Officers. The evening session opened at 8 o'clock. . . . The platform was next occupied by Vivekananda, a monk of Madras, Hindoostan, who preached throughout India."

4. The vow involved not touching money and having no purse. This perhaps explains why he wrapped up the money from his lectures in a handkerchief. Burke, I.113.

the intellect of a scholar, the character of a chaste monk, the courage and temperament of a warrior, the restlessness of an explorer, the energy and organizational ability of a top business magnet, and the missionary zeal of a prophet. And these are qualities not easily harmonized.

India's Representatives at the World's Parliament of Religions

India was also well-represented with illustrious *puṇḍit*s, reformers, and minority religious leaders.[5] Four posed together in one picture with Vivekananda — Narasiṁha Charya (Madras, "Sei Vaishnava" [*sic.*]),[6] Lakṣmī Nārāyaṇa (Lahore),[7] H. Dharmapala (Mahabodhi Society of Calcutta and delegate for Ceylon Buddhists), Virchand Gandhi (Bombay, a Jain), Manilal N. Dvivedi (professor, brāhmaṇa), Protap Chunder Mozoomdar (Calcutta, Brahmo Samāj),[8] B.B. Nagarkar (Bombay, Brahmo Samāj),[9] C.N. Chakravarti

5. John Henry Barrows, (ed.), *The World's Parliament of Religions: An Illustrated and Popular story of the World's First Parliament of Religions. Held in Chicago in connection with the Columbian Exposition of 1893*, Chicago: The Parliament Publishing Company, 1893, 2 vols. List of persons of platform at opening 64-6 pp. One could well argue that the reason India received more than its share of attention at the WPR was this very mix of personalities.

   J.W. Hanson, D.D., ed., *The World's Congress of Religions: The Addresses and Papers delivered before the Parliament and an Abstract of the Congresses Held in the Art Institute, Chicago, Illinois, U.S.A., August 25 to October 15, 1893, under the auspices of the World's Columbian Exposition*, Chicago, International Publishing Co., 1894.

6. Barrows, I.153. Probably also identified as "Nara Sima Satsumchyra" of Madras and a Brahman, Barrows I. 137.

7. *Ibid.*, 153.

8. Churesh Chunder Bose, *The Life of Protap Chunder Mozoomdar*, 2 vols., Calcutta: Nababidhan Trust, 1940, and Sunrit Mullick, Protap Chunder Mozoomdar in America: missionary of a new dispensation, D.Min. dissertation, Meadville/Lombard Theo-logical School, 1988, p. 328.

9. Houghton, 67, 743.

(Allahabad, Theosophy),[10] Jinanji Jamshedji Modi (Bombay, Parsi), and Jeanni Sorabji (Bombay, listed as Parsi but a Christian convert)[11] were present and made magnificent speeches. Pundit Dvivedi's paper on Hinduism was certainly the most comprehensive defense of Vedic religion at the Parliament and the most scholarly by the then new standards of comparative religion.[12] Virchand Gandhi, the Jain, made the most militant defense of Hinduism at the Parliamemt in response to a particularly condescending speech of a Christian missionary.[13] While all the Indian speakers were articulate and favourites of the throngs who came to the Parliament, Mozoomdar's oratory had the most immediate acceptance. After one of his speeches four thousand people stood and spontaneously sang "Nearer, My God, to Thee."[14] And it appeared that at the Parliament itself an Occidental who spoke for India and against Christian missions was the most controversial: and that was Annie Besant, the Theosophist.[15]

Collectively, the speakers from India, Japan and China[16] enjoyed such success that the organizers of the Parliament began using them at the end of the programmes to hold the attention of

---

10. Houghton, 62. But also identified as "G.U. Gyanendra H. Chakravarti," Houghton, p. 926.

11. Houghton, 535; Barrows I.125, 214-15.

12. J.W. Hanson, D.D., ed., *The World's Congress of Religions: The Addresses and Papers delivered before the Parliament and an Abstract of the Congresses Held in the Art Institute, Chicago, Illinois, U.S.A. August 25 to October 15, 1893, under the auspices of the World's Columbian Exposition*, Chicago, International Publishing Co. 1894, pp. 347-61

13. Barrows, I.144-45.

14. Barrows, Cf., Burke,I.90.

15. Winthrop, S. Hudson, *Nationalism and Religion in America: Concepts of American Identity and Mission*, New York: Harper and Row, 197, p. 286.

16. Barrows, I, the welcome to Pung Kwang Yu "were surpassed in the case of no other speaker on platform. . . . wild waving of hats and handkerchiefs."

the audience.[17] Vivekananda would not speak many times, but as an Asian he should actually have more opportunities than most Western delegates. Gathering together all of his contributions indicates a brilliant but minor role. (See Appendix A: Vivekānanda's Speeches).

There is evidence to suggest that Vivekananda did not perceive himself to be either the star of the Indian delegation or its savior. Two weeks after the Parliament Vivekananda wrote to Prof. John Wright of Harvard, who was most responsible for getting him credentialed, and stated that he was proud of his fellow Indian religious leaders and seemed even a little in awe of them and the event itself.

> Dear brother, I was so afraid to stand before that great assembly of fine speakers and thinkers from all over the world and speak but the Lord gave me strength and I almost every day heroically faced the platform and the audience. . . . Oh how I wished that you were here to see some of our sweet ones from India — the tender hearted Buddhist Dharmapala, the orator Mazoomdar and realize that in that far off and poor India there are hearts that beat in sympathy to yours, born and brought up in this mighty — and great country.[18]

---

17. Burke, I.74, "but there they sat enduring with much murmuring, expecting the next speaker might be one of the popular Orientals whose name was usually first on the bulletin board."

18. Burke, I.96. Letter of 2 October 1893. What needs to be pointed out in Vivekananda's letter written closest to the event is that there is no tension with Majumdar of the Brahmo Samāj during or immediately after the WPR.

    "my heart was fluttering and my tongue nearly dried up." Burke, I.59.

    Later he would elaborate further:

    Vivekananda's own remembrance on his first speech: "In my first speech in his country, in Chicago, I addressed the audience as 'Sisters and Brothers of America,' and you know that they all rose to their feet. You may wonder what made them do this, you wonder if I had

→

Vivekananda an the Creation of a Legend

Vivekananda's role at the Parliament must be assessed from three kind of records, the last of which will be ignored for this paper: (1) 'official-type' histories of what happened 'inside' the World's Parliament of Religions,[19] (2) reports by 'outsiders' such as the American press, and (3) 'hindsight storytellers' and their reminisces after Vivekananda's fame.

Large 'offical' histories were compiled within a year of the Parliament. Barrow's history portrays Vivekananda as a young and slightly discourteous minor participant. Barrows even lightly criticizes Vivekananda in more than one passage.[20] Hanson, Houghton, and contemporaneous smaller works give no hint that Vivekananda emerged within the Parliament as a major religious leader or participant. All of these reinforce our earlier conclusion based on Vivekananda's single letter immediately after the conference that India's delegation had starred and not just he.

But to outsiders looking with other eyes Vivekananda was more than a participant; he was a symbol of something larger. Vivekananda's impact on the American press takes up three large volumes totalling 2194 pages.[21] These are the lifework of Marie

→ some strange power. Let me tell you that I did have a power and this is it — never once in my life did I allow myself to have even one sexual thought. I trained my mind, my thinking, and the powers that man usually uses along that line I put into a higher channel, and it developed a force so strong that nothing could resist it." p. 547.

19. Jenkin Lloyd Jones, "Books on the Parliament," *Unity*, vol. 32 (January 1894), pp. 274-75.

20. Barrows, *loc. cit.* Especially Barrows editorial remark after reporting Vivekananda's final address: "Svami Vivekananda was always heard with interest by the Parliament, but very little approval was shown to some of the sentiments expressed in his closing address," I, p. 171.

21. Burke, I, *loc. cit.*, p. 712; Marie Louise Burke, *Svami Vivekananda: His second visit to the West. New Discovers*, Calcutta: Advaita Ashrama, →

Louise Burke, a self-trained historian, who has saved every shred of evidence of Vivekananda's two visits to America. The volumes contain popular press accounts about the impact of Vivekananda's participation at the Parliament and her commentary. What emerges from reading 'outsiders' views of the Parliament are clearly different perceptions or points of view about Vivekananda's participation. One reason for this is that a newspaper article written about a single delegate necessarily distorts since it must foreshorten events, dissolve ambiguities and focus on its chosen figure. Just how Vivekananda emerged as the symbol for the entire 17 day event is another study; but the fact is that he had become the person most identified with the Parliament and its symbol within one year after its closure. The way he functioned as a symbol and some peculiarly American implications will be sketched out in Appendix B.

The Indian press quoted American newspaper articles extensively and magnified the legendary and symbolic content according to Indian needs.[22] When Vivekananda returned from the West in 1897, the legend was so powerful that it could even modify and control his mission and message.

Although the World's Parliament of Religions could make all defenders of Hinduism heroes in India, the temporary unification of its delegation at the event itself was soon lost in the larger struggle for leadership of India's renaissance. Returning from the Parliament were leaders with differing agendas, some for radical displacement of the Indian tradition, others for radical reform, for

→ 1973, p. 843.; and Marie Louise Burke, *Svami Vivekananda in the West: New Discoveries: The world Teacher*, Calcutta: Advaita Ashrama, 1986, p. 639.

22. There is a massive collection of Vivekananda's press coverage in the English language press of India in the National Library in Delhi and it definitely documents this assertion. Also, it can be safely assumed by the missionaries reaction in India, their quotations, and the triumphal welcome from all of India that the Indian press generally in fact had furthered the legend given to them from American reports.

the occult, or for revival of the innate superiority of India's spirituality. Only one could triumph and shape "the majority religion" for the next decades. And that triumphant view presented *dharma* and *sanātana dharma* in distinctive ways.

The young Hindu monk, Vivekananda, could find his way to centre stage on the strength of his vision: Hinduism had to be represented from the ideal plane of universal religion. This sixth of 10 children of Vishwanath Datta (*c.* 1835-84) and Bhuvaneshwari Basu (*c.* 1841-1911) and the first among the spiritual children of the Dakshineswar priest of Kālī, Shri Ramakrishna,[23] could weave together Hinduism, Vedānta and the Religion Eternal, the *sanātana dharma*, in a message not always understood by his hearers.

Why was he so memorial? And yet why did so many different people hear his message so differently but so powerfully?

Vivekananda brought to the World's Parliament of Religions a treasury of interreligious ferment: the Hindu-Christian contact (he attended Scottish Church College in Calcutta), the Unitarian Brahmo Samāj partnership (he was caught up in the Brahmo's struggle to educate the masses and purify Hinduism[24]), the

23. Interview with *Boston Evening Transcript*, September 30, 1893, quoted in Burke, I.67-8. "He has come with pamphlets that he distributes, relating to his master, Paramhansa Ramakrishna, a Hindu devotee, who so impressed his hearers and pupils that many of them became ascetics after his death. Mozoomdar also looked upon this as his master, but Mozoomdar worked for holiness in the world, in it but not of it, as Jesus taught."

24. Spencer Lavan, *Unitarians and India: A Study in Encounter and Response*, Boston: Beacon Press, 1977; David Kopf, *The Brahmo-Samaj and the Shaping of the Modern Indian Mind*, Princeton: Princeton University Press, 1979; George M. Williams, "Svami Vivekananda: Archetypal Hero or Doubting Saint?" in Robert Baird, *Religion in Modern India*, New Delhi: South Asia Publications, 2nd rev. edn., 1989.

From the view that Vivekananda was little affected by his Brahmo Samaj contact, the most comprehensive study is S.N. Dhar, *A Comprehensive Biography of Svami Vivekananda*, Madras: Vivekananda Prakashan Kendra, vol. I, 1975, vol. II, 1976.

rediscovery of India's religion (he was converted from the most radical branch of the Brahmo Samāj by Shri Ramakrishna himself) and the primacy of direct religious experience. Vivekananda had a fine nineteenth-century general education in philosophy and science. He lost no energy in fighting evolution and current scientific trends. Nor was he threatened by or fearful of modern science.

And Vivekananda had sufficient strength within himself to grow in spite of mistakes (that lack of full honesty concerning his credentials and background) and to rise above all types of attacks. His personal morality and spiritual character were identifiable by many Americans and Indians; his presence was unforgettable.

Vivekananda, "the princely pagan" to so many Americans, articulate and insightful but also able to capture the essence of great ideas in memorable slogans, would personify the unresolvable tensions of the Parliament. He came as a universalist but left more a defender of a particular purified, idealized religion. He stood as a living question mark to the American "lively experiment" as the "last great hope of civilization" based upon a Christian and democratic equality of peoples and nations.[25] Here was a native of an older civilization who represented revitalization of its values and vision.

Here is the stuff legends can be made off.

Vivekananda as Preserver and Reformer

Vivekananda's well-known plan to teach Indian spirituality to the West and receive in turn Western help, science and technology is part of the great legend.[26] Vivekananda came with a twofold programme to defend Hinduism from any attack and to reform

---

25. Sidney Mead, *The Lively Experiment: The Shaping of Christianity in America*, New York: Harper and Row, 1963.
26. Williams, "Svami Vivekananda: Archetypal Hero or Doubting Saint?" *op. cit.*

and purify it based on its highest spirituality. That reform would require help from the West and he began collecting gifts even before the parliament.[27]

He defended India from an idealist position in the West, and in India he criticized its actual failures. But he was only able to manage the power of mass media in one direction. The American press did not collect his sayings against Purāṇic practices, 'kitchen religion,' 'don't touchism,' and 'priestcraft.' But the Indian press savoured every word of his idealist message defending Hinduism to the West. The fight that he pursued at and after the Parliament with missionaries and with Christian fundamentalists produced much to glorify Hinduism and India. He actually returned to Detroit in March 1894 to attend the Student Volunteer Missionary Movement's second international convention in order to engage them at the height of their attacks on Hinduism.[28]

While a liberal coalition of spiritual universalists was formed at the Parliament and came together again in Chicago eight months later (May 1894), Vivekananda worked with a lecture company on his own. He followed an invisible network of anti-missionary religious organizations, but failed to strengthen his ties with leading liberal and universalistic religious organizations. Former allies at the Parliament, both from India and in America, worked for a platform for cooperation in the spirit of universalism. They would be in contact for years to come with attempts such as the First American Congress of Liberal Religious Societies (held in Rabbi

27. Burke, I.20-1. Ltr. from Mrs. John Henry Wright, from Annisquam, Mass, August 29, 1893. ". . . Kate Sanborn had a Hindoo monk in tow as I believe I mentioned in my last letter. . . . He stayed until Monday and was one of the most interesting people I have yet come across. . . . Then on Sunday John had invited him to speak in the church and they took up a collection for a Heathen college to be carried on strictly heathen principles — whereupon I retired to my corner and laughed until I cried."

28. Burke, I, "The Christian Onslaught," pp. 289-313 and "Return of the Warrior," pp. 314-76.

Emil Hirsch's Sinai Temple, Chicago),[29] the Free Church movement of Jenkin Lloyd Jones, the free religious association movement of Francis Abbot and Ralph Waldo Emerson,[30] or the International Association for Religious Freedom of Charles Wendte.[31]

The Indian press reports of Vivekananda's defense of Hinduism and his conversion of the greatest minds in America to Vedānta preceded his return to India and made that return like no other.[32] Throngs greeted him. *Mahārājās* competed with each other to pull him in carts to the centre of towns where he received the keys to cities and regions.[33] Later upon his return to America the American press would transmit the growing legend that "he was received [back in India] with honours to be greater than any paid to a religious teacher since the time of Buddha."[34]

---

29. "The Union of Liberal Religious Forces," *Unity*, vol. 32 (Feb. 1, 1894), pp. 340-41; "The First American Congress of Liberal Religious Societies," *Unity*, vol. 33 (May 1894), pp. 135-36. cf. Seager, *op. cit.*, 204.

30. Creighton Peden, "F[rancis] E. Abbot, View of Christianity and Free Religion," a paper presented at the History Section, Collegium: Association of Liberal Religious Studies, p. 23.

31. Spencer Lavan's Study of The International Association for Religious Freedom, a paper presented at ICS, Pittsburg, *c.* 1891; Shinichiro Imaoka, "From Religious Freedom to Free Religion," in George M. Williams, *Liberal Religious Reformation in Japan*, New York: IARF, 1984.

32. Vivekananda survived a battle for his credentials and another with missionaries about his own missionary legend. For the latter, cf. Wilbur W. White (Sec. of Calcutta YWCA), *Svami Vivekananda and His Guru with Letters from Prominent Americans on the Alleged Progress of Vedantism in the United States*, Madras: Christian Literary Society for India, 1897.

33. Svami Vivekananda, *The Complete Works*, Calcutta: Advaita Ashrama, 1964, 9th edn. Volume III contains most of the speeches concerning the triumphal return, "From Colomo to Alomora," pp. 103 ff. The "official history" in *The Life of Svami Vivekananda by his Eastern and Western Disciples*, Calcutta: Advaita Ashrama, 1965, seventh edn., tells the events on pp. 452-78.

34. Burke, I.292, quoting the *Oakland Tribune*, Feb. 24, 1900.

Yet the very success of his defense of Hinduism prevented the completion of his two-fold programme. He was not able to reform Hinduism. He could hardly purify his religious practices of his own fellow monks, *gurubhāīs* of Shri Ramakrishna.[35] His legend as a warrior for Hinduism became so great that he could not control it when he wanted to begin reforming specific practices of Hinduism. It controlled him. He could not be a reformer in India. Even his order, the Ramakrishna Order and Mission, had misunderstood its dual role of preserving the best and reforming the rest, opting to become the example *par excellence* of Hinduism.

Vivekananda's Mission of Preservation and Reform

The message that Vivekananda began to articulate was so complex that it both contributed to the legends produced by its hearers and to religious misunderstandings. This judgement comes from hindsight and must be tempered with an equal comparison to his times. There is an element in his message that is exceptional and must be rediscovered and understood.

Vivekananda's twofold mission as preserver and reformer of Hinduism was articulated according to his ideas about his Western and Indian audiences and a complex heuristic which led him to teach persons according to their spiritual level. (This is summarized in Appendix B) Contextualization requires knowing all of these — plus precise terminology used both for defense and for criticism.

Vivekananda used four terms for two different purposes to express his dhārmic mission. Thus, eight conceptions were used by Vivekananda for the defense and renewal of Indian spirituality.

1. **[Triumphant] Hinduism** [pure, ideal; in the world]*
2. **[Purified] Hinduism** [real; in the world]
3. **Vedānta** [pure, ideal; in the world but somehow transcendent]*

35. *Life of Svami Vivekananda, op. cit.*, p. 507.

4. **Vedānta** [real; in the world]
5. **Advaita Vedānta** [real; in the world]
6. **Advaita Vedānta** [pure, ideal; transcendent yet in the world]*
7. **Sanātana Dharma**; **Religion Eternal** [transcendent yet in the world]*
8. **Sanātana Dharma**; **Religion Eternal** [transcendent]

An asterisk (*) indicates those concepts used almost exclusively to defend Indian spirituality from attacks by Western despisers. On a few occasions these conceptualizations were utilized after the Parliament in India when *guru*-baiters or Indian despisers of their own tradition attacked. Rhetorically and philosophically, the concepts utilize a defense of the actual from the plane of the ideal. Vivekananda did not begin by utilizing any of this defensive arsenal at the Parliament. His first speech is characterized by a local newspaper as "broad as the heavens above us, embracing the best in all religions, as the ultimate universal religion — charity to all mankind, good works for the love of God, not for fear of punishment or hope of reward."[36] Every indication suggests that he began as a universalist, emphasizing the unity and truth of all religions. But he had anticipated from studying under Western teachers in Calcutta that attack would come; and he was ready when it did.

Four conceptions — Hinduism [pure, ideal; in the world], Vedānta [pure, ideal; in the world; transcendent], Advaita Vedānta [pure, ideal; transcendent; classical], and Sanātana Dharma or the Religion Eternal [transcendent; in the world] — are all for defense. Western scholars who write off Vivekananda as a revivalist[37] or

---

36. *Boston Evening Transcript*, September 30, 1893. Cited in Burke I. 67-68.

37. Agehananda Bharati, *Journal of Religious Studies*, February 1970, p. 207.

Hindu chauvinist locate these passages which seem to comprise the larger part of his articulated mission. By defending Hinduism *et al.* from its ideal vantage point and with its best formulations and intentions, he merely pointed to its highest vision. Arnold Toynbee shortly thereafter wrote in the *An Historian's History of Religion* that it was the right of all religions to present their ideal — but not their right to compare that ideal with the actualities of another religion. Ideals are compared with ideals, realities with realities. Those who attacked Hinduism compared their best and noblest intentions with India's worst, and Vivekananda came prepared, presenting the ideal as Hinduism's reality.

Vivekananda's apologetic for idealized Hinduism was so powerful that it would eventually take the wind out of the Hindu reform movements, especially the Brahmo Samāj. It would make them appear disloyal to India's past greatness and would strip them of any authority for leading the renaissance. Idealized Hinduism did not need any traitors who compromised with Western religion and its political oppressors. There was no need for radical reform, only slow and careful education of the masses and a change of attitudes toward 'man-making' religion.

Theologically, this defense was a particularistic universalism, dangerously close to declaring that Hinduism — Vedānta, Advaita, Advaita Vedānta, the Religion Eternal — were all superior to other religions. And this shift came as Vivekananda fought against missionary Christianity. He accepted the ladder model of Śaṅkara's vision of the sacred and forgot Shri Ramakrishna's circle of the equality of religions. The ladder image put Hinduism — or whichever term he chose for its idealized, purified form — at the top or at the highest rung of earthly manifestations of religions. And all other religions could be accepted as lower rungs. It was ironic that it was this same condescension from Christians that brought out this militant defense of Hinduism as true, moral, equal, and good at the Parliament. (The liberal version of this type of particularized universalism with rational Christianity as the epitome of civilization was as irritating to Vivekananda as the exclusively Christian conservative's position.)

The need was so great for a quick fix for India's inferiority and so tempting to lead the Indian renaissance that Vivekananda gave much of his immense talent to this task. Yet he would try, quite unsuccessfully, to attempt his dual mission when he returned to India in 1897. Eventually he would try to lead the defense of Hinduism and focus on teaching higher spiritual levels for personal enlightenment. His second trip to the West in 1899 marks his resignation from the task of evolutionary reform and even his resignation from all organization leadership in the Ramakrishna Order and Mission. The offical histories of the Order do note that Svami Vivekananda had lost interest in these organizations several years after founding them.[38]

The second set of concepts — [Purified] Hinduism [real; in the world], Vedānta [real; in the world], Advaita Vedānta [real; in the world], Sanātana Dharma; Religion Eternal [transcendent] — reveal the aspect of his dhārmic mission which is least understood and was all but lost. Vivekananda wanted to reform Indian religions and life according to a quite demanding transcendent standard. From the vantage point of something which India had not yet become, he would call for its reform. The forgotten part of his message is how he relativized Indian spirituality and called it into account for its shortcomings from the demands of *sanātana dharma* or the Religion Eternal. Briefly, he lost control of this aspect of his dual mission because of a national need for pride in its tradition in order to lift its head from the humiliation of political servitude to begin its fight for political freedom.

Theologically, Vivekananda utilized Ramakrishna's circle of religious equality. All paths are true; all religions are true. One must carefully differentiate this from Śaṅkara's ladder of religious

---

38. *Life of Svami Vivekananda, op. cit.* and Williams, "Vivekananda," in Beard, *op. cit.*, p. 66.

superiority. Vivekananda could use the four terms and maintain the dhārmic transcendent without 'idolatrizing' it in any particular religion or religious symbol. That dhārmic transcendent is left totally transcendent. Particular religious expressions as word, act, symbol, community were human attempts to actualize by approximation to the absolute. Appendix D combines the four conceptions (Hinduism, Vedānta, Advaita, and *sanātana dharma*) to illustrate how they functioned without maintaining a strict dialectic of transcendence.

This is the model that the most radical spiritual liberals at the Parliament apprehended in varying ways. They saw religions as humanizations of the universal or transcendent. Hirai and Kishimoto would take this model back to Japan, and, while remaining good Buddhist scholars and associates of the Japanese Unitarian Association, they would join Shinichiro Imaoka (1880-1986) in founding the Japanese Free Religious Association. Nagarkar and Mozoomdar of the Brahmo Samāj already tried to work from a model of a real equality of religions. They saw the Brahmo Samāj as a particular religion of the Universal Religion, and Universal Religion could never be exhausted in its particular expressions. That is why they resisted conversion to Christianity, even that particularized universalism of British Unitarianism. This is the crux of their argument with F. Max Müller.[39]

Vivekanada knew the implications of Ramakrishna's circle of truth. It meant that all religions are true, in some way approximations of the absolute, the eternal, but in particular cultural and historical forms. (See Appendix E: Ramakrishnaism) It meant that his three categories of *dharma* — Hinduism, Vedānta and Advaita — must not be equated with the Absolute, *sanātana dharma*. They were only particular attempts to grasp or apprehend the transcendent, *nirguṇa Brahman*. Of the four religious conceptions only *sanātana dharma* had any chance of being used in such a way

39. Seager, *op. cit.*, 260-61.

that it would remain absolutely transcendent. For *sanātana dharma* to function as a metaphor for ultimate trancendence, it could not be reduced to or be identified with any particular human expression or practice.

No single religion is the Religion Eternal but merely approximations that must change, grow and evolve. Ralph Waldo Emerson and Francis Abbot have expressed deep approval of Vivekananda's radical critique of *dharma* with *sanātana dharma*.

Appendix A
Vivekananda's Speeches

Day 1, September 11

Opening words by Svami Vivekananda of Bombay. **Barrows I,** pp. 101-2. **Hanson,** 39-40. Bombay, **the most ancient order of monks in the world;** the mother of religion, to all uncharitable feelings between persons wending their way to the same goal. **Burke I, 63.**

***Boston Evening Transcript,* September 30, 1893.**

". . . broad as the heavens above us, . . . embracing the best in all religions . . . as the ultimate universal religion," **Burke I, 67-68.**

Day 4, September 14

Evening reception by Mrs. Potter Palmer, President of the Board of Lady Managers. "The condition of women in India. **Barrows I, 156. Burke I, 81.**

Day 5, September 15

Barrows I, 118-20. Frog story.

Day 9, September 19, Afternoon Session

"Hinduism" **Barrows I, 124.** "Hinduism as a Religion." **Hanson, 366-376.** "Paper on Hinduism." **Burke I, 81.**

September 19 unplanned remarks: [*morning???*]

"patronizing way that we ought to accept Christianity . . . England the most prosperous Christian nation in the world, with her foot on the neck. . . . At such a price the Hindoo will not have prosperity."

in response to *Rev. Joseph Cook and Bishop J.P. Newman* reported in the Dubuque *Times* September 29, 1893. **Burke I, 81.**

Day 10, September 20

brief speech by Vivekananda: "Christians must always be ready for good criticism . . ." **Barrows I, 128-29.** "bread not metaphysical nonsense." **Burke**

I, 86.

evening. brief speech. "Religion Not the Crying Need of India." summarized in *Christian Herald*, October 11, 1893, quoting Vivekananda: "Christian missionaries come and offer life, but only on condition that the Hindus become Christians, abandoning the faith of their fathers and forefathers. Is it right? . . . If you wish to illustrate the meaning of 'brotherhood,' treat the Hindu more kindly, even though he be a Hindu, and is faithful to his religion. Send missionaries to them to teach them how better to earn a piece of **bread,** and not teach them **metaphysical nonsense." Burke I, 86.**

Day 12, September 22

Scientific Sessions: "Criticism and Discussion of Missionary Methods."

September 22 morning. "Orthodox Hinduism." Scientific Session **Burke I, 70.**

afternoon in Hall III, the Scientific Session. **Barrows I, 152-54.** Vivekananda in Conference on the Modern Religions of India. (***September*** 22. possible talk: Condition of Women in India.) Scientific Session **Burke I, 86.**

Day 13, September 23

Vivekananda gave an address. (or did he?)

Day 14, September 24 Sunday

Rev. George F. Pentecost of London on "The Invincible Gospel" asserting the ultimate triumph of Christianity as assured by its essential superiority to all other religions. "Some of the Brahmans of India have been here and have dared to make an attack upon Christianity. They take the slums of New York and Chicago and ask us why we do not cure ourselves. They take what is outside the pale of Christianity and judge Christianity by it." **Barrows I, 143.** They attacked religious systems of India on the point of morality. priestesses who were known as immoral and profligate. They were prostitutes . . . **Barrows I, 143.**

Rev. George T. Candlin of China's address: "The Bearing of Religious Unity on the Work of Mission." **Barrows I, 144.**

It was Gandhi, the Jain, who defended Hinduism. It is not religion but in spite of religion that abuses occur. **Barrows I, 144-45.**

Vivekananda gave semi-public lecture at Third Unitarian Church, Chicago CW VIII **200.**

Day 15, September 25

Vivekananda spoke at afternoon session: "The Essence of the Hindu Religion." **Barrows I, 154.**

Day 16, September 26, Evening Session.

Vivekananda made small remark, probably about Buddhism. **Barrows I, 148.**

Day 17, September 27

closing remarks: (**Barrows I, 170-71**) . . . not dissension." **Hanson, 944:** "Much has been said on the common ground of religious unity. I am not going just now to venture my own theory . . . Harmony, peace, and not dissension."

Barrows disapproval of Vivekananda's closing remarks. **Burke I, 91**

Appendix B
Vivekananda's Misunderstood Mission

Vivekananda's terminology would intend to be consistently inclusive (He would exclude no religion from truth.) and universal (He would hold that Universal Religion or Religion Eternal is apprehended variously by all religions in their particularity.). Several other academic problems have less direct bearing on his solutions to the four-fold problem involved in universality: Vivekananda's religious development,[1] his teaching with a view of the religious level of the hearer,[2] and the problems of hagiography and historical probability regarding his teachings and life.[3]

Vivekananda's two-fold mission as preserver and reformer of Hinduism had three different audiences — the American press, American

---

1. *The Quest for Meaning of Svami Vivekananda: A Study in Religious Change,* New Horizons Press, 1974. "Svami Vivekananda: Archetypal Hero or Doubting Saint?," in Robert Baird (ed.).
2. "Swami Vivekananda's Conception of Karma and Rebirth," in Ronald Neufeld (ed.), *Karma and Rebirth: Post-classical Developments,* New York: SUNY Press, 1986.
3. "The Problem of Religious Experience in the Life of Svami Vivekananda," and "Methodological Problems in Documenting Religious Change When Change is Denied: Svami Vivekananda's Early Years."

religionists, and India. He had a remarkable influence on each, becoming as if he were a Rorschach ink blot test for all three.

Mirror of the American Experience. Vivekananda was a national phenomenon. Never had a "pagan" received such attention. Wherever he went he was in news. Often stories appeared on the front page about his arrival, and later his speech and activities in the community. While some religious interest is evidenced, there is little understanding of his purified religious practices and philosophy. There is something deeply American that the writers are exploring.

The creed of the republic sought liberty, justice, and the opportunity for happiness for all. But immigrants from Europe's warring states, national minorities, and multiplying Christian denominations and sects threatened America's creed. Religious toleration would really be put to a proper test with real pagans. The old question of "how do you turn bigotted, hateful immigrants into good citizens?" paled with paganism.

Newspaper writers and the reading public used Vivekananda as a mirror to reflect on the dilemmas of freedom and toleration. Could Americans spirituality allow this dark-skinned Indian the freedom to speak against Christianity or must he be silenced? They sensed that if religions and religionists could be humanized, if the claims of religion could be brought into the realm of human activity, then even paganism could be tolerated.

Richard Seager is correct when he looks to the early proponents of pluralism and finds them as they have been effected by the Parliament.[4] But the masses and their newspapers are concerned that the creed of the republic will withstand even these religious fights.

Litmus of the American Religious Situation. Vivekananda came to the Parliament as a liberal and a champion of a universal faith. He challenged American religious arrogance, ignorance, and hypocrisy. Vivekananda's contribution in America was less with organizations than with individuals. His breaking off contact immediately with the Parliament, with natural allies in the Bramo Samāj and Theosophy, the Free Church movement of Lloyd Jones, and the quest for a Universal faith left for him no contribution to their development. He certainly did not

4. Seager, *op. cit.*

lessen the evangelical and fundamentalist Christians' desire to convert heathens; he may have added to it. But he did have a personal influence on many Americans' spirituality.

One of the most important contributions could have been to the American concern with religious toleration. He made it a function of acceptance rather than indifference.

Some of the theological issues at the World's Parliament of Religions have general equivalents in the American psyche — America's destiny, its example to the world, its political experiment as the world's last hope, its role as bastion of freedom, tolerance, equality, justice, and the pursuit of happiness.[5]

Translated into Christian theological statements these notions involve some of the most sacred and deep-rooted conceits of America and America's Christians. Perhaps only three issues will suffice to indicate the permanence of the discussion and its power. They involve truth (theologized as what is religion?), equality (What is Christianity's relation to other religions — if there are more than one?), tolerance (as in, how can I allow evil and be religious?), and freedom (what is free religion?)

What is religion? Because this is a convoluted way of asking "the truth question," it raises the greatest passions. It was most convenient for Americans to answer that religion is Christianity; it "is the way, the truth and the light." To use religion as a plural, religions, as in a World's Parliament of Religions, would drive delegates *quo* theologians to look at how they were misquoting a seemingly self-evident scripture.[6]

Are religions equal? Can there be a real parliament with equality of the religions? This seems to be the aspect of the question that America's newspapers unconsciously grasped. Vivekananda's mere presence at the Parliament (i.e., the nine non-Christian religions) raised the fundamental issue of democracy. Citizenship involved equality, and Vivekananda

---

5. Mead, *op. cit.,* This is such a familiar notion that this one citation will provide a suitable bibliography.
6. Karl Barth would find another way around this insularity of truth. Barth would allow a plurality of religions, then exempt God's work in Christ from the category of religion, and finally judge all religions by God's revelation in Christ.

exhibited the finest characteristics of a religious citizen. A World Parliament of Religions presupposed world citizenship.

By the time the theologians had asked the questions of truth and equality they had muddied the discussion with categories that could not provide an "American answer." Religious toleration would have been furthered if theologians would have found common basis for shared truth and perceived equality. But the theological language of the day sought its universals by opposing inclusive with exclusive. The category of universalism was so weak that all sides could claim to be universal. One universalist position at the parliament, a universal religion composed of all other religions, was championed by the liberals and non-evangelicals.[7] But there were also liberals who believed in evangelizing in Chirst's name.[8] And there were hardly any conservatives and evangelicals who did not believe in the universality of Christ's gospel. The offense of the plurality of religions could still be met with the universalism of a particular religion because of its superiority over all the rest. Universalism became the buzz word of the century and thus it would become meaningless.

The new world order of religions, recognizing Universal truth and the coming together as cooperating equal religions, realizing unity in diversity, would still be a dream of some leaving the parliament.[9] While the liberals celebrated their vision at the Parliament, they would still be trying to actualize it a century later. They had no better idea how to achieve it in actuality than did their political cousins trying to put together a commonwealth of equal and free nations.

---

7. Seager, *op. cit.*

8. The Universalists, probably America's sixth largest denomina-tion at the end of the century, would not compromise their vision by officially joining the Parliament but put all their energy in the separate denominational congresses. They were a kind of liberal that would irk more than Vivekananda with their conscending notion that salvation, though universal, was only through Christ and thus from Christianity. Mozoomdar's lengthy debate with Max Müller concerned this very limitation of universality.

9. In May 1894, six hundred signed the call for a fellowship to achieve this end. Seager, *ibid.*, 204. Jones invited Asians to join the Free Church movement. Seager, *ibid.*, 246.

The American experience demanded *tolerance* and *freedom*. Religionists have tended to ask the toleration question poorly and selfishly. When they were in the majority, of course, they would not tolerate evil and untruth. The first Western conception which provided a basis for seeing the partial truth to be accepted and the process of conscience to be tolerated and defended in one's opponent was with Francis David of Transylvania.[10] Vivekananda's articulation of acceptance of the other's religion shifts the ground, incorporates the values of truth and equality, and does not compromise one's own or one's neighbour's freedom. How could it not be heard as a supporting voice for America's cultural achievement.

Religious pluralism may only provide a temporary solution to the four-fold problem. It avoids the truth question but does not compromise the values of tolerance, equality and freedom. Since religious pluralism has often joined with indifference, religionists have assumed it weakens religious sensitivities. Vivekananda's teachings of acceptance of the truth and equality of all religions demonstrate that toleration is an intermediate value to acceptance and understanding. All that needs to be added, then, is religious freedom.

Vivekananda's theological contribution was to teach a way of theologizing without dogma. He did not have to abandon the truth question but based the quest for knowledge and understanding firmly on human experience. Religious doctrines and teachings were attempts at expressing that which was apprehended of life and its transcending process of evolution and perfection or descending slide of error, failure and injury. Adequacy, appropriateness and incompleteness are part of the truth process, not indifference and irreligion.

Acceptance of this human process of the religious quest is shared among equals — worshipping together as Muslims, Jews, Hindus, Christians, atheists, *et al.* This kind of dialogue did not occur at the Parliament; the agenda was controlled by its organizers. And it was a decidedly Western agenda.

---

10. Gellérd Imre, *Truth Liberates You: the Message of Transylvania's First Unitarian Bishop, Francis David*, tr. from Hungarian by Judit Gellérd. Chico: Centre for Free Religion, 1990; John Erdö, *Transylvanian Unitarian Church: Chronological History and Theological Essays*, tr. from Hungarian by Judit Gellérd. Chico: Centre for Free Religion, 1990.

Freedom from the tyranny of sin was offered by the Christian; the purified Hindu wanted freedom for knowledge and bliss. One seemed a contraction of the human spirit while the other expressed a longing for expansion and self-transcendence. Seeming the more beautiful, the higher good, the nobler sentiment, these are but a small apprehension of the task.

Catalyst for Indian Awakening. Vivekananda's two-fold mission to defend and purify India has been assessed by abler scholars of cultural change.[11] What seems abundantly clear is that Vivekananda and the Ramakrishna Mission and Order came to be pigeonholed on the side of preserving Hinduism.[12] As has been mentioned before Vivekananda did not like the *bhakti* emphasis of Brahmanananda (1902-22). The Order seems to vacillate between devotion/liberation and knowledge/service paths.[13]

Appendix C
Vivekananda's Taxonomy of Teaching

He taught four groups: (1) Westerners ignorant of basic Indian notions and often antagonistic to them even when explained, (2) Western disciples, (3) Indian audiences with a wide spectrum of interests usually with one or two guru-baiters, and (4) Indian disciples. These audiences were divided by Vivekananda's spiritual map into differing religious tendencies, capabilities and preparations.

The wide religious, educational and philosophical range of his audiences affected the formulation of his message almost as much as a conception Vivekananda held about the tendencies of each individual.

---

11. R.C. Majumdar, (ed.), *Svami Vivekananda Centenary Memorial Volume*, Calcutta: Svami Vivekananda Centenary, 1963; R.C. Majumdar, *Svami Vivekananda: A Historical Review*, Calcutta: General Printers & Publishers, 1965 and Jean Herbert, *Svami Vivekananda: Bibliographie*, Paris: Advien Maisonneuve, 1938, provide some valuable bibliographic information of the now more than 1500 monographs which have been written on Vivekananda.
12. Agehananda Bharati, *Journal of Religious Studies*, February 1970, p. 207.
13. Williams, "The Ramakrishna Movement: A Study in Religious Change," in Robert Baird (ed.), *Religion in Modern India, op. cit.,* pp. 55-79.

He believed that he needed to be all things to all people because a teacher must teach not only at the level of his audience but also according to the spiritual tendency of each individual in his audience. Vivekananda stated that he presented the discoveries of Shri Ramakrishna. These discoveries taught that: (1) Persons have differing tendencies (*samskaras*, *prakritis*) and require different paths (*yogas* or *margas*), (2) A teacher must teach the correct *yoga* to each individual, and (3) All paths (*yogas*, *margas*) are one.[1]

Some of the apparent inconsistencies in his teachings are caused by these multiple points of view and the varying contexts concerning Hinduism, Vedānta and the Religion Eternal. Vivekananda's apparent inconsistencies were articulated by him in what we might call a twofold paradoxical loop: (1) each religious tendency is true separately for those in that path (*yoga*); (2) all paths are one. Not only will Svami Vivekananda teach at one point as though a particular point of view is the truth, he will also teach that the harmonization of viewpoints which have been taken as mutually inconsistent by earlier Indian philosophers are really in harmony. This set of claims leads to a presentation of his views which will attempt to show unity in diversity.

This is an Indian version of the dilemma experienced by one of the universalist positions at the Parliament. That is, for religions for all shared truths, there must be some universally shared ground. For each to be true separately means that they all share in something "higher than" or transcendent to any and all. This was the grand dream of Jenkin Lloyd Jones and the Free Church idea. And this was the dream that Vivekananda, Jones, Mazoomdar, Hirai[2] and other religious liberals brought to the parliament.

1. Cf., George M. Williams "Svami Vivekananda's Conception of Karma and Rebirth," in Ronald W. Neufeldt, *Karma and Rebirth: Post Classical Developments*, Albany: State University of New York Press, 1986, for a wider discussion of this problem.

2. Kinza M. Riuge Hirai was one of the interpreters for the Japanese delegation and a lay Buddhist. He would join the Free Religious Association in Tokyo and become apart of the Japanese Unitarian movement, to grow into a "better Buddhist." Cf., George M. Williams, *Liberal Religious Reformation in Japan*, New York: International Association for Religious Freedom, 1984.

Appendix D
Vivekananda's Unified Use of the Four Conceptions

The four Concepts in Defense of India's Spirituality.

[Militant] Hinduism [pure, ideal; in the world]*

Vedānta [pure, ideal; in the world but somehow transcendent]*

Advaita Vedānta [pure, ideal; classical; and transcendent]*

Sanātana Dharma; Religion Eternal [transcendent but somehow also in the world]*

The Four Concepts for Spiritual Reform

[Purified] Hinduism [real; in the world]

Vedānta [real; in the world]

Advaita Vedānta [real; in the world]

Sanātana Dharma; Religious Eternal [transcendent]

There is little to suggest in the first speeches of Vivekananda at the Parliament that he would become identified as the one who would attack the arrogance of Christians and espouse "an aggressive Hinduism." His first addresses were filled with so much sweetness and light as not to offend anyone. Even the most particularistic of the Christian evangelicals could reinterpret his remarks about universal religion as a universality under Christ and hear the truths within his speeches as coming directly or indirectly from his education in a Christian college and his use of the English language, which somehow helped one rise above superstition and paganism.

But once he began the brilliant defense of Hinduism at the Parliament, it would prove too much for several different and/or overlapping groups: (1) those who held the uniqueness of Christianity, (2) missionaries to India. Their positions were quite exclusive on issues of Christian goodness and truth. The Archbishop of Canterbury refused to attend, stating: ". . . The difficulties which I myself feel are not questions of distance and convenience, but rest on the fact that the Christian religion is the one religion. I do not understand how that religion can be regarded as a member of a Parliament of Religions without assuming the equality of the other intended members and the parity of their position and claims."[1]

1. Burke, I. p. 53.

A minister from Hong Kong saw the Parliament as a betrayal of Christ: ". . . If misled yourself, at least do not mislead others nor jeopardize, I pray you, the precious life of your soul by playing fast and loose with the truth and coquetting with false religions. . . . You are unconsciously planning treason against Christ."[2]

Hinduism, Vivekananda shouted, must fight for its rightful place among the commonwealth of religions. Hinduism was equal with all other religions, is as good as any, and certainly as true. It had the advantage of being based on the Vedas which are older and more spiritual than other religion's scriptures. Hinduism is the "mother of religion."

Proselytizing of Hindus was condemned, since all religions are true and Hinduism is most appropriate for Hindus. Send true Christ-men as missionaries rather than losers who learn nothing of India, stay a short time and even then with their many servants, and return to the West to slander India and Hinduism from their own shortcomings and failures.

But when Vivekananda used this conception in India it would be populated with components which met Indians' specific needs. Hinduism must again become a "man-making religion," instead of being silent in face of the exploitation and bondage of colonialism. (Statements on economic justice gave Vivekananda a political standing which he could not erase by his denials of political innocence.)

The defense of Hinduism did not specify what was thought worthy or unworthy. It suggested to many hearers that Vivekananda advocated everything Hindu as equal, good, true. It led to a result that he did not approve: the championing of exclusive religion based on dogmas and practices derived from the ordinary and institutionalized on the real level of history.

During Vivekananda's triumphal return to India in 1897, he began to spell out the new dimensions of "Vedānta" as to be lived in a new age or *yuga*. This was perhaps Vivekananda's most suitable term for his Western and Indian audiences.

Yet misunderstanding arose in those hearers of Vivekananda who literalized his statements that "the Vedas are the only scriptures which

---

2. Burke, I. p. 53.

teach this real absolute God."[3] or that Vedānta is the truest and highest of all religions. ". . . all other religions of the world are included in the nameless, limitless, eternal Vedic religion."[4] Vivekananda's use of his Vedāntic ladder would seem to hear what it fought at the Parliament, a universalism based on the superiority of one religion. There are enough of his "militant Hinduism" pronouncements which equate Hinduism and Vedānta to fill a book. And when some *svamis* of the Ramakrishna Mission and Order appear to use these sayings in a sectarian way, it also appears that Vivekananda must have used them in the same way. For example, Svami Satprakashananda stated:

> [The Vedas] do not advocate any dogmatic faith, but enunciate the spiritual truths underlying all religious doctrines, practices, and experiences. Strictly speaking, Vedānta is not a particular religion but the common basis of all religions.
>
> Being derived from Vedānta, Hinduism is identified with it. . . . Hinduism is the Vaidika-dharma (the Vedic religion). It is also called Sanātana-dharma (the Eternal religion), inasmuch as it affirms eternal truths and finds their application in life.[5]

If Svami Satprakashananda's two paragraphs are to be saved from a mixing of transcendent vedānta with an historical Hinduism, then a single phrase, "inasmuch as," must be highlighted. But many of Vivekananda's hearers misunderstood his fiery pronouncements simply because they did not understand the logical necessities of these varying contexts. For them, it sounded like Vivekananda defended their Hinduism as being the culmination of the Vedas which was also the Religion Eternal.

A philosophical objection can be made from the vantage point of observing one century of its usage. 'Vedānta,' as a category to express the dynamics of the transcendent, is not adequate. It does not sufficiently point beyond historical formulations and ethnic conceits to serve its

---

3. Vivekananda, *Complete Works*, IV, 343. "So far as the Bible and the scriptures of other nations agree with the Vedas, they are perfectly good, but when they do not agree, they are no more to be accepted." From "The Vedānta in all its phases" (1897), *CW*, III, 333.

4. *Ibid.*

5. Svami Satprakashananda, *Svami Vivekananda's Contribution to the Present Age*, St. Louis, Mo.: The Vedānta Society of St. Louis, 1978), p. 112.

purpose. (To say this a century after Vivekananda is to build upon his contribution to interreligious communication and not to detract from it. Were he attending the anniversary of the World's Parliament of Religions in 1993, I am certain he would handle the problems of categories for multilevelled ontologies and epistemologies differently.)

If Vivekananda were a classical *advaitin,* the unmodified conception of Advaita Vedānta as the truest expression of *sanātana dharma* would be forthcoming.

While this seems a logical position, Vivekananda's best position is Viṣiśṭadvaita. It does not vitiate real work and service of others.

> Therefore, children of the Aryās, do not sit idle; awake, arise, and stop not till the goal is reached. The time has come when this Advaita is to be worked out practically. Let us bring it down from heaven unto the earth; this is the present dispensation.[6]

If the highest religion is Advaita Vedānta, then Saṅkara's quietism without works is best and truest, most advanced.

> Take off the name and form, and whatever is, reality is He. He is the reality in everything. "Thou art the woman, thou the man, thou art the boy, and the girl as well, thou the old man supporting thyself on a stick, thou art all in all in the universe." That is the theme of Advaitism. A few words more. Herein lies, we find, the explanation of the essence of things. We have seen how here alone we can take a firm stand against all the on rush of logic and scientific knowledge. Here at last reason has a firm foundation, and, at the same time, the Indian Vedantist does not curse the preceding steps; he looks back and he blesses them, and he knows that they were true, only wrongly perceived, and wrongly stated. They were the same truth, only seen through the glass of māyā, distorted it may be — yet truth, and nothing but truth.
>
> . . . Therefore, arise, awake, with your hands stretched out to protect the spirituality of the world. And first of all, work it out for your own country. What we want is not so much spirituality as a little of the bringing down of the Advaita into the material world. First bread and then religion. We stuff them too much with religion, when the poor fellows have been starving. No dogmas will satisfy the cravings of hunger. There are two cures here: first our weakness, secondly, our hatred, our dried-up hearts. You may talk doctrines by the millions, you may have sects by the hundreds of millions; ay, but it is nothing until you have the heart to feel. Feel for them as your Veda teaches you, till you find they are part

6. *CW*, III, 428, taught at Lahore on 12 November 1897.

> of your own bodies, till you realize that you and they, the poor and the rich, the saint and the sinner, are all parts of One Infinite Whole, which you call Brahman.[7]

Majority Religion in Modern India. When combined, the four-fold concepts worked together to define majority religion in modern India. Nine descriptors would populate Vivekananda's complex notion of Indian spirituality.[8]

Monism — Advaita Vedānta was the rational articulation of the Absolute and the principles of oneness. The *māyāvāda* doctrine of Śaṅkara was accepted as definitive. But in the realm of multiplicity, Viṣiśṭadvaita (qualified monism) validated one's involvement in the world. Ramakrishna's radical destruction of the epistemological differences of Advaita, Viṣiśṭadvaita and Dvaita in his experiential harmony of all approaches can be portrayed by the model of the wheel with three spokes coming to the oneness of truth at the centre. Vivekananda, as a solution to the same problem used the model of the ladder and postulated, as Nalini Devdas correctly observed, "a reasoned system in which *Dvaita* and *Viṣiśṭadvaita* are the stages and *Advaita* is the goal."[9]

The thirst for the realization of God and *Brahman* or Shakti or Kālī or even in Ramakrishna as the *avatāra* of the *satya yuga* was relegated by Vivekananda to a subordinate role for intermittent periods of time after 1890. What became more important than realizing God and attaining *mukti* was his "God the poor and the miserable." But as a Viṣiśṭadvaitin the poor and God were the same, only perceived from different levels of reality. For the poor he would forego his own liberation — the traditional reason for the total renunciation of the *sannyasin.* Nor would it matter much experientially, whether or not Sri Ramakrishna was really God. Epistemologically, Ramakrishna's avatāra-nature vouchsafed the unity of Brahman and Shakti, for only an avatāra could return from merger in the oneness of the Godhead and know its identity with the God of form. Yet Vivekananda's ladder model placed Advaita at the top as the truest philosophical expression and relegated *avatāras* to the relatively real of *vivarta* (appearance).

7. CW, III, 432.
8. Cf. Williams, "The Ramakrishna Movement," *op. cit.*
9. Devdas, *op. cit.*, 32.

Monasticism — Narendra became Svami Vivekananda at the suggestion of the Rājā of Khetri. When Vivekananda went to America, he laimed to be a monk of the oldest order of *sannyasi*s in India, that of Shankaracharya.[10] He allowed himself to be known as a Brahmin. He identified himself as being from Bombay or even Madras. He was credentialed to speak before the World Parliament of Religions on the basis of these verbal claims. After his remarks in defense of Hinduism and often at the expense of other Indian religious groups (the Brahmo Samaj and Theosophy, in particular), some attacked him as a liar. These attacks almost aborted his work in America, but he managed to get resolutions of support from the Rājā of Khetri and from lay disciples in Madras proving that he represented pure Hinduism. His former *gurubhai*s did not provide him with the needed credentials.

When Vivekananda returned to India in 1897 and asserted his leadership over the circle of Ramakrishna monks, he accommodated more to their monasticism than they did to his. (This will be treated in the next period.) When they accused him of being Western and said that his teachings were not compatible with those of Sri Ramakrishna, Vivekananda responded "with great fervour":

How do you know that these are not in keeping with his ideas? Do you want to shut Shri Ramakrishna, the embodiment of infinite ideas, within your own limits? I shall break these limits and scatter his ideas, broadcast all over the world. He never enjoined me to introduce his worship and the like. The methods of spiritual practice, concentration and meditation and other high ideals of religion that he taught — those we must realize and teach mankind. Infinite are the ideas and infinite are the paths that lead to the Goal. I was not born to create a new sect in this world, too full of sects already.[11]

Vivekananda's monasticism would lead the movement away from total renunciation of gold to its use for mankind. His was an 'in-the-world' asceticism which was not practised by their Master, Sri Ramakrishna.

Universalism — The nineteenth century quest for the foundation of universal religion which proved the unity of all religions was founded by

10. See footnote no. 2, page 359.
11. *Life, op. cit.*, p. 504.

Svami Vivekananda in Vedānta. He equated the principles of Vedānta and *sanātana dharma.* These were the principles of spirituality with its realization of the One. This was the pure Hinduism.

Toleration — Sri Ramakrishna had realized all religions as true. This was experiential and grounded in the special nature of his experiments with Islam, Christianity and the Hindu sects (such as Tantra, Shākta, Vaishnava, Shaiva). Svami Vivekananda, nor any other monk known to the author, ever carried out their own experiments. They all accepted the truth of all religions on the basis of their Master's work. Svami Vivekananda tried to lead in some comparative studies — reminiscent of those at the Brahmo Samaj. But no one actually went into the practice of Islam or Taoism. The Ramakrishna movement's outer form would be Hindu.

Vivekananda's message asserted that Hinduism is the most tolerant of all religions in the world. It accepted all as true. Unity was the basis of tolerance. But as the defender of Hinduism at a time when cultural inferiority was a bitter reality, Svami Vivekananda often lapsed into what Sister Nivedita (Margaret Noble, a British disciple) termed his "militant Hinduism." Taken out of this historical context, many of his remarks about Christianity, Judaism, Buddhism and Islam appear hypercritical and do little to further this ideal of tolerance. But these critical remarks were often cherished more by his countrymen desiring some area of superiority than the mild statements of unity and tolerance.

Non-sectarian — Vivekananda applied the doctrine of universality to the Hindu tradition and sought to lessen any divisiveness between its sects. He wanted to lead all Indians to a purified Hinduism, diverse enough for all. Following Sri Ramakrishna's realizations about difference resting on the variety of spiritual paths (*mārgas*), Vivekananda taught that there were four tendencies through which mankind sought God. Hinduism was the only religion that recognized that the religious capacities of persons vary according to their inner tendencies (*saṁskāras*).[12] These capacities must be channelled into a proper method or path (*yoga*), and only Hinduism taught the four *yogās* (*jñana, bhakti, karma* and *rāja*).[13] Each of

12. *Complete Works, op. cit.,* VII, 98.

13. *Complete Works, op. cit.,* V, 12, 292, 455; VIII, 152.

these paths had the same goal, oneness with *Brahman.* (He did not seem to notice that *jñana yoga* and *rāja yoga* covered much of the same spiritual territory — the non-traditional or intuitional knowledge of the Absolute[14]) Vivekananda insisted that *karma yoga* was the best path for the present and even *sannyasis* should forsake other paths and work for the awakening of all.

Liberalism — Liberal religion in the nineteenth century was founded on beliefs in universal reason, in progress and in the potential of the masses — democracy or socialism. Justice, liberty and equality were liberal religion's principles. These taught that the lack of food and clothing was unjust and a social rather than a personal ill. Therefore, liberal religion sought social reform through legal redress and educational uplift for the underprivileged and downtrodden. These ideas came to Vivekananda as part of his education in Scottish Church College in Calcutta and through his involvement as a member of the Brahmo Samāj (1878-1885). These ideas were not primary concerns of Sri Ramakrishna — not in these ways. When Svami Vivekananda acted as a liberal, he called for the end of Puranic superstitions and for a reform of the religion of "don't touchism" (a reference to untouchability and defilement by touch) and the religion of the kitchen (a reference to the restrictions on inter-caste dining). At times he even predicted an end to the caste system itself because the principle of *sanātana dharma,* and consequently purified Hinduism, was oneness — even of caste. In the *satya yuga,* which was coming into being through the preaching of "fiery mantras" to the masses, all would become Brahmins. Svami Vivekananda was especially critical of priestcraft. He predicted that it would lose its business. He was hurt deeply when his *gurubhais* resembled Purānic priests instead of Advaita *sannyasis.* He attacked their devotions on many occasions before he finally lapsed into silence:

> You think you understand Shri Ramakrishna better than myself? You think Jñana is dry knowledge to be attained by a desert path, killing out

---

14. *Raja-Yoga* (*Complete Works* I, 119 ff.) taught methods of "psychic control" for "the liberation of the soul through perfection." (pp. 124, 122) Its textual basis was Patanjali's *Yoga Sūtras.* This comprised his major exposition of the mystical path. In *Jñana-Yoga* (*Complete Works* II, 55 ff.) Vivekananda defined the way of philosophy (knowledge). Yet both of these paths utilized as the highest *pramāṇa* direct realization.

> the tenderest faculties of the heart. Your Bhakti is sentimental nonsense which makes one impotent. You want to preach Ramakrishna as you have understood him which is mighty little. Hands off! Who cares for your Ramakrishna? Who cares for Bhakti and Mukti? Who cares what the scriptures say? I will go to the hell cheerfully a thousand times, if I can rouse my countrymen, immersed in Tamas, and make them stand on their own feet and be Men, inspired with the spirit of Karma-Yoga. I am not a follower of Ramakrishna or any one, I am a follower of him only who carries out my plans! I am not a servant of Ramakrishna or any one, but of him only who serves and helps others, without caring for his own Mukti.[15]

Vivekananda demanded that his *gurubhai*s be 'in-the-world' ascetics. He demanded that these *sannyasi*s who had renounced the world to gain *mukti* must become servants of the poor and underprivileged. He called it *karma yoga,* but as A.L. Basham has observed, this respect for physical work is a purely Western idea.[16] Vivekananda's genius was to establish the connection between the *Bhagavad Gita*'s call to action with India's modern awakening, ignoring its demand that all action be given to Krishna as *puja.* This awakening linked social reform in India to liberal, progressive education of the masses. In the nineteenth century liberal religionists believed that this was the formula for world reform. It would end in a brotherhood of mankind and a commonwealth of nations.

Humanitarianism — Svami Vivekananda's liberal principles for social reform were supported by humanitarian commitments. His "Practical Vedānta" taught *yoga* as service to all creatures (*sevā dharma*). He formulated "the Plan" for dedicated *sannyasi*s to teach the masses the industrial and agricultural technology, develop them intellectually, and then raise them to their true nature through the highest principles of Advaita Vedānta. He differed with Sri Ramakrishna in that he believed that even householders could be taught the principles of unity with the Absolute, the relative reality of the One (*māyāvāda*), and renunciation while remaining in the world of duty and toil. He believed that even *sannyasi*s should give up their selfish goal of *mukti* and work to feed, educate, and lift the masses to their true greatness, in full knowledge of the Divine within.

---

15. *Life, op. cit.* p. 507.

16. Cited from Bharati, *loc. cit.*

Progressive — Nineteenth century liberal religion linked social reforms, humanitarianism and progressive education. Education was the key to awakening the masses of the world from the darkness of ignorance. Progressive education was universal in principle and democratic in philosophy. Vivekananda believed that proper study would help in paralysing the ills of poverty and superstitions. The basic content of these studies would be the Vedānta, to learn the principles of true spirituality, and Western science, to utilize the discoveries which would better material existence. First one must eat; then one can explore spirituality's heights.

Scientific — As just mentioned, Svami Vivekananda sought to bring the science of the West to India. He believed that Vedānta was the only scientific religion. Since its principles were grounded in the Absolute, there could be no incompatibility with science.[17]

Appendix E
Ramakrishnaism

Everyone knows about the Ramakrishna Mission and Order's failed attempt to claim to be a minority sect, namely that of Ramakrishnaism.[1] The Ramakrishna Order and Mission abandoned the majority religion and the locus of its reform to protect its own interests. It affirmed that it was both a minority sect but still Hindu; its ontological claim for nearly a century, of being the embodiment of purified Hinduism, had changed fundamentally.

Inferentially, the Ramakrishna Order and Mission had been forced in its legal battles to say that it was new. It was a reform religion and not the majority religion. It affirmed Ramakrishna's circle of equality of all religions, but not unambiguously because of an understanding of radical transcendence. Since Ramakrishna was still affirmed as the embodiment of the Religion Eternal, Ramakrishnaism was uniquely an embodiment of the Religion Eternal. Therefore it was different from Hinduism.

---

17. One should note that Vivekananda's reconciliation of both science and humanitarian work required an epistemological shift from Advaita's posture toward science which would assign it to *vivarta* while Viśiṣṭādvaita would find science and knowledge about God compatible.

1. Affidavit filed by R.K. Mission, District: 24-Parganas, High Court at Calcutta, C.O. No. 12837 (W) of 1980.

Again inferentially, the Ramakrishna Order attempted in the lawsuit to understand its own finitude. Legally, it was Ramakrishnaism and a minority sect. It was legally a particular religion. Perhaps that does not change the fundamental teaching of the Order: that it is both purified Hinduism and the living example on earth of the *sanātana dharma,* the Religion Eternal. That claim could still be made even though 'majority' Hindus have more justification in calling Ramakrishnaism sectarian.

The few Svamis who talked "off-the-record" about this crisis claimed that what the lawyers said in court does not represent the ideal nor have the ideals of the Mission been changed. There may be more truth to this new position than meets the eye. Hinduism has always worked well philosophically with two-level ontologies — appearance and Reality, *māyā* and *Brahman, ajñana* and *jñana,* infinitum. But the Ramakrishna Mission's historical claims were nevertheless compromised in practicality. It is now harder to assert that the gospel of Ramakrishna attempts to embody *sanātana dharma* in its universal form and that it expresses as an institution a purified Hinduism which is neither a sect, nor sectarian.

By clarifying itself as a minority of 1400 monks and 100,000 lay followers, the Ramakrishna Order and Mission accepted an identity of something more like a numerical minority. It abandoned the role thrust upon the Order from its beginning in 1897, that of being the living example of purified Hinduism. It could still affirm that it was both a minority sect and still Hindu but its self-understanding of its ontological essence would now have to be argued on two levels. This dual dialectic of being one with the transcendent and embodying it on the real level both saved it from being ordinary, majority Hinduism and clarified its identity as just a minority religious group.

This identity crisis has forced the Ramakrishna Mission and Order back upon its own foundations to Ramakrishna's circle of equality and into its own particularity. From the shame of having fled the locus of majority religious reform, which it never lead anyway, Vivekananda's vision may now come to be understood: the Ramakrishna Order and Mission's identity and destiny is one of a preserving, reforming approximation of the unity of all religions. As such, it can reaffirm the highest vision of the 1893 Chicago World's Parliament of Religions. Also, it demonstrates the ontological tension between *dharma* and *sanātana dharma.*

17

Strī Dharma: Wife's Duties

A Hindu Textual and Contextual Analysis among the Educated and Professional Women in Contemporary Indian Society and the Diaspora in UK and USA

Annapurna Devi Pandey

Orientalist Perspective

ON June 10, 1998 I read an article titled "Rural child brides fated to illiteracy, exploitation" in our local daily, San Jose Mercury, one of the widely circulated papers in Northern California. It showed a picture of a 4 year old girl, Hansa, and a 12 year old boy Sitaram getting married in a cermony in Rajasthan, one of India's populous northern states where the report says that child marriages are common, though illegal. According to the Indian Constitution, the age of marriage is 18 for girls and 21 for boys and the Child Marriage Restraint Act of 1978, makes child marriage illegal. Still, according to the newspaper article, it is a common practice in these five populous northern States (Rajasthan, Madhya Pradesh, Uttar Pradesh, Bihar, and West Bengal), where child marriages are most deeply rooted, with a combined population of 420 million, about 40 per cent of all Indians. Today in modern India early marriage is not encouraged except for in rural northern states. But marriage among the girls is deeply valued.

That article on the prevalence of child marriage in India may simply reflect on the social ills in some parts of rural India, but it also reflects an Orientalist image of 'helplessness' and 'dependence' of the Indian women on their menfolk, with other meanings and implications regarding women's infantile status, arranged marriage and precarious role in the family in India. The status of women in India has also been described for Western society in the popular writings of Indian-American writers in the diaspora, such as Chitra Devakarni Banerjee's books, *Arranged Marriage*, a collection of stories about women's suffering in the arranged marriage system; *The Mistress of Spices*, which reflects on the abuses and other ills inflicted upon Indian women by their menfolk. These books have been in the bestseller lists in the past couple of years. These works feed into the fractured imagery of Indian women held by Western society.

The Challenge

My aim in this paper is neither to portray the victim status of Indian women, as represented in the popular writings in the Western media, nor to discuss the exotic and romanticized imagery of Indian women in the post-colonial setting. My main concern is to analyse the literary and socio-cultural significance of the Hindu texts, and to show how women in urban India and in the diaspora are reconstructing or shifting traditional values and still reincorporating Hindu traditions through textual reinterpretation and enactment of various life-cycle rituals and religious practices.

I intend to analyse the textual literature on the role of women in marriage and family and to give a contextual study of the life experiences of educated and professional women both in contemporary India and in the first and second generation of Indian women who now live in the UK and USA. As a social scientist and a Hindu, I have my outsider's as well as insider's perspective on the textual and contextual analysis of women in the contemporary socio-cultural context. As a Hindu, I have been a participant observer in several life-cycle rituals performed by the women. As a researcher, I have interviewed a few professional women in India, in the Bay area in California, and in London.

The Significance of Marriage in Hindu Society

Marriage is still the *sine qua non* of Indian life. It provides an identity to the male and female and is considered the most salient *saṁskāra* (life-cycle rite) in the life of a Hindu.[1] The word *saṁskāra* means to 'complete,' 'prepare,' 'make over,' 'fully form' and above all, to 'purify' (*śuddhi*). Since ancient times, Indian texts starting with the Vedas, Upaniṣads, *Manu Smṛti* and *Strīdharmapaddhati* (set of the wife's religious duties and rituals) have focused on a symbiotic relationship between male and female in the context of marriage rituals. Progeny has been the central focus in the Hindu marriage with the expectation to regenerate the society both in ancient times and today.

I would like to make it clear that the texts, even though made widely known by authors such as Wendy Doniger O'Flaherty who translated Vedas from Sanskrit to English (1981); and Julia Lesley who translated Tryambakayajvan's *Strīdharmapaddhati* or *Guide to the Religious Status and Duties of Women* (1989) in her book *The Perfect Wife,* are still not accessible to the millions of Indian masses. These books are highly academic and cater to the taste of a very selected group of people in India and abroad. Also, people in India follow Hindu religion in terms of rituals and practices not exactly according to prescribed books. Hindu religion is not a book-based religion, unlike other world religions, such as Judaism, Christianity, Islam, and Buddhism. These books either written in Sanskrit or any regional language translated in English still are not widely followed because of the constraints of language and regional differences in terms of religious practices and following of these texts in various local and regional languages. Still these texts do portray the normative Hindu tradition and are widely followed

1. Raj Bali Pandey, *Hindu Samskaras*, Motilal Banarsidass, 1969. He explains that marriage is the final *saṁskāra* of a living body, a religious act, sacred and permanent. Here looking at the universal principle of creation and recreation, marriage makes the husband-wife complete, united and one.

and practised in the diverse regional cultures of India in the form of oral traditions, local practices and rituals. The textual interpretations are also reflected in the presentations of the great Indian epics like the *Rāmāyaṇa* and *Mahābhārata*.

Marriage has always been either romanticized or exoticized in South Asian culture. It has been mostly analysed from its textual perspective. Western scholars have done in-depth studies of these texts to reflect on women's status in India.[2] Religious studies scholars, starting with the German Orientalist scholar, Max-Müller and more recently Wendy Doniger O'Flaherty have introduced Vedas to a wide audience with the translations of Vedas in English and have popularized the role of women in Vedas and *Manu-Saṁhitā* in the East and West.[3] The ancient Indian texts on domestic (*gṛhīya*) rituals, primarily those focusing on marriage, tell us a great deal about the subservient position of women at that time. On close examination, several of these texts reflecting on the perceptions of the role of women were recorded and elaborated upon by a literate male elite. The male priestly experts did not evaluate the marriage rituals in terms of women's rights, but focused on "ritual science" and, to some extent, their personal concerns as perceived at that time.[4]

All the literature on marriage focuses on a symbiotic relationship between male and female in the context of marriage rituals. As nature reproduces, so society must also reproduce for its continuity. Without the interaction of male and female, how could there be progeny? Progeny is a central expectation in the context of marriage rituals both in ancient time and today. At the same time, what has been ignored is that irrespective of progeny

2. For example, Julia Leslie's *Perfect Wife*, Oxford University Press, 1989.
3. Wendy Doniger O'Flaherty, ed., *The Rigveda: An Anthology of one Hundred and Eight Hymns*, Harmondsworth, Eng: Penguin, 1981.
4. One such work that puts the orthodox point of view is Tryambakayajvan's *Strīdharmapaddhati*, or *Guide to the Religious Status and Duties of Women* written in the eighteenth century in southern India.

without one sex, the other is not complete. The complementarity between male and female has been totally overlooked by most of the writings. Many studies of Hindu marriage predominantly focus on prescriptive literatures, especially the Sanskrit moral-legal texts (Dharmaśāstras) which interpret marriage as a set of normative rules and attitudes to be pursued in order to achieve merit and ensure social harmony.[5]

A Brief Overview of Literature on the Role of Women in India

In the last few decades there has been renewed interest in women's changing role and status in India. The general observation focuses on women's revered status as goddesses and their disadvantaged status as wives and mothers identified only through their men.[6] Susan Wadley and Doranne Jacobson's *Women in India: Two Perspectives* (1986) and Lynn Bennett's *Dangerous Wives and Sacred Sisters* (1983) portray dichotomous model of women in the South Asian Hindu cultures. These studies are primarily concerned with contrasting two opposite perceptions of women in the roles of wives *versus* the roles of mothers and sisters. This polarized view of female nature as good/bad highlights on the absolute split in female roles. It also presents the view that although women are revered as goddesses, they also have a dis-advantaged status as wives and mothers, to be defined only through men. Raheja and Gold in their book, *Listen to the Heron's Words* (1994), argue that the split-image approach to South Asian women derives largely from the male point of view.[7]

5. Raj Bali Pandey's *Hindu Samskaras*, and Tryambakayajvan's *Strīdharmapaddhati*.

6. R.P. Sharma's *Woman in Hindu Literature*, Gyan Publishing House, New Delhi, 1995; Vanaja Dhruvarajan's *Hindu Women and the Power of Ideology*, Bergin & Garvey Publishers, Inc. Massachusetts, 1989, echo the overall disadvantaged position of women in India.

7. Gloria Raheja and Ann Gold, *Listen to the Heron's Words, Reimagining Gender and Kinship in North India*, 1994, p. 37.

I would argue that the dangerous or destructive imagery of Hindu women as sexual beings is also the reflection of Western Judeo-Christian tradition conceptualizing women in the image of Eve. She is conceived as guilty of committing the original sin. In the Hindu tradition sex is sinful only where it is socially illegitimate. . . . Woman as mother was venerated but woman as an erotic being was not degraded. Far from being seen as sin, the sexual act was symbolic of creative energy. Such an attitude permitted the duality of approach to women.[8] As a result, women are constructed in terms of their body and are secondary to men. It was with the impact of Christianity and Victorian mores that the notion of the guilt complex took root in India. This imagery, in turn, is reflected in the writings about women of the South Asian cultures.

Recently, some Western journalists/writers have spent some time in different parts of India because of their personal or professional interests and have published works catering to the Western audience.[9] Mitter in her book, *Dharma's Daughters* (1991) has portrayed the conflicting lives of urban Indian women caught in a traditional patriarchal society, left with limited choices and boundaries. Bumiller in her book, *May You be the Mother of a Hundred Sons* (1992), also focused on the status of Indian women, looking closely at issues such as dowry, rape and purdah. She concluded, as evident from the title, that women are still valued according to the number of sons they produce for the family.

Reacting to the rigid portrayal of women's subjectivity in Hindu traditions spelled out for the women in India by the role of *pativrātya* and the perfect model of *strī dharma*, some women

8. Romila Thapar, "Looking Back in History" in Devaki Jain, ed., *Indian Women*, Publications Division, Ministry of Information and Broadcasting, Government of India, 1975, p. 12.

9. The works of Elizabeth Bumiller, *May you be the Mother of a Hundred Sons*, 1992; Sara Mitter, *Dharma's Daughters, Contemporary Indian Women and Hindu Culture*, Rutgers Press, 1991; would be obvious examples.

activists and scholars who have been trained in the Western tradition have critiqued the rigid portrayal of women in various religious texts, causing the subordinate position of women in India.[10] Butalia and Sarkar (1995) argue that the Hindu scriptures are being revived by the right wing political parties, which are continuously reminding the women of their appropriate role in the family and mobilizing them against other communal groups in the name of their duties towards their own religion. The Hindu revivalists have their own political agenda to appropriate the interests of these women in the name of religion. As a result, women are used as pawns catering to the interests of the communalist Hindu right wing political groups. The authors are of the opinion that women's interests are overridden in the interests of politicized Hindu religion, which in turn threatens secular democracy in India. Ghadially (1988) argues that, inspite of rapid changes in India in the last few decades, women still are required to conform to age-old traditional images and stereotypes of Hindu normative tradition. Women still have to conform to the stereotyped model of *pativrātya* (husband as the sole duty) portrayed in Hindu myths and this imagery justifies the present-day violence against women.

Some anthropological studies of Indian women, namely Kolenda (1987),[11] Roy (1975)[12] and Fruzetti (1982),[13] among others, have focused on the role of family and religion in the lives of Indian women. They have emphasized the role of family that clearly defines the multiple roles and status of women, and the role of religion that gives the Indian women a feeling of community, self-

10. Tanika Sarkar and Urvashi Butalia, eds., *Women and the Hindu Right*, Kali for Women, 1995; Rehana Ghadially, ed., *Women in Indian Society*, Sage, 1988 reflect on an overall stereotyped images of women conforming to the age-old Hindu tradition.
11. Pauline Kolenda, *Regional Differences in Family Structure in India*, Rawat Publications, 1987.
12. Manisha Roy, *Bengali Women*, The University of Chicago Press, 1975.
13. Lina M. Fruzzetti, *The Gift of a Virgin, Women, Marriage and Ritual in a Bengali Society*, Rutgers University Press, 1982.

identity and a sense of agency as well as support that distinguishes them from their Western counterparts.

Most recently, South Asian studies scholars like Gloria Raheja and Ann Gold (1994), Ann Pearson (1996), Lindsey Harlan and Paul Courtright (1995), among others, have focused on women's agency and their resistance to the textual, normative Hindu traditions through their own personal interpretations of Hindu rituals, customs and other religious practices. Raheja and Gold[14] have focused on women's oral tradition through their folk songs, to reflect on the rural women's agency and personhood in heavily gender segregated communities like Rajasthan and western Uttar Pradesh. Based on her field study in urban Varanasi, Ann Pearson[15] argued that women perform the ritual fasts not just to conform to their sacrificial role in the interests of their family, but to give themselves a sense of satisfaction, selfhood and strength for their own identity in the socio-cultural context. Harlan and Courtright[16] explored various instances of marriages outside or transgressing the normative boundaries of Hindu marriage, deriving examples from various expressive traditions, myths and life-stories. They have provided new perspectives on Hindu marriage in South Asian cultures by focusing on the marginal experiences of women who have resisted the conventional conceptualization of *strī dharma* or the duties of wives. On the whole, these studies have used the oral and expressive genre as a medium expressing the agency of women who are otherwise situated in the normative Hindu tradition.

In this paper, my purpose is to discover how Hindu marriage actually works as a social and actual reality as interpreted from

---

14. Gloria Raheja and Ann Gold, *Listen to the Heron's Words, Reimagining Gender and Kinship in North India*, 1994.
15. Ann Mackenzie Pearson, "Because it gives me Peace of Mind" Ritual Fasts in the Lives of Hindu Women, SUNY, 1996.
16. Lindsey Harlan and Paul Courtright, eds., *From the Margins of Hindu Marriage, Eassays on Gender, Religion and Culture*, Oxford University Press, 1995.

the texts by looking into the varied personal experiences and perceptions of those who have gone through it in the changing social situations. The texts I have relied on are Tryambakayajvan's *Strīdharmapaddhati* or *Guide to the Religious Status and Duties of Women*, the epics *Rāmāyaṇa* and *Mahābhārata* as well as *Manu Saṁhitā*, the central guidelines for Hindus to maintain social order. I will analyse a contextual view on the *strī dharma* as practised among educated, professional women in contemporary Indian society and Indian women who are immigrants to the UK and USA.

Various Hindu Texts and Their Varied Interpretations

TEXTS

Strī dharma (wife's duties) has been defined and interpreted in many Indian moral-legal texts. Before discussing the significance of *strī dharma*, let me focus on *dharma* (virtue) and its significance in the Indian society. *Dharma* is the central notion of Hindu view of life. It is narrowly defined as the art of behaving according to one's own fundamental qualities, and hence the observance of a code of conduct given by nature and birth.[17] To elaborate on it further, if one asks an Indian villager about his religion, he may not describe his rituals or ascetic life but talk about his 'righteousness' (*dharma*). Derived from the Sanskrit root *dhri* meaning "to bear, support, maintain," *dharma* in a broader social context means that which sustains creation, the eternal principle underlying the Universe, the fundamental world order. The concept is both descriptive and prescriptive, indicating both what is, and what should be, the real and ideal. In the realm of individual action (*svadharma* or righteousness for individual), *strī dharma* (wife's righteousness) refers both to what one does and what one ought to do. One's action defined by circumstances is also one's religious duty, for it was ordained to be so and is therefore right. In theory, at least, there is no conflict between the real and the ideal.

17. Alain Danielou, *Virtue, Success, Pleasure and Liberation. The Four Aims in the Tradition of Ancient India*, Inner Traditions International, Vermont, 1993, p. 23.

Coined during the Vedic era, *dharma* extended beyond sacrifice to the moral world, to the realm of conduct. *Dharma* now came to mean any action that conformed to the cosmic order and permitted the individual to realize his or her allotted destiny. Any action contrary to *dharma* brought its own automatic punishment. As Manu writes, "when violated, *dharma* destroys; when preserved, *dharma* preserves, therefore *dharma* must not be violated, lest violated *dharma* destroys us" (Manu V.111.15). Thus the status and role of each individual, man or woman in the society, not only reflects *dharma* but upholds it, and in so doing, maintains the universe.

Keeping the above thoughts in mind, let us discuss *strī dharma* and its individual and wider social and cultural implications. Even though it has been discussed in many texts since ancient times, it has been exclusively dealt with by one text in Sanskrit, Tryambakayajvan's *strīdharmapaddhati* or *Guide to the Religious Status and Duties of Women*. It focuses on *Strī dharma*, what women ought to do in their role of wife. This text was written in Sanskrit by an orthodox *puṇḍit* in the eighteenth century at Tanjore in south India. It is the only major work available on *strī dharma*. This text depicts the ideal role of women in the eighteenth century i.e., before the nineteenth century social reform movements in different parts of India. It serves as the Dharmaśāstric appendix to the portrayal of Rāma and Sītā as the ideal husband and wife from the great Indian epic, *Rāmāyaṇa*. This text has received wide attention in Western academic circles since it was translated from Sanskrit by a south Asian religious studies scholar, Julia Leslie in 1989.[18]

By the eighteenth century, women's situation had already passed through various stages of development and been subject to the various reactionary movements including Buddhism, Jainism

18. Julia Leslie, *The Perfect Wife: The Orthodox Hindu Woman* according to the *Strīdharmapaddhati* of Tryambakayajvan, Oxford University South Asian Series, Oxford University Press, 1989.

and Bhakti movements in different parts of the country. These movements emerged as a result of the supremacy of the Brāhmaṇic rule in Indian caste system. Women's status was already consolidated by the Islamic rule in India. The significance of the present text lies in the fact that there is a culmination of earlier, much celebrated Purāṇic texts like the *Mahābhārata, Rāmāyaṇa, Manu Smṛti* and Kauṭilya's *Arthaśāstra*, among others, reflecting on the position of women in the Hindu society.

Even though this text may not apply to all Hindu women in India today, high caste women were expected and encouraged to conform to the ideals mentioned in the text. The text is based on how women ought to behave as wives. *Strīdharmapaddhati* presents teachings on the ideal women derived from the epics and Purāṇas.

Using the translation of the text *Strīdharmapaddhati* by Julia Leslie, entitled *Perfect Woman*, I shall summarize the main points of Tryambakayajvan's *Strīdharmapaddhati*.

Tryambaka emphasizes that "obedient service to one's husband is the primary religious duty enjoined by sacred tradition for women" (p. 29). He defines "obedient service to one's husband" in three ways: firstly, a wife should serve her husband "without regard for her own life." Secondly, she should accept whatever her husband does "even the sale of herself." Thirdly, she should obey his will "even when it conflicts with other religious duties." Each point is substantiated by various examples from the epics and Purāṇas. It was presumably hoped that such lengthy retellings of favourite and traditional tales would inspire impressionable young women to conform to the highest ideals of *strī dharma*.

Let me explain each point with some examples. On the first duty, "without regard for her own life," Tryambaka cites the example of Sītā, the ideal wife in the *Rāmāyaṇa*. When Sītā sees Rāma and Lakṣmaṇa being carried away by a powerful demon, she begs the demon to release them and take her instead.

On the second duty, "accepting even her husband's trade/sale of the wife," the story of Hariścandra from *Mārkaṇḍeya Purāṇa* explains this point. The king, during his difficult times, even sells his wife to pay for the sacrificial fees to a brāhmaṇa ascetic.

On the third duty, "even if it conflicts with other duties," if two duties conflict, service to the husband comes first. Tryambaka concludes that through devoted service to her husband, the good wife attains the merit of every religious act that he performs. Going even further, Tryambaka postulates that if her husband requires it, a woman should do even what is normally considered wrong. He draws examples from two well-known stories of the *Mahābhārata*. First, he quotes at length the conversation between Pāṇḍu and Kuntī on the subject of *niyoga* [the liaison of a wife with men other than her husband]. Even though Tryambaka does not approve of *niyoga*, he recommends it for Kuntī as a wife's *dharma* to her husband, Pāṇḍu. Pāṇḍu, being unable to father his children, asks Kuntī to find someone to act for him by the ancient custom of *niyoga*. Tryambaka repeats Pāṇḍu's crucial statement that "those who know the law know that whatever a husband tells his wife (to do), whether it is lawful or even unlawful, she should do it." As a result, the highest heaven is attained for the wife.

SUMMARY OF TRYAMBAKA'S TEXT

Tryambaka clearly argues that the husband is thus to be propitiated. Firstly, the wife performs her religious role as the ritual assistant to her husband. Secondly, the wife's devotion to her husband is her foremost religious duty. She should treat her husband as her only teacher, her only God.

I would like to add that Trayambaka has chosen the suitable examples from Purāṇic texts to support his arguments. He knew that the texts are not fixed as evidenced in several examples from the *Rāmāyaṇa* and *Mahābhārata*. Tryambaka admits that he is aware of the contradictions with regard to the duties of a woman towards her husband.

At the same time, we can observe several contradictions in the characters of "Ahalyā, Sītā, Draupadī, Tārā and Mandodarī," known as *pañcakanyās* (five maidens), central to the epics of *Rāmāyaṇa* and *Mahābhārata*. These names are considered auspicious to invoke, name of great women, each of different significance. They were not saints, except for one, they were not goddesses. They were all devoted wives and mothers. Each one of them is the ideal of Indian womanhood, is known for her virtue. As wives, these women are remembered as paragons of wifely virtues. But they are also revered as *pañcakanyās*. All these women have defied their husbands at some point in their life and chose their own duties (*svadharma*) over their *strī dharma*. Each character is tainted. Let me explain.

Ahalyā, the first woman created by Brahmā, was the wife of the sage Gautama. She was seduced by Indra disguised as her husband and then cursed by the sage for her wrong-doing. Even though she became impure, ultimately she proves her virute and fidelity, attaining *mokṣa*, with the touch of the divine feet of Śrī Rāma.

Sītā is perhaps the most widely known figure in Hindu myths. In *Rāmāyaṇa*, the myththology that exemplifies the ideal Indian social order, Sītā is the ultimate example of beauty, graciousness, selfless love and devotion to her husband, Rāma. After many dacades of struggle in her life she ultimately defies her husband, Rāma, and joins her mother earth to avoid the humiliation of tests she was subjected to, to prove her virtue.

Draupadī, wife of the Pāṇḍavas, represents the diverse aspects of Indian life and tradition, the institution of *svayaṁvara* (the bride choosing her husband-to-be from among a number of assembled eligible men), and the institution of polyandry (a wife with more than one husband). Under the circumstances she got married to five Pāṇḍava brothers and lived with them all her life. When she was pawned by her husband Yudhiṣṭhira in a game of dice and was lost to the Kaurava brothers, she questions him in the presence of all the elders what right did her husband have to pawn her when he had already lost himself in the game of dice?

Tārā and Mandodarī, are the great characters from the *Rāmāyaṇa*. Tārā, wife of Bali and later married to his younger brother Sugrīva and Mandodarī, wife of the mighty king Rāvaṇa and later married to her husband's younger brother, Vibhīṣaṇa, in the epic *Rāmāyaṇa,* were devoted wives. But to maintain justice and social order they questioned their respective husbands Bali and Rāvaṇa respectively in the pursuit of their *dharma* and opposed their husbands as the reminder of ultimate truth and virtue.

So these are the *pañcakanyā*s and they certainly provide a colourful variety of examples that deviate from the ideal *strī dharma*. They are neither saints nor virgins. They are remembered not as virtuous wives, but as ideal women performing their *dharma,* even to the extent that it contradicts their *strī dharma*. These examples suggest that women played varied roles and were recognized for their rightful action. From this overview now we will move on to instances of modern women playing the role of wives in our Hindu tradition.

Contextual Evidence: Hearing the Voices of Women

What bearing do these texts have on the lives and experiences of Indian women set today? Observing contemporary women's lives both in India and in the West, we find that marriage is still the ultimate goal in an Indian woman's life. Women are still considered the bearers of Hindu tradition. They keep the religious tradition alive through their innumerable rituals — songs, dances and other religious practices. Women are still considered auspicious in the roles of *kanyā* (maiden), wife (*dharmapatnī*) and mother (*mā*). Various roles and duties of women have continued as part of an oral tradition and socialization practices. But in the performance of *strī dharma* and the notion of *pativrātya* (husband as the *dharma*) we can see an incongruency in the orthodox, textual, normative interpretation of *strī dharma* and its practices in various cultural contexts. In the context of the religious duties and experiences of women, I would like to introduce different voices of women and their own evaluations of the textual normative tradition. It is not that women are deviating from the prescribed norms as suggested by Julia Leslie,[19] but that they are reconstructing the norms and are recreating their wifely duties according to their own experiences in terms of education, profession and different social exposure in the changing socio-cultural setting.

I would elaborate on this by looking at some case studies. Here I would confine my study only to the urban educated and career women in the metropolitan cities in India and in the immigrant communities in England and USA. I have talked to many educated and professional women extensively on their duties as a wife and mother and whether they experienced any conflict with the traditional notion of a wife and their role in the family. My urban sample has its limitations. At the same time it is a fact that this group is experiencing changes in the society through industrialization, different cultural exposure (for the immigrants in UK and USA) and change in the family set-up (from extended to nuclear). The studies that I have reviewed above focusing on women's agency, resistance and challenge to the traditional norms through their oral tradition such as Leslie (1991), Raheja and Gold (1994), Harlan and Courtright (1995), among others, are mostly confined to rural women and limited to various regional areas.

Some Examples

Let me give some examples to illustrate the experiences and views of Asian women living in the UK and the United States. I begin with Shraddha, my niece, who just got married in London in the summer of 1997 at age of 31. A high caste brāhmaṇa, Shraddha, is

19. Julia Leslie, ed., *Roles and Rituals for Hindu Women*, Rutherford, 1991. Leslie argues that "It is the small deviation from the norm which may be crucial, perhaps the way the apparently negative is transformed into something positive and powerful." p. 3.

an accomplished chartered accountant, teaches at the University of London, and is working on her doctoral dissertation. She came to London at the age of two with her parents and a twin brother and has lived in UK ever since. Unlike her parents who grew up in India, her home is England. When she was in college she met her future husband, a Kāyastha by caste (ritually inferior to the highest order of brāhmaṇas) whose parents also migrated from Bihar to UK when he was very young. With their parents' approval, they courted each other for a couple of years and their relationship finally culminated in marriage.

Both the bride and groom went through a traditional Hindu wedding ceremony according to the north Indian customs. Before the wedding the bride even had her ritual auspicious bath with the pure ingredients like turmeric and sandalwood paste. Seven married women helped her with this act of purifying her body and mind. Also the groom had to go through similar purifying process to be transformed into an auspicious state. The wedding took place for a long two hours (even though abbreviated to suit the modern restless mind). The priest, a university-educated Kāyastha, performed the ceremony eloquently, keeping an eye on the minute details. He recited all the marriage *mantras* chanting beautifully, explaining the significance of Hindu marriage and the assigned roles and responsibilities of both husband and wife. The bride and groom took a vow to live together not only in this life but also in many more to come, for eternity. They took the *saptapadī pherā* (seven steps in circle) around the sacred fire, the groom following the steps first taken by the bride. It symbolizes living the life together through thick and thin and taking every step in life in consultation with each other. The sacred fire is the witness to this bond which is transformed as sacred with the purification of self, performance of the ritual with the help of a priest and taking a vow together to look after each other in this life and in the lives occurring after this one.

After the ritual, the priest spelled out the essence and significance of Hindu marriage in which husband and wife will perform three *puruṣārtha*s (aims of life), out of total four, together. As regard to *puruṣārtha*s, there are four main aims of life for a Hindu. These are *artha* (success), the economic goal; *kāma* (pleasure), the physical or bodily satisfaction; *dharma* (virtue the spiritual goal) and *mokṣa* (liberation) the ultimate union with the divine. The priest explained that as husband and wife they would attain economic, physical and spiritual well-being together. But for *mokṣa*, the ultimate liberation from this recurring life-cycle, each of them will attain it individually based on their *karma* (action) in this birth and in the past ones.

Following the Hindu patrilocal residence order, the bride moves to her in-laws. In the present setting she will be with her husband, about 60 miles from her own workplace and will commute to her work. Even though in the figurative sense, she moves from her natal family to her affinal family, she is assured that she has a permanent place at her parents' house. According to the custom of transferring her own family name to her husband's, she is looking forward to changing her surname from Pandey to Verma. The change of last name affirms to the concept of *parāyā* (outsider) once the daughter gets married and is identified with her husband's family. In the patriarchal system in India, a daughter, once get married, belongs to her in-laws relinquishing all her rights in her parental family and inherits the family name of her husband's.

Answering my questions on her *strī dharma* she does not see any significant change in her lifestyle. Both the bride and groom have been engaged to be married for the last several years. Now she is going to live with her husband as his legally married wife. She defines her marital relationship based on equal partnership and divison of labour on the family front. He loves to cook, speaks very good Hindi and is very shy. She is overly protective of him.

Her educational and professional achievement gives her a sense of pride and financial security that she is not economically dependent on him. At the same time she does not question her role of wife as redefined in her present context.

In a second case study, in December of 1996, Pragati, daughter of a very close family friend, born and brought up in the Bay area in Northern California, got married to an American Catholic young man. The bride, an Oriyā brāhmaṇa, an attorney by profession, in her late twenties and the groom half French, half Panamian, a software engineer, also in his late twenties, went through Hindu and Catholic marriage ceremony. The wedding was grand, the ceremonies carefully planned and well-organized. The celebrations lasted three days on the bride's side. The bride and groom were married in a traditional Catholic ceremony in the morning. The bride was dressed in a magnificent ivory wedding gown and was a spectacular sight when she entered the church accompanied by both her parents. She, with her parents each at each of her side met the bridegroom at the aisle. Then the priest performed the wedding in the conventional Catholic way.

Later elaborating upon the ritual, she commented that unlike in the Catholic tradition, she was not "given away" by her father to the bridegroom. The very fact that both her parents walked with her and joined the bridegroom explains that they brought her up to this point, but that now she would grow with her husband. Similarly, the groom was also escorted by both his parents (to the front of the church) instead of waiting at the altar as the father of the bride transferred ownership. The couple met at the end of the aisle, after being escorted by their respective parents and together they walked arm in arm to the altar. The seemingly insignificant detail was symbolic of the couple's philosophy together. They viewed their ceremony as the beginning of the life together as partners, friends and companions — not husband as the master and wife as the docile chattel to be passed from one owner to the next. Here both set of parents accepted the bride and groom into each other's family, making it a complementary union of not just two individuals but of two families.

The Hindu ceremony followed the Catholic one in the afternoon. Again an enlightened priest, an Oriyā brāhmaṇa and university professor, presided over the ceremony. He elaborated on the meaning and significance of Hindu marriage and the respective roles of the couple based on mutual sharing of duties and responsibilities. What was significant in the marriage ritual was that there was no mention of the husband's rights. Rather, at each step of the ritual, the priest spoke to the bride and groom about their duties and responsibilities towards each other, their family, community, and God.

As I observed, these marriages represent a redefined and revised *strī dharma* according to the changing socio-cultural context. In the contemporary situation women opt for higher education and demanding professions. In the marriage relationship both parties are aware of each other's commitments outside the family. Also both have an inherent understanding of marriage as a two-way process not that the wife is a chattel and responsibility of the other. *Strī dharma* in the conventional normative tradition is not questioned or negated, but it is conceptualized in terms of mutual cooperation, commitment and division of labour keeping with the demands of the two responsible partners in the present-day society. The marriages in the Hindu tradition are serious attempts to reconcile individualized desires and rights to emotional commitment and responsibilities to one's family as well as to the spouses.

At this point I would suggest that these modern, accomplished and enlightened professional women make a conscious choice of *strī dharma* based on mutual commitment, responsibilities to their marriage relationship, to their parental family as well as to their newly constructed affinal family. These women conceptualize their marriage relationship on the basis of sharing, compassion and mutual commitment rather than holding a subordinate relationship to their spouse.

Here I would like to refer to the South Asian Studies scholar, Karen Leonard who has been working among the East Indian Americans for more than 20 years. Being a specialist in South Asian and Asian American history and culture, she recently published a book, *The South Asian Americans* (1997), that focuses on the history, culture and the process of adaptation of the South Asian communities to the American culture since the early 1900s. In her study of second generation Indian women and marriage in California, she observes that "the generational clash is strongest on the issue of marriage."[20] She argues that these women are torn between their sexual desires and their responsibilities to their own family and they often keep their marriage secret. She further elaborates on the conflicting management of desires of the young generation *versus* their love and responsibility towards their parents. Being brought up in America and culturally different from their parents, these women's sexuality and marriage are crucial sites for their self-assertion and resistance, although that resistance may be hidden and not openly expressed.[21] She goes on citing several examples from different discussion groups among the second generation South Asians, as well as local Indian newspaper articles and other conference discussions.

I find her observations very limited and narrow. I would rather argue that the young professional Indian women are aware of their identity struggle in a different cultural context. At the same time they internalize the Indian values through the oral tradition, e.g., religious rituals, practices, songs, music, dance form and continuous social gettogethers keeping the community spirit alive. As my examples show, and Leonard's study elaborates further on the diversity of South Asian culture, "South Asian culture and

20. Karen Leonard, *The South Asian Americans*, The New Americans Series, Greenwood Press, Westport, 1997, p. 159.

21. *Ibid.*, p. 160.

identity in the United States must be seen as flexible and to be respected in its many incarnations; no constructions or voices should be judged as "inauthentic."[22]

Some Conclusions

I would conclude that the marriages of these Indian women in the diaspora represent resistance to the age-old subordination of women to their menfolks. They reconstruct their *strī dharma* in the changing socio-cultural context based on sharing, compassion and mutual commitment rather than holding a subordinate relationship to their spouse.

The material that I have presented here is confined to the educated, professional women in the Western context. But I suspect that my findings may apply to the same class of women in the Indian situation as well. I see a kind of alliance between the textual presentation of women's duties and a contextual representation of women practising their religion, portraying "a constitutive aspect of their relevance to the contemporary project of women's self-representation."[23] Sunderrajan (1995) observes that with the reincorporation of Indian myths and reenactment of national history through the state sponsored television accessible to the majority of Indian masses, the traditional roles of women as model wives in the *Rāmāyaṇa* and *Mahābhārata* are revered, and accepted as our national heritage. Also in other state sponsored serials, for example in *Rajni* or *Udaan*, the "contemporary liberated female figures, elite, Westernized, educated and professional — simultaneously and effortlessly hold on to the traditional values of husband worship, family nurturance, self-sacrifice and sexual chastity."[24]

---

22. Karen Leonard, *The South Asian Americans*, The New Americans Series, Greenwood Press, Westport, 1997, p. 169.
23. Rajeswari Sunderrajan makes this point too in a different context in her book *Real and Imagined Women*, Routledge, 1993, p. 142.
24. *Ibid.*, p. 135.

Rajeswari Sunderrajan analyses the role of the state in forming a national womanhood, saying,

> In the representation of both kinds of women — women in history and myth who are 'modern' as well as contemporary women who are 'traditional' — women (and religion) are made to serve as harmonious symbols of historical continuity rather than as conflictual subjects and sites of conflict.[25]

I would say that the state plays a very important role in the media presentation of an ideal woman. At the same time, although a professional woman is very aware of the state's overpowering attempt to cast her in traditional roles, she tries to negotiate between her duties of a wife and her rights as an individual, and successfully combines both with a well rounded conceptualization of marriage.

---

25. Rajeswari Sunderrajan makes this point too in a different context in her book *Real and Imagined Women*, Routledge, 1993, p. 135.

18

Women in the East and Women in the West

Ashmita Khasnabish

> Divinty is what we need to become free, autonomous, sovereign. No human subjectivity, no human society has ever been established without the help of the divine. There comes a time for destruction. But, before destruction is possible, God or the Gods must exist.

If women have no God, they are unable either to communicate or commune with one another. They need, we need, an infinite if they are to share a little. — *Divine Women*, 62

> I am Durga, goddess of the proud and strong./And Lakashmi, queen of the fair and fortunate;/ I wear the face of Kali when I kill, I trample the corpses of the demon hordes.
>
> — *Savitri*, book seven, canto four, 509

I REALIZE as a post-colonial feminist that we have reached a critical time when women could speak globally on certain issues or problems and for my purpose I intend to use the French feminist Luce Irigaray's theories of *jouissance* and "divinity" (they overlap) to read problems of women both in the East (India) and the West and negotiate certain solutions. But, I must make it clear that in articulating the problems of Indian women, obviously, I have recourse to the Hindu philosophical texts. In this regard, I would like to articulate my position as a post-colonial feminist trying to bridge the hiatus between the East (India) and the West and use Luce Irigaray's theories of *jouissance* and divinity which have a great deal in common with the Hindu philosophy; *jouissance* being identical in a way with the Hindu notion of *ānanda* and the rich tradition of the Hindu Goddess buttressing Irigaray's concept of the female divinity.

What is the problem of the East when it comes to women? The problem of the East is that in many religious scriptures of Hinduism, woman has been given an equal status with man, but in reality women are dominated by patriarchy. Although there are women godesses and male gods cannot exist without them, there are Books of Laws as well which relegate women to the role of subordinates. There are two serious problems here: first of all, the Hindu religious texts are self-contradictory: secondly, there is a hiatus between the theory and the practice.

Upaniṣads are authentic religious texts which have a great deal to say about the status of women. In the *Bṛhadāraṇyaka Upaniṣad*, "the creation of the manifold world from the unitary self" is described through the splitting of the self into two pieces. It has been said: "He caused that self to fall into two pieces. Therefore, arose a husband and a wife. Therefore this [is true]: "Oneself is like a halffragment, . . . Therefore this place is filled by a wife" (*BU*, 78). Here, it is being described that without existence of the sexual partner, in this case, the wife, one cannot thrive. Otherwise, "Oneself is like a halffragment." One more interesting aspect is that the wife is considered to originate from the same self. It alludes to the general prevailing theory of the Hinduism, that woman is the betterhalf of man. In the same passage of the Upaniṣads, it has been observed: "Verily, he had no delight. Therefore one alone has no delight. He desired a second" (*BU*, 78). So, the wife is created from the same self, "the unitary self" from which the husband is also created.

In the *Chāndogya Upaniṣad*, the sexual act is described as a religious rite: "The woman is the fire, her womb the fuel, the invitation of man the smoke. The door is the flame, entering the ember, pleasure the spark. In this fire Gods form the offering, from this offering springs forth the child." It talks about the high status of woman's body ascribed to it by Hinduism, in contrast to the female body abnegated by Western phallocentrism. The *Chāndogya Upaniṣad* (*CU*) also alludes to the stage of a society in the Vedic period where patriarchy did not seem to play a dominant role which is exemplified by the story of Satyakāma and Jābāla described in this Upaniṣad.

1. Once upon a time Satyakāma Jābāla addresed his mother Jābāla: "Madam! I desire to live the life of a student of sacred knowledge. Of what family, pray, am I?"
2. Then she said to him: "I do not know this, my dear — of what family you are. In my youth, when about a great deal serving as a maid, got you. So I do not know of what family you are. However, I am Jābāla by name. So you may speak of yourself as Satyakāma Jābāla." (*CU*, 66)

Satyakāma's mother tells him that he could be introduced to society by his mother's name since she got him as a maid when she was serving various people. But she was hesitant to articulate the truth that her son did not have a father. Even more interesting is the way Satyakāma is accepted by his *guru*, (teacher) because when he tells him the story of his genealogy that his mother does not know who his father is and he should go by his mother's name, Haridrumata Gautama was pleased and said, "A non-brahmin would not be able to explain thus. Bring the fuel, my dear. I will receive you as a pupil. You have not deviated from the truth" (*CU*, 66)

The Upaniṣads contain references which testify to the high status of women in that society which does not seem to be dominated by patriarchal influence. But, there are other texts and Book of Laws in Hinduism which reduce her to the role of a subservient. First, I would like to talk about Vātsayāyana's *The*

Kāmasūtra. *Kāma* means senses and so *Kāmasūtra*, means a book of erotic. At the outset, I must also clarify the divine or the religious origin of this book. According to the Hindu concept of perfect life, there are three postulates which one has to obey: *dharma, artha, kāma*. *Dharma* means a life of religious activity, *artha* means social welfare, "economic and political activity" and *kāma* means a life of senses or sensuous pleasure. Each of them was equally important and it was essential to pursue each of them. The life of *kāma* or senses was considered sacred. The historians speculate that this book was written between first and fourth centuries AD. The main point is that the book advocates the Hindu view of sex that it is only "necessary" and "normal" but "sacramental." Vātsyāyana's code of marriage is highly advanced and is based on the assumption that the marriage is successful when both the partners respect each other.

> A man acting according to the inclinations of a girl should try to gain her over so that she may love him and place her confidence in him. A man does not succeed either by implicitly following the inclination of a girl, or by wholly opposing her, and he should therefore adopt a middle course. He who knows how to make himself beloved by women, as well as to increase their honour and create confidence in them, this man becomes an object of their love. But he who neglects a girl, thinking she is too bashful, is despised by her as a beast ignorant of the working of the female mind. Moreover, a girl forcibly enjoyed by one who does not understand the hearts of girls becomes nervous, uneasy, and dejected, and suddenly begins to hate the man who has taken advantage of her. (*Kāmasūtra*, 130-31)

Vātsyāyana has described the art of winning a woman's heart and also suggests that he thinks that the man-woman relation is based on mutuality. The abovementioned quotation postulates that a man should approach a woman according to her desires and know how to honour her. A man should never neglect a woman thinking her fastidious or forcibly enjoy her either. If he does that he will be held in scorn. Vātsyāyana has attached a great deal of value to the mind of woman and advocates the importance of the woman's mind in the play of erotic senses and how man should be cautious about that. He has also talked about kneeling at a woman's feet; to induce her by 'conciliatory words,' 'entreaties,' 'oaths,' and 'kneeling at her feet.' He observes: "for it is a universal rule that however bashful or angry a woman may be, she never disregards a man's kneeling at her feet" (*Kāmasūtra*, 129). In spite of all these good points, the book is prejudiced against women. In the chapter "On Marriage," Vātsyāyana describes that when a girl reaches the age of marriage, every afternoon she should be dressed in a becoming way by her parents and sent to different social gatherings including marriage ceremonies because he thinks her to be a kind of merchandise. Vātsyāyana considers women as a kind of merchandise and an object of exchange between two families. No matter how much importance he ascribes to women's mind and body when he talks about the sexual relationship, he is prejudiced against women. It is a pity that the Hindu religious texts are full of ambivalences; it is doubly tragic because not only the books are full of ambivalences, there is a hiatus between theory and practice. That means even when some of the ancient texts foreground the position of women as an active agent, in reality or in practice they are still subalterns. When it comes to marital relationship between man and woman, woman is most of the time given the status of the subordinates.

The most atrocious comments about women have been made in the book called *The Laws of Manu*. One of the codes of Manu suggests that a woman should be under the custody of her father during her childhood, under her husband during her youth and under her son's custody during her old age. It has been said: ". . . a woman is never fit for independence" (*The Laws*, 190). It further says, "By a girl, by a young woman, or even by an aged one, nothing must be done independently even in her own house" (*The Laws*, 190). *The Laws of Manu*, seems too much biased by the stringent patriarchal rules. Even when it talks about the duties of a wife, it leaves no space or freedom for women. It gives too much allowance to a husband at the cost of his wife. It says that a husband who is "destitute of virtue," or "or seeking pleasure (elsewhere)," or does not possess any good qualities at all must "be constantly worshipped as a god by a faithful wife." According to Manu, the remarriage of the widow is not allowed but the remarriage of a widower is allowed. It has been said that after the death of her husband a wife should lead a rigorous and an ascetic life on "pure flowers, roots, and fruits" and she must not mention the name of another man after her husband's death. But as far as man is concerned, it has been said, "Having thus, at the funeral, given the sacred fires to his wife who dies before him, he may marry again, and again, kindle (the fires)" (*The Laws*, 192). The husband has been repeatedly equated with the God and a wife has been intimidated and controlled by the following observation: "By violating her duty towards her husband, a wife is disgraced in this world, (after death) she enters the womb of a jackal, and is tormented by diseases (the punishment of) her sin" (*The Laws*, 191). What more, in the famous book *The Kāmasūtra*, a man is allowed to commit bigamy or polygamy during his wife's lifetime, under some outrageous conditions:

> The folly or ill-temper of the wife
> Her husband's dislike to her
> The want of offspring
> The continual birth of daughters
> The incontinence of the husband (147)

This was more or less the picture of the status of women during pre-colonial India, and since those times India has gone through many upheavals and changes but the status of women has not changed even in the post-colonial India, especially in certain classes.

Now I would like to give an account of the different categories of women in the post-colonial period. A greater and greater number of women have been able to cross the boundary of patriarchy and come to this country for higher studies. But there is another category of women in this country, I mean immigrant women, who bought the ticket for this country leaning on their husbands. This category of women has been deftly portrayed in Bharati Mukherjee's writing. It's not that I am castigating them but given the circumstances in India, they have no other alternative.[1] If they had rebelled they could have saved themselves but they chose not to, may be under patriarchal pressure.

There is another category of women in India, who belong to the educated middle-class and they have their independent position in society, apart from their husband's affiliations. This group is comprised of doctors, engineers, high government officials, school teachers, college and university professors, etc. It just reminds me that there is a similar group in North America who are highly established professionals and economically independent. I cannot help alluding to a quotation from Gayatri Spivak's article, *A Literary Representation of the Subaltern* where she alludes to a passage from the article, "The Betrayal of Superwoman" by Binita Parry and suggests that the passage which is talking about the established

1. This (the problem of marriage) is quite a complicated question to be resolved too soon. As post-colonial women we are trying to resolve it in multiple ways. A lot of Indian women have entered into interracial marriages and some are successful, some are not. A lot of women have access to USA through marriage, or more specifically through arranged marriage; again some of them are successful, some of them are not. A lot of women have come to this country for higher studies being accompanied by their lovers or companions (they eventually get married) and most of them are successful. So, my open-ended conclusion is that comparatively women are more successful in marital relationships if they value their education, financial independence and combine it with marriage, instead of sacrificing their own independence. Again, as I have said earlier, it is far more complicated than could be resolved in a single footnote. For, further reference and discussion in this matter, see the writings of Madhu Kishwar, Ruth Vanita and Taslima Nasreen.

professionals in USA is suffering from a sense of history. It is implied that this article does not portray the suffering of the other non-elite classes of women. I defend Binita Parry and critique Spivak by saying that we should always give credit to ourselves if we have been able to liberate ourselves at least to a certain extent. However, I feel now it is incumbent on me to report about the other categories of women in India. I have not talked about the lower middleclass and working class women who suffer most through lack of education and poverty. If they are abused they do not know how to articulate themselves and they are sometimes beaten and burned to death by their in-laws and husbands when their parents fail to meet their expectations about dowry. But, here one thing must be made clear that women irrespective of any class could be victim of this kind of situation, dowry-death could be likened to the *satī-dāha prathā* (the custom of women being burnt along with their husbands in the eighteenth century). Spivak in her article, *Can the Subaltern Speak* has spoken about this heinous rule about women in India, which is described by her as a case of "self-immolation."

Spivak has dealt widely with the issue of the subaltern and the importance of being sensitive not only to the subaltern group in general but the status of women as subaltern in the context of the entire subaltern group:

> Within the effaced itinerary of the subaltern subject, the track of sexual difference is doubly effaced. The question is not of female participation in insurgency, or the ground rules of the sexual division of labor, for both of which there is 'evidence'. It is, rather, that, both as object of Colonialist historiography and as subject of insurgency, the ideological construction of gender keeps the male dominant. If, in the context of colonial production, the subaltern has no history and cannot speak, the subaltern as female is evermore deeply in shadow. (Spivak, 287)

The passage makes it clear that both as a subaltern and as a subject of Colonialist historiography, the ideological construction of gender always prioritizes the male. The truth is that women as subalterns are doubly effaced, and doubly repressed. They are once removed because they are the subject of colonial production; they are twice removed because they are repressed by partriarchy. An interesting example of the subaltern woman (working class and non-elite) would be Spivak's representation of Jashoda in her translation of the Bengālī female writer Mahashweta's story, "Stanyadayani" (meaning "Breast-giver") where the crude reality of the subaltern woman is portrayed. In the story, everything relates to the breast-milk produced by the character Jashoda. Her job is to breast-feed the children of her master's family in addition to breast-feeding her own children and finally she is devoured by cancer.

> The milk that is produced in one's own body for one's own children is a use-value. When there is a superfluity of use values, exchange values arise. That which cannot be used is exchanged. As soon as the (exchange) value of Jashoda's milk emerges, it is appropriated. Good food and constant sexual servicing are provided so that she can be kept in prime condition for optimum lactation. The milk that she produces for her children is presumably through 'necessary labor'. The milk that she produces for the children of her master's family is through 'surplus labor'. (Spivak, 248)

Here is a portrait of the subaltern woman whose body is being used as a commodity, as an exchange object. The female is being used for exchange-value when her body's use-value has been exhausted. I fully agree with Spivak that this is the picture of a subaltern woman who is a victim to partiarchal society, yet she is ignorant about it. The tragedy is that women are often idolized and are being exploited by patriarchy for its own use. Women are idolized as Divine Mothers, so that they could be taken advantage of, which is exemplified in Mahashewata Devi's story. I would like to quote just one simple line from Spivak's translation of Mahashewata Devi's story, "Stanyadayani" which exemplifies this:

> Such is the power of the Indian soil that all women turn into mothers here and all men remain immersed in the spirit of holy childhood. Each man the holy child and each woman the Divine Mother. (Spivak, 225-26)

Spivak interprets this as the "hegemonic cultural self-representation of India as a goddess-mother," and her comment is that as long as this kind of the "goddess-mother" image persists there is no hope for Indian women, "she will collapse under the burden of the immense expectations that such a self-representation permits" (Spivak, 244). Two things I want to refute here: first of all, I want to refer to Partha Chatterjee's account in the "Whose Imagined Community" that the distance between the two domains, 'the elite' and the 'subaltern,' are not rigorous any more and there is an easy traffic between these two spheres; thus Spivak's attachment to the term as the only true category to describe Indian women does not remain valid anymore. Secondly, although it is true as Partha Chatterjee also depicted the nineteenth-century middle class women being used by new patriarchy as spiritual beings robbed of her sexuality, Indian women in the twenty-first century cannot just remain concealed under the category of the 'subaltern' or 'divine mother' but could use 'divinty' as a new category, to create a new space.[2] Contrary to Spivak, I suggest a rereading of the image of the 'divine mother' or 'goddess-mother' image. The image of

2. It is quite pertinent here to look at Partha Chatterjee's comment on the contiguity of the spheres of the 'elite' and the 'subaltern' in the current era: ". . . it is rather a recognition in the elite domain of the very real presence of an arena of subaltern politics over which it must dominate and yet which also had to be negotiated on its own terms for the purposes of producing consent. On the other hand, the domain of subaltern politics has increasingly become familiar with, and even adapted itself to, the institutional forms characteristic of the elite domain. ("Whose Imagined Community,"? p. 13)

   In the light of the statement it could be claimed that the time also has come to demystify former divine-woman-mother image and install a new movement along that line, since the old world has collapsed any way and we are heading for a new universal ideology and space.

the 'goddess' I invoke as a concept of infinity which is distinctly different from patriarchal concept of it as a scapegoat — a mother figure doing all the sacrifices. One more caveat is that I am not saying that materialist version of feminism or Marxist feminism cannot offer any solution but I am suggesting that oriental women can have recourse to the theory of divinity, since the notion of feminine divine is rooted in Indian culture in spite of all contradictions embedded in it. I will enter into more detailed account of this aspect later in this discussion.

What is the problem of the West when it comes to women? Luce Irigaray has argued in the "Volume-Fluidity," chapter of *Speculum* that woman is identified in terms of negation, non-entity, but ironically it is from her that men draw their resources but always fail to acknowledge her. She comments: "Woman remains thus nothing at all, or thus all at nothing, in which each (male) one seeks to find the means to replenish the resemblance to self (as) to same." (*Speculum*, 227) This is the main lacuna of the West that women's position or subjectivity is not acknowledged at least theoretically in this culture, whereas in the East, woman's place is theortically or in an apparently contradictory way acknowledged in the culture but hardly practised. According to the Hindu philosophy it is thought that the world cannot exist without the co-existence of *puruṣa* (male) and *prakṛti* (female), or without the union of Śiva and Śakti. At the same time it nurtures the cult of *satī-dāha* (burning of the widow in her husband's pyre). In the Western phallogocentric culture, woman's position remains unacknowledged in religion, in philosophy and the branch of knowledge called psychoanalysis places her in a disadvantaged position. Irigaray is castigating psychoanalysis which denies women access to society, language and culture. Irigaray points out the loophole in Lacanian psychoanalysis[3] which relegates women to the realm of the unconscious and the

3. According to the Western Lacanian psychoanalysis, mainly there are two orders — the imaginary and the symbolic. The imaginary order is associated with the unconscious and as such the female or →

imaginary and denies her access to the symbolic which represents patriarchy and the way culture, religion and language are manifest. Irigaray is rereading the Lacanian imaginary by attributing a status which has not been attributed to it so far in the Western discourse. Irigaray is unravelling the imaginary or the woman's unconscious in terms of consciousness and her theory of *jouissance* helps her to elucidate that. The imaginary has always been associated with the unconscious. But the problematic lies in the fact that whereas men's unconscious or the imaginary was justified by his access to the symbolic order or language or the phallus — women's unconscious remained unrepresented. Rather women remained men's unconscious in the Western psychoanalytical theories. In "God and the Jouissance of the Woman," Lacan is almost making fun of the "good old God," by identifying both God and woman as Other — he is attributing the position of a second class citizen to both God and Women. He is describing God as a third party between man and woman:

> Today, however, my objective is rather to show you precisely, in what he exists, this good old God. The mode in which he exists may well not please everyone, especially not the theologians who, as I have been saying for a long time, are far more capable than I am of doing without his existence. Unfortunately, I am not quite in the same position because I am dealing with the Other. The Other, while it may be alone, must have some relation to what appears of the other sex. ("God and the Jouissance of the Woman," pp. 140-41)

→ the feminine; whereas, the symbolic order stands for the patriarchal order or the phallus meaning language. In Lacan's world, the reality could not take place without language. Unfortunately, this language is associated with patriarchy or the male world, and the imaginary which is identified with the unconscious does not have any access to language or the patriarchal order and as such defined as the female, which is highly damaging for the Western women. For further reference, see the article "The Rationality and the Imaginary" in *Philosophy in the Feminine* by Margaret Whitford and *Lacan, a Feminist Introduction* by Elizabeth Grosz.

He is quite certain to distinguish him from the theologians, but he accomplishes more than that. He makes it quite clear that he is dealing with the Other — or in other words God is positioned as an other to him, or God is a mode of defining woman as other. What is most disturbing is the fact of woman being inscribed as non-existent — even when Lacan mentions God as Aristotle's supreme being from which everything originates — He (God) is situated in the "opaque place of the *jouissance* of the other" again connecting that other with woman, "that other, which if she existed, the woman might be." Lacan always expresses his misgiving about the "existence" of the "woman," he is not sure if "that other" existed!

Irigaray points out other assumptions of Western phallogocentrism which undermine and deny women's proper place in society and culture. She regrets that the Western theological tradition lacks any female Goddess and does not offer the culture any female trinity: "mother, daughter, spirit." If women are not provided with any female Goddess, they are unable even to communicate within themselves.

> . . . the relationship among women is governed either by rivalry for the possession of the 'male organ' or, in homosexuality, by identification with the man; the interest that women may take in the affairs of society is dictated of course only by her longing to have powers equal to those of the male sex, and so on. Woman herself is never at issue in these statements: the feminine is defined as the necessary complement to the operation of male sexuality, and more often, as negative image that provides male sexuality, with an unfailingly phallic representation. (*Irigary Reader*, p. 119)

This is the picture of Western phallogocentric society, of what happens if women live in a culture and society which rules out the role of any female God. She is driven by the desire to possess and sometimes she is engaged in competition with another woman for the "male organ," to identify with a man since she has no access as a female to this male sexual imaginary, or in Irigaray's term "homosexual imaginary," "hommo" meaning men in French.

The sad thing is that women are not desiring power on their own, but are motivated "only by her longing to have powers equal to those of the male sex." In this society, the image of woman is projected as a negative image, that offers the "homosexual" or male-dominated world, with a "phallic-self-representation," where women cannot conceive of them having their own system and language. So, Irigaray offers the argument that this is happening because women do not have a divine, some horizon of accomplishment for her gender which will liberate her from patriarchy. She argues, "If women have no God, they are unable either to communicate or commune with one another. They need, we need an infinite if they are to share a little" (*Divine Women*, 62). I think what Lacan or psychoanalysis in general overlooks or omits is the naked truth that they are still promoting the role of the Father — what Luce Irigaray tries to do is to rehabilitate the divine. This 'divine' which Irigaray writes with a small letter and which Lacan chastises as "good old God" serves two roles for Irigaray. First of all, Irigaray is rehabilitating God from the condemnation of psychoanalysis; secondly, she is pointing her finger to Western logocentric culture, which deprives women of any Goddess.[4] So Irigaray is defending the divine first from psychoanalysis and then put it in the context of women. Whereas, Lacan associates God with supplementary *jouissance* in women or the absence of God as women's vagina hidden, Irigaray perceives that the concept of God or God is the only person who could save women.

To me Irigaray uses the concept of God to give women whatever they need and whatever is not given to them by the so-

4. Here, I must clarify one thing that by saying that Irigaray talks about the issue of women's divinity because the Western culture does not have any female goddess, does not preclude Greek goddesses but it must be remembered that Greek goddesses or European Goddesses have been extinct in terms of cultural or religious practice.

called patriarchy which is always already constructed for women. According to Irigaray, the implication of the term God or the concept of God needs to be realized in two different contexts; in the first place, contrary to psychoanalysis Irigaray thinks of God as a concept of infinity, as a "horizon of accomplishment" — a way out of the phallus-patriarchy-psychoanalysis — an instrument to help create women a new space in the symbolic order. In the *La Mysterique* of the *Speculum of the Other Woman* Irigaray talks about the divine love which could save women which is in a way reminiscent of the Hindu religious love for the divine [*cf.* Rabindranath Tagore (*tomarei koriachi jivaner dhrubatara, sumudre ar kabhu habonako pathahara*, 18) meaning that once God is the supreme goal like a fixed star in one's life, one does not get lost. Or (*amar sakol niye base achi, sarbanaser asaya, ami tar lagi path cheye achi, pathe jejan bhasaye*, 332) meaning that one is waiting with all of her/his wealth material and spiritual] as if one is awaiting a danger since God is looked upon as somebody for whom one could sacrifice anything. Or (*amar je sab dite habe seto ami jani; amar jato bitto prabu amar jato bani*, 378) meaning that one is ready to surrender everything to God out of love. Thus, the theme of all these songs is the total identification with God in surrender, love and giving.

In *Speculum*, Irigaray talks about this kind of union with God:

> Each becomes the other in consumption, the nothing of the other in consummation. . . . Thus I am to you as you are to me, mine is yours and yours mine, I know you as you know me, you take pleasure with me as with you I take pleasure in the rejoicing of this reciprocal living — and identifying — together. (*Speculum*, p. 196)

Later, in talking about the ethics of sexual difference or about the love relationship between men and women Irigaray invokes this kind of love in which one partner does not consume the other, and there is always a residue. She is using the relationship between God and women as prototype for the relationship between men and women. But she also talks about God in pure religious terms — she is critiquing the Western logocentric culture, according to which there is only God, and no goddess. It must be remembered here that there were many European goddesses and Irigaray mentions different Greek goddesses; but the problematic lies in the fact that Goddess cult has been submerged under and supplanted by Christianity. Irigaray further suggests that:

> Man is able to exist because God helps him to define his gender (genre), helps him orient his finiteness by reference to infinity. The revival of religious feeling can in fact be interpreted as the rampart man raises in defense of his very maleness. (*Divine Women*, p. 61)

So, women need the help of infinity to measure her finiteness and that Irigaray provides through her theory of female *jouissance*.

The other lacuna of Western theology and culture, according to Irigaray, derives automatically from the fact that the culture which is two thousand years old presents a male trinity and a virgin mother. She regrets, "a mother of the son of God whose alliance with the father is given little consideration. . . . The virgin's relations with the Father always remain in the shadow" (*Divine Women*, 62). The result of this is that women's sexuality or corporeality is looked down upon and undermined by this theology, and this does not ascribe any importance to warm, human, corporeal man-woman relationship.

In the *Marine Lover* Irigaray hurls the question: "When a body becomes a barrier that cannot be crossed, something closed off inside its own skin, or place or world, isn't this the work of hatred? Doesn't Christianity forget this?" (183). Irigaray is not accusing Christ but condemning the tradition which has changed the image of Christ according to their will. This is analogous to the apparent contradictions of Hinduism which offers the image of the Goddess Kālī, the creator and the destructor; the Goddess Durgā, the protector; the Goddess Lakṣmī, the Goddess of Fortune; and the

Goddess Sarasvatī, the Goddess of Learning. But it is the same theology which restricts women to her widowhood throughout her life in the name of religion, and used to force women to ascend to their husband's pyre — the modern version of which is dowry death. So, it seems that every culture nurtures a group of people who monopolize it and makes rules to their advantage. This group of people could be defined as wielding patriarchal power over society.

Irigaray offers the theory of *jouissance*, and the theory of divinity (they overlap) as emancipatory strategies. The theory of *jouissance* offers women the ability to feel both their bodies and their minds. This gross disrespect for the imaginary and the body which associates it with the feminine by Lacan has been positively rendered by Irigaray in terms of the female *jouissance*.[5] Phallic *jouissance* has three attributes which characterizes it as typically male: it is located in the symbolic or at the intersection of the real and the symbolic, it has no connection with the body (which has everything to do with the female), and it has the grasp of all the

---

5. Here I would like to allude to the Bangladeshi writer in exile Taslima Nasreen's book (*Nirbachita Kalam*) meaning *Selected Columns*, where gross disrespect is shown to the female body by associating it with the rottenness of milk, egg, etc. "The milk gets rotten, egg gets rotten, so women." The commodification of the female body seems to be present in every culture.

   In Hindu culture it is not possible to get an exact parallel of the word 'imaginary,' since according to this culture the unconscious is not given much importance; the unconscious is primarily understood positively as 'intuition' or 'extra-sensory perception' in harmony with the rhythm of the universe (cf. Sudhir Kakar). Thus, the unconscious is independent of any gender. The emphasis in Hindu culture is on the conquering of the self and merging with others in complete identification. My point is that although the unconscious is not ascribed any gender, the gender distinction still remains, but in other forms, or manifestations through rigorous rituals and rights and prohibitions. The 'phallus' still dominates the Hindu culture in terms of 'phallus-worship' by Hindu women to get good husbands and by married women to get sons.

signifiers. Irigaray's definition of the female *jouissance* could be characterized as an attempt to redefine the imaginary or the female imaginary of the Western discourse in terms of the symbolic — or an attempt to define the female unconscious in terms of the conscious. According to Irigaray, *jouissance* has two dimensions — corporeal and spiritual. Her theory of corporeal *jouissance* advocates that the multiple sexuality of the female body is the site of her *jouissance*. Thus, the corporeal aspect of *jouissance* helps women to valorize the body which has been abnegated by the Western theological tradition.

The spiritual aspect of *jouissance* could be inscribed as "An indefinite overflowing in which many a becoming could be inscribed . . . Without any conceivable end. With neither telos or arche" (*IR*, p. 55). It would be possible only if women have their *jouissance*, own *jouissance* which they could feel through different parts of their body — and then connect it to their inner heart, and make journey upward or ascend as necessary for their survival. As I have suggested earlier in my discussion this female *jouissance* ". . . which would be of the order of the constant and gradual creation of a dimension ranging from the most corporeal to the most celestial"[6] (*IR*, p. 190) seems to be located not in women's unconscious but in the conscious mind or heart. There is another

6. Irigaray's definition of *jouissance* ranging from the corporeal to the celestial is reminiscent of the Indian philosopher Sri Aurobindo's concept of the 'Supermind' or 'Supramental Consciousness' — which talks about a transformation of the body from the descent of a supramental light above. According to this concept, body and mind are intimately connected and for any spiritual transformation to occur, the body or matter will ascend upwards, and the supramental light will descend downwards and through this two-fold process the transforma-tion could take place. "A spiritual Ananda (meaning joy, pleasure) can flow into the body and inundate cell and tissue; a luminous materialization of this higher Ananda could of itself bring transformation, a total transformation of the deficient or adverse sensibilities of physical nature" (*The Life Divine*, 1989).

important dimension to this kind of love or *jouissance* — this love is independent of any child, or independent of procreation — this takes place between the persons of two opposite sexes in which ". . . that ecstasy of ourself in us, that transcendence of the flesh of one to that of the other become ourself in us, at any rate 'in me' as a woman, prior to any child" (*IR*, p. 180).[7] Thus, another important dimension of this *jouissance* is to liberate women from being tied to the role of mothers. This joy is independent of motherhood — an emblem of a woman's existence as a woman — in which her lover looks at her for what she is.

Now the question is how this theory of *jouissance* is going to work for women's liberation both in the West and the East. In the West, especially in North America, even feminists are overwhelmed by Lacanian psychoanalysis and foregrounds it. Irigaray has not been acknowledged to that extent and she is rather accused to be an essentialist for coming up with her theory of the female *jouissance* which links feminine corporeal *jouissance* to the divine. Irigaray has been questioned as an essentialist because she attaches such great importance to the female body but fortunately she is not without her supporters. I could not help mentioning here Naomi Schor's article, *This Essentialism Which Is Not One* which 'de-hystericizes' the debate about 'essentialism,' by suggesting that Irigaray's emphasis on the female body (the multiple sexuality of the female body being the source of pleasure, or her theory of *jouissance* ranging from the corporeal to the celestial) is based on materialism rather than essentialism, meaning her emphasis is not

7. When Irigaray describes this *jouissance* as ". . . an engendering associated with the world and the universe" or ". . . a mere expenditure of fire, of water, of seed, of body and of spirit" it seems identical with the Hindu notion of cosmic bliss or divine Ananda (meaning in harmony with the universe). The ideal love relationship through which this female *jouissance* could be expressed would be Rādhā (Indian Goddess) and Kṛṣṇa (Indian God) whose relationship is portrayed as outside of marital relationship. Their pleasure could also be expressed as the divine love.

so much on physiological, as on physical. But, my point is that instead of engaging in a debate on essentialism, the Western feminists should acknowledge their debt to Irigaray for trying to recuperate female body and mind from the realm of the Western 'imaginary' and the unconscious.

Now when it comes to the East, it seems to me that the East has its own tradition of *jouissance.* Irigarayan theory of *jouissance* could be interpreted in the light of the modern Indian philosopher Sri Aurobindo's theory of the "Supramental Consciousness." Let me quote from Sri Aurobindo:

> An aspiration, a demand for the supreme and total delight of existence is there secretly in the whole make of our being. . . . In the body-consciousness this demand takes shape as a need of bodily happiness, in our life — parts as a yearning for life-happiness, a keen vibrant response to joy and rapture of many kinds and to all surprise of satisfaction; in the mind it shapes into a ready reception of all forms of mental delight; on the higher level it becomes apparent in the spiritual mind's call for peace and divine ecstasy. This trend is found in the truth of the being; for Ananda is the very essence of the Brahman, it is supreme nature of the omnipresent Reality. (*The Life Divine*, p. 8)

The female *jouissance* which Irigaray defines to be ranging from the corporeal to the celestial is similar to what Sri Aurobindo defines as *ānanda* and according to him it ranges from the "body-consciousness" to the "higher level of consciousness."

Unlike Lacan, Sri Aurobindo is not discriminating against women saying that this flow of *ānanda* ranging from the "body-consciousness" to the "supermind" could take place only in men while women are inferior or have lower level of consciousness and cannot have access to *ānanda*. This *ānanda* is similar to the *ānanda* conveyed in Upaniṣads, *madhu bata ritayate, madhu kharanti sindhava, . . . madhumat parthivam rājāḥ madhu daurastu naḥ pitā*. Also, in the Hindu culture consciousness of mind is valorized more than the unconscious (cf. Sudhir Kakar, and Ashis Nandy).

It is important to mention here the first Indian psychoanalyst Girindrasekhar Bose who practised psychoanalysis as the science of "the philosophy of Consciousness."[8] Thus, my point is that in the East (in India) we have this tradition of *jouissance* — but we need to learn how to practice it for women's liberation. In the present era women could claim to have access to this *jouissance* in terms of *ānanda* by looking at the tradition of Indian psychoanalysis according to which women have equal claim with men and unlike Western psychoanalysis taught by Lacan, Indian psychoanalytic practice never associates women with the pure unconscious. Woman is rather the 'Ādya-Śakti.' But, we need to fill out the gap between the theory and the practice.

Now the question is how Irigaray's theory of divinity could work as an emancipatory strategy both in the West and in the East. First of all, the theory of divinity offers a concept of infinity against which women can posit them-selves and liberate themselves from the pressure of phallo-centrism because, if women are not presented with any "horizon of acomplishment," they get embroiled in a fight among themselves. Irigaray argues, "If women have no God, they

---

8. In this regard, I would like to allude to Ashis Nandy's article *The Savage Freud: The First Non-Western Psychoanalyst and the Politics of Secret Selves in Colonial India*, where he refers to Girindrashekhar Bose as the first Indian psychoanalyst who practised psycho-analysis as "science as a philosophy of consciousness." I would like to quote from Ashis Nandy: "Acceptance of the unconscious does not secularize one's world, for the unconscious is not particularly incompatible with spirituality, but it cures one of pseudo-spirituality" (*The First Non-Western Psychoanalyst in Colonial India*, 129). In Indian Hindu culture, the emphasis is on the conquering of the unconscious, or using unconscious as the source of intuition.

   Girindrashekhar Bose had correspondence with Freud, and as Ashis Nandy tells us, Bose like Freud believes that "the unconscious" stands for a lower level of "personality functioning," but, contrary to Freud and like a Hindu, believed in the conquering of the unconscious and self-knowledge. Bose said in his "sattava, rajah, tamah," that the realization or the awareness of the self is identical with the "awareness of the ultimate reality of being and God."

are unable either to communicate or commune with one another. They need, we need, an infinite if they are to share a little." (*Divine Women*, p. 62). It leads to Irigaray's theory of the "sexual difference," which could also be claimed as a part of the theory of divinity. The term "sexual difference" is not a pleasant term to feminists, mainly to the social and materialist feminist and they want to obliterate the term, because according to them it is associated with patriarchal discourse and gender difference.[9] But, Irigaray keeps the term intact and develops her theory on the "sexual difference," which points towards the harmónious relationship between man and woman.

> Each sex should be considered in relation to its corresponding ideal, its transcendental. If each sex does not strive to realize its powers, an alliance with or an encounter between the energies of both remains impossible. One always encroaches on the other, without fulfilling its own destiny, without finding the blossoming of its becoming and its fertilization by the other. (*IR*, p. 107)

The concept of divinity is important not only for the emancipation of women but also for the flourishing of the perfect man-woman relationship. Each sex must have an independent connection with the divine, so that each has one's own space. The truth is that unless each sex realizes his or her own power, any proper sexual encounter between them remains impossible. What Irigaray means is that the perfect man-woman relationship is based on mutuality, both on alliance and freedom, in which one partner does not consume the other and one is not reducible to the other. But for this, the first stage is to realize the divine, so that one has a "horizon of accomplishment" which will help each to realize his or her own power and then only the perfect relationship can evolve.

9. Here, I could not help clarifying a little bit more about the debate between the gender theorists and the sexual difference theorists. Whereas, the gender theorists talk about neutralizing the female body, the sexual difference theorists emphasize the female body should be valorized and women's liberation could not take place if female body is not taken into account in conjunction with female mind.

Irigaray advocates that procreation is not that important between man-woman relationship; but what is important is they produce together an energy and ecstasy, "but an energy produced together and as a result of the irreducible difference of sex."

The third angle of the Irigarayan theory of divinity touches upon the theme of "carnal ethics," which stresses that the relationship between man and woman should be based on both corporeal and spiritual aspects. She argues, "In this way it would no longer be a meeting within a shadow or orbit of a God the Father who alone lays down the law, or the immutable mouthpiece of a single sex" (*IR*, p. 174). Irigaray resents the fact that the female body is not properly respected and this respect will be restored once the sexual relationship is established on both corporeal and spiritual aspects.

That the Western logocentric world will be greatly benefited by the Irigarayan theory of divinity, there is no reservation. She is trying to come up with the notion of the divine as a philosophical concept — positing a concept of infinity, "a horizon of accomplishment" which will help women to establish themselves in their own rights. Women in the West lack an image of God in the female gender which deprives them of any horizon against which they can measure themselves. Once, the West succeeds in conceptualizing women in terms of divinity, the emancipation from the custody of the phallus or the supreme signified will take place. How about the woman in the East, since the East already has the tradition of female goddesses? The irony lies in the fact that although the culture is given with the image of Goddesses, it is somehow not reflected or represented in everyday life; in everyday life, woman is still beaten to death; used as an exchange object between families and not given proper value. It also happens because of the apparent contradictions in the Hindu religion, which worships the image of Goddesses and at the same time forces women to ascend their husband's pyre, or lead a life of celibacy after her husband's death, or causes dowry-death. So, how do we read Irigaray's message in the Indian context? I suggest a rereading of the Indian concept of the 'divinity' or the goddesses and also of *jouissance* as *ānanda* or bliss. Once, Indian women learn to inculcate their own tradition and live in that circumambience (which might be little difficult to learn initially) the transformation would take place to a greater extent.

References

Chatterjee, Partha, *The Nation and Its Fragments: Colonial and Postcolonial Histories*, Princeton, New Jersey: Princeton University Press, 1993.

Ghosh, Sri Aurobindo, *The Life Divine: Book One and Book Two Part one*, Sri Aurobindo Ashram, Pondicherry, India: All India Press, 1973 (8th Indian Printing).

Grosz, Elizabeth, *Jacques Lacan: A Feminist Introduction*, London and New York: Routledge, 1990.

Irigaray, Luce, *Marine Lover*, tr., Gillian C. Gill, New York: Columbia University Press, 1991.

———, *Speculum of the Other Woman*, tr. Gillian C. Gill, Ithaca, New York: Cornell University Press, 1985.

———, "Divine Women," tr. Gillian C. Gill, *Sexes and Genealogies*, New York: Columbia University Press, 1993.

Kishwar, Madhu and Ruth Vanita (eds.), *In Search of Answers : Indian Women's Voices From "Manushi"*, Totowa: Biblio Distribution Center, 1984.

Kakar, Sudhir, *The Inner World: A Psychoanalytic Study of Childhood and Society in India*, Delhi, Oxford, New York: Oxford University Press, 1978.

Mukherjee, Bharati, *The Middleman and Other Stories*, New York: Ballantine Books, 1988.

Nandy, Ashis, "The Savage Freud: The First Non-Western Psychoanalyst and the Politics of Secret Selves in Colonial India," in *The Savage Freud and Other Essays on Possible and Retrievable Selves*, Princeton, New Jersey: Princeton University Press, 1995.

Nasreen, Taslima, *Nirbachita Kalam* (Selected Columns), Calcutta: Ananda Publishers Private Limited, 1992.

Rose Jacqueline and Juliet Mitchell, ed., and tr. Jacqueline Rose, "God and the Jouissance of the Woman," *Feminine Sexuality*, New York, London: W.W. Norton and Pantheon Books, 1985.

Radhakrishnan, Sarvepalli, and Charles A. Moore, (ed.), *A Source Book in Indian Philosophy*, New Jersey: Princeton, UP, 1957.

Schor, Naomi, "This Essentialism Which is Not One: Coming to Grips with Irigaray," *Differences: A Journal of Feminist Cultural Studies*, vol. 1, no. 2 (Summer 89).

Spivak, Gayatri Chakravorty, *In Other Worlds: Essays in Cultural Politics*, New York and London: Routledge, 1988.

Whitford, Margaret, (ed.), *The Irigaray Reader*, Cambridge, Massachusetts: Basil Blackwell Inc., 1991.

———, Luce Irigaray, *Philosophy In the Feminine*, London and New York: Routledge, 1991.

Vātsyāyana, *The Kāmasūtra*, tr. Sir Richard Burton and F.F. Arbuthnot, ed. W.G. Archer, Berkeley: G.P. Putnam's Sons Inc., 1966.

List of Contributors

R.S. **Bhatnagar** retired Professor of Philosophy, Rajasthan University, has published: *Berkeley Darśana: Ek Paricaya* (1962), *Ādhunik Pāścātya Unāni Dārśanika* (1991), *Darśanika Samasyāen: Tattva Mīmāṁsā* (1997), *Jñāna: Vividha Paridṛśya* (2003). He has also published several papers and reviews in *Darśanika Traimāsika, Unmilan, Journal of Indian Council of Philosophical Research* and contributed papers to various anthologies [address: 10/558 Kaveripath, Mansarovar, Jaipur 302020, Rajasthan].

S. Cromwell **Crawford,** born and reared in India, has British family ties through the East India Company of 1760s. He received a Bachelor of Divinity degree from Serampore University, West Bengal. Coming to the USA in the 1960s, he earned a degree of M.A. in Philosophy and Ethics from Indiana University, Bloomington, and a Doctor of Theology degree from the Pacific School of Religion, Berkeley. Crawford is Chairman of the Department of Religion, University of Hawaii. He teaches in the areas of Comparative Religions, Comparative Ethics, and Religion and Medicine. As a bioethicist, he lectures internationally on the subject of Hindu biomedicine. His latest publication is *Hindu Bioethics for the Twenty-First Century,* published by The State University of New York Press, 1963 [address: 261, Anapalau Place, Honolulu, Hawali 96825, U.S.A., E-mail: <scrawfor@hawaii.edu>].

Kathryn **Castle** is Principal lecturer in History at London Metropolitan University and a fellow of the Royal Historical Society. She is the author of *Britannia's Children,* in the Studies in Imperialism series, Manchester University Press, 1996. She has also contributed to numerous publications in the area of racial representation and children's literature. She is currently working on a monograph which examines the history of Blackface Performance in Britain, 1836-1978 [address: Department of Humanities, Arts and Languages, London Metropolitan University, 166-200 Holloway Road, London N7 4DB (UK), E-mail: <k.castle@un>].

Bart **Gruzalski,** left a tenured associate professor position at Northeastern University in Boston, Massachusetts, to help found the Pacific Center for Sustainable Living in Redway, California. His two recent books are *On the Buddha* (2000) and *On Gandhi* (2001). Since 9/11 he has been lecturing at universities across the United States on why nonviolence alone can defeat terrorism [E-mail: <pcslgruz@humboldt.net.>].

Pushraj **Jain,** is the Head of the Department of Sanskrit in PG DAV College (E), University of Delhi. He has written extensively and lectured in several parts of the country on Gandhi. His books *Sanatana Dharma aur Mahatma Gandhi* and *Vedic, Jaina aur Adhunika Jivana* are acclaimed by critics and general readers alike. His manuscript on Jaina Philosophy and Religion is ready for publication [address: PG DAV College, University of Delhi, Nehru Nagar, New Delhi].

Ashmita **Khasnabish,** Ph. D. in English literature from Bowling Green State University, is currently a visiting scholar at the Brown University Pembroke Center for Teaching and Research on Women and teaches at the University of Massachusetts, Lowell. A scholar in feminist postcolonial theory, and postcolonial literature, she is the author of the book *Jouissance as Ananda: Indian Philosophy; Feminist Theory and Literature* (Lexington Books, Lanham, Boulder, New York, Oxford, 2003). She has also authored articles in the journals *South Asian Review* and *C. L. R. James Journal* [address: 18, Patterson Road,Lexington, MA 02421, USA, E-mail: <Ashmita_Khasnabish@uml.edu>].

V. **Kutumba Sastry,** after getting trained in the traditional style of recitation of *Rigveda* at Tirumala, has studied Alaṅkāra Śāstras and Advaita Vedanta at Machlipatnam and Madras respectively. He worked for his research under the guidance of eminent Sanskritist Dr. V. Raghavan on Dharma Suri's *Sāhityaratnākara.* After serving Rashtriya Sanskrit Sansthan for more than 12 years as Lecturer and Reader he joined Pondicherry Central University as Professor and Head, Department of Sanskrit in 1990 and continues to be so till date. At present he is the Vicechancellor of Rashtriya Sanskrit Sansthan, Deemed University under MHRD, New Delhi. He has authored two books and 50 research papers [address: Director, Rashtriya Sanskrit Sansthan, 56-57, Institutional Area, Janakpuri, New Delhi - 100 058, E-mail: <rsks@nda.vsnl.net.in>].

Mahesh M. **Mehta** teaches Hindu and Buddhist Philosophy, Comparative Mysticism and Yoga in the Departments of Religious Studies and Languages, Literature and Cultures at the University of Windsor, Canada. He has also taught at the Universities of Pennsylvania and Michigan. He has authored two books on *Mahābhārata* Text-Criticism and Sanskrit Grammar, and contributed numerous articles to books and journals on Advaita Vedānta, Mādhyamaka, Mysticism and Yoga [address: 10955 Brentwood Cres, Windsor, ON N8R 2H4, Canada [E-mail: <sanatana@hotmail.com>].

Mrinal **Miri** is currently Vicechancellor of Northeastern Hill University. Miri has taught philosophy in Delhi University and Notheastern Hill University. His philosophical publications include several books and many articles in professional journals both in India and abroad. Prior to his present assignment he was, for six years, Director, Indian Institute of Advanced Study, Shimla [E-mail: <mirimrinal@hotmail.com>].

Godabarisha **Mishra** is Professor, Department of Philosophy, University of Madras. He worked as the Editor at Kuppuswami

Sastri Research Institute, Chennai between 1985-1988. He specializes in Advaita Vedānta and has published thirty research articles besides a few books including *Anubhūtiprakāśa of Vidyāraṇya*. He has recently co-edited *Paramparā* (ICPR, New Delhi, 2003) and *Breaking the Barriers* (Asian Humanities Press, Fremont, California, 2003). He has visited Oxford University, UK on Charles Wallace Fellowship in 1995 and on Sivdasani Visiting Fellowship in the fall of 2003 [address: Flat 1, "Murali Krishna", 38, 5th Trust Cross Street, Mandavelipakkam, Chennai - 600 028, Tamil Nadu, E-mail: <gmisra19@hotmail.com>].

Annapurna Devi **Pandey** received her Ph.D in Sociology from Jawaharlal Nehru University, New Delhi. With a post doctoral degree in Social Anthropology from Cambridge, UK, she has been teaching in the Department of Cultural Anthropology at University of California, Santa Cruz. Dr. Pandey's research is focused on Women's organizing at the grass roots level, the role of various NGOs focused on women's issues and their varied experiences of self empowerment, social awareness and wellbeing in the process of globalization in Orissa. She also studies the diasporic issues of identity among the bay area Indians as expressed through the practices of religious rituals and celebrations [address: Verite, Auroville, Tamil Nadu - 605 101, E-mail: <annapurnadpandey@yahoo.com>].

Makarand **Paranjape** is Professor of English at Jawaharlal Nehru University. A poet, novelist, critic, and columnist, he is the author of *The Serene Flame, Playing the Dark God,* and *Used Book* (poetry); *This Time I Promise It'll Be Different* and *The Narrator* (fiction); and *Mysticism in Indian English Poetry, Decolonization and Development*, and *Towards a Poetics of the Indian English Novel* (criticism). The books he has edited include *Indian Poetry in English; Sarojini Naidu: Selected Poetry and Prose; Nativism: Essays in Literary Criticism; The Best of Raja Rao; The Penguin Sri Aurobindo Reader; In Diaspora: Theories, Histories, Texts;* and *Saundarya: The Perception and Practice of Beauty in India.* He is also the founding editor of *Evam: Forum on Indian Representations* [address: School of Language, Literature and Culture Studies, Jawaharlal Nehru University, New Delhi-110067, E-mail: <makarand@mail.jnu.ac.in>].

K. Dad **Prithipaul,** born in Mauritius and accomplished with Master's Degree in Indian Religion and Philosophy from Banaras Hindu University and Doctorate from Paris University, has formerly worked as Senior Research Fellow at the Institute of Advanced Study in Philosophy (BHU) and as a lecturer at the Harvard University. Retired as Professor Emeritus in 1992, he is presently engaged in completing a philosophical commentary on the *Mahābhārata.* He has been an elegant and renowned author, and has to his credit several published works, namely *Action & Contemplation in Advaita Vedanta; Moha — The Notion of Spiritual Error in Brahmanical Thought; Bhagavad Gita: A Translation and verse by verse Commentary* (2 *Vols.*). Besides these, his works of translation too deserve mention: *Spiritual Aspects of Islam; Philosophy of Nagarjuna; The Yogasutras of Patañjali;* and *Colonization — A Global History* [address: 10335 - 137, Str. NW, Edmonton, Alberta T5N 2H2, Canada, E-mail: <prithi@shaw.ca>].

Prof. Bisraam **Rambilass** after completing his M.A, and Ph.D in Sanskrit currently teaches in the Department of Languages at the University of Durban, Westville. Beside publishing more than a dozen articles in professional journals and anthologies, he has authored two books, edited five volumes and published five compilations on Hindu rites and *saṁskāras.* He has been an active member of Ārya Samāj and is currently the President of Arya Pratinidhi Sabha, and editor of *Veda Jyoti* [address: 183 Umhlangane Road, Avoca, Durban, 4051, South Africa, E-mail: <aps@apssa.co.za>].

Alan **Roland**, Ph.D., is a practicing psychoanalyst in New York city. He is a Training Analyst, Member of the Faculty and Board of Trustees, National Psychological Association for Psychoanalysis. He is author of *In Search of Self in India and Japan: Towards a Cross-cultural Psychology* (Princeton University Press, 1988); *Cultural Pluralism and Psychoanalysis: The Asian and North American Experience* (Routledge, 1996); and *Dreams and Drama: Psychoanalytic Criticism: Creativity and the Artist* (Sage Publications, 2002). He has also edited and contributed to three books and published over fifty papers [address: 274 West II Street, New York, NY 10014, USA, E-mail: <alanroland@aol.com>].

Srinivasa **Rao** retired from the Department of Philosophy of Bangalore University after serving as Professor and Chairman for nearly 25 years, before that he had served for a decade in the Department of Philosophy, University of Mysore. He obtained his M.A. and Ph.D. in Philosophy from the University of Mysore, of which the latter work has been published by the University of Hawaii Press, USA, in 1998 under the title, *Perceptual Error: The Indian Theories.* Besides this thesis, he has also authored a highly acclaimed work *Advaita: A Critical Investigation.* He has served as the Vice-chairman of the Indian Philosophical Congress for one term and has been repeatedly invited for lectures and seminars in several universities in USA and Germany. He is currently Emeritus Professor of Philosophy [address: B-406, Gagan Vihar Apartments, Raja Rajeshwari Nagar, Bangalore — 560 098, Karnataka E-mail: <srirao@vsnl.com>].

Arvind **Sharma**, formerly of the I.A.S., is Birks Professor of Comparative Religion in the Faculty of Religious Studies at McGill University in Montreal, Canada. He has published extensively in the fields of Hindu Studies and Comparative Religion and is currently engaged in promoting the adoption of a Universal Declaration of Human Rights by the World's Relgions [Address: 3520 University Street, Montreal, Qubec H3A 2A7, Canada, E-mail: <Arvind.Sharma@staff.mcgill.ca>].

Shrinivas **Tilak** (Ph. D. McGill University) is author of *The Myth of Sarvodaya: A Study in Vinoba's Concept* (Breakthrough Communications, New Delhi 1984); *Religion and Aging in the Indian Tradition* (State University of New York Press, Albany, New York 1989); and *Understanding Karma in Light of Paul Ricoeur's Philosophical Anthropology and Hermeneutics* (forthcom.). An independent scholar living in Montreal, Canada, his research interests include Cultural Gerontology, Hermeneutics, and Indology [address: 4910 Walkley, Apt 14, Montreal, Quebec H4V 2M2, Canada, E-mail : <shrinivast@hotmail.com>].

Saranindranath **Tagore** is Associate Professor in the Department of Philosophy, National University of Singapore. His teaching and research interests are in the areas of Indian Philosophy and European Philosophy. Apart from publishing papers in academic journals and anthologies, he has published (with Professor Wendy Barker), *Rabindranath Tagore: Final Poems* (New York: George Braziller, 2001), which won the Sourette Diehl Fraser Award. Before joining the National University of Singapore, he was Associate Professor at the University of Texas at San Antonio [address: National University of Singapore Department of Philosophy, 3 Arts Link, Singapore 117570, Singapore, E-mail: <phisnt@nus.edu.sg>].

George M. **Williams**, Ph.D., Professor Emeritus of California State University, Chico. Author of numerous books and articles on religion in India, including The Quest for Meaning of Svāmī Vivekānanda (New Horizons, 1972) and Handbook of Hindu Mythology (ABC CLEO, 2003). He has also made a number of educational films and videos on topics for religious studies. He has been awarded two honorary doctorates for his work in interfaith understanding [address: Department of Religious Studies, California State University, Chico, CA 95929, USA, E-mail: <georgewilliams2@mac.com>].

Ashok Vohra is Professor of Philosophy at the University of Delhi. He was the Member Secretary of Indian council of Philosophical Research during 1995- 98. He is the author of *Wittgenstein's Philosophy of Mind,* (Croom-Helm, London, Sydney); co-author of *Radhakrishnan: His Life and Ideas* (State University of New York Press, New York) and co-editor of *The Philosophy of K. Satchidanada Murty* (ICPR, New Delhi). He has translated Wittgenstein's three books *viz., Philosophical Investigations; On Certainty;* and *Culture and Value* into Hindi. His Hindi translation of Wittgenstein's *Tractatus Logico Philosophicus* is ready for publication. In addition he has published more than seventy articles and research papers in Indian and foreign professional journals. He has been writing columns on Indian Philosophy and religion in leading national dailies [Address: 10 Commissioner Lane, Civil Lines, Delhi - 110 054, E-mail: <ashok_vohra@hotmail.com>].

Index